SECOND EDITION

80+ Customer Ratings on Amazon with over 50 Five-Star reviews

"*The Business of Venture Capital* is a comprehensive book with data, industry trends, and insights from leading VCs and LPs – a must have for practitioners."
—*David York, Managing Director, Top Tier Capital Partners, a Fund-of-Funds with over $2 billion under management*

"Whether you are a practitioner or a student of the venture capital industry, this book offers innumerable insights into the art of the deal."
—*Scott Kupor, Managing Partner, Andreessen Horowitz*

"A valuable resource for beginners and experts alike, *The Business of Venture Capital* addresses the complexities and challenges of being a successful venture capitalist."
—*Michael Kim, Managing Partner, Cendana Capital, a next generation Fund-of-Funds*

"Mahendra's research into today's most active investors reveals how the Venture Capital model is evolving. It's the closest book I've found to a User's Manual for VCs."
—*David Cowan, Bessemer Venture Partners*

"Combines concrete examples and deep insights of industry leaders – a must-have for any venture investor or practitioner."
—*Karim Faris, General Partner, Google Ventures*

"Mahendra demonstrates how skill, discipline, and often luck and intuition can help to create successful venture capitalists. This is engaging and enjoyable."
—*Jon Callaghan, True Ventures*

"Detailed yet accessible description of the many facets of venture capital – from the nuanced considerations of LPs to the intricate mechanics of the entrepreneurial companies they bet on."

—Amish Jani, Founder and Managing Director,
FirstMark Capital

FIRST EDITION

"If you read only one guide to becoming a successful VC, this is the one to read."

—Paul Maeder, Chairman, National Venture Capital
Association (NVCA)

"Captures the LP mindset succinctly – any GP or aspiring VC can benefit from this book."

—Timothy Recker, Chairman, Institutional Limited Partners
Association (ILPA)

"... packs the insights and wisdom of those who have done it, not once but multiple times."

—Frank Caufield, cofounder, Kleiner Perkins
Caufield and Byers

"An immensely useful and comprehensive guide."

—Mark Florman, CEO, British Venture Capital
Association (BVCA)

The Business of Venture Capital

THE BUSINESS OF VENTURE CAPITAL

THE ART OF RAISING A FUND, STRUCTURING INVESTMENTS, PORTFOLIO MANAGEMENT, AND EXITS

THIRD EDITION

Mahendra Ramsinghani

WILEY

Library of Congress Cataloging-in-Publication Data

Names: Ramsinghani, Mahendra, author.
Title: The business of venture capital : the art of raising a fund,
    structuring investments, portfolio management, and exits / Mahendra
    Ramsinghani.
Description: Third edition. | Hoboken, New Jersey : John Wiley & Sons,
    Inc., [2021] | Series: Wiley finance series | Includes bibliographical
    references and index.
Identifiers: LCCN 2020030565 (print) | LCCN 2020030566 (ebook) | ISBN
    9781119639688 (hardback) | ISBN 9781119639718 (adobe pdf) | ISBN
    9781119639701 (epub)
Subjects: LCSH: Venture capital.
Classification: LCC HG4751 .R36 2020 (print) | LCC HG4751 (ebook) | DDC
    332/.04154068—dc23
LC record available at https://lccn.loc.gov/2020030565
LC ebook record available at https://lccn.loc.gov/2020030566

Cover Design: Wiley
Cover Image: © piranka/Getty Images
Author Photo: Courtesy of Mahendra Ramsinghani

SKY10083135_082924

In the memory of my parents,
who reminded me to put
knowledge above wealth,
people above profits,
truth above power,
and service above self

For Amar and Geeta, who gave me wings

&

for Deepa and Aria, who bring the light and the song

Contents

Foreword

Now in its third edition, *The Business of Venture Capital* builds on the foundational best practices in venture investments, offering new, valuable tools along with some wit and wisdom. The scope of the venture capital business is wide, and often opaque. For example, how do *our* investors (limited partners or LPs) make decisions? What challenges do they encounter, and how should a general partner (GP) understand their universe? How can a practitioner build a "point of view" on the market, identify emerging trends, compete to win the best opportunities, and nurture them to success? What biases and cognitive traps spring up in our business? How should we think probabilistically? What skills are critical to our business, and how does one develop such skills? Which parts of our business are at the mercy of the markets?

In this book, you will find answers to many of these questions. But, as with any good book, it will leave you thinking about many other questions. You'll ultimately need to figure out how to apply many of the mental models about which Mahendra writes to your own situation.

Over the past decade, Mahendra has had to answer many of these questions, both as an investor and a practitioner. When the first edition was released nearly a decade ago, there was no book on VC and the blogosphere was just in its infancy. So, he heeded Nobel Prize winner Toni Morrison's advice: "If there's a book that you want to read, but it hasn't been written yet, then you must write it."

This book includes views of over 50 leading LPs and GPs, compiled in a jargon-free, digestible format to benefit all those exploring VC as a path, whether you're a solo-GP getting ready to raise a fund or a venture partner on your first board.

This book covers the arc of investment and blends lessons from Silicon Valley as well as other parts of the country. Over the past decade, much has evolved — the amount of capital flowing in venture has increased tenfold by some estimates. Besides mainstream LPs, hedge funds, sovereign wealth funds, and corporate VC funds have helped shape this growth trajectory. At the same time, the presence of new and large players, including Softbank, have impacted the nature of the venture business overall.

Indeed, our business is changing rapidly and, with it, we continue to evolve. But our singular goal remains the same — to help entrepreneurs in their journey to build important and lasting businesses, along the way generating superior returns for our investors. It is my hope that this book will not only set the foundation for you but make a meaningful impact in your journey as a practitioner.

Scott Kupor
Author, *Secrets of Sand Hill Road: Venture Capital and How to Get It*
Managing Partner, Andreessen Horowitz (A16Z)
Former Chair, National Venture Capital Association
(2017–2018)

Preface

WHY SHOULD YOU READ THIS BOOK?

Thank you, dear reader, for arriving at the doorsteps of this somewhat lengthy tome. I hope you reached here, at the doors of this career after some thought and planning, unlike me, who stumbled in the VC wormhole and got sucked in 20 years ago.

Do you really need a big, fat, expensive book on venture capital, when a thousand blogs can give you answers instantaneously? Surely, in this day and age of free content, why would you want to pay an ungodly amount to buy a book? And who has time to read these days?

And you must surely know, no book will teach you how to be a great investor — you have to get out there and start investing. Like learning to ride a bicycle. A book can only do so much. The learning comes from doing.

But what is the best way to become a good investor — to build a structured approach, to build your foundation, and to build a strong core? Maybe this book can help. The business of venture capital not only presents basic principles, checklists, and frameworks, but also shares philosophies and wisdom of the ages. At its very core, an investor has the ability to understand risk and then make a probabilistic bet against that risk. We do this to achieve outstanding "venture-like" returns, well above some other asset classes.

On the face of it, the business sounds easy. I mean — how hard can this be? As they say, any fool can write a check. Everybody knows the obvious of investing: "Buy low, sell high." But how many can do it consistently across macroeconomic changes, with evolving technology cycles, competitive landscape, regulatory dynamics, and management teams? The sands of time keep shifting. Entropy prevails. All that is valuable is being eroded by the new waves. Your role as an investor is to make sure you can stay balanced, find music in this cacophony, and find the right signal.

In public equities, trading strategies include a "momentum" driven approach. You invest in a stock that has a high level of buy–sell activity. This momentum drives the price. In a frenzy, everyone jumps in and the price starts to go up, but very few pause to step away from the herd. To ask, "Why is this happening?" is not the mind-set of the momentum investor. They are well trained to make several short trades and know when to get in, when to get out. The "value" investor — someone like Warren Buffett — studies the company's financials, its value proposition, the ins and outs of the sector, competition, product pricing, defensible moats, and more. The intellectual effort for understanding value is much more different and strenuous than the herd mentality momentum-based trade. Bear in mind that we are not here to make moral judgments against momentum trades nor demonstrate superiority of any kind — we are merely choosing a path, based on our strengths to get to a destination. I was a herd trader, too, until I could develop my own muscles and confidence. Success can come from many paths, and you have to choose what works best for you. I have tried both approaches and can tell you one is far easier than the other, but the rewards of a well-planned strategy are immensely gratifying — both intellectually and financially. It is like a game of chess — only in this case, you have n number of opponents.

One of the primary goals of this book is to help you to build the muscle — manage risk effectively, shield yourself from all the biases, and get to the promised land.

The second goal is a bit more subtle — what kind of a person will you become in this journey? As a venture capitalist, we are not just trading stock — we work with people. That indomitable human spirit in founders comes to you. They bring their dreams, their life-time aspirations — if we cannot look beyond their fancy PowerPoint decks, we are to blame. Those dreams are a part of this package. If we only chase financial outcomes, are we being short-sighted and self-serving? Wall Street may choose to operate that way, not Sand Hill Road. Not venture. A typical VC interacts with the portfolio founder multiple times a week — a Wall Street trader may never know the name of the management team members. We become intimately aware of the founder's day-to-day dilemmas and their sleepless nights, their joys, sorrows, anxiety, and depression — all of these come with this package as well. So the next time you make an investment, remember that you are not just making a trade — you are putting on fertilizer to help sprout the founder's dreams. Of such dreams will come a better tomorrow. If there is a gale storm in the middle of the night, you better get out of bed and get out there. Do your best to protect those saplings.

And this business will not disappoint — you will find the best and worst of human behaviors when you make (or lose) big money. Because there are two primal drivers — those imposters called greed and fear. This business brings all the highs and lows of these two demons. Dysfunctions within venture funds, their founding teams, CEO desire for global dominance, street fights with competition, slick maneuvers, politics, ego, drama — you name it, and this business has it all. Not getting caught up in this theater and still staying true to yourself can be a challenge. I could share some great stories of power, greed, backstabbing, and more, but I will save the gossip and entertainment for *People* magazine. My goal was to bring out the best of this business and leave the reader empowered and inspired. To stay persistent and focused over the long haul despite all these primal challenges requires some tenacity. How do you build a fair and balanced core in your ethos, your DNA, and your daily persona?

Until our portfolio company becomes an enduring milestone, we must fight their fight with every inch of our lives, blood, sweat, and soul. Our work is done not when we make great returns but only when we help fulfill the dreams of founders. To forget this basic rule of venture investments is to forget our purpose. For it is not our goal to mindlessly multiply small pieces of green paper and proclaim Midas list ranks on our resume — that is a fool's errand for those who, while getting rich, leave behind a trail of carcasses of broken dreams. We are here to help those dreams come one step closer to reality. We are here for empowering the crazy ones with our gifts of time, money, intellectual insights, and our wonderful relationships. All of this to serve for the greater good of society. That should be our singular goal.

To find the founder whose vision is to serve for the most good of the society is not an easy task. In the beginning, all founders sound alike — their mission statements filled with zeal and passion. They serve up PowerPoints to our demand for "billion-dollar" markets. It is your job to dissect the frothy shapeshifters from the authentic forces of good. How do you make value judgments when faced with the promise of fantastic returns? Juul — the e-cigarette vaping company — grew the fastest in recent years, raised the most amount, and can generate the best returns for their portfolio. But if you were to make a lesser return in another company, say one that's addressing cancer, would that align with your values? Would your limited partners (LPs) be happy? Would you be satisfied with the trajectory of your career?

Indeed, "values over valuation" has been one of our larger business challenges — if we chase the promise of an IPO and triple-digit IRR but damage the socioeconomic fabric, where do we draw the line? I know one prominent investor who chooses to not use the portfolio company's technology for defense markets. The CEO was blunt — *our technology can kill a lot of people, but we will never sell it for that purpose*. The company would be valued at least 10 times more if it went down that path, but its bedrock values keep it on course, staving off the monkeys of greed. If you do not establish the foundation of values, you could make money, lots of it — but then you might feel purposeless, adrift in the sea of capitalism.

What set of values will become your internal compass to help you make the right decisions when you stand at the tougher crossroads of our business? As you build a framework of values, this work is like a journey, best illustrated by C. P. Cavafy's poem "Ithaka":[1]

> *Better if it lasts for years,*
> *so you're old by the time you reach the island,*
> *wealthy with all you've gained on the way,*

And we are here only for a short while, even though VCs are desperately trying to solve for death.

> *Come now, you who say, "Today or tomorrow we will go into such*
> *and such a town and spend a year there*
> *and trade and make a profit" —*
> *yet you do not know what tomorrow will bring.*
> *What is your life?*
> *For you are a mist that appears for a little time and then vanishes.*[2]

So this book weaves in lessons from these three areas — managing risk, service to founders, and above all, developing a framework of values.

AND WHO AM I TO WRITE THIS BOOK?

There are no experts (nor will there ever be) in the world of venture capital. It's like the list of top Hollywood stars or top-performing mutual funds — each year, you have someone new at the top. In this constant churn, we are all learning this craft, and apprenticeship is the name of this daily practice. Those at the top are humbled by the forces of the unknown: risk and uncertainty. In recent times, their own arrogance and exploitative behavior have brought their downfall. And those at the bottom of the pyramid are striving — a combination of luck, some skill, huge networks, and the advantages of market timing lift them up.

Jorge Luis Borges wrote, "I am all the writers that I have read, all the people that I have met, all the women that I have loved; all the cities that I have visited, all my ancestors."[3] With all that and more, being a storyteller at heart, exposure to this business makes it easier for me to share the lessons. Having tasted all three layers of the founder-GP-LP cake as a practitioner in Silicon Valley and having invested in over a hundred companies over the past decade, I have made a lot, lost a lot, and learned a lot. These lessons, some very expensive ones, are offered in this book. In my quest to learn the nuances of this business, I have compiled insights of proven investors from firms like A16Z, Benchmark, First Round, the Foundry Group, True Ventures, Sequoia Capital, and Union Square Ventures, to name a few. I have also woven these with the wisdom of investment giants like Warren Buffett, Charlie Munger, and Nicholas Nassem Taleb because their observations can be applied to most parts of our business and life. And finally, I sprinkled in some wisdom from philosophers and Nobel Laureates (like Bob Dylan).

Having co-invested with some of the best-in-class, and occasionally with the pseudo-intellectuals, opportunists, and carpetbaggers, you experience the *people problem* in our business. You never know the true nature of a person until you reach the extremes of success or failure. Big exits drive greed. Failure gets everyone scampering away. Blame is pinned on some macro-event, China, or circumstance. Amidst these roller-coaster rides, I learned two things well: (a) how to avoid the self-serving and the greedy and (b) where I could not avoid, I mastered the art of projectile vomiting.

As Rudyard Kipling wrote in his poem, "If":[4]

If you can make one heap of all your winnings
And risk it on one turn of pitch-and-toss,
And lose, and start again at your beginnings
And never breathe a word about your loss. . .

Yup, I've experienced a bit of that. So those are some good reasons why I'm qualified to write such a book.

If you feel the ROI on this book has not been to your high expectations, dear reader, I am sorry I have wasted your time with this rambling repository of riffs, anecdotes, and generally available kitschy stuff. And yes, I'm happy to refund you a full amount. Or make a donation to a charity of your choice. For all others who get featured on that *Forbes* Midas List after reading a page or two of this book, do feel free to send me a few points of that carry. I'm saving up to buy a winery in Hawaii as I approach my retirement years. Aloha to health, happiness, harmony, peace, abundance, and carry.

WHAT SHOULD YOU KNOW ABOUT THIS BUSINESS OF VENTURE CAPITAL?

It's not as easy as it looks. And not as hard as you might think it is. But I'm sure you expect a bit more than that. So here are seven pointers:

1. *The VC business is changing, growing, and even maturing a bit.* There are over a thousand VC firms managing about $400 billion in assets under management (AUM). This has doubled in the past decade, which is a good thing. Money is flowing in this asset class, and our business is about deal flow and cash flow — and with LPs pouring in the cash, VCs can continue to make investments. In any given year, 200+ funds raise their capital, and the average fund size raised is now at $200+ million. The largest VC fund raised was Sequoia Growth at $8 billion. The $100 billion Softbank Vision Fund is in a league of its own — more capital than all venture funds combined, promising trillions in return. Such a leap in the punctuated equilibrium of funds is a once-in-a-lifetime event, where it leaps 100X over the average fund size of $1 billion. A billion no longer brings a sense of awe, but a $100 billion fund might be trending alongside #respect and #unicorns. With COVID pandemic, we are forced to make investment decisions without much face-to-face interactions. I am sure such a shift will eliminate a lot of meeting room

theatrics, posturing, and above all — the nonsensical CEO assessments, where VCs make leadership judgments in a few hours and are always wrong.

2. *Veni, Vedi, VC.* Let's conquer and disrupt everything. The final frontier is death. Brave scientists and founders, armed with capital, have raised capital to mine asteroids, live on Mars (the planet, not the chocolate factory), and solve for every problem — existent or imagined. One startup was launched so that we could just say "yo" to each other. It raised a few million and then died. Investment thesis have expanded from software and technology domains, to new promises and fertile lands. Like nomadic farmers, VCs are rushing into new territories — artificial intelligence, robotics, blockchain, finance and insurance technologies, and an alphabet soup of buzzwords that include 5G and IoT, sprinkled with quantum, edge-computing. The opportunity set is broad. GPs have a hard time focusing — we are all kids in this global candy shop of innovation. This is the best time to be in the business of VC.

3. *More money = more competition = higher entry valuations = lower returns.* With additional flows of capital, we are reminded of the basics of economic theory. Supply and demand, prices and elasticity — as VCs chase risk-adjusted returns, the valuation curves in later-stage companies have started to bend dramatically. Or let me put it another way — valuations have become crazy pricey. And as one side goes up, another goes down. This impacts potential for generating returns. Increased valuations have got very little to do with higher acquisition values or superior exit outcomes — it's merely a function of more money chasing a few good opportunities. So as the competition heats up, we need to improve sourcing skills, engage with founders via disciplined processes, and understand how we can deliver higher probabilistic outcomes. Boy, this game just got a lot more serious. So it's time to hone your investment skills.

4. *Honing your skills beyond term sheets and balance sheets is important.* Are you good at probability? Playing poker? Nerdy enough to bet on technology trends? How do you want to play — are you fiercely competitive? Or are you like Peter Thiel, who likes monopolistic hidden gems and operates like a chess grandmaster? He is also good at probabilistic betting and snagging big outcomes — his $500,000 investment in Facebook generated a 10,000X return. Even his $1.5 million bet on Donald Trump's election campaign paid off big time, while CRV, an East Coast venture firm, blazoned its website home page with **"F*ck Trump"** on election day. So as an investor, you have to decide which part of the playground you want to play in. Business, finance, politics, power — or a mix of all. This will define your investment thesis or strategy and help you to hone your areas of focus. With pandemics, trade wars, and geopolitical shifts, new opportunities continue to arise, and the world is indeed your oyster. Try to make sense of all these trends and then do the most difficult part — develop some unique points of view, not widely understood or accepted. You make money only when you find hidden gems in non-obvious places.

5. *We take ourselves too seriously, and imitate each other mindlessly.* Most VCs like to portray themselves as super-intellectuals when all they do is rinse and recycle ideas, picked up from others. Most VCs mindlessly imitate a handful of top-tier investors, chasing their investments while positioning themselves as thought leaders. HBO launched a parody... er ... a comedy show on the antics of VCs and founders in Silicon Valley. We have come a long way indeed when we have our own show — a sign of maturity. It's not just investment strategies or authoring blog posts and essays that are being mimicked. Be it office space or fashion, VCs herd together from Sand Hill Road to South Park. Patagonia vests are so popular with VCs in Silicon Valley, *Fortune* magazine ran a

parody post titled "Group of White Men in Patagonia Vests Confused for VC Fund, Raise $500 Million,"[5] where one fictitious VC, Evan, says, "At first I tried to tell people we don't work in venture capital. . .But then I got to thinking, how hard can it be? I can always tell which ideas are good ideas, and now I have a few hundred million dollars to prove it." One of their investments was in Patagon.io (no relation to Patagonia), which is experiencing hockey-stick growth. To make their job really easy, they backed a group of data scientists who have found a way to use drones and artificial intelligence to geolocate groups of white men wearing Patagonia vests in order to predict future investment opportunities. Amen!

6. *We rationalize in hindsight, and don't fully understand our biases.* One of the finest books on human behavior, *Thinking Fast and Slow* by Daniel Kahneman is fat and dense, but it can give you insights in your own mind's operating system (or the OS and the BS in our heads). Or *Workplace Poker* by Dan Rust can help you play politics better, and even gracefully tackle your smiley-faced backstabbing partners. Try to understand your special skills and unfair advantages that can help you win — you may be able to spot technology trends while others are busy elsewhere, or know people that can bring value to your world in creative ways. You may be a well-connected princeling or have access to the corridors of power. Improving your game involves maintaining a student mind-set, understating human psychology, biases in decision-making, spotting groupthink, avoiding false starts or flash trends, and catching big waves.

7. *The VC business model is evolving, but slowly — very slowly.* When Fred Wilson was asked how the VC model will evolve in 20 years, he said, *"All I know is that it will be different."* He was humble enough to avoid making grandiose predictions. The only significant innovation in the past decade has been that carry has gone from 20 percent

to 30 percent for some firms, while losses have worsened. In recent years, we have seen the rise of online platforms to facilitate more transactions and liquidity (AngelList, SecondMarkets) and the use of big-data and AI (just Google "Chris Farmer and SignalFire" and see how his data-driven VC approach can disrupt the disruptors), and the distributed ledger. It can shift the flow of capital from the LP-GP-founder trickle to a game-changing peer-to-peer funding model. Fun times ahead.

Build on these last 50 years of VC legacy and create your own recipe for VC in the next 50 — your own brave new world. And don't compare yourself to the VC heroes and gods, but carve your own authentic path.

As advertising guru David Ogilvy once said, "Aim for the company of immortals."

Acknowledgments

Each of us bears the imprint
Of a friend met along the way;
In each the trace of each.
For good or evil
In wisdom or in folly
Everyone stamped by everyone.

—Primo Levi

And so, this book bears an imprint of many brilliant minds, friends good and wise. This labor of love would not have been possible without the help of all those who shared their experiences, insights, and wisdom — in sharing tactical and strategic, they also show us how to become better people, living their lives with the precepts of #givefirst. Thank you, Brad, for sharing your knowledge, abundance of spirit, and generosity of the soul. You are, indeed, the silent force that works relentlessly for the greater good, like the Gandhi of Venture Capital. I am deeply grateful to Scott Kupor, managing partner at Andreessen Horowitz (A16Z) and former chairman of National Venture Capital Association. Scott is a gifted and empathetic leader. His big heart and rigorous intellectual engagement have helped and guided many, including me. Having good role models in our business is important, so thank you to all those who spent time with me — too numerous to name — your quotes, wisdom, insights, and fingerprints are all over this book. You have helped shape the minds of investors of tomorrow with your ethos, behavior, blog posts, and tweets.

This book, in its third edition now, has stood upon the shoulders of investor-giants. When the first edition came out a decade ago, I had no idea where all this was going. You, dear reader, have made this journey an absolute delight. I am grateful to you for all the numerous emails, reviews, feedback, and comments for the previous editions. All your kind words are rightfully deserving of the VCs mentioned in this book. They are the lead singers who deserve the applause and gratitude. That I get to hang out with such smart, generous people is a blessing.

Above all, I thank the Great Spirit — the mysterious unknown that inspires and guides us to pursue greater good, gives us the tenacity to stay the course in tough times, and helps us to bring our gifts to society.

Part One

The Making of a VC

Most good beginnings in this land of venture capital careers involve some planning, some luck, and not taking yourself too seriously. How does this business work — what does an average day look like — how do you get in and how do you grow — and what are the pitfalls? Is it just about making money — multiplying green pieces of paper and filthy lucre?

Should you try to keep improving every day? "If you are under the impression you have already perfected yourself, you will never rise to the heights you are no doubt capable of," Kazuo Ishiguro, wrote in his book, *The Remains of the Day*. It is no wonder that Jeff Bezos, founder and CEO of Amazon, refers to this book as one of his favorites.

What makes a good VC? Is it skill, tenacity, or that mysterious stroke of luck? Is it a network of relationships, or is it market timing? And who decides what is good? If you follow the industry standards, then it's largely returns — cash-on-cash multiples you can generate as fast as you can. That will get you a place on the vanity charts of Forbes Midas List of Venture Capitalists, which can elevate your brand and career prospectus. How do you grow as a person? Should VCs think about their role in society — to support and enhance systems of governance, better education, role of arts, and a healthier environment? Or should we pretend that those problems do not belong to us nor affect us?

As my mama said, never trust anyone who tells you how to get in but does not show you how to get out — be it a swimming pool, a dark cave with supposedly hidden treasures, or the business of venture capital. Hanging out with cool founders every day, discussing the latest bleeding-edge trends, can be fun, even addictive. You need to know how to get out of this business. Alcoholics Anonymous has a 12-step program to recovery — but for investors addicted to the adrenalin rush of cool-tech and exit-highs, there are no support groups. On that note, I have added a chapter on your own exit strategies — just as you get in, you should know how to graciously find your way out of the maze.

1

The Business of Cash and Carry

INTRODUCTION: AN OPERATIONAL PRIMER

For Masayoshi Son, raising a $100 billion Softbank Vision fund was easy. As he quips, it was "$45 billion in 45 minutes" — his 45-minute meeting with Saudi Arabia's crown prince kicked off the fund raise. To the prince, Masa offered a gift. "I want to give you a Masa gift, the Tokyo gift, a $1 trillion gift. Here's how I can give you a $1 trillion gift: You invest $100 billion in my fund, I give you a trillion." Son left the meeting with a commitment of $45 billion, and other investors followed soon thereafter. The world's largest venture fund was off to the races.

But if raising $100 billion was that easy, the doyens of Sand Hill Road venture firms would have done it long ago. For Softbank, the journey started in the year 2000, with a $20 million investment in Alibaba, a startup that would eventually grow into a Chinese e-commerce giant. Alibaba went public in 2014, and at that time, Softbank's 28 percent stake in the company was valued at $58 billion. Son had also invested in Yahoo! in 1996 and reaped its rewards, following the company's IPO four years later. Son's fascination with the world of technology started with the microprocessor. "When I was 17 years old, the very first time I saw a photo of a microprocessor, it made me cry. I was overwhelmed," he would say. As the waves of innovation rose and fell, the teeny microprocessor spawned into the World Wide Web in the 1990s, followed by the cloud and mobility a decade later. Son kept surfing along and is poised to ride the next trend — be it technological changes like robotics, automation, and artificial intelligence (AI) or societal changes such as ridesharing, vertical farming, and food delivery.

Those who have analyzed his historic investment track record point to the fact that even if you slice off the biggest win — his Alibaba investment — the rest of his portfolio shows above 40 percent internal rate of return (IRR). When the industry average performance is in the mid-teens, having such a significant edge in investment performance helps. Combine that with a boldness of vision and the ability to execute on a global investment strategy and voilà — you have $45 billion in 45 minutes.

The venture capitalist's journey often begins with the ability to raise a venture fund (Exhibit 1.1). The universe of investors in any venture fund includes two broad categories: (a) institutional investors such as pension funds, foundations, university endowments, sovereign wealth funds, business corporations, and (b) high-net-worth individuals (HNWIs) and their family offices (see Exhibit 1.2). Institutional investors primarily view venture funds as an asset class, a money-making machine that promises to deliver an annualized "risk-adjusted" IRR.

Exhibit 1.1 **Venture capital business model.**

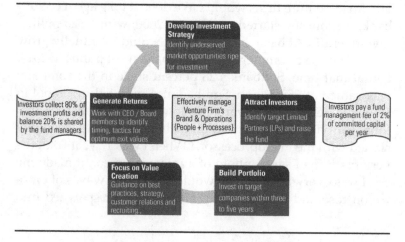

Exhibit 1.2 **Limited partners.**

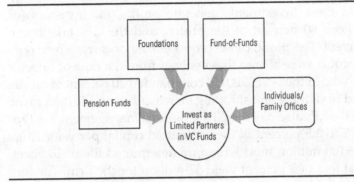

The VC business model is simple: a venture capitalist, or general partner (GP), knocks on the door of various investors, known as limited partners (LP), to raise a fund. LPs agree to invest in venture funds based on the venture capitalist's background, investment expertise and past performance, a compelling investment strategy, and, to some extent, that mystical X factor — an amalgamation of ability, skills, and luck that defies any logical construct and makes one practitioner more successful than the others.

The two groups — the GP as the investment manager and the LP as the provider of capital — form a 10-year partnership. The LP agrees to pay the GP a management fee each year and a share in a percentage of the profits. In turn, the GP agrees to work night and day to find hot, blazing startups, to invest the capital, turn them into unicorns (billion-dollar valued companies), and harvest the money back in large multiples. The end game for the LP is to make a superior risk-adjusted financial return. The primary measure of success for the venture firm is the IRR and cash-on-cash (C-on-C) return, a multiple of the original investment amount or multiple of invested capital (MOIC). Venture firms and GPs live, and are slaughtered by, these two metrics.

To better understand the economics, take the example of a $100 million fund. The GPs of the fund would invest this capital in, say, about a dozen companies and after building value aspire to "exit" the investments, meaning to sell the ownership. Should these investments generate profits, the investors (or LPs) keep 80 percent of the profits, and the GPs take home 20 percent. The profit, called *carried interest* or carry, where one-fifth profits were shared, has evolved from the time of Phoenicians, who in the year 1200 CE commanded 20 percent of profits earned from trade and shipping merchandise. In addition to the carry, the LPs also pay the GPs an annual management fee, typically 2 to 2.5 percent of the committed capital per year. Thus, for a $100 million fund with a predetermined life of 10 years, annual fees of 2 percent yield $2 million for the firm. The fees provide for the day-to-day operations of the firm and are used to pay for salaries, travel, operational, and legal expenses. The responsibilities and compensation packages are determined by the professional's responsibilities and experience.

A *venture fund* is defined as a fixed pool of capital raised for investing per an agreed-upon investment strategy. A *venture firm* manages this fund, and, over time, a firm can manage multiple funds. The GPs are the primary investment decision makers and are supported by a team of investment and administrative professionals.

To get a venture fund off the ground, several such investors have to be pitched, engaged, convinced, cajoled, and even threatened to commit to a fund. This is often a long, arduous journey for most venture professionals. Fundraising stretches every thread — salesmanship, tenacity, and fortitude. To start with, it's never easy to identify the right target set of investors. It's like searching for a black cat in a dark room — often, the cat does not exist and you can spin around in the dark room. Assuming you can build a target list of fund investors, all the classical challenges of any sales process come into play. Getting in the door, engagement with the decision makers, pushing to a close with not one but at least a dozen or more investors requires special talents. Seldom do investors respond promptly, offer clear feedback on their decision-making criteria, process, and time lines.

Building momentum amongst a group of disparate investors to reach a satisfactory fund size takes as much as 18 months and is often compared to an uphill crawl on broken glass. Attracting, engaging, and assembling a large number of investors is often like a game of house of cards. If one of them pulls out early in the process, a cascading effect can occur. For every fund that makes it to the finish line, at least three die a premature death, littering the venture graveyards with unfulfilled ambitions, ill-timed strategies, and broken partnerships that never got off the ground.

Once the "fund" is subscribed to its target amount, it is closed and no new investors are admitted. The life of such a fund is typically 10 years, during which the venture professionals build a portfolio of companies and aspire to generate returns. The fund is typically dissolved after the tenth year, or when all portfolio investments have been liquidated.

After the fundraising process is complete, venture professionals are under pressure to deploy the capital. During this investment period, startups come in, investors check them out, and the mating dance begins. Pitch decks, term sheets, valuations, and board seats are negotiated as a venture fund builds a portfolio of 20–24 companies within three to five years. A typical portfolio size for any fund can be 10–30 companies, based on the sector and stage of investment.

ROLES, RESPONSIBILITIES, AND COMPENSATION

In any venture firm, the cast of characters includes the GPs (also known as managing directors or managing GPs), vice presidents, principals, associates, and analysts (Exhibit 1.3). These primary investment professionals are responsible for generating returns. Newer titles have evolved as fund operations have become more focused. For example, in larger funds, roles such as director of business development or the head of deal sourcing have emerged. The administrative team, also referred to as the *back office*, is responsible for the day-to-day operational aspects. This team includes chief operating officer, chief financial officer, general counsel administrative, and human resources.

Exhibit 1.3 **Fund organization chart.**

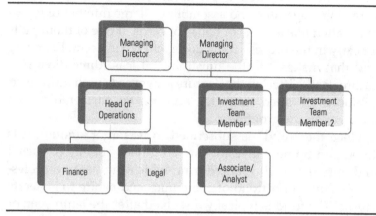

The primary responsibilities of the investment team differ along the lines of seniority. On any typical day, the GPs would juggle a number of activities: negotiating terms for investment opportunities, participating in boards of current portfolio companies, responding to any LP/investor requests, and putting out a few fires along the way. On a rare day, exit negotiations may occur. An entry-level analyst is expected to source investment opportunities and conduct the first screening of due diligence. At the other end of the spectrum, the partners keep a close watch on portfolio construction, governance, exits, and strategy and timing of the next fund. The typical compensation package includes a salary, annual performance bonus, and a share of the profits called *carry*, which stands for carried interest.

As they say, any fool can write a check, but it takes some skill (and luck) to generate financial returns. To select and win the right investment opportunity in a highly competitive environment calls for a blend of analytical rigor and speed, with a strong brand and network of relationships. Yet despite all the front-end challenges, almost 80 percent of all investments fail. Unproven technologies, shifting market dynamics, management team challenges, competition, and regulation can kill a company. Any venture fund's portfolio will eventually end up with a mix of successes, some average outcomes, and flame-outs. A typical rule of thumb is that one-third of the portfolio companies return 5X to 10X multiple of invested capital; one-third will generate lower outcomes — say 1X to 2X of invested capital, and the final one-third of the portfolio will fail — be the scars on the back, relegated to the "experience" bucket as total losses.

Returns are measured by MOIC and IRR. While the multiple of invested capital is often touted as a metric of success, it is equally important to demonstrate speed. The IRR is a function of time. Its underlying notion of time-value of money implies that a dollar today is more valuable than a dollar tomorrow. Put a different way, time is your enemy. The faster you can sell, or exit, a portfolio company, for as high an amount, the higher the IRR. As seen in Exhibit 1.4, the holding period of an investment can have a significant impact on IRR, while the multiple on invested capital remains the same.

A fund's portfolio companies are reduced to a single line statistic — measured primarily by multiple of invested capital and gross IRR. See Exhibit 1.5.

On the surface, the business looks like a fascinating game, where you can write large checks, dole out advise to founders, and write blog posts in media touting your investment thesis. Beneath the surface, there is a fair amount of uncertainty, stress, competition, and turmoil. As Sir Michael Moritz of Sequoia Capital once said, "It is a business of a thousand soap operas."

Exhibit 1.4 **The Advantages of Shorter Holding Periods.**

Company	Capital Invested ($m)	Realized Value ($m)	Holding Period (years)	Multiple on Invested Capital (MOIC)	Gross IRR (%)
Company 1	$1.0m	$5.0m	2	5X	123.6 %
Company 2	$1.0m	$5.0m	6	5X	37.9 %

Exhibit 1.5 **Fund Portfolio Returns.**

Portfolio Company	Capital Invested ($m)	Current Value ($m)	Multiple on Invested Capital (MOIC)	Gross IRR
Company A	$6.50	$39.20	6.08X	60.60 %
Company B	$2.10	$2.10	1X	0.00 %
Company C	$9.60	$33.10	3.8X	46.20 %
Company D	$6.80	$0.60	0.09X	−53.00 %
Fund	**$25.00**	**$75.00**	**3.00X**	**51.2 %**

Top Takeaways

Launching a venture firm requires:

- A bold vision aligned with market forces
- Compelling and timely investment strategy
- Investment performance/track record
- And above all, the ability to be persuasive

2

Why Choose a Career in VC

Fueling the frontiers of innovation, being an agent of change, supporting the next generation founders, asymmetric financial gains, freedom/autonomy from the 9-to-5 drudgery, or the thrill of building companies — the role of venture capitalists is never dull. If anything, it is like a drug — easy to get hooked and high, harder to let go.

CREATIVE CONSTRUCTION

One of the influential economists, Joseph Schumpeter, coined the term *creative destruction*, where industries are decimated when innovative trends occur: The *"gale of creative destruction"* whips through the *"process of industrial mutation that incessantly revolutionizes the economic structure from within, incessantly destroying the old one, incessantly creating a new one."* On the other side are where the forces of creative construction, entrepreneurs and venture capitalists, are at work. When a paradigm shift occurs in any technological ecosystem, it is more likely that a founder and some venture capital investors are stoking that disruptive entrepreneurial fire. "See, venture capital is reducible to a few words. You have to be interested in managing change, and you have to recognize that change is *necessary*,"[1] says Donald T. Valentine, founder of Sequoia Capital. To be a part of creating that new *new thing* can be immensely satisfying.

INTELLECTUAL STIMULATION

A career in venture capital investing is "the most fun you can have with your clothes on," says Deepak Kamra of Canaan Partners.[2] A day in the life of a venture capitalist is full of stimulating conversations with entrepreneurs who are changing the world. At various points in their startup journey, entrepreneurs seek investors, not only for the moolah but to test assumptions, validate their concepts, and prepare for the road ahead. Amid all these caffeine-laden dreams, the investor is exposed to a steep learning curve of technological changes, the shifting sands of market dynamics, sources of opportunity, and competitive constraints. For those who thrive on comfort in ambiguity, a rapid pace, headbutting with type A entrepreneurs, and "those crazy ones," the career path of venture capital offers it all. Elizabeth "Beezer" Clarkson, managing director of Sapphire Ventures, says, "We forget how unusual this career is. We are privileged. Other sectors seem pale in comparison when we look at the range of energy and creativity that flows to us. It can be addictive."

MENTOR CAPITALISTS

Those who have had a successful entrepreneurial journey often see venture capital as a pathway of imparting their lessons to the founders and entrepreneurs. "At a certain point in your career, it is more satisfying to help entrepreneurs than to be one," says Marc Andreessen, co-founder of Andreessen Horowitz.[3] Scott Weiss joined Andreessen Horowitz after selling his company, IronPort Systems, to Cisco. "Being a venture capitalist gives me the opportunity to mentor and offer direction to the entrepreneurs. They trust my judgment because I have been down this path before," he points out. Several practitioners agreed that the VC career path allows them to continue to live vicariously through supporting other entrepreneurs.

ASYMMETRICAL REWARDS

Venture capital is an "antifragile" career with fundamental asymmetry. Hourly wage earners get paid for time, not value. This may be one of the few career paths that offer exponential financial returns while bringing innovation and positive change to society. In his book *Antifragile*, author Nicholas Naseem Taleb defines asymmetry to be when you have more upside than downside and tend to gain from volatility,

Exhibit 2.1 **The perks of being a VC in Silicon Valley — reserved parking.**

randomness, stressors, errors, time, and uncertainty. Venture capitalists thrive on information asymmetry. They have a ringside view of the technological future, and the companies they have funded are often the ones to become the next-generation behemoths. Financial gains are expected as a byproduct of value creation, but only after asymmetry is identified and realized.

In Silicon Valley, where parking is a perk reserved for the rich, you even find spots that are for exclusive use of venture capitalists. Along with pregnant mothers-to-be, disabled and handicapped, and the environmentally conscious Tesla owners, you find a spot reserved for the VCs (Exhibit 2.1). I once parked at such a spot to see how it might be enforced — do uniformed parking police officers come by, check my LinkedIn profile, my assets-under-management (AUM), and approve with a stern nod? And under what circumstances would I get a parking ticket?

Anyone who wants to be a VC but says it's not for the money is lying. Trying to get-rich-quick in this business has caused more destruction and career implosions. In a rush, naive investors have made decisions that have hurt companies, founders, and their own psyche. VC is a long game, where results prove out after a decade. If you want to see your financial returns at 4 P.M. every day, join a hedge fund.

3

Attributes of Successful VCs

Success in the world of investing boils down to the ability to pick "good" investments. "You have to become a great buyer," says Mike Maples of Floodgate Fund. Yet the ability to pick the good investments sounds deceptively easy, as any fool can write a check. And we typically realize our folly after making a lot of bad investments. Or as they say, good judgment comes from experience, and experience comes from bad judgment.

The primary goal for any venture capitalist is to create value — for their entrepreneurs and their fund investors. "We are in the business of helping a company achieve critical path milestones. Being able to determine what is critical path is a matter of survival — our job is to be insanely rigorous about what the critical path is." A definitive characteristic about a venture capitalist is being analytical about these milestones, says James Bryer, former chairman, National Venture Capital Association.

Successful venture capitalists have an entrepreneurial mindset, the ability to understand the basics of value creation. Yet, the background of some of the leading venture capitalists demonstrates no clear pattern. You could have operational expertise. Or not. To become better at the art of investing, here are a few attributes.

STRONG AWARENESS OF TECH TRENDS

As any candidate who aspires to be a VC someday, new entrants can bring new insights in an ever-evolving technology world. Where are the new hidden opportunities? How best can we gain access to them? The only way you would be able to add value to the venture firm is if you live, breathe, and surf on the edge of those technology waves. As a newly minted investor, try to build a list of 10 key technology trends that will impact our society over the next decade. Identify three to five trends that appeal to you, and in which you might have an edge. The best way to validate your thinking is to seek some guidance from seasoned investors. Never hesitate to send a cold email, but make it respectful and well-crafted. "I am always happy to help — it makes it easier when I get a thoughtful request," says Brad Feld, of Foundry Group. But know that most VCs are spread very thin on time. To make a strong impact, a deep and a thorough level of preparation is essential.

When I interviewed Terry McGuire of Polaris Ventures, a VC of 25 years, he said, "I like it when a candidate says, why did you invest in this company as opposed to that one? Not only did you check out our website but combined that with an awareness of technology waves and other opportunities therein." So while you can get in the door of a VC, what will keep you there is your level of thinking, preparation, discipline, and homework.

"A lot of good venture capitalists have 'situational awareness' — they can walk into just about any kind of meeting and, in about five minutes, figure out who's doing what to whom and exactly what the issues are, sort of cut through it and figure out what's going on. You can look at a given situation and project its trajectory reasonably well," says James R. Swartz, formerly of Accel Partners. "You need to build a frame of reference by which to judge people and to judge opportunities and to be able to judge markets and what's going on in the economy," says Reid Dennis, founder of Institutional Venture Partners.

Christopher Rizik, a former VC who now manages Renaissance Venture Fund, a fund of funds (FoF), says, "Have a good sense of the world around you and how it is changing. After all, we put money behind ideas that change the world — the demographic, technological — unfilled needs. You have to be open and curious to look out into the future."

ABILITY TO PICK WINNERS

Entrepreneurial expertise matters, but not as much. What matters is the value you create. Venture capitalists love it when a potential candidate has some entrepreneurial expertise — has built a product, attracted investor capital, managed teams, and led a company to an exit. Those very skills can sometimes become a handicap to an investor. One of the operator-turned-investors shared with me that the hardest part of their role is to stay on the sidelines. "It is not your role to be the CEO. I am always trying to run the company in proxy — jump in to save the company, steer it in the right direction or drive it faster." There is indeed no predictor of success in VC, so don't let the lack of entrepreneurial experience stop you. Investment bankers, McKinsey consultants, lawyers, and journalists have made successful forays in the VC world. Your resume does not count anymore as much as value you may have created for founders. As the founders sing your praises, other founders will soon hear about it and start to call you, as opposed to you chasing opportunities all day. As you sift through these opportunities, becoming a good judge of human character and entrepreneurial abilities is critical. "We see a lot of executives who have a vision. Our job is to decide if it really is a vision or a hallucination," one VC remarked. Once you can pick the winner, you have to move fast. "Having a great brand is a good start. Speed of decision-making is equally important," says Jeff Clavier of Uncork VC. If you like the startup, you have to move quickly to seal the deal. If you don't, someone will gladly do so. This is a highly competitive business, especially in Silicon Valley.

OPTIMISM, PATIENCE, AND STABILITY

"You have to believe that the world can change . . . be optimistic and at the same time, be realistic and guarded, not romantic," says Terry McGuire, co-founder, Polaris Ventures and Emeritus Chairman of National Venture Capital Association. "You've got to be a good listener. I find if the venture capitalist does all the talking, he doesn't learn very much about the people he's thinking about investing in. Very important to listen . . . and judge who looks and feels like they have the makings of making a real company. Eventually, it becomes instinct if you do it often enough," says Paul "Pete" Bancroft, former CEO of Bessemer Securities, former chairman of National Venture Capital Association. It's a combination of innate skills (optimism, judgment, comfort in ambiguity) combined with real-world experience. "Good instinct, well honed by experience, makes a good venture capitalist. The most difficult part is dealing with uncertainty," says C. Richard Kramlich, chairman and co-founder, New Enterprise Associates (NEA). Chris Rizik adds this:

> Nothing will be as fast as you want. A smart practitioner never panics or gives up when companies hit a bump. Those who are patient will not only profit but will ultimately succeed at the expense of those who panic. Patience should be married with intelligence — if you can no longer achieve the end game, it takes discipline to walk away and say, we are just not going to get there. Swallow hard and realize you just lost a few million. Along the way, we have to be fair with one and all. What goes around comes around. In the end, the best VCs are people who were fair, were smart, and treated everyone well. People seldom want to work with those who are out only for themselves.

ABILITY TO LEARN AND GROW

While there is no good predictor of what makes a good venture capitalist, some patterns are obvious. Those without substantial startup or operating experience can be successful in the profession. Although domain expertise may be good, it certainly is not of significant importance in the long run. Your performance eventually matters. "In my 20-year career as a venture capitalist, I have invested in all kinds of domains and companies. For long-term success in this business, you have to think more generally and push yourself out of your comfort zone. You should be willing to reinvent yourself," says David Cowan, Bessemer Venture Partners.

It's not just a few skills that matter but the ability to "adapt/grow" with the company and reinvent oneself. Promod Haque of Norwest Venture Partners echoes this sentiment:

Being a venture capitalist requires a varying degree of skills. At a seed stage, the skills required are different from say, investments at a mid or later stage. At the seed stage, we have a founder. The venture practitioner needs to have the ability to understand risk, validate ideas, and connect these to the market. Exploration and validation are key steps at this stage. A startup is a no-name entity — the credibility and track record of the venture practitioner can be a tremendous asset in recruiting management talent and customers. Talent that can grow the company is usually in high demand and otherwise would not be available. In the early stage, the practitioner's ability to help the startup to find customers is very important. The Fortune 100 companies — those marquee customers that all startups seek — unfortunately avoid startups. They are trying to minimize the number of vendors and stick with the proven ones . . . even if you get your foot in the door, these companies need time and ability to assess the new product. It's a significant commitment . . . these are extremely busy executives and asking them to check a new product out requires strong suite of skills. As the company evolves further, the ability to syndicate the investment becomes critical. Other investors will look at how you are putting the investment rationale and leading the round.

AN INHERENT BIAS FOR ACTION

Seth Levine of the Foundry Group says that a good practitioner needs to have some attention deficit disorder (ADD) to be a good venture capitalist:

> The core of being a good VC is the ability to move from one thing to the next, often completely disconnected thing, quickly and without slowing down. Rare is the time when I sit down and spend a few hours doing something (anything) without interruption; so much so that I generally interrupt myself these days if I'm spending too much time on any one thing, but mostly because in any given day things just seem to come up constantly. With something like eight companies that I actively work with these interruptions are all over the map — I may be helping one company sell its business, another raise capital, another plan for a strategic offsite and another with an executive search. Keeping all of this straight in my head is a bit of a task, as is shifting gears from talking about the tax considerations of a particular merger structure with one company to looking at moving into a new vertical market for another.

To summarize, a good VC has the ability to pick good investments and help build great companies. VCs with a mix of business experience and empathy, a supportive mindset can be "the investor of choice" and magnet for entrepreneurs. As long as your internal axis is tilting toward supporting, as Steve Jobs would say, those crazy ones, the journey will be a joyride.

4

Welcome to the Land of Ad-Venture

In a business of 10X outcomes, there are 100X applicants for every open position. And within the best venture firms, there are no openings posted publicly. Firms are small, tightly knit groups — a rock band, or a sports team of high performers — and bringing in a new team member requires careful thought, planning, and execution, else the whole thing blows up. Partners are vetted carefully over multiple engagements and long dating periods and are hired within known circles. Philosopher and author Joseph Campbell once wrote, "A bit of advice, given to a young Native American at the time of his initiation — As you go the way of life, you will see a great chasm. Jump. It is not as wide as you think."

There are no barriers at all to entry, indeed, to get into the business of venture capital. The veritable pipeline of wanna-be investors is infinite and never-ending, with eager-beavers, gold-diggers, carpet baggers, opportunists, and some very few prepared minds. To practice law or medicine, you have the bar examination. Or enroll in a residency, put in grueling hours and start at the bottom of the proverbial ladder. The venture capitalists' career path is not barricaded in any way, except intellect and investable capital. Some VCs have both.

ROLES AND RESPONSIBILITIES OF A VC

*". . . you need a license to drive a car or buy a gun,
but not to be a venture capitalist."*

—Marc Andreessen, co-founder,
Andreessen Horowitz (A16Z)

At New Enterprise Associates (NEA), one of the leading venture firms on Sand Hill Road with over $10 billion under management today, a bright associate level candidate shared his travails with me. After spending two years in investment banking, he joined NEA, where he is focused on enterprise software investments. The young man was adept and spoke fluently on all the major technology trends and the alphabet soup of IoT, 5G, and AI. "I was stunned to see how hard working most partners are at our firm," he says. To newcomers seeking to dip their toe in venture capital, he says, "You have to prepare for a set of radically different tasks each day. Don't let anyone tell you this is easy. And you learn quickly to not take the first opportunity that walks in the door, but rather analyze the universe for the best." Getting into a Sand Hill Road firm takes a bit of luck, experience, and skills. Yet for others, the challenges of getting in can be significantly higher.

Take the example of a pre-MBA analyst position posted at Bessemer Venture Partners, one of the longest-standing venture capital firms in the country (the firm started in 1911). More than 650 resumes, 42 first-round interviews, and 7 second-round interviews later, one offer was made. That's about 0.15 percent odds for an entry-level position! Such odds are daunting for any aspirant. Other positions on LinkedIn attract a large number of applicants, as many as 300 applicants for each position.

An investor with an international venture firm bemoaned the fact that post-MBA, getting in VC is not as easy. "We over-optimize for getting into venture but rarely does a candidate get two competing job offers from two firms. Unlike consulting, investment banking or other career paths where you have multiple choices, this is a narrow road." Compare this with a career in investment banking and you get a very different picture. Alice Easton writes in the *Daily Princetonian*:

> After months of dressing up in suits and ties, making their way to New York or the Nassau Inn and trying to impress panels of interviewers with their technical and social skills, juniors applying for summer internships in finance and consulting can now reap the benefits of their work: elaborate "sell days" to convince them to accept the job. . . . They paid for two nights at a fancy hotel in New York. . . . They rented out a museum and had a cocktail party, and then rented out the VIP room in a nightclub in Soho. . . . They even send chocolates in the mail. . . . They showed recruits a whole lifestyle. When Goldman Sachs CEO gave a keynote speech to Wharton MBA students, the first point he made after stating Goldman Sachs's $23 billion in revenue in 2004 was the importance his firm places on "hiring and retaining the best people" in order to maintain a "culture of excellence."[1]

Brant Moxley, managing director at Pinnacle Group International, an executive recruiting firm that focuses on private equity and venture capital career opportunities, says, "There are 10 times the number of applicants for every job opening in the venture capital arena. The demand is staggering. Strong operating experience and technical and financial skills, or experience in the investment banking business may also be a badge of honor at the entry level. What I find fascinating is while everyone wants to get in the business of venture capital, not many understand what it takes to stay in the business."

Sarah Tavel, a partner at Benchmark, wrote, "People who tend to rise to the top during the selection process do so because of their passion, not just for venture capital but for the entire ecosystem."[2]

A pre-MBA position is, by design, established for two years. "Ninety percent of the time, these positions are not partner

A Typical Venture Capitalist's (VC's) Responsibilities

A typical position description for investment professional would read as follows:

Key tasks and responsibilities. Participate in and contribute to all aspects of the investment process with responsibility for all quantitative and qualitative analysis of portfolio companies.

Sourcing and Analysis. Develop a sourcing strategy and identify key competitive elements in developing a sustained long term advantage. Evaluate potential opportunities, including sector research and trend analysis. Conduct due diligence, assist with deal execution and transaction management.

Structuring and execution. Negotiate investment structure in close liaison with the legal team. Prepare and coordinate the execution of term sheets, investor rights and share purchase agreements, and other legal documentation.

Portfolio management / Post-investment monitoring. Support the CEO, identify value-add levers and carry out portfolio company analysis on a quarterly basis. Stay up to date on performance variances, top challenges for each company. Prepare returns forecasts and updates for limited partners. Awareness of relevant legal aspects of corporate governance is essential.

Marketing and fundraising. Marketing, positioning, and fundraising via strong relationships with GPs/investors/consultants/advisers.

Skills. Knowledge of relevant (health care, technology, fintech) sectors. Transactional experience and analytical abilities. Advanced financial, business modeling, and writing skills.

Competencies. Results-driven, ambitious, and highly motivated. Strategic and commercial acumen. An entrepreneurial approach, initiative, and adaptability. Team player with a strong work ethic. Excellent networking skills.

tracks. At best, an analyst would stay with the firm for three years, instead of the usual two," declares Brant.

One "associate"-level job position that got lit up on Twitter was symptomatic of an entitled overlord seeking a slave or even a grateful piss-boy, ideally on-call round the clock. Qualifications listed include "someone who grew up poor or very close to poverty" and has an MBA with experience at a top consulting firm. But after all that and the ginormous student-debt, you would start as an executive assistant. Don't lose hope, because someday. . .yes, someday you will be the CEO. Until then, be a slave. "You are someone who understands and accepts they are working for a boss. . . . You should be able to build order from chaos, be able to create structure for someone who has zero" structure, available 24/7, grew up poor (yes, this was listed as a qualification in the ad), and provide concierge like service. If all goes well, you could be the CEO, "make enough for generations to come."[3] Would you apply for such a finely crafted position?

And if you get in, the instability and the churn factor in this career path are high. C. Richard Kramlich of NEA, once remarked, "Below the surface there's a huge amount of turnover."[4] When Bill Gurley graduated, he wanted to be a venture capitalist. He went to New York for the first time in his life to beg for meetings with venture capitalists and was told, "Don't even think about it, kid. Go work for 20 years and then come back." Gurley went on to become one of the biggest sell-side analysts on Wall Street, quickly narrowing his focus to "this thing called the internet, which no one knew anything about at the time." Microsoft founder Bill Gates recommended Gurley for his first venture job with Hummer Winblad. Gurley jumped at the opportunity and said yes before even hearing the entire offer.[5] Soon Benchmark would come knocking and recruit him away.

John Doerr of Kleiner Perkins Caufield & Byers (KPCB) once remarked, "I cold-called Silicon Valley's venture groups, hoping to apprentice myself to one."[6] His cold-calling efforts did not get him a job at KPCB, but eventually, after five years at Intel, John would land at this firm. Brooks Byers, who had asked John to get some experience, famously invited John Doerr for a 5:30 a.m. jog to see how motivated he was. John was at the track the next morning and landed the role.

Like Doerr, Robert Nelsen chased Brooks, too, but found his calling elsewhere. "I remember cold-calling Brook Byers, founder of Kleiner Perkins Caufield & Byers, about a hundred times. . . . I was always interested in venture capital," says Robert (Bob) Nelsen. Nelsen went on to be the cofounder of ARCH Venture Partners (ARCH), which has now grown to manage multibillion in assets. In his 20-year investment career, Bob has led nine companies to valuations of $1 billion or more. "Venture capital was my first career choice," he says. In his first year of business school, Bob read about the launch of ARCH Venture Partners and approached the founder, Steve Lazarus. "I told Steve I would work for him for free." Nelsen started with ARCH as soon as he finished college.[7]

"I heard once that all venture capitalists operated from 3000 Sand Hill Road," says David Cowan. Sand Hill Road was the mecca and Andreessen Horowitz, NEA, Sequoia Capital, Draper Fisher Jurvetson (DFJ), Battery Ventures, and more were all stationed in the same neighborhood. David, who had a brief two-year stint at Oracle, was eager to explore possibilities in the venture universe. One fine afternoon he drove to Sand Hill Road and walked unannounced into one of the venture firm's offices. The lady at the front desk was firm: "No, we don't have any openings." But David persisted. "I am sure you know a few firms who would be looking." The lady pulled out a copy of the Western Association of Venture Capitalists directory and circled a few names. "I wrote letters to five firms. Two of the five offered me a position," recalls David, who has been with Bessemer Venture Partners, for over two decades years.

Cold-calling a venture capital firm rarely works — especially in the modern day. "I don't think that approach will work today. The business is much more complex and competitive," warns David.[8] What might work is likely a web presence. Famously, Union Square Ventures recruited a two-year rotational analyst position by not seeking resumes but asking for "web presence." Union Square defined web presence as "anything accessible via a URL. It could be a blog, a social networking profile, a portfolio, a company, a social bookmarking archive. . . . It is whatever you think best represents who you are online."[9]

At the entry-level position, differentiators can be few and competition fierce. A web presence can be a head start in building your path into a venture career. Building a network of mentors can also allow for rapid growth. "A good mentor in this business can be a huge asset," advises Brant Moxley, who manages a placement firm, working with some of the leading investors. "But realize that in a classic venture firm, the senior partners do not have all the time to mentor juniors. A junior is like a remora feeding on the leftovers of the shark meal — you have to make sure you are in the right feeding ground," he adds with a chuckle.[10]

INTERNSHIPS AND CAMPUS RECRUITMENT

Investment banking trumps VC when it comes to campus recruitment. Taufiq Rahim, a *Daily Princetonian* columnist, wrote of what he called the "hunting season" on campus of the elite. "They're here. I can see them. I can smell them. They're in my inbox. They're in my mailbox. They're on my voicemail. They're outside my door. They're on campus, and they smell blood. . . . They're the investment banks, the consulting firms — McKinsey, Goldman Sachs, Bain and Company, Merrill Lynch"[11] But venture firms rarely conduct campus recruitment drives — the pace of hiring and volume of open positions is

Interviewing for Your VC Position

Preparation:

- Investments: Research the venture firm's profile. Understand the sector and stage of investments, assets under management, and its latest fund size.

- Look up the key portfolio companies, and map their progress. Have these companies signed up strategic partnerships? Have they raised follow-on rounds of capital?

- Performance: Research any major exits.

- Philosophy and culture: Read the founders' and senior partners' blogs. Understand their mind-set and philosophies well.

- Reference checks: Call founders, co-investors, ex-employees ... get to the bottom of how the firm treats people.

Examples of questions you can ask the venture firm:

1. What is the fund's investment strategy?

    - Of course, you have done your homework, checked out the websites and online data sources. You know the firm's history and the background of the founders.

    - Research one or two specific investments, and assess the competitive universe of similar investments made by other venture firms. Dive into the investment rationale and find out why this opportunity was chosen over others.

    - Ask how the fund's investment strategy has evolved over time. What challenges has the fund faced, if any, in sourcing opportunities? In raising capital?

    - Find out the life cycle of the current fund. All venture funds have a three- to five-year investment period from the time the fund is raised. Thus, depending on the timing of your entry, you could be involved in making investments, managing the portfolio, or preparing for the next fund raise.

2. What is a typical day at the firm? To whom would I report, and what self-development opportunities exist for an entry-level person?

   - Look for opportunities where you will participate in all facets of the business.

3. Is this a collaborative environment or a field of cowboys who thrive going solo? How do the team members collaborate with each other, especially when the portfolio companies are in trouble? When has the firm let go of any staff, and why?

   - **Look for troubling situations.** How were these handled by the internal team? Be prepared to get smooth-talked and do not believe everything you hear. You will rarely hear honest statements like "We screwed up on that investment" or the GP "is a Machiavellian despot, who screams his head off and throws things around, muttering obscenities." Talk to the industry peers and CEOs of portfolio companies to get a true sense of the culture of the firm.

   - Can you see yourself having fun with this team? A beer on Friday night?

4. How will my performance be measured? Will we have clear milestones established? Will I be able to measure my own progress? Beware of any firm that does not offer clarity in performance metrics, as ambiguity can be used to hurt you.

5. At what point will I be eligible to be on a partner track? In some firms, candidates are elevated to partner status after successful exits, while in other firms, it's a function of time.

low, and when a MBA graduate has significant student debt to worry about, they are rarely picky.

Rajeev Batra, partner at the Mayfield Fund, says, "When I was finishing up my MBA at Harvard, I was approached by a few venture firms. I did not even realize I was being interviewed till we met for the third time." Rajeev had a few entrepreneurial gigs, and a PhD in electrical engineering

Mind Your Language . . . and Your Handwriting

When Forbes profiled Arthur Rock, a young investment manager in Boston, Dick Kramlich read the article with great interest. Arthur was hiring. "Well, I'm gonna find a younger partner . . ." Dick sat down and wrote him a longhand letter. "I never had ever done anything like this before" he would recall. "The following Monday I got a telephone call. "Mr. Rock's on the line."

Arthur hired Dick shortly thereafter. "I found out there were over a thousand responses to the article. And that Arthur had a handwriting expert that analyzed my letter. Isn't that funny? So that's how I got in the venture business." Later, Dick Kramlich went to found New Enterprise Associates (NEA), a multibillion-dollar global venture fund.

Terry McGuire, a venture capitalist of 25 years and Emeritus Chairman of National Venture Capital Association, spent a year in Ireland soon after college, where he learned to speak Gaelic. Coincidentally, at his first job interview, the interviewer spoke fluent Gaelic. He muttered, *"An bfhuil se fluic, amach?"* which is Gaelic for "Is it wet outside?" Terry promptly responded in Gaelic. The two hit it off, and Terry landed the job.[13] But was it just a stroke of luck? It certainly helped that Terry was the president of the Harvard Business School Venture Capital Club. "It's a combination of training, the network, and opportunity that presented itself," says Terry. Terry went on to start Polaris Ventures after a seven-year stint at this Chicago-based venture firm.

demonstrated his domain knowledge. "In my business school essay, I had written that eventually, I wanted to be a venture capitalist when I grow up," he says.[12]

Candidates often underestimate the power of internship opportunities. Many practitioners would be open to a thoughtful email or a call along the lines of "Hi, I am graduating next year and wanted to explore a summer internship. I have studied your investment thesis and have identified a few opportunities that may be of interest. Let me know if I can come by and discuss these." That kind of an opening gambit is bound to get a response.

Often, those at a junior level may wonder if entrepreneurs will engage with them. The debate is rife with opinions of a thousand bloggers: entrepreneurs should only talk to those professionals who can make decisions. While various blogs emphasize the important attributes of the investor's stature, experience, decision-making abilities, or getting the deal done, to get to the decision makers, the starting point is often a junior person. Pat Grady, partner at Sequoia Capital for over 12 years says, "When I joined Sequoia back in 2004, I was the youngest in the firm but my title was partner. For Sequoia, this was never about a 'sourcing' gimmick, making sure that founders 'talk only to partners' hence this title. It was a genuine intention to align everyone for the same outcomes. We do not have hierarchies in this firm and we work closely with each other."

THE FELLOWSHIP OF INVESTORS

For experienced professionals, the Kauffman Fellows Program can be one potential path to enter the hallowed halls — a two-year, hands-on training program designed by the VCs for the VCs. The program offers structured learning opportunities with evolving module to explore themes of innovation, investing, leadership, and self-awareness.

Punit Chiniwalla, MD, with a corporate venture firm pursued the coveted Kauffman Fellows Program, which eventually

Junior Partner, Hungry Partner

Paul Graham of Y Combinator writes, "Junior persons scour the web looking for startups their bosses could invest in. The junior people will tend to seem very positive about your company. They're not pretending; they want to believe you're a hot prospect, because it would be a huge coup for them if their firm invested in a company they discovered. Don't be misled by this optimism. It's the partners who decide, and they view things with a colder eye."[14]

Peter Thiel, investor and entrepreneur, points out that the junior person is often an advantageous starting point for entrepreneurs. "Tactically, the first thing to do is find someone who *does* need to make investments. That can mean finding a senior associate or a principal for your first pitch, not a senior partner. This contravenes the conventional wisdom that holds that you should not pitch to junior people. ("Don't pitch someone who can't write a check themselves.") That wisdom is wrong. Junior people will give entrepreneurs a fair shake because they need good deals to their name. If they don't find those deals, they won't become senior, and they very much want to become senior. So seek these people out: they are motivated in a way more seasoned VCs are not. . . . No senior VC *needs* to do an investment. You should never forget that. Any senior VC that you're talking to is already wealthy and has many famous deals to show for it. Your company is probably not going to make a material difference to him but does present a significant chance of adding to his workload and failure rate; there will therefore be a certain amount of inertia against the deal . . . on average most deals don't pan out but do take time.[15]

helped him land smack in the center of the hypercompetitive venture universe of Sand Hill Road. Punit had made his first investment at a university venture fund, even before he had graduated from business school. This experience, combined with a PhD, enabled Punit to land in the Kauffman Fellows Program. After a brief stint on Sandhill Road, Punit manages the US offices of an international corporate venture fund. The much-sought-after program, whose mission is to "identify, develop, and network emerging global leaders in venture capital,"[16] is a near-guaranteed entry ticket into the world of venture capital.

While working full-time at a venture capital firm, each Kauffman Fellow engages in a two-year, hands-on apprenticeship that includes professional coaching in seven modules, mentoring by seasoned venture partners, and triennial sessions of industry and leadership curriculum. The program claims that the fellowship's value can be measured along three axes of investing: apprenticeship, leadership development, and being a part of a global network.

Each year, about 20 to 30 fellows are picked from a pool of about 200 applicants. The application process is a two-step dance, which is rigorous by any measure. The written application and the interview — reviewers include leading venture capitalists — look for a prior track record of accomplishments that are significant. Entrepreneurial background trumps operational background; in fact, it trumps everything else.

At the interview stage, the universe of 200 applicants narrows down by about a third. Each candidate is grilled by panels of four to five venture capitalists. The next stage is the finalist stage, where candidates who cross the finish line are then matched with firms who are seeking to bring on fresh talent. If any firm does not pick up a finalist, the process ends. For those selected, the sponsor venture capital firm pays a hefty tuition in addition to the salary for the two-year internship. These would-be Fellows are assigned mentors from established venture firms who, over the course of a two-year period, will provide insights and formal training into the art and science of venture investing.

Some of the common characteristics of Fellows include "a bias toward entrepreneurs; deep scientific, technology, or business domain expertise; an aspiration to contribute to the building of companies, either as an investor or as a startup leader; an appetite for risk, ambiguity, and unstructured environments; and humility, empathy, a sense of service, and unquestioned integrity."[17]

ADJACENT ENTRY POINTS

Getting in to a top-tier venture fund is tough. Yet, practitioners have found ways to meet their career goals by starting in an allied universe. These pathways are not as competitive, and each one has its pros and cons. As they say, there is no straight path into venture capital.

About 6 to 8 percent of all venture capital investments in United States come from corporate venture capitalists (CVCs). Besides a financial return, corporations invest in startups to gain a view of the newest new thing. Corporate venture capital funds are sponsored by the mother ships to help generate financial returns. Allied objectives for CVCs include identifying novel technologies to enhance revenue streams and amplify a corporation's competitive position. Other corporate objectives include validation of new market segments as well as leveraging relationships between the corporate venture capital portfolio and corporate business units. About 60 percent of corporations invest in venture funds as LPs, and 90 percent of CVCs invest directly in startups. Getting in a corporate venture capital firm of repute such as Google Ventures or Intel Capital can be a strong starting point for practitioners. Angel networks also offer excellent opportunities to entry-level candidates and are forgiving playgrounds where skills can be honed.

Opportunities in the institutional investor (LP) universe can be a starting point. Pension funds — both private and public — Fund-of-Funds, university endowments, foundations, and insurance companies have to deploy assets in the universe of venture funds. Family offices also offer a strong starting point for practitioners. These are addressed in greater detail in Chapter 8.

Investment banking firms, law firms, marketing firms, and even journalists have seen talent transition into venture capital.

From Entrepreneur to VC

The recent wave of investors has come from a demonstrated entrepreneurial background. Having started a company, raised capital, and generated an exit eminently qualifies you to serve other entrepreneurs well. But that does not guarantee success as an investor.

Exhibit 4.1 illustrates the pros and cons of each pathway.

Exhibit 4.1 **Entry Points in Venture Capital.**

Pathway	Opportunities	Challenges
Entrepreneurial/ startups	Engage with entrepreneurs. Ability to understand value drivers, technology challenges, and team dynamics.	Shifting from player to coach — managing temptation to jump in and drive when companies underperform. Sector expertise can be narrow. Pace can be too slow. As one entrepreneur-turned-VC remarked, "As a CEO, I was used to six emergencies before 9 a.m. As a VC, I am getting so bored and lazy."
Investment banking/ consulting	Wider horizon of sector knowledge and exposure to opportunities	Lack of founder network/awareness of investment dynamics/risk-taking abilities
Corporate VC/ micro VCs/ angel networks	Develop investment experience, sharpen due diligence abilities, and establish track record of investments	Differing agendas and conflicts. Investment activities may be limited by corporate agenda or angel interests. Speed of decision-making can be a concern.
Institutional investors	Ability to understand the LP/investor perspectives. Build relationships and have knowledge of new funds. Ability to time the entry.	Risk of being perceived as an asset manager versus an investor. Number of investments may be limited. Process is often slow and involves buy-in from various stakeholders.
Service providers	Ability to function as a resource to entrepreneurs.	Lack of domain expertise, lack of deeper understanding of financial dynamics.

When Jan Garfinkle, founder of Arboretum Ventures Fund, decided to be a venture capitalist, she polished her resume and approached several early-stage venture funds. But every fund turned her down. So she decided to start her own fund.

Jan had spent two decades cutting her teeth at two venture-backed cardiovascular device companies. A large publicly traded company acquired both these companies, leaving Jan a bit richer, wiser, and hungrier. She started off as a product manager with Advanced Cardiovascular Systems (ACS), a forerunner in over-the-wire angioplasty — a technique that reopens narrowed or blocked arteries in the heart (coronary arteries) without major surgery. The founder of the company, John Simpson, once remarked, "When we started the company, there was no interventional cardiology device sector."[18] C. Richard ("Dick") Kramlich, founder of NEA, had then invested in Advanced Cardiovascular Systems. Dick once said of ACS, "The procedure was entirely noninvasive . . . the body didn't have to go through the trauma it once had to endure."[19] At Advanced Cardiovascular Systems, Jan spent six years in marketing and sales of angioplasty systems. When Eli Lilly came knocking and acquired the company, the foundation stone for Guidant Corporation was laid. "We were the largest single shareholder in Advanced Cardiovascular Systems. . . . The company did extremely well,"[20] Kramlich would say. That was over 25 years ago, when Jan was at the threshold of her career. To be in an NEA-backed startup was certainly fortuitous for Jan's career path.[21]

Like all good serial entrepreneurs, Jan moved on to John Simpson's next company, Devices for Vascular Intervention. The same founder who had built Advanced Cardiovascular Systems was now leading the charge in the next wave of the cardiovascular sector. Devices for Vascular Intervention laid its bets on atherectomy — a procedure to remove plaque from arteries. Here, Jan wrote the first business plan, and over the next six years, as director of marketing and clinical research, she dove deeply into the universe of regulatory trials and approvals. Again, Eli Lilly had been watching closely and came knocking at the door. These two companies acquired by Eli Lilly became the foundation for Guidant Corporation, which was eventually spun off by Eli Lilly as a separate company and listed as GDT on the New York Stock Exchange (NYSE). Boston Scientific acquired Guidant in 2006 for $27.2 billion. At that time, the vascular intervention business was valued at $4.1 billion.[22]

When venture firms turned her down time and again, Jan decided to do what any entrepreneur does — never take no for an answer! She decided to raise her own fund and launched Arboretum Ventures, a fund focused on early-stage health care and medical device companies. Having lived close to Nichols Arboretum in Ann Arbor, and with her own DNA of a nurturing type, she found the name to be the appropriate encapsulation of her philosophies and style.

Like Jan, John Hummer, cofounder of Hummer-Winblad, interviewed at five venture firms. "All five turned me down — on the same day," reminisces John with a smug smile. John went on to start his own fund. "I climbed in from the window, as most do to get in this business of venture capital," comments the towering John, who once was a professional basketball player.

Most venture professionals agree that there is no straight path into the business of venture capital. You have to climb in from the window, if that's what it takes! Jan and John were able to raise their own funds: for others, the starting point is often at an entry-level position.

GETTING LUCKY — WHEN OPPORTUNITY MEETS A PREPARED MIND

For a few chosen practitioners, the entry into venture capital was not an uphill crawl or a series of grueling interviews. It was a calling — a blaring siren. Bryce Roberts was planning to go to law school and in the interim decided to start a ski company in Jackson Hole, Wyoming. "One of my neighbors, a venture capitalist, invited me to sit in on pitch meetings and offer feedback," he says. Bryce went on to be the co-founder of O'Reilly Alphatec Ventures, which has led investments in a number of prominent technology startups.

Jack Ahrens, co-founder of T-Gap Ventures, has been in the venture business for over 30 years. While he was employed at a bank in Illinois, one afternoon he stumbled upon an internal memo that suggested his department was being shut down. "I was irritated and told my boss I would be leaving." His boss promptly jumped in: "We have a venture capital arm — what if we made you the president and gave you a raise?" "I took it — I barely knew what the heck venture capital was, but here I was a VC for three decades," says Jack. In these three decades, Jack has led over 35 successful exits, including 20 IPOs. Interestingly, neither Bryce nor Jack has the desire to grow his fund size beyond what is manageable. My own observation is that if they wished, they could easily raise a lot more capital and increase their fund size, but so far they have curbed any such inflated ambitions. For those who followed their calling, the ability to find strong investment opportunities, generate returns, and stay on the growth trajectory is not difficult.

There is no way of knowing whether you are a natural, as Sanford Bernstein puts it. Bernstein, founder of the investment banking firm Robertson Stephens and Company, had invested in venture funds for 20 years. "Some do it, some can't, and like with athletes, there is no way of telling 'till they take the field," he once remarked.[23]

To prove they are good athletes, venture capitalists need to pick good investment opportunities. John Doerr used to say that training a new venture capitalist was not unlike preparing a fighter pilot for battle. It takes six to eight years, and you should be prepared for losses of about $20 million.[24] Yet in its first fund, Hummer-Winblad invested in 17 companies, of which 16 yielded a positive return. Jan Garfinkle's Arboretum Ventures Fund I had two exits in quick succession that yielded strong returns — comfortably landing the fund in the top quartile.

It does help to have a reasonable measure of luck on your side. When Jan Garfinkle decided to raise her first fund, Arboretum Ventures, she met a leading LP over Chinese food to discuss her game plan. The LP committed, and the fortune cookie, now pasted in Jan's journal, said, "You will soon get something you've always wanted." Fifteen years later, Jan is raising her Fund V, which is 10 times the size of her Fund I. When she launched her Fund I, she expressed the desire to serve this industry and be on the board of the National Venture Capital Association.[25] Ten years later, she served as the chair of this association.

David Cowan of Bessemer Venture Partners adds it all up nicely: "The one most important quality of a successful venture capitalist is *luck*."[26] Arthur Rock, who was an investor in Apple, Intel, and some of the formative companies of the technology era, says, "You gotta be lucky. Everybody's gonna be lucky at some time or another. I was lucky to be lucky early in my career."[27]

In the business of venture capital, luck is necessary but not a sufficient condition.

5

Developing Your Investment Career

"Every discipline has its top 1 percent — how do the top VCs operate? What can you learn from these — because, in early years, you will fund companies you shouldn't. You will try to fix things you can't," says Mike Maples, founder of Floodgate Fund.

BUILDING YOUR STRENGTHS

How does one build a career as an investor and rise to the top? Making rational bets while being aware of psychological biases and emotions is a good starting point. Whether you choose to emulate the path of Bill Gurley, Brad Feld, or Warren Buffett or follow the principles of Ray Dalio, there are no predetermined paths, instant premix concoctions, formulas, or silver bullets. When you develop your own views of this craft, you will stand on a strong foundation.

- *Build on first principles, not blind imitations.* Elon Musk, when forced to rethink the cost of building a $65 million rocket, observed that the materials required to build the rocket were only 2 percent of the overall costs. That was the trigger for starting SpaceX. Scientists are often trained to think along such lines, but the vast majority rarely develop this skill. Indeed, thinking is the hardest part of our jobs, and very few people do it well. Most of us imitate others, often without realizing it. Aristotle's view said, "In every systematic inquiry (methodos) where there are first principles, or causes, or elements, *knowledge and science result from acquiring knowledge of these;* for we think we know something just in case we acquire knowledge of the primary causes, the primary first principles, all the way to the elements." The Socratic method of questioning (discussed in due diligence section) can be applied here, where we ask ourselves, "What data and evidence do I have — why do I think this way?"

- *Hang your observations together in simple mental models.* Charlie Munger, investment partner at Berkshire Hathaway, described mental models and frameworks as follows: "The first rule is that you can't really know anything if you just remember isolated facts and try and bang 'em back. If the *facts don't hang together on a latticework of theory, you don't have them in a usable form.* You've got to have models in your head. You've got to hang experience on a latticework of models in your head." Mike Maples, Floodgate Fund, encourages investors to "Build your insight hypothesis on selections you make — founders or companies." For example, an observation can include a hypothesis like *immigrant founders are hungrier as they have burnt all bridges, hence they have a higher chance of success.* Or you could develop a hypothesis around certain market segments, adoption patterns, buyer behavior, and so on.

- *Build your circle of competence using probabilistic thinking.* As investors, we can operate in some areas really well. And we can do poorly if we try to get into every corner of the marketplace. Because our entire business is based on outcomes, we need to make quality decisions that separate skill from luck. In her book *Thinking in Bets,* author Annie Duke writes, "We are betting against future versions we are not choosing." We suffer from hindsight bias (after the outcome is known, we of course knew it to be inevitable) blind-spot bias (where we cannot see our own bias and shortcomings), and self-serving bias (attributing wins to skill and failures to luck). We need to build a good process for decision-making. We gather details, build our knowledge, but also are aware of what we do not know. We apply uniform standards to data and watch for conflicts and self-interest. In making venture investments, "we should understand the power law," Mike Maples reminds us. The power law states that outsized returns come from a handful of companies while the vast majority of investments yield an average outcome. "How can we know which risks are worth taking? I passed on Airbnb — what questions should I have asked instead?" he says.

What Makes a Good Investor?

Personality, Brains, Energy

For a venture capitalist, I think you want brain power and you want energy and you want personality. Want somebody who is going to attract people . . . It goes without saying you want somebody dead honest, and you want somebody that's got really good ethics, and you want somebody who's got a strong sense of pride in getting the job done. And then I didn't mention the analytical side. . . .[1]

—William Draper III, founder,
Sutter Hill Ventures

- *Study game theory.* In the game of VC, you have competing investors, follow-on and strategic investors, founders, competition, partners . . . the whole gaggle where interests can diverge. As the simplistic definition of game theory goes, you are trying to predict the next move in any strategic interaction between multiple players where everyone knows the rules and outcomes.

Game theory can be a powerful tool to understand possible outcomes where you sort out messy situations. You often have the following dynamics at work:

- *Game:* Any set of circumstances that has a result dependent on the actions of two of more decision makers (players). Assume the CEO and the board/investors are players, aiming for a certain outcome.

- *Players:* A strategic decision maker within the context of the game. In VC, the primary players (CEO, board) as well as secondary players (competition, regulatory forces) can impact the outcomes.

- *Information:* All sides have varying, and partial, information of the state of the business, market, competitive dynamics and moves being plotted.

- *Strategy:* Actions and circumstances that might arise along the way.

- *Outcomes:* Win, lose, or continue to build — these dynamics can vary with any number of moves made by the players.

Though performance matters, politics and power dynamics can kill you. Many VC careers have died a premature death, thanks to ego, greed, and politics. While you may be innocent, know that this is a high-stakes game. Self-preservation and "jumping in front of the right deal/parade" occurs all the time. One investor reminds us that you have to earn your political capital in any firm — know who is in charge and understand the power dynamics. You could be the smartest person with top-decile returns, but if they don't like you, they will find a way to kick you out. In another firm, a young but insecure power-hungry partner played diabolical moves and eliminated a senior partner because he felt threatened. The senior partner had a proven track record, strong network of relationships, and could source better opportunities. But he was eliminated because, according to the party line, *he was not a "team player" and did not follow the firm's "culture and processes."* "I had to make a decision — should I keep my $500,000 a year position to become a lap dog? I chose self-respect and peace-of-mind instead. . . ." this GP bemoaned.

Let us look at two examples where investors were able to build their venture careers rapidly.

How to Hit the Ground Running

Foundation Capital, a Silicon Valley venture firm with two decades of investments in companies such as Netflix, Uber, Chegg, and Graphcore, was getting ready to raise its next fund — the ninth fund since it started in the late 1990s. The firm had survived and thrived across major innovation and economic cycles such as the emergence of the World Wide Web and the dot-com bubble, Web 2.0 and the mobile revolution, the rise of Big Data, software's ascension to the cloud, and the birth of blockchain. As the technology waves evolved, the three senior partners at the firm were eager to recruit the next generation of the investment team. Fund IX focused on enterprise software, finance, and consumer and marketplace opportunities. One of the candidates it homed in on was a rising star in cybersecurity investments, Sid Trivedi. For Foundation Capital, cybersecurity had been a lucrative arena. As the firm continued to build on its successes, it needed some fresh blood. With his investment experience of three years, Sid brought a healthy blend of insights, self-confidence, and more importantly, a growing network of over a hundred executives in the cybersecurity universe. During his interview, one of the senior partners at Foundation Capital asked him that dreaded curveball question: *"Give me the names of five people you know well in three categories — prospective founders, current founders, and investors. Tell me why you picked them and how you got to know them."*

A quintessential networker, Sid walked up to the whiteboard and put down names in each of the three categories. The senior partner then picked five names from this list of 15 and asked for an introduction. In the meantime, the rest of the team at Foundation Capital engaged with Sid for over 25 hours, conducted over a dozen reference calls (several of them were blind checks), and could see the potential edge Sid brought to the team. Soon after, Sid had an offer from Foundation Capital. "Besides having developed a point-of-view in cybersecurity, I can help our portfolio companies secure their first dozen customers quickly. For any founder, that can be an advantage," says Sid.

Soon after joining the firm, Sid hosted a dinner with security founders, buyers, and professionals. The guest speaker, a chief technology officer of a publicly traded company with over a hundred-billion-dollar market cap, sat down to have a fireside chat with Sid. For the founders who attended, the value of the investor and the firm was evident — access to a potential customer and seasoned security investors who had invested across multiple cycles and their views on market trends and challenges. Within six months of joining the firm, Sid was able to close on his first investment — a security team had spun out from a multibillion-dollar networking company to develop the next-generation AI-driven security platform. "In our business, feedback cycles are long, as it takes 10 years to realize returns. In the meantime, I have developed the muscle of seeking constant feedback from my partners, founders, and peers in the business. Gotta get better every day to stay ahead in this game."

Moon Shots in Emerging Technology — Bets in Quantum Computing

The arc of Andrew Schoen's VC career begins with Sid, where he founded the Cornell University's Venture Club to gain exposure to the world of venture capital. Young MBA students could work alongside seasoned investors and learn the craft, hone their skills. As Andrew and Sid built the club, they engaged with leading firms such as Sequoia, Bessemer, and others who came in to work on projects with the students. With the ringside view of the venture world, both of them were able to find an entry point.

Soon after graduation Andrew, who has spent five years at the multibillion-dollar venture firm New Enterprise Associates (NEA), moved to Beijing, China, for three years. There, he was able to build out the portfolio and subsequently moved to New York, where he set up the firm's East Coast offices. "The job of a venture capitalist is to identify and invest in opportunities with immense potential — ours is distinctly a mission of value creation (as opposed to value capture). *We foster innovation that occurs in leaps and bounds, with progress that looks more like a step-function graph than a straight line,*" he writes.[2] One of the companies Andrew led an investment in is a category defining opportunity in quantum computing. With the end of Moore's law in sight, we need a punctuation mark in the path of semiconductor development. For Andrew, this is a moon shot, but as a first mover, he was able to study the entire landscape of opportunities in quantum computing and make a bet on an opportunity that has significant potential.

For him, it's not the risk that matters but the scale of the outcome. As he muses:

> For investors who are able to lean in with their eyes wide open and fully understand the bet, an investment in quantum computing could be a moon shot worth taking. A moon shot can go awry. But venture capitalists make moon shot investments when they are convinced that the potential rewards outweigh the risks. The question is not whether investments will be made in quantum computing. Multiple governments around the world, and multiple government agencies domestically, are already directing funds and technical efforts toward this challenge. Several private investments have already been made in the field. *The question is whether the rewards will be worth the financial risk, and the wait.*

What Makes a Good Investor?

Comfort Ambiguity, Uncertainty, and Change

Good instinct, well-honed by experience, makes a good venture capitalist. The most difficult part is dealing with uncertainty.[3]

—C. Richard Kramlich, chairman and co-founder,
New Enterprise Associates

See, venture capital is very reducible to a few words. You have to be interested in managing change, and you have to recognize that change is *necessary*.[4]

—Donald T. Valentine, founder,
Sequoia Capital

BEWARE: BIAS AND PSYCHOLOGY

The Misconception. *You calculate what is risky or rewarding and always choose to maximize gains while minimizing losses.*
The Truth. *You depend on emotions to tell you is something is good or bad, greatly overestimate the rewards, and tend to stick to your first impressions.*

–David McRaney, Author of
You Are Not So Smart

Every practitioner should aim to be a student of human psychology and behavior. We are primal beings and we function in ways that cannot be fully explained within the logical construct. This section addresses a few challenges that are likely to occur while making investment decisions, primarily due to randomness of human psychology and emotions.

Let's start with David McRaney's observation that we are not as smart as we think we are. His book points out as many as 48 ways we delude ourselves. But for the sake of brevity, let's focus on the few that are relevant in the context of venture capital investments.

- *Emotions versus logic.* In any investment decisions, practitioners create elaborate logical labyrinths to minimize risk or justify actions — but as human beings, we have equal parts emotion. Or mostly emotions, if you start to scratch beneath the surface. We have a tendency to ignore odds in our favor and often rely on gut feelings. Snap judgments. Love at first sight. You had me at hello. . . . we could go on and on. At work, we do stuff because we like someone. We want to earn points or be liked. Or we want to reciprocate, to feel good about ourselves. Research shows that when

What Makes a Good Investor?

A Good Therapist

The part that is really overlooked is that a VC needs to be a good therapist. Any CEO will tell you that it's the loneliest job in the world. You have to lead, be upbeat and confident . . . every CEO has doubts of hitting the next milestone, the next customer or the next capital raise. A good VC is someone who can host an open, transparent discussion and even give them a pep talk. At times, the founders get at each other's throats. It's very easy for VCs to get prescriptive and that's not helpful — what is helpful is giving them the tools to manage the issues and become stronger.[5]

—Rob Hayes, managing partner,
First Round Capital

You've got to be a good listener. I find if the venture capitalist does all the talking, he doesn't learn very much about the people he's thinking about investing in. Very important to listen . . . and judge who looks and feels like they have the makings to be a real company. Eventually it becomes instinct if you do it often enough.[6]

—Paul "Pete" Bancroft, former CEO
of Bessemer Securities, former chairman
of National Venture Capital Association

it comes to identifying risk, our brains are hardwired to respond from the gut. Investor Chris Sacca one said, "Never forget that underneath all the math and the MBA bullshit talk, we are all still emotionally driven human beings. We want to attach ourselves to narratives. We don't act because of equations. We follow our beliefs. We get behind leaders who stir our feelings. If you find someone diving too deep into the numbers, that means they are struggling to find a reason to deeply care about you."[7]

In his book *How We Decide*, Author Jonah Lehrer points out that "our best decisions are a finely tuned blend of both feeling and reason — and the precise mix depends on the situation." Now, there is nothing wrong in healthy emotions but as students of human behavior, we need to recognize that sometimes, it's not necessarily logic that's at work. Without emotion, it becomes incredibly difficult to settle on any one opinion. We would endlessly pore over variables and weigh the pros and cons in an endless cycle of computations, writes McRaney.[8] Thus, in any situation where the decisions don't add up, know that emotions, not logic, may be at work.

- *Reciprocation, obligations and indebtedness.* In a classic book on human psychology, *Influence — Science and Practice*, author Robert Cialdini writes that reciprocity is one of the most widespread and basic norms of human culture. Quite simply put, reciprocity is exchange — if someone wishes you well on your birthday, you do the same on theirs. Holiday cards, dinner invitations, horse-trading where politicians vote on bills just because the other politician supported their bill. Lobbyists play this game pretty well. Pharmaceutical companies are especially notorious, and curry favors at the cost of innocent patients — leading doctors snag "consulting agreements" or paid vacations to Hawaii, where they are gently reminded to prescribe more medication. It even extends to international aid. So why is this relevant to venture capital investments?

Most venture capitalists have relationships — professional investors who are often aligned philosophically, intellectually. Such investors often syndicate investments, and may have made (or lost) money, standing side by side. If a VC "refers" or "brings you in" on a deal, this ritual of reciprocity starts. This creates a web of obligations that you may not necessarily be aware of. But this obligatory dynamic could very well impact decisions. The best antidote for such behavior is to raise it upfront, at the time of investment, and put it bluntly to investors: "Knowing that you have a longstanding relationship and a history of working together, it could work well in our advantage. How do we make sure this opportunity stands strong on its merits and our emotions do not hurt us?"

- *A VC with ego — Why should I eat your leftovers?* VCs tend to compete, often mindlessly. Paul Graham, founder of Y Combinator, one of the world's leading accelerators, writes:

A while ago, an eminent VC firm offered a series A round to a startup we'd seed funded. Then they heard a rival VC firm was also interested. They were so afraid that they'd be rejected in favor of this other firm that they gave the startup what's known as an "exploding term sheet." They had, I think, 24 hours to say yes or no, or the deal was off. What surprised me was their reaction when I called to talk about it. I asked if they'd still be interested in the startup if the rival VC didn't end up making an offer, and they said no. What rational basis could they have had for saying that? If they thought the startup was worth investing in, what difference should it make what some other VC thought? Surely it was their duty to their limited partners simply to invest in the best opportunities they found; they should be delighted if the other VC said no, because it would mean they'd overlooked a good opportunity. But of course, there was no rational basis for their decision. They just couldn't stand the idea of taking this rival firm's rejects.[9]

- *Pain + Reflection = Progress.* One of Ray Dalio's principles is often quoted but rarely practised in the business of venture capital. VCs often talk about pattern-matching for success. But pattern-matching for failure is rare. Losses are often buried deep and quick, unless you need a favorable tax treatment. Logos vanish from websites and LinkedIn profiles. In a business where speed and "hit-rates" matter, the LPs suffer the pain, while GPs rarely reflect. Nor do LPs ask questions about lessons learned. Getting inside a "hot fund" matters more. Asking tough questions may not yield access to the elite funds. Venture investing still remains a game of hit-or-miss, with more losses than hits. But as VCs, we do injustice to our own ethos when we do not reflect on our own losses and mistakes. How will our hit-ratios ever improve? One VC told me about their first loss — it occurred when they got a call at 10 p.m. from a portfolio CEO. "I cannot do this anymore," said this exhausted, overworked, underappreciated, and totally burnt-out CEO. The VC reflected that they had not worked hard enough to understand the CEO's personal challenges. And it was too late to offer support now, when the CEO had pulled the plug. Another VC's loss occurred when a company ran out of cash. In this case, the CEO was a quintessential salesman who could get orders but did not understand the implications of poor cash management, leading to a flameout. The VC blamed it on their own rushed fervor to invest in this company. Speed, trust, blind optimism can destroy any portfolio quickly. And therein lie the root causes of all investment losses. To address these, following a radically open-minded decision-making process can help.

- *Decisions, biases, and harmful emotions.* In the VC business, we often make rapid decisions with limited knowledge. Ray Dalio's fundamental decision-making principle asks to build deeper knowledge sets with utmost humility. In practicing humility, we assume we are not as smart (as we think we may be). If we reach out to as many people to gather as much data, we might make better-informed decisions.

What Makes a Good Investor?

Good Judgment

VC doesn't necessarily take technical talent — it doesn't hurt — but it's more about people skills and the ability to assess whether there's a market for something,

—C. Richard Kramlich, founder,
New Enterprise Associates (NEA).[10]

They see into the future, and they see what I call "situational awareness." A lot of good venture capitalists, most venture capitalists — the good ones — can walk into just about any kind of meeting and, in about five minutes, figure out who's doing what to whom and exactly what the issues are, sort of cut through it and figure out what's going on . . . You sort of look at a given situation and project its trajectory reasonably well.[11]

—James R. Swartz, founder,
Accel Partners

It really pays off to come into [venture capital] after you've had a fair amount of experience doing something else. I think it's a business that you're probably better off entering in your thirties and forties than you are entering it in your twenties, because you need to build a frame of reference by which to judge people and to judge opportunities and to be able to judge markets and what's going on in the economy.[12]

—Reid Dennis, founder, Institutional
Venture Partners

Venture capitalists should guide companies based on real-world experience . . . if you had a good marketing job at Intel, that beats an MBA. An MBA is a little bit general for the venture business. . . . The partners [at our firm] can say to entrepreneurs, "We've been where you're going," and really mean it.[13]

—William K. Bowes Jr., founder,
US Venture Partners

We should often ask, "How do I know I am right?" VCs only know if they are right after a longer period — say, five years, when portfolio companies succeed or die. But we can ask this question at every stage of our investment process. All investors go through two phases — gathering information and conducting analysis — before we commit. During these phases, a lot of opinions clash with facts. And we can be rushed into saying yes or no. Emotions and impulses can drive this instead of knowledge, data, and analytical skills. To develop and follow a rigorous weighted and probabilistic model of decision-making is not easy.

Brian Armstrong, CEO of Coinbase, has written a post about an anonymized decision-making framework that can bring a level of discipline in any politically charged, ego-driven process. Such an approach can reduce the role of harmful emotions in decision-making. Ego, greed, status-plays, and one-upmanship are rife in the VC business. Our own psychological biases will never vanish completely, but at least we can become more self-aware. The notion of radical transparency may seem idealistic but needs to be inculcated in our lives.

- *Conformity (or groupthink).* In groups, we like to conform rather than act independently. Time and again, studies have shown that our behavior changes, at times dramatically, when we are in groups. This might explain why you have some investors who say one thing in a one-on-one session but change their views when they are in a group. This is group dynamics at work — people don't usually want to be seen as renegades. Conformity is default behavior in human beings indeed, as it is seen as essential to survival in tribal contexts. McRaney points out that our desire for conformity is strong and unconscious — like the desire to keep everyone happy around a dinner table. But *beware the dark place conformity can lead to — dishonesty.* If you see groupthink and weak spines around the table, raise your hand and ask, "Are we conforming to look good to each other? Or do each of us believe this is a good decision?"

The other interesting aspect of group dynamics is that it can decrease the quality of decisions, writes Dan Ariely in his book, *The (Honest) Truth about Dishonesty*. We have all seen this happen in large organizations and government entities: it's called *bureaucracy*, and it results in decisions being made via the lowest-common-denominator approach. No one gets fired. It's all good, but nothing ever gets done. It is rare for such a challenge to occur in a startup, but be watchful.

- *Halo effect: Hero worship.* Every business has its heroes. The lead singer of the rock band U2, Bono is a venture capitalist with TPG Growth and Elevation Partners. While we have not seen such star power in a startup's boardroom, it would be fun to speculate what a board meeting would be like. Bono walks in, sits down, removes his shades and says in his gravelly husky voice, "We really should move away, really, really move away from that strategy." Would there be a chorus of "ayes" followed by, "And now can we get your autograph, picture, and a hug?" We often subconsciously gravitate toward people who look like us, who agree with or compliment us, or are physically attractive, writes author Robert Cialdini. It's called similarity, compliance, association, and cooperation. Such psychological nuances often make one board member persuasive over others, creating a halo effect. These aspects of human behavior may be especially troubling in the context of a venture capital. While these cannot be avoided, we need to recognize them and make sure that we can tackle them effectively. Watch for pandering when one board member excessively grovels at the feet of another VC demigod. They are setting the stage for groupthink.

- *Networks: That overhyped Rolodex is not as useful as you think.* VCs may have 1000+ connections on LinkedIn but a human brain only has the capacity to keep track of about 150 connections. Beyond that, it's all a pile of data. Research shows that the size of our brain determines the size of our "active" network, where we maintain these relationships in a meaningful fashion. And our prefrontal cortex can process only about 150 connections. Noted author Malcolm Gladwell pointed out in *The Tipping Point* that productivity declines once the size of the company grows beyond 150 people.[14] In such networks, the grease of information and activities — getting together for a beer, a hike, or a game — keeps it running smoothly. The power of reciprocity works well and the network is *alive*. But if we try to expand the network without being able to nourish it meaningfully, the ability to impact and reciprocate in such a network crumbles. Bottom line: Don't believe in your own ability to tap in your 1,000+ LinkedIn contacts — keep your expectations low.

What Makes a Good Investor?

A Guarded Optimist

You have to believe that the world can change. . .be optimistic and at the same time, be realistic and guarded, not romantic.[15]

—Terry McGuire, Co-Founder, Polaris
Ventures, and former Chairman of the National
Venture Capital Association

The goal of this chapter is to help practitioners improve their game while appreciating the softer undertones of how we behave. We are complex, emotional beings, each motivated by different drivers and insecurities. Is your investment decision driven by independent, honest analysis and supported by facts? As investor Peter Thiel points out, "Humans are massively cognitively biased in favor of near-term thinking. VCs are no different."[16]

6

A Business Where Enemies Accumulate

CHALLENGES OF A VC CAREER

Steve Jobs was not impressed by venture capitalists and once said of VC that it "sounds like a bullshit job to me."[1] Ironically, this was reported by none other than Sir Michael Moritz, who was then a journalist and would become a venture capitalist and chairman of Sequoia Capital. Of his own experiences as a VC, he would say, "Every day is composed of a hundred soap operas — it's an exhilarating place to live and work."[2]

As a venture capitalist, you are not creating anything new, but rather fueling the creation of new innovations and businesses. Often regarded as a commodity, a VC is often compared to a role of a slick, glorified financier — most of whom take credit for the entrepreneur's successes and hide their losses or blame them on others. On the other hand, some practitioners find a way to take credit for all successful outcomes.

This chapter looks at a few challenges of being a venture capitalist.

Emotionally and Intellectually Demanding, a Business of Thousand Nos

The business calls for a mental tenacity — not becoming exhausted by the times you must say no to entrepreneurs, turn people down, or turn someone's great idea down without being abrasive. Roelof Botha, Partner at Sequoia Capital says:

> Friends come and go; enemies accumulate. At Sequoia, we meet with thousands of companies every year, and only partner with 15–20. That's thousands of interactions where we run the risk of making a negative impression. Regardless of whether we end up partnering with them, we always want founders to know we respect them and their ideas. I'm mindful of how I treat people and I think about the long-term consequences of my interactions. The people we meet with will tell others about their experience, good or bad.

To handle multiple investment opportunities and complex situations; to maintain your drive and discipline; to prioritize tasks; and to be comfortable with ambiguity are the hallmarks of this profession. "I have stopped trying to

"No, Thursday's out. How about never—is never good for you?"

manage my calendar," says Jack Ahrens, a VC of 30 years. "Rather, I keep a prepared mind for emergencies that may arise on any day."

High Level of Churn

Once you get in, staying in the business of venture capital is easy only as long as you can generate superior returns. Successful practitioners continuously need to adapt themselves to economic cycles. Besides performance, the business is rife with partnership challenges, greed, and politics. Often, people leave and firms fall apart.

Performance of Partner

The one and only measure of the business is financial returns. Returns are a function of capital invested and time. Time is your enemy. As the clock keeps ticking, the measure of performance — internal rate of return (IRR), which is a function of time — keeps dropping. Worse, in bad markets and recessionary times, the ability to exit an investment slows down, not to mention the potential value of the return. But investors really don't care for any excuses. When asked what keeps him up at night, Roelof Botha of Sequoia Capital said, "Suffice it to say that you're only as good as your next investment."[3]

Performance of Funds

In a world of one-hit wonders, consistency matters. Top-tier venture capitalists who generate returns get to raise their next funds quickly and charge higher profits — as much as 30 percent, as opposed to the standard 20 percent. Marc Andreessen once said, "I don't believe there is such a thing as a VC industry. There are about 40 firms that really do well as investors and over 600 firms that will break your heart as an investor. A handful of firms generate all the returns and a lot of firms want to generate those returns."[4]

The Business of Home Runs

Only a small number of startups are meant to be successful. The same goes for venture firms. I expect most VCs to fail. The entire business is about finding exceptional, awesome companies. If you find one of them every five years, nothing else matters.

—Mike Maples, Floodgate Fund[5]

Market Forces

At times, changes in market trends can hurt highly specialized firms. Not too long ago, clean-tech investments were at an all-time high. As the waves receded, the green practitioners had to tweak their resumes. Some repositioned themselves as generalists. Others went back into the technology sector and sought "clean web" opportunities. Often, when technology/software investments are on the upswing, life science sectors take a beating. Technology sectors have a shorter path to exit, while the time horizon of life sciences investments is longer, often mired with technological, regulatory, and financial risks.

No Payday

Of the 8,000 practitioners in the business in the United States, very few have seen any financial profits, or as they say, a "carry check." In other words, most practitioners have survived on salaries coming from management fees. This is yet another cause of heartburn for VCs who feel frustrated that their bets have not paid off fast enough, and for limited partners (LPs), who think incentives are misaligned when VCs get paid fees for poor performance. One investor with over nine years of experience says, "We need to own up to the fact that there may never be a big payday."

Ego, Greed, and Intellectual Dishonesty

Any LP will regale you with stories of bad VC behavior. But at its very core, what irritates these investors is how VCs play around with numbers to bloat their performance. It's an age-old tactic: slice and dice the data to make sure your performance looks good and then find the next sucker who can invest in the fund. VCs, with their inflated egos, hubris, and biases, rarely do a *mea culpa*. No VC in their right mind will say, "We lost your money and we learned a few lessons." Often, VCs find someone to blame for poor performance. Several limited partners described this behavior as disingenuous. A fund of funds (FoF) summarized it as the Lake Wobegon[6] effect, where in a VC land, all the women are strong, all the men are good looking, and all the children [and all the venture capitalists] are above average.

VC CAREER AS A CALLING

The VC business is subject to pressures from multiple ends: the supply of capital, the availability of investment opportunities, liquidity time frames, and regulatory dynamics. Elizabeth "Beezer" Clarkson, managing director of Sapphire Ventures Fund-of-Funds, says, "Often, you don't know if it's you or its luck. Having humility is essential."

In any career where those two imposters of fame and fortune prevail, you can be assured of petty politics, backstabbing, and opportunistic behavior. Ego, greed, and hubris have often turned practitioners into primal beings — ask any founder and they will share plenty of VC horror stories.

At its core, venture capital is truly an apprenticeship business. It takes years of mentoring to learn how to assess

Being Reasonably Nice Can Be a Competitive Advantage

I've heard entrepreneurs say, "I don't want to talk to that firm because they are such jerks." In almost all cases, these are well-known, older firms who come from the era when capital was scarce.

Every experienced entrepreneur I know has a list of 'toxic' VCs they won't deal with. There are still plenty of VCs to pitch to get a fair price for your company and only deal with decent, helpful investors. It sounds kind of crazy, but being a reasonably nice person has become a competitive advantage in venture capital.

—Chris Dixon, partner, Andreessen Horowitz[7]

investment opportunities, set pricing, and strategy, build and motivate management teams, deal with inevitable and unpredictable threats to the businesses, source additional capital and strategic partners, and finally, divest (for better or worse) these illiquid investments. "The good ones view it as a calling, not a career," says Diana Frazier of FLAG Capital Management, a fund of funds.

Singer Bob Dylan once said, "I accept chaos. I'm not sure it accepts me." That sums it up nicely — you can accept venture capital, but will it accept you?

7

Generational Transfer
and Succession

"Succession in venture funds is like a Shakespearean tragedy —
it involves money, ego, fame, and emotion," says Paul Holland
of Foundation Capital. Some describe the adrenaline-laden
world of venture investments as in the song "Hotel California" —
where you can check out any time you like, but you can
never leave.

Hanging out with cool kids, doling out large sums of
money, playing rich Daddy power trips, and feeling mighty
invincible can be heady. Yet how best should you plan to get
out? And where do you go from the world of venture — where
you get to see a thousand great startups each year? Most career
paths sound mildly interesting after venture, and worse, you
might be ill-qualified to do any meaningful operational role.

MANAGING SUCCESSION - NOW MY WORK IS DONE

Succession and generational transfers in venture firms is
hard — nearly impossible. When firms are successful in generating returns, ego and greed take over. Rainmakers and top
performers get the "God" syndrome, and they are the ones
carrying the weight of this world, while others are socialists.
Even the legendary investor Warren Buffett has not been able
to find a suitable replacement to run Berkshire Hathaway and
continues to run the firm at the age of 89. But Sequoia Capital

has mastered the art of passing the baton to the next generation without missing a beat — over the past nearly 50 years,
Sequoia has done it not once, but twice.

When Don Valentine decided to start a venture firm in
1972, he did not call it "Valentine Capital" — partly because he
wanted the firm to last well beyond his years. The California
coast is abundant with Sequoia trees, an evergreen variety, typically living 1,200–1,800 years, among the oldest living things
and also one of the tallest trees on Earth. That sounded like an
apt name for the firm he had in mind. For five years, he ran
the firm largely by himself, making investments in early-stage
technology companies.

Pat Grady, who co-leads Sequoia's Growth business, a
role he assumed as part of the firm's most recent generational
transfer, describes the firm's first succession — the transition of Sequoia Capital from Don Valentine to Sir Michael
Moritz and Doug Leone. Pat says that Don walked in one
morning and sat down with Sir Michael and Doug. "He pulls
out this sheet of paper. He had made notes in two separate
columns — *duties he could do* and *duties he no longer wanted to
do*. He asked them to make a checkmark next to those duties
they would still like Don to do. Then he said, all of this is now
yours." Pat chokes up as he recalls Don's words, "But make
sure when you leave the firm, it is in a better place than when
you took over Sequoia."

Within months, the worst public market debacle occurred
when the internet dotcom bubble burst of the year 2000, leaving behind some deep losses. Both Moritz and Leone were
proven investors, having returned investor capital multiple
times over. "It would have been an easy decision for Sequoia
to hide behind the fact that everyone in the market lost their
shirt. But that's not the spirit — Doug and Sir Michael fought
for every inch and made our investors whole." Sequoia has
never lost money for its investors. They did not let the Don
down — on performance or generational transfer. They built
a team, and when the time came, Moritz and Leone would go
on to pass on the baton to Jim Goetz, who would remind other

Generational Transfer at Sequoia:
Letter to LPs

Subject: Time to pay it forward

Disruption is at the heart of our business. It's what creates opportunities for Sequoia entrepreneurs, and it's what helps them produce extraordinary returns for our LPs. Ironically, it's also the force that many venture capital firms resist, often contributing to their own decline.

Sequoia is the exception.

Over the past 45 years, starting with Don Valentine, Sequoia has embraced change as much within our partnership as outside it. That willingness to renew and reinvent — often by empowering the less experienced among us — has been the foundation of our success. I am deeply indebted to Doug and Sir Michael for the trust they placed in me, first as a Sequoia-backed entrepreneur, later as co-lead of the venture business, and more recently as a Sequoia Steward. Implicit in that arc is an obligation to pay it forward to the next generation. That time has come.

During the coming week, I plan to step aside from my leadership responsibilities. I do so with great confidence in this next generation of leaders. They represent a gifted cohort who bleed Sequoia, and their fresh ideas will spur the next wave of reinvention. More to come on these well-deserved changes from Doug.

To ensure a smooth transition and encourage change, I am going to decamp from the Menlo office for a few months. I will remain a GP in existing funds and continue to represent Sequoia on boards. When I return, I intend to sponsor new investments, but I plan to reduce my workload, so that I can start saying "yes" to some of the other aspects of my life that have been on hold over the past twenty years.

Forever grateful.

JJG

(Jim Goetz)

Sequoia partners to rise up to the challenge. "I'm not going to be here forever," he would often say. Emotion wells up, yet again, as Pat talks about the second generational transfer. "Jim Goetz was at the height of his game, when he decided to step down . . . saying, my work here is done." Today, Roelof Botha leads the US business.

The first wave of establishing its brand and superior performance, and the second of successfully expanding globally, now enters the third inning for Sequoia. And for Sequoia to stay ahead in the game, it has to constantly innovate and reinvent itself. "Our partnership will be a reflection of the future that we all want to live in. If we lose our edge, it's over — we are dead. But we are working to make Sequoia a firm that is beloved," says Pat, as he mulls about the future. "We reflect on how we can democratize access to capital, so that any founder can win, not just someone with a Stanford degree and a warm intro. We look around the table and wonder how we can build a partnership that is representative of all groups of founders — our customers — not just diversity of thought and experience.

Christy Richardson, director of Private Investments, Hewlett Foundation, has been a Sequoia LP for over two decades. "The best indicator of a well-executed succession plan is when the senior partner wants to leave, but the younger partners ask them to stay and continue to share their knowledge and experience. We have often watched for how the leaders are building the next-generation team, and stepping away at the right time. Sequoia works hard to help their next-gen and newest partners succeed," she says.

We'll Turn the Lights Off When We Leave

"At Foundry Group, we have no succession plan. We will turn the lights off when we are done, and leave."

—Brad Feld, Foundry Group

THE ART OF LETTING GO

While the transition for teams at Sequoia was a planned move, for Jerry Colonna, author of *Reboot* and a CEO coach, the exit from the world of VC investments was abrupt. He was co-leading investments for a fund with $23 billion under management. His prior partnerships include stellar names like Fred Wilson, of Union Square Ventures, and JP Morgan. He volunteered to help the New York City Olympic bid in 2012. Indeed, Jerry was at his peak. And then the Twin Tower attacks occurred. "My home had been attacked," Jerry said. "I came out of an Olympic bid committee meeting and I stood across the street from the pile, as they referred to it — Ground Zero, which was still smoldering. It all felt like it was falling apart. It felt like there was a complete charade." At that moment, Jerry contemplated suicide. He called his therapist, who urged him to "get in a cab and come see me," and that was a pivotal point, which led him to spend years in reflection. He emerged from all the hurt and ashes as a mensch and a mentor to startup founders.

"Doing yet another deal will not help me grow. VC business is always there — it's not going away, and I can always come back to it," says one investor, who walked away from an investment role after nine years to try something different, something new. Author and angel investor Tim Ferris stepped away, taking a hiatus investing, because the noise simply wasn't worth it. The cortisol-fueled, unnecessary hurrying associated with that culture was causing more harm than good.[1]

Igor Taber left Intel Capital after a decade of making investments in Silicon Valley startups. "I loved to see multiple flowers bloom," he said. Growing up in Ukraine, he was the first in his family to go to college and get a formal education in the United States. "I spent 10 years in Intel in a business development role and another 10 as investor in the VC arm — no one should stay in one company for 20 years — it feels like a lifetime," he quips. "My transition out of venture was driven by a great CEO and a phenomenal opportunity — it was just too good to pass." Igor had invested in a machine learning platform and served on the board for four years. "The CEO's determination, work ethic, vision, and importantly a team builder of giants got me excited," and he joined Datarobot, heading up corporate strategy and acquisitions. At Intel Capital, Taber had funded and served on boards for more than 20 companies, but one caught his eye.

For Paul Holland, the role was reversed. He started his career in an operating role after a chance meeting with Reed Hastings, founder of Netflix. "It was at a hot tub party 30 years ago," recalls Paul, and he ended up working with Reed, shaping the trajectory at Netflix. After eight years of investing at Foundation Capital, and as a GP for six funds, Paul plans to transition out of the fund. "The third generation of management is coming in at Foundation. We need to make it easy for them. Transitions need to be structured and respectful for both sides. At 35, you don't know what it is like to be 58," he says. And on his way out, he did a parting favor to a junior partner. He helped shepherd a particularly risky seed investment that the junior partner would work on. As he heads off to his next phase in life, Paul has made some lasting contributions, not just to his LPs but to the industry as whole. He produced a documentary — *Something Ventured* — which memorialized the views of some of the legends of the first generation — these include Arthur Rock, Don Valentine, and even the late Tom Perkins, founder of Kleiner Perkins.

For some that got out, it was triggered by a life-event, for others, boredom. And we should ask of ourselves, as Don Valentine did, can we leave behind a better firm — a better society or a better tomorrow? Or did we try to enrich ourselves one last time as we head out that door? In one of the Silicon Valley firms, a retiring GP presented an elaborate NPV calculation and a payment stream that the junior partners had to commit to pay to the retiring GP. The departing partner planned to collect a "royalty for using his name" for several years, and after all that, he even retained a percentage of the GP. The new members of the firm were bonded labor, albeit Tesla-driving Stanford-graduates.

Paul Holland, who has designed his own transition at Foundation Capital, says, "As an industry, we can certainly do better — for the most part, it has not been done right." To which we say, true, and read aloud, one more time Shakespeare's Sonnet 60:

> *"Like as the waves make towards the pebbl'd shore,*
> *So do our minutes hasten to their end;*
> *Each changing place with that which goes before,*
> *In sequent toil all forwards do contend."*

Part Two

Raising Your Venture Fund

It's easy. It's not easy.

The hardest and the most humbling part of a VC's journey is often raising a venture fund. And in raising a fund, you make an explicit promise to serve your LPs. Whether you give them a ticket to the ringside view of the technology circus, or empower them to play an active role in shaping the future, as a fund manager, the first thing you do is serve your LPs. Bob Dylan's song "Gotta Serve Somebody" is a gentle reminder that no matter how high you go, there is always someone who we serve.

You may be a business man or some high-degree thief.
They may call you doctor or they may call you chief.
But you're gonna have to serve somebody. . .

So in this section, let's figure out the basics — who you serve, your fund strategy, targeting the right fund investors and LPs, the arcs of story-telling, decks and data rooms, road shows, and more.

Might I suggest that you wear that humble hat. Knee-pads are optional but often recommended. Groveling may be required, and is often expected in the high corridors of power. Over some fine whiskey at the Battery Club in San Francisco, one LP humble-bragged that he has anchored many venture funds, being the first money in first-time funds. "I am the quintessential GP king maker," he muttered. And then he continued with a pompous smirk, "I love it when they come begging to me. I own them."

Just as smart founders select the right VCs on their board, the best fund managers are able to pick the LPs that matter, can add value, and shape their journey. Unfortunately, there are very few of these. Pick the wrong LP and you have a toxic problem. Some are like absent parents — who show up for an occasional annual sporting event. The best ones build rich, collaborative, two-way networks.

The business of VC is like a two-sided marketplace. On one side are the investors — your LPs and your shareholders. On the other side are your founders. You cannot serve just one side well — you have to ensure both sides get some love, respect, and, above all, performance. You want LPs for life — not just for one fund. But it's often the first fund that counts — if you do well, the rest becomes easier.

8

LP Universe

The universe of limited partners (LPs) includes a range of institutional investors such as foundations, university endowments, pension funds, fund of funds, family offices, and sovereign wealth funds. Each institution has its own DNA. Each institutional class has its own framework and investment criteria. Each institution has different sources of capital, investment criteria, constraints, and return expectations. To achieve their target returns, institutions have to constantly juggle with different types of assets.

The four major asset classes competing for investor capital are stocks (public equities), bonds (sources of fixed income), alternative assets (private equity, venture capital, hedge funds, real estate), and the safest class: cash. Based on global economic trends and risk–return potential, investors establish strategies to deploy optimum allocation of capital in each of these asset classes.

Asset allocation, a prudent method to manage risk and returns, is driven by each investor's appetite for risk, rewards, and liquidity. Consider Exhibit 8.1.

Venture capital is a sub-asset class of private equity and falls under the alternative investment asset class, and for most LPs, it is a smaller fraction of the overall portfolio. Typical LPs in any VC fund include a mix of LPs, as seen in Exhibit 8.2.

Alternative assets include a growing array of options, are listed in Exhibit 8.3.

Certain types of alternative assets, such as private equity/ venture capital, are illiquid and contractually locked up for

Exhibit 8.1 **Major asset classes in an investor portfolio.**

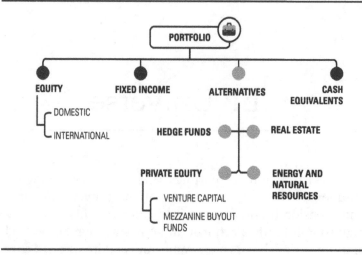

Exhibit 8.2 **Typical mix of LPs in venture fund.**

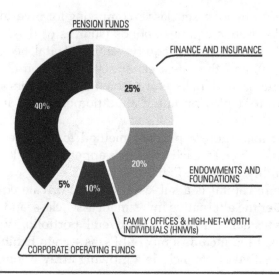

Exhibit 8.3 **Alternative Investments.**

Class	Sub-asset Class	Investment Goals
Private equity	**Venture capital**, leveraged buyout funds (LBOs), distressed debt, mezzanine funds, special situations	Higher returns and diversification
Hedge funds	Global macro, absolute return, market neutral, long/short, event driven, and derivatives	Higher returns and diversification with better liquidity, as compared to private equity
Real estate, infrastructure	Real estate investment trusts (REITs), private real estate funds	Diversification
Commodities	Energy, oil, gas, timber, agriculture, and managed futures	Returns/cash income streams from other assets

10-year horizon. Such assets do not provide the same advantages to investors as do equities and hedge funds. Secondary sales of alternative are not efficient. Lack of liquidity affects allocation outlays, and often investors seek an illiquidity premium, a higher return from such illiquid asset classes.

In this chapter we will look at each institutional investor and understand their modus operandi. Let's take a closer look at the pension funds.

PENSION FUNDS

By far, the largest source of capital for the VC universe is pension funds. Employers create pension funds to manage employees' investments. Employees set aside a certain amount of their paycheck in a separate account, with the goal of savings for retirement. Employers, with an objective of attracting talented employees and incentivizing savings, match the employee contribution into the pension plan. Thus, the two sources of cash inflows into pension funds are a sum of contributions made by individuals and employers. With a larger pool of employees, the steady trickle of contributions grows to a significant amount over time. The goal of any pension fund is to provide financial security to the employees and their beneficiaries.

The pension fund is typically a separate entity and is governed by a board of trustees. The typical asset allocation strategy for this pool of capital depends on the cash needs of the pension plan. Pension funds need to maintain a larger cash pool to meet their monthly obligations to retirees. Consider California Pension Retirement System (CalPERS), the largest public pension fund in the United States, which has over $300 billion in assets in management. CalPERS has allocated about 10 percent or $28 billion to the private equity asset class. Often, the government prescribes language requiring that pension funds "maximize returns without undue risk of loss." Pension funds are also subject to political pressures, and interference can severely affect a pension fund's returns and viability.

ENDOWMENTS AND FOUNDATIONS

University Endowments

University endowments invest heavily in private equity and venture capital. Like every financial institution, they have to manage inflows, outflows, and returns on their capital. A university's cash inflows include student fees, grants, and contributions. On average, student fees and grants constitute 48 percent of a university's revenues; as these sources are uncertain, universities seek to insulate their position by creating endowments. Less than 10 percent of revenues at Yale University have resulted from tuition, but over 40 percent of the university's operating income comes from its endowment. An endowment generates investment income and provides a cushion against any potential uncertainties. With it, a university can focus on its primary goals of providing education and conducting research (or building a football stadium, depending on priorities) — activities that further social causes and knowledge. The grants and contributions are fickle and insufficient — neither of these is tantamount to predictable revenue streams. More than 90 percent of endowments typically spend around 5 percent of their assets each year. They use these cash outflows for university operations or capital expenditures. The rest is often set aside for investments. *Due to limited demands on their cash outlays, endowments are better suited for investments in alternative strategies.* At Yale University Investments Office, as much as 33 percent of the assets are set aside for private equity. Recall that with CalPERS, it was less than 10 percent.

Typical asset allocation for US college and university endowments is shown in Exhibit 8.4. Yale endowment's private equity asset allocation has increased steadily to over 30 percent over time.[1]

Kimon G. Pandapas, member of the Global Investment Team at MIT Investment Management Company, says, "We invest in venture capital to generate multiples of invested capital. It's an added bonus that in doing so, we also are supporting technological innovation, as technology after all, is in our name."

In comparison with pension funds, endowments have invested as much as four times the percentage of their assets in alternative assets. In a perfect world, endowment funds can

Exhibit 8.4 **Yale Endowment's Asset Allocation.**

Asset Class	Yale University	Educational Institution Mean
Absolute Return	23.2 %	20.6 %
Domestic Equity	2.7 %	20.8 %
Foreign Equity	13.7 %	21.9 %
Leveraged Buyouts	15.9 %	7.1 %
Natural Resources	4.9 %	7.7 %
Real Estate	10.1 %	3.4 %
Venture Capital	**21.1 %**	**6.6 %**
Cash & Fixed Income	8.4 %	11.9 %

Note the difference between Domestic Equity and Venture Capital allocations
Source: Yale Endowment, Asset Allocation as of 2019.

potentially last forever, while pension funds can run out of money due to demands of current liabilities.

Foundations

Like endowments, foundations are a significant force in the world of private equity. Foundations exist to support charitable and nonprofit causes. Governed by federal laws and regulated by the US Internal Revenue Service (IRS), foundations are managed by their trustees. Foundations support programs that are likely not supported by federal or state grants, such as childcare, arts and education, health care, climate and environment, and religious and social causes. The emphasis placed on health care by the Bill and Melinda Gates Foundation is one such example. Foundations offer grants to various nonprofit organizations to conduct these programs.

Over 75,000 foundations in the United States manage over $500 billion in assets. Private foundations are established and endowed by corporations (e.g., Ford Foundation, W. K. Kellogg Foundation) or families or individuals (e.g., Bill and Melinda Gates Foundation) and fund programs that are important to the donors. To meet IRS eligibility, private foundations must give away as much as 5 percent of their assets each year. The balance, 95 percent, is invested using asset allocation strategies. Foundations have to report their financial information publicly, as IRS guidelines mandate this disclosure. Besides private foundations, other types of foundations include community foundations, which attract a large number of individual donors from a geographic region, and corporate foundations. Corporate foundations exist to further the cause established by the donor corporation and are funded from the corporation's profits. Over 2,000 corporate foundations in the United States hold over $10 billion in assets. Larger endowments with $1 billion or more in assets are more aggressive with private equity investments, with as much as 57 percent of capital invested in Alternative Strategies. The number falls to 10 percent with smaller endowments below $25 million.

Eric Doppstadt, VP and CIO, Ford Foundation, which has over $12 billion of assets, says, "Venture capital was once a small cottage industry, has now become a global force, similar to other asset classes within the alternative universe. Bear in mind that 20 years ago, venture was a not a standalone asset class — it was a small subset of private equity within alternatives. The LPs in a VC fund would fit around a small conference table. Today, you need the largest ballroom in a hotel to host the annual meeting of a typical VC fund." Foundations have aggressively stepped up their commitments to venture capital over the past decade.

Other forms of foundations include operating foundations, which conduct research or provide services, as opposed to grant-making activities. Compared to a pension fund, the short-term cash needs of a foundation are not as significant. Hence, the allocations toward long-term assets, such as alternative assets (which includes VC), tend to be higher.

SOVEREIGN WEALTH FUNDS

Sovereign wealth funds (SWFs) collectively manage upward of $15 trillion and are beginning to play a much larger role in shaping the venture industry dynamics. Approximately 15 percent of the global alternatives market is owned by SWFs. Exhibit 8.3 shows a few examples. State-owned investment funds that use government surplus capital to invest in a variety of assets, SWFs can be an incomprehensible beast or a boon. In engaging with such entities, two characteristics rise above — due to their sheer scale and governance and political dynamics, investment decisions take longer and are fraught with uncertainty. And this is no place for smaller venture funds. Sovereign wealth funds increasingly rely on private markets to diversify away from oil and gas, into new technology frontiers offered by the venture asset class. However, decision-making cycles can be long, uncertain, and riddled with political and macroeconomic dynamics.

Exhibit 8.5 **Sovereign Wealth Funds — A Growing Opportunity for Venture.**

Country	Entity	Assets Under Management (AUM)	Year Established	Sources of Capital
China	State Administration of Foreign Exchange (SAFE)	~$3 trillion	1978	Foreign Exchange Reserves
Norway	Government Pension Fund	~$1 trillion	1990	Oil/Petroleum
USA	California Public Employee Retirement System (CalPERS)	~ $360 billion	1932	State employee pension reserves
Saudi Arabia	Public Investment Fund (PIF)	~$320 billion	1971	Government
Singapore	Temasek Holdings	~$308 billion	1974	Government

Objectives of sovereign funds are also often tied closely to government and socioeconomic factors. Some of these objectives may not be stated publicly but become evident after a few operating cycles. While primary goals for most funds are financial returns, others are subtle about economic growth, diversification, or stability of their home countries. Start by asking about the entity's sources of capital, mandates, governance structure, and decision-making processes. Look closely at their operating timeline and current portfolio, as that will tell you if the entity has already executed on building its VC portfolio plan. With some newer sovereign entities entering the market, unestablished funds have gotten lucky and managed to get away with large commitments without meaningful performance or a sustainable strategy. One GP snickered, saying we are all guinea pigs in this grand experiment: "We are teaching them about venture, so they should pay us the fees, correct?"

According to a PwC report, four regions dominate the landscape in terms of total number of entities and total assets: Asia Pacific (specifically China), the Middle East, Europe (specifically Norway and Eastern Europe), and North America. Asia Pacific and the Middle East account for two-thirds of total assets.

As seen in Exhibit 8.6 (a), the average SWF size grew to $170 billion, but assets are concentrated between a small number of funds. Motivation for sovereign wealth funds to invest in private markets continues to grow steadily.

See Exhibit 8.6 (b). Asset allocation to private equity has grown from about 9 percent to 27 percent since 2002.

Exhibit 8.6 **(a) Average sovereign wealth fund size.**

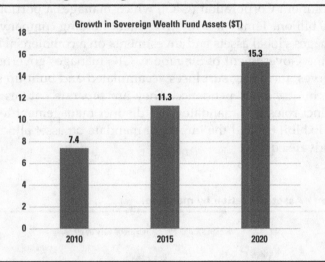

Source: Modified from PwC Study, Sovereign Investors 2020, A Growing Force

Exhibit 8.6 **(b) Asset Allocation - The shift to Private Equity.**

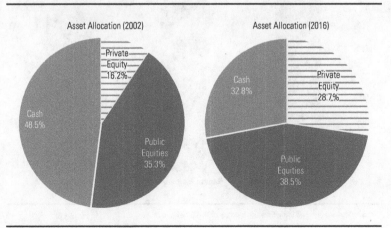

Source: State Street Global Advisors Data, 2019[2]

Though the allocation to private markets grows, the emphasis on stabilization drives some funds to invest in cash and long-term, fixed-income portfolios, while those seeking growth are more aggressive. Take the example of two entities headquartered in Singapore: Temasek Holdings, which has a portfolio of $300 billion, and Government of Singapore Investment Corporation (GIC), which manages a portfolio of $100 billion. Temasek is an investment holding company and manages global assets and investments on a commercial basis for the Government of Singapore. GIC manages government reserves, including surpluses accumulated and built up since the country's independence. They are separate entities with distinct roles and mandates and distinct management teams. See Exhibit 8.7 and the impact of mandate on asset allocation to private equity.

Exhibit 8.7 **Asset allocation by mandate.**

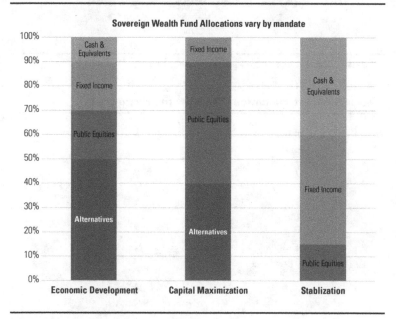

Source: Modified from PwC Study, Sovereign Investors 2020, A Growing Force

FINANCE AND INSURANCE COMPANIES

Within the LP universe, finance and insurance companies provide as much as 25 percent of the capital for venture capital and private equity. Finance companies are treated as a catch-all category to ensure clarity of presentation in this book. These include banks, nonbank financial companies, and fund of funds. Each finance company defines its own internal criteria such as target returns, volatility, holding period/time horizon, which helps develop their asset allocation plan.

Like pension funds, insurance companies manage a large amount of cash inflows and outflows. Any insurance company is in the business of managing risk. An insured party pays a premium at a fixed time interval — say, monthly, quarterly, or annually. Insurance companies invest the premiums, but the underlying driver is to meet a potential obligation that may occur in the future. If an accident occurs, the insured receives compensation. The business model of any insurance company can be reduced to inflows via premium payments and investment income. Underwriting expenses and incurred losses are primary outflows. The scope of the insurer's business and required guarantees drives the target rate of return. These factors determine an asset allocation strategy for any insurance company. As the demand for liquidity is high, the insurance companies do not wish to lock up their capital in VC funds for 10 years. The appetite for VC/PE is often low.

Insurance companies have a unique advantage as a business model: The customer pays up front and eventually, at some point in the future, may receive benefits. In some cases, all a customer may ever get is the proverbial peace of mind. The primary mechanism to generate investment income for insurance companies is management of "float" — the amount of money that "floats" with the insurance company as premiums arrive and sits around, waiting to be paid out in the event of any claims. Insurance companies need to maintain certain levels of capital; if they fail, regulators can swoop in. Solvency requirements are an important factor; hence the need to

That's One Happy Family...

The Hillman family office of Pittsburgh, Pennsylvania, helped launch Kleiner Perkins Caufield Byers (KPCB) Fund I, with a $4 million investment in an $8 million fund. KPCB Fund I invested in 17 companies such as Applied Materials, Genentech, Tandem Computers (and one called "Snow-Job"), and returned $345 million to its investors. The estimated 43X cash-on-cash return made the Hillmans very happy, thank you very much.

maintain a certain level of cash is important. Thus, insurance companies have to model their cash needs based on an actuarial assessment of risk and liabilities. In any insurance company, the accounting and actuarial teams develop the overall plan that determines cash inflows and outflows. Inflows are predictable, but outflows are not entirely predictable. Actuaries invest an enormous amount of time in modeling demographic patterns of fire, floods, accidents, and other acts of God to derive a co-relationship between premiums and claims — or risks and rewards. Hence, insurance companies attempt to manage their cash positions and liquidity effectively, as unanticipated events could occur and affect their solvency. Thus, asset allocation for insurance companies is heavily weighted in low-risk investments such as bonds. Venture capital investments are lower on the totem pole and fall in the "Other" category for most insurance companies.

FAMILY OFFICES AND HIGH-NET-WORTH INDIVIDUALS

According to World Wealth Report, worldwide, wealthy families and individuals control about $42 trillion. More than 100,000 individuals in the United States are estimated to have assets in excess of $10 million. Family offices and HNWIs contribute as much as 10 percent of all capital in venture funds. A family office is a private company, established to manage investments of any single wealthy family. A single-family office (SFO) or a multifamily office (MFO), as their names suggest, are professionally managed investment companies that serve the needs of wealthy families. One of the primary functions of a traditional family office is to consolidate financial management with a view to preserving wealth, generating returns, and minimizing the tax impact for any family's fortune. Small teams of confidants, including professional investment managers, are responsible for managing the family's assets and the family office.

Among the other major tasks handled by the family office are the management of taxes, property management, accounting, payroll processing, and other concierge-type services such as travel arrangements. Family offices are classified as Class A, B, or C, depending on their administrative structure. Class A family offices are operated by an independent company with direct supervision from a family trustee or an appointed administrator. Class B family offices are operated by an accounting firm, bank, or a law firm, and Class C family offices are directly operated by the family with a small support staff. MFOs consolidate activities for several wealthy families with the objective of minimizing operational costs.

The Family Wealth Alliance estimates there are approximately 3,000 US-based single-family offices and 150 multifamily offices. SFOs manage assets ranging from $42 million to $1.5 billion. Total assets under advisement by MFOs are upward of $350 billion, with an average client relationship size of $50 million. Median asset size at any MFO is close to $1 billion.

According to a study conducted at the Wharton School, the most important objective for the SFO is transgenerational wealth management. Having an SFO also allows the family members to pursue their own careers, while enjoying the benefits of professionally managed, effective money management strategies. As the wealth comes from family business, 58 percent choose to remain involved in operating the businesses, and 77 percent are majority stakeholders in their holding companies. This has implications from an investment decision-making perspective. Cap Gemini World Wealth Report reports typical asset allocation for family offices is 8 percent in alternatives. However, some family offices have a strong propensity to invest heavily in venture capital asset class.

In Europe, 63 percent of SFOs manage asset allocation in-house versus 47 percent of SFOs in the Americas. Thus, investment decisions and process timelines may differ if professionals manage the office. Due to the size of assets and the conservative undertones, the decision-making cycle for investment in PE and VC is comparatively longer. Family offices are a significant source of capital for venture funds.

In terms of the total global high-net-worth family population, it remains highly concentrated, with the United States, Japan, and Germany accounting for 60.3 percent of the world's population. The fastest growth of high-net-worths is in Asia or "Ch-India."

CORPORATE OPERATING FUNDS

Corporate investments in venture funds make up a bare whisper of 2 percent of all capital flowing into venture funds. A number of corporations, such as SAP, Cisco, Dow Chemical Company, and IBM, invest as LPs in externally managed venture funds. Others establish internally managed "corporate VC (CVC) funds" such as Google Ventures, which invest directly in companies. CVCs invest about 6 percent of annual VC investments in companies.

COMPARISON OF LIMITED PARTNERSHIPS

In comparing the various LPs in Exhibit 8.8, the allocation to alternatives varies, as does their primary motivation for investing in the VC asset class. Any venture practitioner seeking to raise capital needs to consider the size of an investor's alternative asset pool, decision-making criteria, and timelines of each investor. Family offices and foundations make decisions

Exhibit 8.8 **Comparing the LP Universe.**

Investor Type	Typical Percentage of Assets in Alternatives	Decision Maker(s)	Drivers	Constraints
Endowments and foundations	51%	CIO	Financial returns	Size of investment staff; social and political views
Pension funds	14%	Portfolio manager, chief investment officer (CIO), investment committee; state treasurer may be the final signatory	Financial returns	Liquidity and risk management, size of investment staff, regulatory, political perspectives
Sovereign Wealth Funds	N/A	Concentrated within small trusted circles	Diversification of assets, access to technology and innovation	Lengthy processes, opaque and driven by political and cultural constraints
Family offices	8%	Managing director; family member may be the final signatory	Financial returns, a seat at the innovation table	Limited bandwidth; strategy and allocations are highly fluid
Insurance companies	6%	CIO	Capital conservation	Liability, liquidity, solvency, regulatory
Corporations' operating funds	Opportunistic	Corporate development, CFO, or CEO	Insights into developing technologies and new revenue streams	Limited percentage allocation, board approvals; long-term participation is unlikely

at a faster pace while pension funds and SWFs have longer approval cycles.

For any venture practitioner, it is imperative to understand the universe of alternative asset investors because each one has its own set of constraints. Endowments and foundations are highly aligned toward the venture asset class, while insurance companies are the most risk-averse.

While considering an investment in any venture capital fund, each LP assesses the opportunity based on the following criteria:

- *Asset allocation strategy.* A set of investment principles and portfolio construction guidelines designed to generate an overall target rate of return for the LPs. Venture capital is treated as a sub-asset class of private equity that falls under alternative assets.

- *Investment strategy and criteria.* The factors that help LPs choose target investments within each of the asset classes.
- *Investment process.* Timelines and steps each LP needs to follow to make an investment decision within each asset class.

Capital flows into venture funds from limited partners (LPs), which include pension funds, university endowments, foundations, finance companies, sovereign funds, and high-net-worth individuals. Once we understand LP profiles and their constraints, we can identify which LP may be best suited for a venture fund.

While pension funds are the largest contributor, these are also conservative with respect to VC allocations. Endowments and foundations are comparatively more aggressive and allocate larger portions to VC asset classes. Finance companies act as specialized intermediaries and follow the guidelines established by their sponsors. A fund of funds (FoF) is one such example — it is established as an intermediary to allow larger institutional investors to research, gain access to, and manage VC fund investments.

The universe of LPs is vast, with each LP seeking different risk-to-return goals. A seed-stage fund may be better suited in targeting family offices, whereas a national/global fund with an established track record can attract pension funds and endowments. As in any sales process, understanding LPs will help you to manage your "somewhat hellish" fundraising process. A fund of funds is a separate "mini-LP-universe" discussed in the following chapter.

9

LPs of Choice: Fund of Funds

Some large, really large institutional investors (like pension funds and endowments) invest in venture capital funds using an indirect investment approach. They pick an intermediary — a fund of funds (FoF) — as opposed to investing in venture funds directly. Now the obvious question is, why do smart, institutional investors bother adding a middleman — yet another layer in this mix? After all, they could bypass this step and invest in funds directly.

ADVANTAGES OF A FUND OF FUNDS

The fund of funds (FoF) model was established to meet the asset allocation and diversification demands of larger financial institutions. OK, let's try that in plain English — large, multibillion-dollar institutional investors have to sprinkle money in different buckets. Each bucket is an asset class and has risk associated with it and offers a different financial return. As we saw earlier, there are many buckets such as stocks, bonds, and real estate — even bitcoins. Venture is one such bucket. It's a smallish bucket when you compare it with other buckets like hedge funds, but it's getting bigger.

The venture bucket competes with a lot of other buckets for attention. As a result of risk-reward trade offs, not all buckets are equal. VC is the riskiest of them all — indeed, we often brag that 9 out of 10 companies in any fund's portfolio will fail. That's 90 percent of your LP capital squandered away. Not too long ago, eager investors put $1.5 million in a social media startup that built an app that would allow us to say "Yo" to each other. That's all. Nothing more.

VC is risky but also suffers from lack of consistency of returns. You see wild swings in the returns, and for those who expect predictable behavior, this can be a problem. The *standard deviation* (a fancy term for a inconsistency of returns, or a measure of risk) varies as much as 150 percent in VC asset classes, and that's a big headache for investors. On top of that, every VC fund claims to be a top performer. As noted in Chapter 6, a fund of funds bemoaned in one of its newsletters that VCs sound like that mythical town called Lake Wobegon, where all the women are strong, all the men are good looking, and all the children are above average. Another fund of funds manager said, "When every VC fund tells us they are top quartile, I wonder where the rest of three quartiles managers are — I just cannot seem to find them."

So when you have (a) high risk and inconsistent returns coupled with (b) less than 10 percent of your assets allocated to VC and (c) everyone is a rock star VC, you end up with a challenging situation. To avoid this theater and madness, institutional investors have "outsourced" the selection process of

Fund of Funds: Bridging Institutions and Venture Firms

Funds of funds raise approximately $30 billion in any given year. The first fund of funds was raised in the 1980s, when a firm that would eventually become Adams Street Partners raised $60 million. Today, Adams Street Partners raises $2 billion each year and manages over $25+ billion. It typically invests in 15 to 30 new partnership commitments. Its target allocation typically includes 30 percent in venture capital, with the largest slice allocated to buyout funds 40 percent and the rest set aside for mezzanine and distressed debt funds.

VC funds to fund of funds. To institutional investors, a fund of funds offers the following advantages:

Efficiency. For a $50 billion pension fund with less than 10 percent of its assets in private equity, the world is further sliced into mezzanine, buyouts, and venture. Apply another set of layers of risk diversification — sectors, geography, size, and vintage year — and what you have is a fairly complex matrix of relatively small investments. The ability to manage such investments effectively becomes a challenge for the pension fund managers. In such situations, fund of funds allow these larger institutions to efficiently participate in the venture capital asset class without substantially increasing their workload and overhead.

Access. Fund of funds offer access to elite funds and have deeper knowledge of emerging funds with higher potential for performance. They are actively engaged, often keeping a close eye on the market dynamics, tracking emerging managers and high performers. Institutional investors often lack the abilities or resources to conduct research and proactively build relationships. Fund of funds offer specialized expertise to track and monitor industry trends, identify winners, build relationships with key managers, and stay current with investment themes and market terms.

Diversification. The universe of the venture capital fund managers evolves with the ebb and flow of economic trends and opportunities: sector-focused funds, geographic funds, and stage centric funds. As investors diversify and spread out risk over a range of different assets, a fund of funds can reduce their burden by managing a portfolio of venture funds.

Cost structure. Fund of funds are cost-effective solutions for institutional investors because the due diligence, negotiations, and post-investment portfolio management

Exhibit 9.1 **Fund of funds business model.**

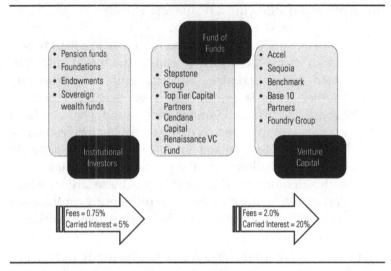

is outsourced to the managers. A typical fee structure is 5 percent carried interest, combined with approximately 0.75 percent annual management fee, as seen in Exhibit 9.1.

FUND OF FUNDS INVESTMENT STRATEGIES

Let us look at three funds of funds in Exhibit 9.2, each focused on venture capital funds, yet their investment strategy differs based on focus, geography, capital under management, and value provided to their fund portfolio.

Top Tier Capital Partners is a San Francisco–based niche-focused fund of funds. The firm makes primary and secondary investments in venture capital funds. Its experience, relationships, and reputation within the venture capital community have enabled a portfolio that includes the who's who of venture fund managers, such as Andreessen Horowitz, Accel Partners, Battery Ventures, Kleiner Perkins Caufield & Byers (KPCB), and True Ventures, among others.

Exhibit 9.2 **Fund of Funds Strategies: A Comparison.**

	Top Tier Capital Partners	Cendana Capital	Renaissance VC Fund
Assets under management	$3.3 billion	~$250 million	$200 million
Average investment size in a venture fund	$25 million	$5 million to $10 million	$5 million to $10 million
Manager focus	Established funds	Micro VC funds	Blend of early regional and established national funds
Geographic focus	US only, with higher concentration in California and New York	Silicon Valley and New York City only	Bicoastal funds investing in Michigan and the Midwest.
Sectors of interest	Primarily technology, with select life sciences	Technology only	Technology and life sciences
Current portfolio	~ 60 venture firms	~ 25 venture firms	~ 25 venture firms

Cendana Capital invests in institutional seed funds or micro-venture capital funds. Micro-venture capital funds (typically fund size of less than $100 million) target companies at a seed stage. Michael Kim, who launched Cendana Capital, the first fund of funds to target the micro-venture space, was the former chair of the Investment Committee of the San Francisco Employees Retirement System (SFERS), a $17 billion public pension fund. At Cendana Capital, Michael meets around 250 fund managers each year but invests in only 10 funds. "Most of the funds we have invested in are managed by former entrepreneurs. Having spent the past decade as both an LP and GP, it is clear that there are significant incongruities in how LPs and GPs seek to generate returns," says Michael.

Renaissance Venture Capital Fund (RVCF) is a fund of funds that invests in venture capital funds with a geographic focus on Michigan. Besides generating returns, the fund of funds aims to foster innovation by connecting its investors — primarily Fortune 500 corporations — with startup companies. "As fund-of-funds model evolves, two factors come into play — access to superior VCs and the ability to add value to three constituents — our LPs, our venture funds and the portfolio companies," says Christopher Rizik, CEO of the fund of funds, who has been a former GP with a $100 million venture fund. The driver to launch such a fund came about with a simple realization that the two sides need each other:

> Corporations need a line of sight in new technology developments, and startups need access to Fortune 500 customers. A single such customer can often change the course of any startup's trajectory and turn failure into success. What's attractive is that unlike government-sponsored funds, there are no restrictions on the amount of investment to be made locally. On the other hand, the Renaissance model follows the premise that there are enough opportunities, ideas, assets, and talent in their states, and there's no need to burden venture capital firms with rules and regulations. . . .We tore up the old arcane, protective rules of many similar funds and focused instead on aggressively bringing together the assets that made our region so special.

In comparing all LP types, the fund-of-funds model stands apart from classical institutional LPs such as endowments/pension funds because they bring a much higher level of insights, context, and intellectual rigor to the business.

They can (a) guide VCs on various best practices/processes, (b) connect VCs with relevant counterparts, and (c) be driven to succeed as much as VCs are. After all, if they don't generate returns, they go out of business. I have found that some fund of funds managers are excellent thought leaders — they keep a close watch on the technology frontiers; review a lot of funds, strategies, and inflated internal rate of return (IRR) data; and gently but firmly challenge every assumption. They hold VCs to a higher standard. These are the "super LPs of choice" — you want them on your side!

10

How LPs Conduct Fund
Due Diligence

Investors and limited partners begin and end fund diligence by assessing the strength of the investment team — the general partners (GPs) and their investment strategy. If the investment team has a demonstrated performance track record and relevant expertise and is pursuing a compelling strategy, fundraising can be a lark. Limited partners (LPs) proactively seek prudent and experienced fund managers who can be good stewards of their capital and generate strong returns. Some seek established managers, while other focus on *emerging managers* — a new crop that may bring a fresher approach, energy, and malleability to the business.

PRIMARY AND SECONDARY INVESTMENT CRITERIA

Institutional investors evaluate venture firms on two primary criteria: the fund managers' expertise and their investment strategy. Secondary criteria include investment terms and market conditions, as presented in Exhibit 10.1. Primary criteria can be evaluated as follows:

- *Fund managers' expertise.* As the primary criteria, limited partners seek to understand entrepreneurial/domain expertise. Investment track record and performance is one of the foremost criteria. And track record comes

Exhibit 10.1 **Limited partner investment criteria.**

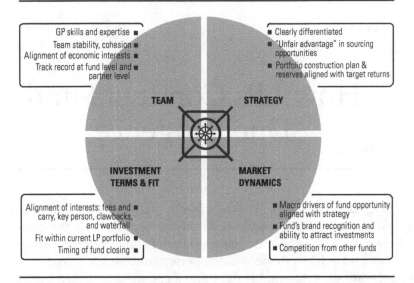

from experience, which comes from losses. The first few investments for any professional are often considered as an expensive learning exercise. As LPs often groan, "It takes $10 million to make a good VC, and that $10 million better come from the LP next door — not from me, thank you."

- *Investment strategy.* What is a fund's investment strategy, and how does it stand apart from the rest of venture funds? What unique factors/differentiators or "unfair advantage" does this combination of investors and their strategy bring to the venture capital arena?

In a study titled "What Drives Venture Capital Fund Raising?," authors Paul A. Gompers and Josh Lerner concluded that fund performance and reputation were the key determinants of fundraising, in addition to macroeconomic and regulatory factors.[1] In another survey of over 200 US-based LPs, they described fund performance as a starting point of their diligence.[2] LPs aspire to get an internal rate of return with a minimum floor of 12 percent, and ideally closer to 20–30 percent, to be considered for investment. The returns are typically tied to a benchmark index for comparing performance. A performance of 400 basis points above the benchmark index (such as Russell 3000, or S&P 500) is often a threshold established by institutional investors.

FUND SELECTION CRITERIA

In their book *Beyond the J Curve*, authors Thomas Meyer and Pierre-Yves Mathonet propose qualitative scoring criteria, which ranks the fund management team and fund strategy as the top weighted factors, as shown in Exhibit 10.2.

Lisa Edgar of Top Tier Capital Partners, a fund of funds, starts her screening process with performance. "In an environment defined by change, it is important to assess the fund manager's ability to produce superior returns across various technological and economic cycles," she says.[3] Top Tier Capital Partners has established relationships with some of the leading

Exhibit 10.2 **Fund Selection Criteria.**

No.	Dimension	Weight (%)	Remarks
1	Management team skills	30	Investment and operational experience, sector expertise, regional connections, size of team, and complementary skills
2	Management team stability	10	Clear roles, responsibilities, decision-making, historical relationships and stability, economic alignment of incentives, financial stability of fund, and succession planning
3	Management team motivation	10	GP commitment percentage, incentive structure, reputation, team independence, outside activities, and conflicts of interest
4	Fund strategy	15	Sourcing, stage/sector, fund size, exit strategy, and overall strategy fit
5	Fund structure	10	Costs/fees, governance, and compliance
6	External validation	10	Track record of previous funds, performance of comparable funds, quality of co-investors, and recurrence of investors
7	Overall fit	15	Considers the overall picture — for example, the fit between the team, fund size, and the strategy

Source: Adapted from Thomas Meyer and Pierre-Yves Mathonet, *Beyond the J Curve — Managing a Portfolio of Venture Capital and Private Equity Funds* (Chichester, UK: John Wiley & Sons, 2005), 221. © 2005 John Wiley & Sons

venture funds in Silicon Valley. For some LPs, investing in a first-time fund is a risky proposition. Fisher Lynch Capital, a fund of funds, seeks proven GPs. "A roman numeral V or higher is a good start," says Georganne Perkins, a senior advisor with the firm.[4] Such a fund would have established a track record over the past four funds and demonstrated its ability to withstand changes in its team, strategy, and technology cycles. But some LPs actively seek first-time fund managers who may be hungrier, driven, and bring a unique point of view to the investment climate. "Like any entrepreneur looking for the next best opportunity, we are always seeking the most promising managers of the future,"[5] advises Kenneth Van Heel, who manages $10 billion in assets as the head of the corporate pension fund for Dow Chemical Company.

Beyond performance, the top due-diligence criteria included team stability and a consistent investment strategy.[6] "My primary goal is to understand the partnership dynamics," says Lindel Eakman, who manages Foundry Group's fund of funds business. As an LP for over a decade, Lindel has seen partnerships fall apart due to interpersonal dynamics and bad chemistry. Acrimonious lawsuits between investment partners create unnecessary headaches for all LPs. Hence, one of the first criteria LPs try to ascertain is stability of the management team. As there is no simple way to predict if marriages and partnerships can survive for long, institutional LPs often avoid the ones who have just begun dating.

11

Defining Your Fund's Investment Strategy

An investment strategy — the *raison d'être* of any venture firm — combines fund managers' skills and expertise with a given market opportunity. Most venture capitalists use emergent strategies, in which the firm adopts a sandbox but remains flexible enough to deal with exceptions. Boundaries are adjusted periodically, and when exceptions occur, they are driven by the potential for return.

A well-established strategy blends macro-trends data with the fund managers' expertise, relationships, insights, and analysis. Synthesizing this information, a fund manager points to the future, where opportunities may grow and generate significant returns.

MARKET OPPORTUNITY

Certain sectors show promise as underlying technologies evolve, while others run out of favor. As the bulky mainframe computer transitioned to the ubiquitous desktop, the ecosystem of hardware and software opportunities emerged. In the late 1970s and early 1980s, the first computing wave attracted eager investors, who backed over a hundred hardware start-ups that focused on disk drives, desktop computers, and allied products. Apple, Intel, Tandem Computers, LSI Logic, and others were amongst the first venture-backed winners. As the networking wave emerged, investors found companies like Cisco, Juniper Networks, Bay Networks, 3Com, and others.

Soon thereafter, the internet boom (and bust) occurred followed by the disruptive forces of cloud computing, and mobile innovations, and now, artificial intelligence has found its way in every investment theme.

Let us consider the inherent drivers of market opportunity. Do structural shifts in the market create new investment opportunities? Management guru Peter Drucker would have said yes. Drucker defined systematic innovation as the "purposeful and organized search for changes, and . . . systematic analysis of the opportunities such changes might offer."[1] He outlined seven sources of innovative opportunity and said that the lines between these sources are blurred and overlap considerably (see Exhibit 11.1).

Exhibit 11.1 **Drucker's Seven Sources for Innovative Opportunity.**

Sources	Definition	Examples
Unexpected	Unexpected events, successes, or failures lead to opportunity.	Financial crisis and the rise of bitcoins, AirBnb, and the sharing economy, Pandemic
Incongruities	Discrepancy or dissonance between "what is" and "what ought to be"; composed of four areas: (1) economic realities of an industry and marketplace, (2) other realities of an industry (optimization of local, nonessential areas), (3) customer expectations versus the industry perception of customer expectations, (4) internal process incongruity	Costs, processes, and quality of health care in the United States Investing in China despite political and regulatory challenges
Process needs	Missing links or unmet needs in a process that could make the process cheaper, easier, or technologically or economically possible	Artificial intelligence, Payment processing/credit cards
Industry and market structures	Changes in industry or market such as new competitors, new customers, more differentiated products, new manufacturing or marketing processes, new substitute, or complementary products or services	Multi-cloud adoption, New applications in cybersecurity
Changes in demographics	Changes in population structure, age structure, cultural composition, employment, education, and income	Aging population and health care needs
Changes in perception	Perceptional shift: "the glass is half full" versus "the glass is half empty"	Crypto-currencies, Cleantech
New knowledge	Discovery of new knowledge such as a new technology or materials	Quantum computing, 3D printing

Source: Adapted from Peter F. Drucker, *Innovation and Entrepreneurship* (Oxford: Butterworth-Heinemann, 1985).

Opportunity is embedded in four sources (the unexpected, incongruity, process needs, and structural changes), and three external factors (demographics, changes in perception, and new knowledge) are drivers of opportunity.[2]

It is not so much as identifying the market opportunity but, rather, tying the opportunity in a cohesive manner with the fund manager's expertise and their ability to execute the investment strategy. As Bob Dylan once sang, "You don't need a weatherman to know which way the wind blows."

Other factors that impact investment strategy include geography (underserved regions yield opportunities due to pricing advantages) and the stage of investments (earlier-stage companies need less capital but are riskier investments). Ultimately, an investment strategy is a combination of the fund manager's expertise, the market opportunity within the sector, geographic advantages, stage of investments, and the size of the fund. No single element stands out as much as the GP expertise. A few examples of fund strategies are laid out in Exhibit 11.2.

Once a strategy is established, leading practitioners not only seek existing opportunities but also lead the formation of companies based on the white spaces, road maps, or the open avenues in the market. Adrian Fortino, Partner at Mercury Fund, says, "In my first year at Mercury Fund, the most exciting part of the job was to build my own investment theme. It was a clean sheet

Exhibit 11.2 **Variations on a Theme: How Strategy Differs in Venture Firms.**

Fund	Sector	Stage	Competitive Advantages
Arboretum Ventures	Health care	Early	One of the largest venture fund in the Midwest, with established track record of investments, exits, and IPOs
Base 10 Partners	Automation and AI technology	Early	Hyperconnected GPs, with Silicon Valley access to founders and top-tier investors
Switch Ventures	Consumer technology	Seed	Ex-McKinsey GP, with operating expertise and data-driven sourcing approach
Brick and Mortar Ventures	Construction and real estate technology	Early	First-mover investor in a rapidly growing sector. GP has ties with Bechtel family, with access to construction sector customer network, market challenges, and usage patterns

approach, and I could build on my experience of seven years in the manufacturing world. As we studied the impact software could have on this arena, it led me to develop our Intelligent Manufacturing investment theme." Using this framework, Adrian went on to search and invest in a number of companies that brought efficiencies to the world of industrial processes. Mercury Fund also positions itself as serving the vast Middle America, where paucity of capital can allow for realistic valuations.

When investor Arthur Rock raised his first fund in the early 1960s, he would recall, "The scientists who had moved from the east to the west had all the ideas. So I saw a great opportunity in bringing the East Coast money out. . .backing these people on the West Coast. 'Go West, young man.'" In 1961, Arthur Rock raised $5 million from East Coast investors and moved to San Francisco to start his own venture capital firm. The fund returned a tidy sum of $90 million back to its investors.

"Even with a great roadmap, it's always necessary to maintain an open mind to great opportunistic investments," writes David Cowan, who rues Bessemer's inability to exit telecom investments at the right time.[4]

COMPETITIVE ADVANTAGES

"VCs don't understand their competition as well, nor do they run their business like a typical startup. You should know

Exhibit 11.3 **Midcontinent US attracts 12% of total VC spend. Mercury Fund's strategy focuses on this underserved market.**

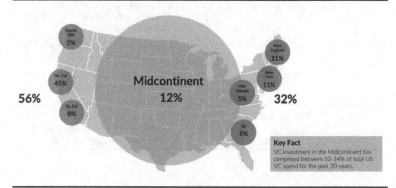

The Top-Down Approach to Building Your Thesis: Roadmap Investing

"Each Bessemer investment road map begins with an analysis of disruptive catalysts that have the potential to cause major displacements in our economy. Those disruptive catalysts might be technical (e.g., network vulnerabilities), demographic (e.g., aging US population), regulatory (e.g., spectrum auctions or Sarbanes Oxley), psychographic (e.g., consumer concerns about security), or geopolitical (e.g., China's reception to foreign investment). We at Bessemer try to take the road map investing approach more seriously than most," writes David Cowan of Bessemer Venture Partners.

"Fresh out of business school, I joined Bessemer and proceeded to fall in love with every crappy pitch I heard. Fortunately, before I did any damage, my bosses intervened. I developed a comprehensive list of 38 potential investment sectors of high technology, and I spent the next three months whittling it down. I crossed off sectors that required deep domain knowledge — sectors that were too early, too crowded, or too unproven. . . . I solicited advice from the smartest experts I could find. I went to conferences, surveying buyers," writes Cowan.

This resulted in sharpening the saw, which allowed him to focus, narrowing down his investment horizon to the data and communications subsectors. Cowan's road map lays out specific strategies, or "initiatives," to exploit the disruption. "For each of these initiatives [Bessemer] made one investment in the best team we could find attacking the problem — some were follow-on rounds . . . and some were new teams that we incubated in our offices." Creating a road map allows a practitioner to spot the growth opportunities and the opportunities in ever-evolving the technology landscape.[3]

Investment Thesis: Union Square Ventures Describes the Power of Network Effects

Venture firms operate a bunch of different ways. Some have a geographical focus, others have a sector focus, still others have a stage focus. Union Square Ventures' (USV) focus was summarized in a simple statement:

Large networks of engaged users, differentiated through user experience, and defensible through network effects.

The partners write, "When we are organizing our activities and thinking about investment decisions, then we parse that a little finer, we unpack some of the components. 'Large' obviously requires scale — Twitter is a great example. But it can also mean large relative to a specific problem set or community. Stack Exchange is comprised of over 80 question and answer sites. Some of those sites, like Server Fault, are designed for very specific communities, but aim to have most of the potential members of that community as active participants. Similarly, Behance is designed for the world's creative professionals."

"Networks" are, of course, interconnected groups or systems, but they also come in a few flavors. For example, networks can be centered around person-to-person sharing of an activity (foursquare, Soundcloud), facilitating a transaction (Dwolla), enabling creativity (Tumblr, Wattpad), person-to-person marketplaces (Etsy, Kickstarter), or business and personal finance marketplaces (Lending Club, Funding Circle). Marketplaces have some of the more interesting network components and use the efficient exchange of information to produce superior economics and create new economies in their area of focus. Examples include the creative projects that wouldn't otherwise come to fruition if the Kickstarter marketplace was not active, the individuals finding work through Workmarket's labor resource market, or the active secondary market in small business loans (and pieces thereof) being traded through Funding Circle. Finally, networks can also be networks of data, such as what

DuckDuckGo (search), Indeed (jobs), and Flurry (mobile apps) are doing that then provide aggregate data-level benefits to users from that data network aggregation.

We will also look closely at the "user experience" of these networks, being most interested in novel ("differentiated") web and mobile native interface ways to engage users around a solution to the particular problem, one that is consistent with the fabric of the users' experiences. With Etsy, USV believes that "the best long-term steward of a network will be a company that focuses on value creation for all participants in the network instead of solely for its shareholders."

Businesses that create barriers to entry through "network effects" — the value of a service to a user increases as others use it. This can potentially arise in a number of ways: for example a proprietary data asset; the marketplace dynamics of having a robust set of sellers and buyers; or through the development of a community that openly shares and exchanges information. In an era where the initial cost to develop the prototype of a product has been dramatically reduced, where there are mature and scalable open-source tools and services to utilize for that development, and where cloud infrastructure is available on demand and at a variable cost, defensibility may no longer be found in the technology underpinnings — the code or IP — of a service. Defensibility may, however, arise through the growth of service that gets more valuable, and more interesting, with each new participant. One nice example of this is Twitter, which is so potentially valuable because, put simply, that's where the Tweets as well as the personal follower/following relationships reside. The value of these businesses tends to be composed of the very networks they have created.

Taken together, these components comprise how USV looks at the Internet at large to find places where we should invest and where we can be good partners. Of course, the components are not monolithic and are subject to nuance and interpretation, but again, of course, that's what makes them most interesting.

where you fit into the market," says Lindel Eakman, who heads the fund-of-funds practice at Foundry Group. "It's easier to start companies, and that has led to an explosion of technology opportunities. As a result, we have seen a large number of technology-focused early-stage funds with no clear differentiation. After a while, they all sound the same," says Chris Rizik, former VC and CEO of Renaissance Venture Capital Fund, a fund of funds. In building competitive advantage, VCs need to research the funds actively investing in their target markets. While this is obvious, very few fund presentations include a competitive analysis. Most VCs assume that there is "so much opportunity" that everyone can live happily.

In building their competitive advantage, VCs can define their edge based on (a) how they will attract the best founders, (b) stage of investment, (c) sector, (d) target geography, (e) network of relationships, (f) industry insights, and (g) past track record.

There is no single factor that defines a competitive edge, but often it's a combination of many. "I believe many strategies are the same, and rarely do funds have a truly ground-breaking investment strategy," Igor Rozenblit, LP with a multibillion-dollar fund pointed out. Most LPs boil down the venture firm's competitive advantage to one question: "Why would founders want to work with you?"

CASE STUDY: SOLO GP GOES INSTITUTIONAL

When Paul Arnold started to test his appetite for venture, he had already paid his dues and done his time. After his stint at McKinsey, Paul had joined a rapidly growing venture-backed technology company, which raised over $200 million and is valued over a billion dollars, a unicorn in venture parlance. Yet as he tried to navigate his way into venture firms, he found it challenging. One VC told him bluntly, "Every venture firm out there is like a dysfunctional family. Don't waste your time."

The next day, Paul decided to strike it out on his own and start his own fund — Switch Ventures. Having grown up in Wyoming, his soft approach, thoughtful yet understated and low-key style, was engaging, and founders flocked around him. But some LPs would dismiss him for not "demonstrating enough passion."

At Switch Ventures (Exhibit 11.5), Paul developed a data-driven approach to identify the founders who will outperform in building stellar companies. Fund I was on track to generate 62 percent IRR while the top quartile for the same vintage year was at 10 percent. The top 5 percent of the performers were at 44 percent. Cambridge Associates has ranked Switch as the second-best fund of the vintage. This performance got the attention of a fund of funds, which jumped in to anchor Switch Fund II with a 10 percent commitment. "It took over a dozen meetings and two years of relationship building," says Paul. "The LPs' biggest area of concern was *(a) can you scale your investment check sizes, and (b) does this have potential to be a long-term partnership?"* On selling to LPs and fundraising, Paul says, "A real pro would have a very organized sales process to bring LPs through the funnel. But I am terrible at this part of the business. I just focused on what I am good at — making investments."

Exhibit 11.5 **Switch Ventures.**

	Fund I	Fund II
Fund Size	$5 m	$25 m
Portfolio	17 companies	25 companies
Average investment	$150,000	$1 m
LP mix	Individuals and families	50% institutions and the rest from individuals/families 100% LP retention from Fund I

Lessons from a Solo VC

- **On fund strategy:** Don't differentiate yourself for marketing reasons. That never holds up over the long-term. Find differentiation that you truly believe will beat the market, and that you are positioned to execute.

- **On fundraising:** It's a long game. Talk to the right LPs. Family offices may be able to make a decision within a few weeks. But large allocators like endowments take years of trust and relationship building. Set reasonable targets. You lay the foundation before you scale AUM.

- **On investing:** It's a power law game. Understand what it means to be cultivating outliers. It's very likely that a single investment or two in your fund will be all that matters. Don't miss them! Have conviction. A herd investor will at best achieve mediocre results.

It's easy to be a dick. Don't be dismissive of founders. Don't ghost. Respect their time. Recognize the inherent power dynamics at play and don't abuse them. If you need a reminder, recall LPs who might have done this to you and course correct. A quick no is much better than a long maybe. Treat each deal like it's your only one. Bet on founders that inspire in some way. NEVER invest in someone whose integrity is suspect.

And get lucky, but separate good/bad decisions from good/bad luck. How can we improve our thinking in a business where it's easy to confuse luck and skill? The problem is that most investors learn from their outcomes and not from evaluating their decisions, regardless of the outcome. They take the wrong lessons from experience when they have a loss (which happens all the time in VC). This loss could be due to a bad decision AND a bad outcome, or a good decision AND a bad outcome. The key is to assess decisions (instead of just outcomes) or we end up with a flawed learning process, where many of the narrative fallacies of the business originate.

- **On building an institutional grade fund:** Overinvest a bit on infrastructure: back-office, audits, legal. If

> you want to be in this for the long haul, it comes back around. Make a 20-year plan, and then start walking.
>
> Have strong mentors who will go to bat for you. Ideally, find people who are the best in your business and 10–20 years ahead of you in the journey. Your reputation is the most valuable thing you have.
>
> - **On building momentum with LPs:** I did what I was good at — making great investments. And by sharing my performance with Cambridge Associates, I got an outside independent source of authority that could say compare my performance.
>
> **On staying tenacious through dark times of fundraising:** Early on, I knew where I wanted to be in 5 and 20 years, which I think made it easy to work through the small things along the way. And my wife was very supportive and trusting (sorry, but she's taken).

CASE STUDY: OVERSUBSCRIBED FIRST FUND — HOW A $30M FUND ENDED UP WITH OVER $100M IN COMMITMENTS

Nigerian-born Adeyemi Ajao had built and sold two companies and made over 50 seed investments when he started to mull over raising his first fund. "Maybe $30m to $40m fund would be a good start," he told me over coffee when I first met him. Ade had built his first startup in Madrid, Spain — a social app called Tuenti, which soon became like the Facebook of Spain and was snapped up by Telefónica for a tidy sum of $100 million. One of the restless kind, Ade then decided to get an MBA at Stanford University. While getting acquainted with the heated belly of the startups in Silicon Valley, Ade got bored and founded another company called Identified — which was a career networking site targeting young professionals, built on the Facebook platform. Business software company Workday soon came knocking, and

Following the Power-Law of Returns: Success Begets Success

Paul Arnold of Switch Ventures believes that there are only three truly distinct venture fund strategies, and all of them boil down to one point: Can you change the distribution of the companies in which you invest? Among the many approaches in venture capital, there are fundamentally only three ways to do this. The best funds pursue all of them.

1. Add value.
2. Source better.
3. Invest better.

That's it. Everything else is tactics and execution. Any strategy that doesn't achieve one of these is puffery, marketing, or confusion. The power law of returns — where very few companies generate solid outcomes — dominates startup investing, as seen in the data presented in Exhibit 11.4 by Co-relation Ventures. After analyzing 21,640 companies between 2004 and 2013, we can see some interesting patterns.

Exhibit 11.4 **The power law of venture returns.**

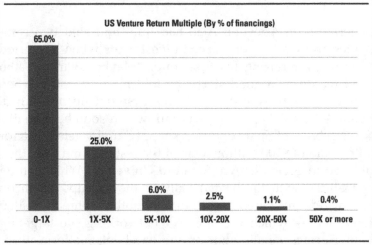

US Venture Return Multiple (By % of financings)

0-1X	1X-5X	5X-10X	10X-20X	20X-50X	50X or more
65.0%	25.0%	6.0%	2.5%	1.1%	0.4%

Nothing is more determinative of a fund's success. Power-law distribution is the architecture of the whole game.

I measure any investing approach against its impact on the power-law distribution. This is the acid test of what is actually effective. And while it is true that adding value, sourcing better, and investing better are all good strategies for other investing situations, the effects, especially of 2 and 3, are especially significant in venture where the power curve has a large exponent. Most VCs invest somewhat randomly along the power curve of opportunities they see. Over short periods of time, this randomness can result in good or bad funds. Over longer periods, mediocrity will set in as their investments regress to the mean. They will have weak persistence of performance.

Improving portfolio company operations is the most common approach. Recruitment, marketing, partnerships, sale, operations, and board support are common areas to help. Most often, this takes the form of coaching founders or rolling up your sleeves to help them get work done. Some funds institutionalize value-add through software or platform teams. Startup studios are interesting, blurring the lines between founders and investors. Adding value is absolutely necessary — it's the promise to your founders to be their partner. And it earns you the right to be involved with great founders. Ultimately, great founders in great markets build great companies. You won't make it in venture if you don't work with them. And you won't work with them if you don't bring value to the table. For founders, an investor's ability to add value is obviously important. Great founders are choosing their investors and want to bring in people who will help build the company. Of the three strategies, adding value is the least unique in impact here. In a much flatter distribution, as you see in, say, leveraged-buyout private equity, adding value will create about the same level of value that it will in the power-law distribution. The

(continued)

(continued)

next two strategies, however, have markedly higher impacts in the power-curve setting.

Sourcing better rescales the distribution of the power law, as seen in the graph. Even a random selection of investments from a better-sourced distribution of companies will have a higher expected return than an average venture fund. Fishing in a better pond can make as much (or more) difference as being a better fisherman. A classic way to source better is to build a better network. This works for firms with a strong general reputation. It can also work if you are deep in a particular group of exceptional people — say, globally elite artificial intelligence researchers. Focusing on a geographical region can create strong networks if a fund establishes regional dominance.

Quantitative venture investing can have a huge impact on picking the right investments. Admittedly, I'm biased. A predictive-analytic approach to teams, companies, and industries stacks your hand from the start. It changes all the investment odds. This takes much work to do well but has attractive returns for the effort. Outbound sourcing is an underappreciated approach in early-stage venture. Because inbound referrals are plentiful, investors often ignore outbound efforts. The key is being able to target founders who actually are exceptional. But if you can, why would you not make sure you are talking with the best out there? Switch aspires to take several of these approaches: using a mathematical and predictive approach to sourcing, building high-quality and selective networks of founders that spin out many great companies, and proactively reaching out to the founders who excite us most.

Invest better and you end up in bigger winners. It increases the frequency in the upper tail of outcomes. Picking better is the dominant way to achieve outsized results at the seed stage. And the most important factor for picking better is, by far, good judgment. Good judgment is hard to describe. It's a somewhat ephemeral quality, which only reveals itself over time. As Bill Gurley of Benchmark says, *picking is the single most important quality he looks for in a new investing partner*. Picking better is also a function of doing research and developing insights. Having a correct industry thesis is a perfect example. If you can predict major technology and economic trends, you will be rewarded with more hits. Art and science (or guts and brains) both play into picking. And both are hard. In most firms, there is a huge variance of performance between partners.

Access becomes a much more important factor in the later stages of venture. This is because the winners start to become very obvious as time goes on. Most Series C investors have very similar lists of the top 10 companies they would like to invest in. Brand and reputation have increasing payoff as you move into later stages. Founders want to work with VCs who invest better for the same reasons they want to work with VCs who source better — they want people to associate them with the best. It sends a positive signal to customers, employees, and other investors. And it's a more valuable network to be a part of.

PUTTING IT TO WORK

There are many ways to execute, and the winning approach depends on the investment stage and people involved. While all three strategies add portfolio value, resources are limited, and a fund should think through which one can add the most for them. Finally, there is some logical order to developing capabilities. For example, if you can't source at least some great deals, you really won't be able to pick great ones, either.

Grounding venture strategy in power-law thinking has consistently been helpful for me, and hopefully, it can help others add a frame to their approaches, too.

after selling Identified to Workday, he ended up launching Workday Ventures, a corporate venture arm. Identified had pioneered the use of *gamification* strategies to make professional networking fun and engaging for its users, who are almost all below the age of 30 years old.

But as market timing and luck would have it, Ade soon found a partner in his friend TJ Nahigian. After spending five years in the investment world with venture firms like Accel, Summit Partners, and Coatue, TJ had the founder itch and formed a company called Jobr, a mobile app that was like Tinder — swipe right to connect with recruiters. Ade knew enough about the hiring space, and TJ opened up his previous round to bring Ade as an investor in Jobr. After Jobr was acquired by Monster, Ade and TJ reaped the rewards of the journey — a partnership in the next big thing. "My next leap in the world of venture came with Ade" says TJ.

As the two started to put their heads together, they concluded that a $75 million fund would be a better target. They decided to call it Base 10 partners — after the decimal system of 10 digits, while pursuing their investment in the world of binary outcomes. Between Ade and TJ, they had done 70 investments, 15 exits, of which 10 were valued over $1 billion. This, combined with their entrepreneurial experience, created a strong foundation.

Ade, who was in the middle of planning his marriage, would find TJ hanging out with him and his fiancée at most times. As these two major events occurred — his marriage as well as launch of the fund — they would joke that starting a fund is no different from starting a new relationship. You have to complement each other's strengths. The analytical TJ shrugs his shoulders, saying, "I don't do feelings," which balances Ade, whose high EQ and love is evident for his founders and LPs alike.

Both would dig into their networks for their Fund I, work tirelessly, and build their thesis (see the Appendix for sample). They would end up with much more than $75m. Base10 Partners Fund I closed at $135 million (Exhibit 11.6). And within two years of launch, their Fund II was being raised, thanks

Exhibit 11.6 **Growth of Base 10 Ventures.**

	Fund I	Fund II
Fund size	$135 m	$200 m
Portfolio	18 companies	18 companies
Stage of investment	12 seed stages companies and 6 Series A	No change in strategy
Average investment	$500,000 (Seed) Up to $5m (Series A)	No change
LP mix	Endowments, Silicon Valley entrepreneurs	Endowments, international institutional investors, and entrepreneurs

to the stellar performance of Fund I. It was considered to be in the top 2 percent of all funds of the vintage year. "We are highly data driven, work as hard as founders, bring operational efficiencies to our companies like a private equity fund, and serve our LPs by delivering the higher returns of a VC fund" says Ade.

Not many first-time funds have had such a solid start. But the foundational elements — team, strategy, market timing, and, above all, performance — worked to their advantage.

CASE STUDY: STARTING ALL OVER. . .

Peter Bell had seen it all — the rise and fall of the dot-com wave at Highland Capital, which started in Boston and soon had a global presence. The sheer scale and cross-cultural team dynamics, not to mention geographic and stage preferences of each region, economic macro-factors, and capital flows was not something he enjoyed. And so he started all over again from scratch and launched Amity Ventures. "I hired one of my partners, CJ Reim, when he was 19 — his intellectual curiosity was off the charts. He built his thesis on the Connected Home vertical over a period of one year and invested in Smart Things, a company that got acquired by Samsung for $200 million, which was a very nice outcome. And my other partner, Patrick

Yang, did the same for autonomous vehicles and invested in Nutonomy. That company got snagged for $450 million, making our investors happy," says Peter.

Even if CJ Reim did not have operating experience, his ability to engage with founders and build a portfolio is compelling. "We have found our place, by being responsive to the founders." For Peter, starting from scratch was not easy. Most LPs try to pick new fund managers, as they do not have to dig into years of track records and team dynamics. But Amity raised $75 million and has started to build a strong portfolio. "We built the firm on three precepts — see the best opportunities, win them with strength, and partner to make our founders successful."

CASE STUDY: WHO HAS TIME FOR THIS? I DON'T NEED NO LPS ANYMORE. . .

In what can be described as a victim of his own success, this fund got started but never took off. "It took me well over a year to build my investment thesis, gather the market data, and construct my fund documents," says this Silicon Valley GP, who prefers to remain anonymous. "After developing the pitch deck, I did two things in parallel — I started to raise the fund and make build my portfolio of investments to put my strategy in action. This was to demonstrate that I had the ability to (a) build my thesis, (b) find the best companies, and (c) win an allocation in hotly contested rounds. My life was extremely stressful during these times — I borrowed money from as many friends as I could, maxed out my credit card debt, and became a madman. In one situation, a lender asked for my primary home as collateral. My wife concluded I was depressed and was putting the family at risk. These were retirement savings that were being put in these high-risk illiquid investments. These would not even serve as collateral in a pawn shop, she reminded him."

The GP must have pitched 50 LPs during this time. He says that not one would give him a straight answer. Their processes were opaque, and there was this "man behind the curtain" thing. He says, "One of them didn't even have any money but strung me along for six months. She was trying to raise her fund of funds at the same time and was using my deck to show off to her own LPs that she had access to great managers. What a scammer! In one family office in Chicago, the head of the family almost yelled at me — 'Why do you think you will be successful?'" In another strange situation, the GP says, "I was invited to meet this hedge fund fat cat at his fancy home sitting on a five-acre plot in upstate New York. When I reached his front door, no one answered the doorbell. This was a remote area and there was no cell signal. I couldn't even call anyone. I stood there feeling like a lurker and a petty beggar, waiting for the proverbial doors to open. But then it started to pour . . . I was drenched standing there and could not even summon an Uber. That was it – I called off the whole fundraising charade and gave up."

The GP continues: "Two years after my first investment, I got a 10X exit — a nice fat check — liquidity. I had invested in a startup at a $6 million valuation, and it got acquired for $60 million. Which was nice. I was able to pay off some of my debt. And within 12 months, another company was sold. My modest investment made me rich. And the best part — I did not have to share 80% of my profits with any LPs."

And then the fun began. The GP started to get inbound calls from LPs as soon as these exits occurred. "They, who never believed in me when I needed them most, were now chasing me. Ah . . . the best form of revenge is success. Such is the irony all founders and first-time GPs face — once you are successful, they all come running to you and groveling. Who needs them now? My portfolio is well above five times cash-on-cash. The flywheel has started, and I will never ever raise any outside capital." The GP says that the LP world is filled with lazy, opportunistic, fickle, and weak people who "should not room with the brave. They should work for the government, collect their paychecks, and stick to a two-hour, low-risk workday."

12

Investment Team Diligence

From any institutional investor's or limited partner's (LP's) perspective, a venture capital partnership is like being locked in a 10-year blind pool — a long relationship in which the investors have very little control, limited ability to exit the relationship, and no clarity of outcomes. Thus, investors seek proven fund managers. Exhibit 12.1 depicts the stacking order of professionals.

EVALUATING FUND MANAGERS

A proven fund manager is one who has generated consistent returns across multiple economic cycles. Few practitioners have demonstrated the ability to source opportunities, invest capital over multiple rounds, add tangible value as a board member, and generate exits. Proven managers do not have to amplify or sell their background, expertise, or scientific domain knowledge. LPs don't really care how they got there as long as they rack up the returns. Rookies eager to enter the business have to establish their credentials.

If a newcomer has entrepreneurial experience — started a company, raised multiple venture rounds, and led the company to an exit — the fundraising path becomes a bit easier. A demonstrated nose for choosing good investments is what matters.

Exhibit 12.1 **GP expertise.**

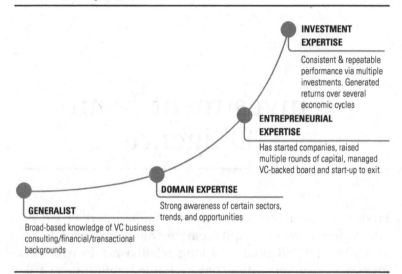

"If you belong in the 'first-time manager/first-time fund' box, what are the investors going to base their decisions on?" asks Kelly DePonte. Some investors are blunt and discourage rookie fund managers. "After all, why should you train to become a venture capitalist on my nickel?" Others are quick to point out that it takes about $10 million of investor capital to train a general partner (GP). "I'd let the other LPs pay for this education," they say. "Experienced managers who have attained returns over multiple funds are attractive to any LP," says DePonte.[1]

Some key criteria for evaluating fund managers and the investment team include the following:

- *Performance*. Does the individual have an investing track record? Are the managers proven top-quartile performers? Emerging? Or somewhere in between?
- *Team skills:*
    - What are the operating qualifications and background? Has the individual played a relevant role in an operating capacity?

- What is the individual's domain expertise: Is she a generalist or a specialist? Can she spot a trend or analyze opportunities?

- Does the individual have any experience as a board member? If yes, describe the person's specific value/role.

- What are the role and investment focus of each individual? In larger multisector/multistage firms, this criterion has higher importance.

TEAM DYNAMICS: STABILITY, SKILL SET, AND ALIGNMENT

Investors assess the team stability, alignment, and dynamics using a number of techniques. Team stability — the ability of the partners to work together through thick and thin — is considered a substantial risk with unproven managers or newer funds. Lindel Eakman, who manages fund investments for Foundry Group, says, "My primary goal is to understand the partnership dynamic." Lindel has seen partnerships fall apart due to diverging career paths, team chemistry, and health issues. Christy Richardson, director of Private Investments, Hewlett Foundation, says, "We look for team dynamics and want to make sure the team will stay together for the next two to three fund cycles — the connective tissue is economic split, but I worry about relationships that have not been stress-tested through challenging times. In a rising tide, everyone is happy and gets along fine. Teams only get tested in tough times."

Alignment of interests shift when senior managers choose to retain most of the profits, leading to potential break-ups of younger partners. Finally, how the members of teams align with each other with respect to roles and responsibilities is a key question LPs often ask.

Here, we describe stability, alignment, and skill sets (soft skills, specialists, and social networks) to help develop deeper insights into a fund manager's due diligence.

Stability and Alignment: Will the Family Stay Together?

Newly minted partnerships are seen as risky. Team cohesion or stability risk is paramount in such firms. If partners cannot get along and quit for any reason, it can be a death knell for the fund. LPs frequently assess each individual's background and expertise, and, more importantly, how these cohesively tie together to form a symphony.

Redundant skill sets or incompatible personalities are red flags. But while functional attributes can be easily ascertained, no LP can predict whether a marriage can last. Thus, the first-time funds have to demonstrate track records as well as intangible elements like cohesion and stability.

To assess team cohesion, LPs look at the following:

- *Alignment of incentives.* Compensation structure, responsibilities, and rewards for each team member. Just as VCs ask for a cap table for their management teams to assess option pools for leading team members, LPs often ask for a view of carry split to ensure that the economics are aligned.
- *Duration of relationship.* How long have they worked together? What circumstances or crises have strengthened these relationships?
- *Alignment with LP's financial goals.* Fund managers own capital or "skin in the game" — what is the amount of fund managers' investment as a percentage of their net worth?
- *Distractions.* What are sources of other income, time horizon to retirement? In one fund, the partners were conducting part-time investment banking activities. This became a huge distraction, as it offered current income and short-term gains over long-term carry.
- *Stability.* Clint Harris, managing partner at Grove Street Advisors, says, "Are the junior members in a fund talking to headhunters? If they are, then you know there is something wrong. . . . The team member can make five phone calls and he will get an honest answer very quickly. . . ."[2]

Stability and alignment of interest are closely tied — should a senior partner be unwilling to share meaningful portions of carry, the junior team members will often vote with their feet and get out the door.

Rock Star Partner Comes on Board

GPs need to treat their partners with respect both on and off stage. At a recent meeting, I complimented a senior partner for having attracted a star. He leaned forward and whispered, "You don't understand, he is our servant."*

*From an anonymous LP with investments in over 50 venture funds and over $1 billion under advisement.

Exhibit 12.2, a format developed by Pension Consulting Alliance (PCA), demonstrates alignment of interest of various principals in an early-stage fund. Red flags include the following:

1. No significant capital contribution from fund managers.
2. Disproportionate carry allocation, especially to senior partners.
3. Excessive compensation from other sources.

Exhibit 12.2 **Sample Format: Assessing Alignment of Interest.**

Principal Name	Expected Capital Contribution	Carry Points (20%)	Total Annual Expected Compensation		Carried Interest Compensation
			From This Fund	From Other Sources	
Managing Director 1	$450,000	10%	$400,000	None	$10,000,000
Managing Director 2	$450,000	8%	$300,000	None	$8,000,000
Principal	$100,000	2%	$200,000	None	$2,000,000

Identifying Complementary Skill Sets

Venture capital investments call for a varied skill set in a team: raising capital, sourcing investment opportunities, adding value as board members, and leading exits. These skills are prefaced by entrepreneurial expertise, technological strengths, and the ability to perceive future market trends and maintain an even keel in somewhat ambiguous and rough times. LPs also closely look at the duration and the intensity of GP interactions — as investment professionals, not golf buddies.

Exhibit 12.3 shows a complementary skill set of a team at an early-stage health care fund. Note the ability of the managing directors to attract junior as well as senior partners across two separate fund cycles.

The Importance of Soft Skills

In a survey of over 145 leading VCs (venture capitalists), leading practitioners agreed that listening skills were considered more important for success in venture capital than quantitative skills.

The skills that were rated most important were as follows:

- Listening skills
- Ability to recruit talented management
- Qualitative analysis skills
- Coaching/counseling/advising skills

"You've got to be a good listener. I find if the venture capitalist does all the talking, he doesn't learn very much about the people he's thinking about investing in. Very important to listen . . . and judge who looks and feels like they have the makings of making a real company. Eventually it becomes instinct if you do it often enough," remarked Paul "Pete" Bancroft, former CEO of Bessemer Securities and former chair of National Venture Capital Association.[3]

Financial and technical skills were rated least important by practitioners, while possessing a CEO perspective was

Exhibit 12.3 **Complementary Skills in a Venture Firm.**

Title (Years with Firm)	Fundraising	Investments	Operating Qualifications	Board Positions	Exits
Managing Director 1 (Founder – 8 years)	Successfully led raise of two prior funds totaling $100 million	Completed 20 investments over 8 years	20+ years, launched 8+ products in medical device companies; marketing, clinical research, and sales expertise	Seven board positions	One exit; as operator, two startups were acquired by publicly traded company
Managing Director 2 (8 years)	Co-developed investment strategy; Supportive role.	Completed 12 investments over 5 years	Nine years in consulting services; investment banking expertise	Five board positions	Two exits: one IPO and one acquisition
Principal (4 years)	N/A	Completed 3 investments over 4 years	Eight years in large automotive company; product development, manufacturing, and strategy	Three board positions	N/A
Venture Partner 1 (1 year)	N/A	N/A	Former CEO of publicly traded company	Three positions	Two exits as CEO of venture-backed companies
Venture Partner 2 (1 year)	N/A	N/A	13 years as cardiac surgeon; development of medical devices and FDA regulatory trends	Observer	N/A
Associate (2 years)	N/A	Completed due diligence for 2 investments	Investment banking with a bulge bank	Observer	N/A

considered a valuable asset.[4] While conducting reference checks with portfolio company CEOs, LPs are able to identify GP strengths in these areas.

LPs also are able to grasp a deeper sense of the culture of the firm. "Naturally, GPs project that all is great within the firm, but while talking to associates, I get a different picture. I have learned how to get to the bottom of that quickly," explains Christopher Rizik. One institutional LP who has made investments in funds across the country would set aside time to speak with the front-office staff, including the administrative staff and the receptionist. "These people may seem irrelevant but are on site every day. They see the entire family at work — the senior partners and the junior partners — and how they interact with entrepreneurs. And they are candid in sharing the true picture."

Generalists versus Specialists

In a study, Paul A. Gompers et al. demonstrated a strong positive relationship between the degree of specialization by individuals at a firm and the firm's success. A specialist investment professional in a specialist firm will outperform a generalist. The poorer performance by generalists appeared to be due to both an inefficient allocation of funding across industries and poor selection of investments within industries, concluded the authors. In other words, the generalists made bad choices across the board. But if you put a specialist individual in a generalist firm, the performance was weak.[5] Thus, the LP emphasis on domain expertise is intuitively high. Another interesting study of 482 venture practitioners in 222 first-time venture funds asserts the same proposition: *The specialists outperform the generalists*. The specialists were superior, especially when it came to early-stage investments. The study also concludes that the two strongest predictors of fund performance were entrepreneurial experience and domain expertise.

Yet the predominance of MBAs in the business of venture capital is evident. In 80 larger venture capital firms, of the 615 general partners, 58 percent had MBAs. Of these, 64 percent came from Harvard, Stanford, and Wharton.[6] But an MBA is not necessarily an indicator of strong performance. On the contrary, a research study shows that funds with more MBAs on board performed poorly as compared to others. "We found at least one place where having an MBA can be a disadvantage," summarized the authors.[7]

VC is a Relationship Business

Who you know matters, in venture investments as well as in life. Access new opportunities quickly, conduct due diligence, syndicate investments, and accelerate exits — all of these can become a lot easier within a strong network. Do strong networks among venture capitalists improve their bargaining power over that of entrepreneurs? According to a study, yes indeed![8] LPs often assess a VC's ability to break in the elite networks, for syndication and follow-on investments, and ascribe an intangible value to a VC's networks.

For any LP, venture capital networks are an indicator of sector expertise and financial strength. Needless to say, the stronger networks were able to extract value from a pricing perspective: lower valuations were evident in more densely networked markets. *Empirical evidence that better networked VCs enjoy better performance has already been established,*[9] but lower valuation at the point of entry was also identified as a function of networks.

"My success, frankly, was mostly due to two things: One, as a CFO . . . I was a corporate finance expert at a time when biotech and medical devices were becoming very capital-intensive models. . . . I had an expertise that the industry needed; and I had these great relationships. Everybody needs an angle, so that was my angle; I knew people,"[10] Alan Frazier, founder, Frazier Healthcare Ventures, once remarked.

Steve Bird, of Focus Ventures, writes on the importance of networks in the business of venture capital. "Quality of management" really means *the quality of the relationships that GPs build over years in the business. Management means forging relationships with other top VCs that allow both parties to repeatedly form syndicates on the best deals.* It means building a network among the entrepreneurial community so that the GP hears about a revolutionary technology when it's still in the lab, not after the company has landed its first round of financing. It means knowing important customers, suppliers, and scientists that can help a fledgling company reach its first quarter of profitability. And it means building trust with the broader financial community so that when the time comes for a portfolio company to get a loan, raise more capital, or go public, company management doesn't have to re-create the wheel.[11]

In summary, LPs want to know if and how the investment team stays motivated — can they outperform at all times? "Doug Leone, partner at Sequoia Capital, would say that 'we have a problem at Sequoia — we have been successful.' The team has ingrained an ethos of zero overconfidence and an utter lack of hubris. They follow the *'only the paranoid survive'* motto and are constantly evolving with time, staying hungry and agile," says a long-time LP in Sequoia Capital, Christy Richardson, director of Private Investments at Hewlett Foundation.

13

Fund Size and Portfolio Construction

What is the correct fund size? How much should you raise? Ask Masayoshi San of Softbank and he will raise his hands up in the air: "A hundred billion," he might say. The short answer is raise as much as you can, to effectively execute on your investment strategy.

A bottoms-up approach can start with the stage of investments, and capital needed to build a well-balanced portfolio. Let's look at the point of investment — what will be the typical first check size? What capital reserves will be set aside for future/follow-on investments? What stage of investment as well as ownership and dilution are you modeling for?

Some fund managers adopt a highly concentrated approach — fewer companies with much higher ownership — while other fund managers build a large portfolio with small ownership. Some sectors — such as life sciences — tend to be capital intensive compared to technology.

The size of follow-on investments with the view of maintaining ownership can impact fund returns.

Exhibit 13.1 summarizes the factors that impact fund size.

While the life of the fund is legally established for 10 years, the capital is deployed during the investment period, typically the first 5 years. Fund managers actively seek to invest and build the portfolio during this period. The goal is to generate returns rapidly, say, within 4–6 years from the time of investment.

Exhibit 13.1 **Factors Determining Fund Size.**

Risk	Remarks
Target sector	Funds targeting capital-efficient sectors such as technology/software can be smaller, while funds targeting capital-intensive sectors need larger amounts.
Stage of investment	Seed and early-stage funds are smaller, versus growth stage funds.
Number of portfolio companies	Typical portfolios can be small and concentrated with 10–12 companies or large with as many as 30–50 companies.
Reserves/Follow-on investments	Some funds reserve at least 2X capital for follow-on rounds, to maintain ownership across multiple rounds, while other funds invest more capital in earlier stages, to get as much ownership at lower cost.
Geographic dynamics	In certain regions, capital supply and demand dynamics are different. In Silicon Valley, due to large demand for capital in a small, concentrated region, fund sizes can be larger. In other regions, investors have to deploy capital across multiple locations, increasing operational complexity.
Potential to generate target returns	Multiple studies show that larger funds tend to generate lower returns. However, fund managers often try to design fund sizes driven by fee calculations as opposed to the ability to generate returns.

Let us look at a seed fund, say $10 million in size (Exhibit 13.2). Typically, management fees of an average 2.0 percent per annum of assets under management are applied for the investment period of the fund, say five years. After this investment period, the fees drop down each year, as the portfolio is in maintenance mode. For the sake of simplicity, let us assume that management fees are $1 million. With investable capital of $9 million, assume you will build a portfolio of nine companies and make three new investments each year.

Before you start to deploy capital, it is important to model and project ownership, entry valuations, and exit outcomes. *You have to establish disciplined thresholds of ownership and*

Exhibit 13.2 **Portfolio Assumptions.**

Fund size	$10,000,000
Fund management fees	$1,000,000
Total investable capital	$9,000,000
Portfolio (Total # of companies)	9
Follow-on investments in portfolio companies	3

Exhibit 13.3 **Ownership Assumptions.**

	Seed	Series A	Series B
Premoney valuation	$6,000,000	$25,000,000	$40,000,000
Round size	$2,000,000	$6,000,000	$15,000,000
Fund investment	$500,000	$1,500,000	$0
Postmoney valuation	$8,000,000	$31,000,000	$55,000,000
Round dilution	25%	19%	27%
Fund ownership	6.25%	5.04%	7.2%
New ownership purchased by fund		4.84%	0.00%
Postround total fund ownership	6.25%	9.88%	7.18%

ensure that you do not get too carried away by hot deals in super-priced rounds. In the following ownership modeling exercise (Exhibit 13.3), we take industry averages and see that a typical $500,000 investment gets us a 6.25 percent ownership in the company at seed stage. As the next (series A) round occurs, we purchase an additional 4.84 percent for $1.5 million and have invested $2 million in a company. We now own 9.8 percent of this company. Some funds will *cap their risk by establishing a ceiling of no more than 10–15 percent of the fund will be invested in one company.* Let us commit this cardinal sin of investing 20 percent in a company for the sake of simplicity and test the portfolio. At series B, we are tapped out and do not invest further. Our ownership gets diluted down to 7.2 percent at this round.

It is important to pace your investments over time, as market conditions change. Many an eager investor has jumped into this business with much enthusiasm and deployed too much too soon. Being disciplined and patient matters. At an average investment of $500,000 per company, deploying $1.5 million, the fund would have deployed 50 percent of its investable capital in the first three years in nine portfolio companies. Further, let us assume that three of these nine companies start to grow nicely, and you deploy an additional follow-on investment of $1.5 million in each portfolio company between year three and year five (Exhibit 13.4).

Exhibit 13.4 **Portfolio Construction.**

Year	Year 1	Year 2	Year 3	Year 4	Year 5
Number of new investments	3	3	3	0	0
Amount per investment	$500,000	$500,000	$500,000	$0	$0
Subtotal – Capital invested (A)	$1,500,000	$1,500,000	$1,500,000	$0	$0
Follow-on investments					
Number of follow-on investments			1	1	1
Amount per follow-on investment			$1,500,000	$1,500,000	$1,500,000
Subtotal – Capital invested (B)			$1,500,000	$1,500,000	$1,500,000
Total invested (A+B)	($1,500,000)	($1,500,000)	($3,000,000)	($1,500,000)	($1,500,000)

In making return assumptions, look at industry data to understand typical exit outcomes and develop your model conservatively. *The mean value of exits is in the range of $293 million.*[1] *As you start to aim for higher exit values, the probability of generating returns drops.* In Exhibit 13.5, we assume exits can occur at a low value of $25 million, mid-range of $100 million, and the $300 million.

Further, we assume that of the nine companies, we will have three as total losses, three exits in the $25 million low range, two exits in the mid-range of $100 million, and one exit at $300 million. These exits are modeled out to occur between years 7–10, generating an internal rate of return (IRR) of 30.1% and 4.36X gross cash-on-cash (C-on-C) return (Exhibit 13.6).

Exhibit 13.5 **Exit Values.**

	Low Range	Mid Range	Upper Range
Acquisition value	$25,000,000	$100,000,000	$300,000,000
Fund return	$1,562,500	$9,879,032	$21,554,252
Cash-on-Cash multiple	3.13	4.94	10.78

Exhibit 13.6 **Exit Range Assumptions and Distribution Waterfall.**

	# of Companies	Exit Value	C-on-C Multiple	Cash-in	Cash-out
Upper range	1	$300,000,000	10.78	$2,000,000	$21,554,252
Mid-range	2	$100,000,000	4.94	$4,000,000	$19,758,065
Low range	3	$25,000,000	3.13	$750,000	$2,343,750
Loss	3		0	$2,250,000	0
				$9,000,000	$43,656,067

The distribution waterfall would look as follows:

Distribution	
Gross cash-on-cash return	$43,656,067
Principal to LPs	$10,000,000
80% carry to LPs	$26,924,853
Balance to GP	$6,731,213

In this example, we modeled for a $10 million fund and its portfolio of nine companies. The exits are projected in three separate value outcomes: (1) low range — $25 million; (2) mid-range — $100 million; and (3) upper range — $300 million. Despite three total losses, of the six exits, we model one outcome at $300 million, two at $100 million, and three exits at $25 million. The projected returns fall in the IRR range of 30% and 4.36X gross C-on-C return. Put it differently, to achieve this outcome, a $10 million fund has to generate $575 million of total portfolio value amongst its six successful exits.

Smaller Is Better

Take a typical $400 million fund. To get a 20 percent return over six years, you have to triple your capital, turning $400 million into $1.2 billion. It's going to take longer than six years, and you have to add management fees and carry, so that $400 million fund roughly has to return $1.5 billion to the investors to get a 20 percent return. On exit, that fund will own at most 20 percent of a company. That means that a $400 million VC fund has to create $7.5 billion of market value to return $1.5 billion to its LPs in order to deliver a 20 percent return.

—Josh Koppelman, First Round Capital

Exhibit 13.7 **Fund Size and Gains.**

	Gains Required in 10 Years to Generate		
Fund Size	15% IRR	20% IRR	30% IRR
$50 m	$38.4 m	$62.3 m	$123.5 m
$100 m	$76.9 m	$124.6 m	$247 m
$400 m	$307.6 m	$498.4 m	$988 m

As we grow the fund size, the pressure to yield high exits increases. In Exhibit 13.7, we see that for a fund of $50 million, a 30 percent IRR in 10 years requires a total output of $123 million. For a $400 million fund, it's almost a billion. Probabilistic thinking combined with market exit data can help develop a good fund size and portfolio construction strategy.

A fund's portfolio is a demonstration of fund managers' ability to execute their own vision. Consider the portfolio construction strategy of an early-stage life sciences company. At Arboretum Ventures I, a fund of $20 million was established to focus on the health care sector. This fund size would allow investments of up to $2 million in 8–10 early-stage companies. In comparison, a technology fund is expected to invest in as many as 25–30 companies, as the sector is capital efficient. On the other end of the spectrum is a large, billion-dollar fund such as Norwest Venture Partners (NVP). NVP targets multistage (venture and growth stage) companies across the globe. Technology investments have shorter market cycles and follow established patterns of capital needs, company maturation, and exit timing. On the other hand, medical devices and biotech investments require larger amounts of capital and have longer maturation timelines.

Institutional investors, especially those managing multibillion dollars, prefer to invest in funds that are at least $100 million in size. This allows them to maintain efficiency and manage relationships appropriately.

"The portfolio is your strategy in action: you can touch the portfolio, taste it, and see it. I spend a lot of my time visiting portfolio companies. I can tell when something is going well, and the portfolio companies share the value of VC and how it is

actualized. This is the prism: I see the whole symphony being played out, and hopefully it is a harmonious interplay of the various elements," says Chris Douvos, who has been an institutional investor for over a decade.

Lisa Edgar of Top Tier Capital Partners summarizes the art of portfolio management as follows:

> As experienced LPs, our decision-making process relies upon pattern recognition in order to identify the characteristics of success and of failure — something [general partners] GPs should be able to do, too. What I'm looking for is the fund manager's view of which companies look like winners and which companies aren't quite cutting it, so that they can manage the portfolio to support only those that deserve additional capital. I understand this is an extremely difficult exercise — especially for very early-stage companies or when the outcome is truly binary. I would suggest that picking the winners from the losers — and more importantly, effectively managing the fund's capital — is specifically the role of the GP (and for which the limited partners pay a management fee). . . . *I want to know how the VC's micro views on each company and macro view of the exit environment is directing overall capital allocation. That's what we call "portfolio management," and to LPs, effective portfolio management is one of the core criteria we use to evaluate managers.*[2]

Key Takeaways

Fund size is a function of portfolio design, target ownership, market dynamics, and ability to generate returns. It should not be a function of fee-income and manager lifestyle choices.

A small, high-quality concentrated portfolio is indicative of a well-designed thesis. A large, scattered portfolio is akin to a *spray-and-pray* investment strategy.

Staying disciplined matters — smaller fund sizes can consistently generate outsized returns. However, as investors taste success, their ego, greed, and hubris often take over, and soon small funds lose their edge.

14

Performance Analysis

"By far, performance is the number one reason why we say no," says Chris Rizik, who heads fund investments as Renaissance Venture Fund. Assessing performance of funds, fund managers, and the fund's performance against a set of industry benchmarks is a critical step toward an LP commitment.

At the heart of it, LPs look at fund managers who can engage in a true partnership. Eric Doppstadt, VP and CIO, Ford Foundation, says, "My motto is quite simple — *"Treat your investors as partners and your partners as investors."* In other words, try to form a long-term partnership with your limited partners, and try to create true 'skin in the game' for your general partners. With this mindset, we seek to operate for the long term, with our interests aligned with our GPs. We have been with some managers for almost 50 years. We build these relationships over time and we feel fortunate that *venture capital is one of the few parts of the financial markets that has not yet become purely transactional, in which long-term relationships still matter."*

Let us look at the ways LPs rank performance and understand the challenges therein. But before we dive into fund level performance, let us start with individual-level performance.

INDIVIDUAL PERFORMANCE AND ATTRIBUTION

At the heart of it, the business of venture capital is akin to skydiving — small teams form pretty patterns, but each diver has to hold his or her own. Splinter groups are formed frequently. While some glide along, navigating the strong winds, others often crash. The rest of the divers can do little to prevent a crashing partner, so they move on and form a different pattern. Inherently competitive at an individual level, this business is one of hero worship and also-rans, where personal brands often tend to rise above the brand of a firm.

When it comes to individual attribution, practitioners often add a string of successes to their bios. For presentation to limited partners (LPs), individual performance of practitioners is typically presented with one-page case studies of each portfolio company. Investors should not only resist the urge to cherry-pick the best opportunities but be prepared to share *details of all the investments*. "Cherry-picking can hurt your credibility: we live in a world where we are a few degrees away from ascertaining the facts," says Christopher Rizik, fund manager at Renaissance Venture Capital Fund, a fund of funds. For investors, it is not just a listing of opportunities that matters, but the general partner's (GP's) role in value creation.

Attribution challenges can also cause internal competition within a firm and destroy its chemistry. In a business where hero worship trounces teamwork, it is easy to see why a partner would want to be on the board of a fast-rising portfolio company. In one firm, a newer partner, seeking instant attribution nirvana, assigned himself to the board of a rapidly growing portfolio company, edging the younger partner out. The younger partner eventually left the firm and took his skills elsewhere. The opportunity that was once rising cratered, scarring the senior partner's track record. "Attribution ambiguity can be sorted out quickly; in most cases, the person who sourced the opportunity and nurtured it is the CEO's primary touch point. We talk to the CEOs of portfolio companies to verify the fund managers' claims. In these discussions, the CEOs also help us understand who a true value creator was versus who showed up for the Christmas parties," says Van Heel.

Exhibit 14.1 depicts another sample format, a summary table that constitutes the list of portfolio companies managed by each professional.

Exhibit 14.1 **Sample Format: Individual Performance.**

Company	Amount of Investment	Current Value		Total Value to Paid In Capital	Internal Rate of Return (IRR)	Multiple of Invested Capital (MOIC)
		Realized	Unrealized			
Company A	$18.6	$60.0	—	$60	38.1%	3.2
Company B	$8.20	$1.0	$3.1	$4.1		0.5

The Alphabet Soup of Performance: IRR, C-on-C, TVPI, DPI, or PME?

An informal survey conducted by McKinsey found that only 20 percent of executives understand the critical deficiencies of IRR.[1] IRR has its allure, offering what seems to be a straightforward comparison of, say, 30 percent returns with 8 percent. IRRs appear favorable but do not consider reinvestment risks and the redeployment of capital in other investment opportunities in the calculation for investors.

Because IRR is expressed as a percentage, a small investment can show a triple-digit IRR. While this looks attractive at first glance, a larger investment with a lower IRR can be more attractive on a net present value (NPV) basis. To interpret IRR as an annual equivalent return on a given investment is easy and intuitive, but this is only true if there are no interim cash flows. This may be the case with most venture investments, but in any biotech or a pharma exit, where earnouts are negotiated, the IRR may become misleading quickly.

LPs often gauge fund performance by analyzing a combination of IRRs (dollar-weighted returns, which are influenced by the timing and magnitude of cash flows) and cash-on-cash investment multiples, either total value to paid-in capital (TVPI) or distributions to paid-in capital (DPI). Each can tell a different story and is important in its own right. But *none is sufficient by itself to tell the whole story.*[2]

LPs are watchful of poor performance as well. If a partner's performance is uninspiring, LPs candidly share their concerns with the stronger partners and even establish preconditions for investments. This leads to elimination of weaker partners much in advance of the LP commitments.

In one example, a new fund was set up by a number of practitioners who had worked at other brand-name firms. But when potential LPs really dug in and got off-the-record evaluation, the luster faded. In fact, these individuals had been pushed out of their firms. "These GPs were not the stars they made themselves out to be," remarked Clint Harris of Grove Street Advisors, a fund of funds.[3] Despite this, a number of LPs had quickly lined up at the new fund's doors, eager to throw money at these underperformers.

PUBLIC MARKET EQUIVALENTS

While IRR and C-on-C are primary measures, public market equivalent (PME) measures a venture capital fund performance against an investment in S&P 500, an index of public market performance. If PME of a VC fund is greater than 1, then the investors did better than investing in publicly traded stocks.

Professor Steven Kaplan of University of Chicago Booth School of Business studied the various venture capital data sources and cross-checked investment histories for nearly 1,400 funds derived from the holdings of over 200 institutional

Exhibit 14.2 **Do VC Funds Outperform Public Markets?**

Vintage Years	No. of Funds in Dataset	Capital Realized (%)	IRR*	Multiple of Capital	PME
Average of all	775	85.8	19.3	2.46	1.45
2000s	423	33.0	0.3	1.07	0.95
1990s	251	97.8	38.6	3.76	2.12
1980s	101	100.0	15.8	2.37	1.08

Source: Robert S. Harris, Tim Jenkinson, and Steven N. Kaplan, "Private Equity Performance: What Do We Know?" *Journal of Finance* (July 2013)

* IRR presented is weighted average (capital committed for each fund as a proportion of the total commitments for each vintage year).

Public versus Private: Why PME Matters

PME is the simplest and the most effective measure of venture capital performance. Consider an example where an investor deploys $100 million in a venture fund and receives $200 million. In comparison, if $100 million were invested in S&P 500 during the same period, the investor would have received $207 million. Thus, gross PME = $200/$207 = 0.97, and net PME = $180/$207 = 0.97. In this case, the investor lost money by investing in this venture capital fund.

investors.[4] Exhibit 14.2 presents some of the findings. VC outperformed S&P 500 public markets index on an average across the three decades, and did so handily in the 1990s, while in the 1980s was a whisper better.

FUND-LEVEL PERFORMANCE

LPs assess investment track records rigorously at the fund level as well as the contribution of each investment professional. Fund performance is measured using two primary metrics: internal rate of return (IRR) and cash-on-cash (C-on-C) multiples. While Exhibit 14.3 shows fund-level performance in a stand-alone format, LPs typically assess stand-alone and benchmarked comparisons, but it is the LP who prefers to choose the benchmark. (See Exhibit 14.4, early-stage funds with a US regional focus.)

LPs slice performance data in a number of ways, but it all begins with the returns. "Instead of giving us the aggregate performance numbers, it would be a lot easier if GPs gave us the cash flows for each portfolio company," says an institutional LP, who has managed over 75 GP relationships. LPs often grumble about the fact that data are not shared to the level of their satisfaction. The Institutional Limited Partners Association (ILPA) has developed reporting guidelines and templates for fund performance that address these challenges.[5]

Exhibit 14.3 **Sample Fund Performance: Stand-Alone Format.**

Company Realized investments	Date of Investment	Date of Realization	Total Capital Invested ($M)	Total Realized Proceeds (A) ($M)	Unrealized Value (B) ($M)	Total Value = A + B ($M)	Multiple of Invested Capital (x)	Gross IRR (%)
Company A	Dec 08	Nov 09	$18.6	$60.0	—	$60	3.2	38.1%
Company B	Jan 09	Jun 10	$8.20	$1.0	$3.1	$4.1	0.5	--
Total			$26.8	$61.0	$3.1	$64.1	2.39	24.2%
Unrealized investments								
Company C	Mar 09	--	$5.0		$9.0	$9.0	1.8	9.2%
Company D	Jun 09	--	$8.20		$4.1	$4.1	0.5	--
Total			$13.2		$13.1	$13.1	0.99	--
Total fund investments			$40.0	$60.0	$17.1	$77.1	1.92	24.2%

Exhibit 14.4 **Sample Fund Performance: Benchmarked Format.**

Fund	Vintage	Fund Size ($M)	Called (%)	Realized (%) Value	Unrealized Value (%)	Multiple (X)	Net IRR (%)	Benchmark IRR (%)	Quartile
ABC Fund VI	2015	9	100.0%	748.0	0.0	7.48	47.7%	25.3%	1
ABC Fund VII	2018	75	94.6%	1.2	95.6	0.97	-1.2%	-4.6%	2
ABC Fund VIII	2020	150	36.5%	0.0	378.5	3.78	182.0%	-10.9%	1

Exhibit 14.5 shows sample analysis tables of a venture firm that has raised three funds. The data is analyzed by the fund, by partner, by stage, investment size, MOIC range, sector, and investment year. All of this helps an LP to get to the root cause of performance. As a GP, you should be prepared to offer this level of data to help LPs analyze performance quickly.

Investors assess general performance metrics as well as specific data points. These data points are sliced in a number of different ways to understand the risk and GP's ability to adhere to the stated strategy:

- *Sourcing.* Did the opportunity originate through your proactive efforts? Or through a proprietary set of

Exhibit 14.5 **Performance Analysis: Slicing the Data a Hundred Different Ways.**

All Funds

By Fund

				Total					Fully Realized				Unrealized			
# of Inv	% of Inv	Board Seat	Lead Role	Total Cost	% of Cost	Avg. Inv Size	Total Value	Gross MOIC	# OF Inv	Total Cost	Total Value	Gross MOIC	# of Inv	Total Cost	Total Value	Gross MOIC
15	7%	-	12	4,316	4%	288	4,362	10x	12	3,160	528	0.2x	3	1,156	3,835	33x
85	41%	23	25	42,774	41%	503	94,804	2.2x	55	15,424	17,906	1.2x	30	27,350	76,898	2.8x
106	51%	49	66	56,604	55%	534	86,248	1.5x	21	4,538	2,127	0.5x	85	52,066	84,121	1.6x
206	100%	72	103	103,695	100%	503	1855555,415	1.8X	88	23,122	20,561	0.9X	118	80,573	164,854	2.0X

Fund I, Fund II, Fund III, Grand Total

By Partner

				Total					Fully Realized				Unrealized			
# of Inv	% of Inv	Board Seat	Lead Role	Total Cost	% of Cost	Avg. Ticket	Total Value	Gross MOIC	# OF Inv	Total Cost	Total Value	Gross MOIC	# of Inv	Total Cost	Total Value	Gross MOIC
8	4%	4	3	3,528	3%	441	3,504	1.0 x	3	764	624	0.8x	2	2,764	2,890	1.0x
1	0%	-	-	719	1%	719	764	1.1 x	-	-	-	-	1	719	764	1.1x
70	34%	10	39	13,459	13%	192	19,762	1.5 x	46	5,800	734	0.1x	24	7,659	1,9029	2.5x
206	100%	72	103	103,695	100%	503	185,415	1.9x	88	23,122	20,561	0.9x	118	80,573	16,4854	2.0x

Partner 1, Partner 2, Partner 3, Grand Total

(continued)

Exhibit 14.5 **(Continued)**

By MOIC Range

Write-off	62	30%	15,288	15%	247	-	0.0k	62	15,288	-	0.0k	-	-	-	-
0-1.0x	37	18%	21,861	21%	591	14,091	0.6k	13	2,658	701	0.3k	24	19,202	13,389	0.7k
1.0-2.0x	75	36%	39,168	38%	522	52,938	1.4k	5	835	1,035	1.2k	70	38,333	51,903	1.4k
2.0-3.0x	8	4%	6,915	7%	864	17,456	2.5k	1	750	2,070	2.8k	7	6,165	15,386	2.5k
3.0-4.0x	6	3%	6,702	6%	1,117	21,942	3.3k	1	1,000	3,040	3.0k	5	5,702	18,902	3.3k
4.0-5.0x	4	2%	2,239	2%	560	10,521	4.7k	2	1,624	7,817	4.8k	2	615	2,704	4.4k
5.0-10.0x	12	6%	11,274	11%	939	66,202	5.8k	3	918	4,715	5.1k	9	10,356	67,488	5.8k
+10.0x	2	1%	249	0%	124	3,264	13.1k	1	49	1,183	24.3k	1	200	2,082	10.4k
Grand Total	206	100%	103,635	100%	503	185,415	1.8k	88	23,122	20,561	0.9k	118	80,573	164,854	2.0k

By Stage

Pre-seed	127	62%	41,131	40%	324	64,343	1.6k	72	15,194	10,036	0.7x	55	25,937	54,307	2.1x
Seed	66	32%	56,927	55%	863	109,017	1.9k	16	7,928	10,525	1.3x	50	48,999	98,492	2.0x
Early A	1	0%	200	0%	200	2,082	10.4k	-	-	-	-	1	200	2,082	10.4x
Series A	2	1%	2,657	3%	1,329	4,697	1.8k	-	-	-	-	2	2,657	4,697	1.8x
Other	10	5%	2,779	3%	278	5,277	1.9k	-	-	-	-	10	2,779	5,277	1.9x
Grand Total	206	100%	103,695	100%	503	185,415	1.8k	88	23,122	20,561	0.9x	118	80,573	164,854	2.0x

(continued)

Exhibit 14.5 (Continued)

By Inv. Size

	Total									Fully Realized				Unrealized			
	# of Inv	% of Inv	Board Seat	Lead Role	Total Cost	% of Cost	Avg. Ticket	Total Value	Gross MOIC	# OF Inv	Total Cost	Total Value	Gross MOIC	# of Inv	Total Cost	Total Value	Gross MOIC
$0–50k	31	15%	5	8	5,484	5%	177	11,910	2.2x	23	2,006	1,816	0.9x	8	3,478	10,094	2.9x
$50–100k	53	26%	5	34	12,139	12%	229	17,057	1.4x	33	6,423	1,047	0.2x	20	5,716	16,010	1.5x
$100k–250k	46	22%	6	20	18,688	18%	406	21,217	1.1x	16	5,075	444	0.1x	30	13,613	20,773	2.4x
$250k–500k	48	23%	29	22	40,464	39%	843	91,141	2.3x	14	7,868	12,144	1.5x	34	32,596	78,998	1.5x
$500k–1mn	26	13%	26	19	23,471	23%	903	38,593	1.6x	2	1,750	5,110	2.9x	24	21,725	5,498	1.6x
+$1mn	2	1%	1	–	3,445	3%	1,723	5,498	1.6x	–	–	–	–	2	3,445	5,498	1.6x
Grand Total	206	100%	305	429	103,695	100%	503	185,415	1.8x	88	23,122	20,561	0.9x	118	80,573	164,854	2.0x

By Sector

	Total									Fully Realized				Unrealized			
	# of Inv	% of Inv	Board Seat	Lead Role	Total Cost	% of Cost	Avg. Ticket	Total Value	Gross MOIC	# OF Inv	Total Cost	Total Value	Gross MOIC	# of Inv	Total Cost	Total Value	Gross MOIC
SaaS	61	30	22	27	26,849	26	440	43,606	1.6x	26	9,130	12,861	1.4x	35	17,719	30,746	1.7x
Commerce	34	17	7	12	11,190	11	329	16,502	1.5x	23	3,201	1,688	0.5x	11	7,989	14,814	1.9
Marketplace	16	8	6	11	9,279	9%	580	24,299	2.6x	7	2,929	5,110	1.7x	9	6,350	19,189	3.0
Mobility	13	6%	5	7	7,104	7%	546	8,304	1.2x	9	2,339	20	0.0x	4	4,766	8,234	1.7
FinTech	9	4%	6	8	8,065	8%	896	15,889	2.0x	1	52	*	0.0x	8	8,013	15,869	2.0
Security	7	3%	1	6	4,878	5%	697	8,013	1.6x	5	2,155	–	0.0x	2	2,723	8,013	2.9

(continued)

Exhibit 14.5 **(Continued)**

Media	6	3%	-	2	850	1%	142	630	0.7x	6	850	630	0.7x	6	-	-	-
Health care IT	6	3%	2	2	1,502	1%	250	763	0.5x	2	500	-	0.0x	4	1,002	763	0.8
EdTech	5	2%	2	3	2,622	3%	524	3,068	1.2x	1	104	-	0.0x	4	2,519	3,068	1.2
AdTech	5	2%	2	4	5,845	6%	1,169	4,591	0.8x	1	797	212	0.3x	4	5,048	4,379	0.9
Other	44	21%	19	21	25,510	25%	580	59,751	2.3x	7	1,066	40	0.0x	37	24,444	59,710	2.4
Grand Total	206	100%	72	102	103,695	100%	503	185,415	1.8x	88	23,122	20,561	0.9x	118	80,573	164,854	2.0
2008	8	4%	-	8	1,726	2%	216	2,080	1.2x	7	1,346	72	0.1x	1	380	2,008	5.3x
2009	4	2%	-	4	1,484	1%	371	2,061	1.4x	3	1,119	456	0.4x	1	365	1,605	4.4x
2010	5	2%	1	5	4,230	4%	846	2,121	0.5x	3	2,639	-	0.0x	2	1,591	2,121	1.3x
2011	26	13%	7	13	14,899	14%	573	30,628	2.1x	1	8,765	5,986	1.0x	8	9,134	24,642	2.7x
2012	36	17%	5	9	12,431	12%	345	21,258	1.7x	25	5,388	8,696	1.6x	11	7,043	12,561	1.8x
2013	26	13%	14	15	17,825	17%	686	48,722	2.7x	11	2,327	3,224	1.4x	15	15,498	45,498	2.9x
2014	8	18%	17	38	23,487	23%	618	46,029	2.0x	15	3,586	2,072	0.6x	23	19,901	43,956	2.2x
2015	40	19%	17	40	20,074	19%	502	24,888	1.2x	5	848	55	0.1x	35	19,226	24,833	1.3x
2016	23	11%	11	23	7,538	7%	328	7,629	1.0x	1	104	-	0.0x	22	7,434	7,629	1.0x
Grand Total	206	100%	11	23	7,538	100%	328	7,629	1.0x	1	104	-	0.0x	22	7,434	7,629	1.0x

Source: A US-based fund of funds.

relationships? How well did the opportunity fit within the core investment criteria of the fund?

• *Investment analysis.* For established funds, LPs look into returns and analyze these by fund, year, industry subsectors, stage of investment, lead/co-lead roles, and board representation. "At times, a fund's track record may be due to a 'one-off' event — we seek consistent performance over economic cycles," says Van Heel. A one-off event, also called a one-hit home run, occurs when one portfolio company generates the majority of the returns for the entire portfolio. "This business is about home runs indeed, but we aim to dissect the overall approach and strategy of the fund. At times, we remove the outliers from the venture fund portfolio and stress test it to see how the rest of the portfolio stacks up. And during the frothy times, we even take it one step further — we set aside the top two and bottom two outliers to see how resilient the returns are." Chopping off each end of the spectrum allows a rigorous investor to review the portfolio in a more balanced light. Several LPs agreed that this approach is used to stress test the returns. Others do not necessarily subscribe to this approach. "You are investing in VC for their best-performing companies: the returns come from the top decile, whether it is in a fund, firm, or the industry. There is no consistency of return," says Perkins of Fisher Lynch Capital. Some LPs also seek to assess the loss ratio: the amount lost vis-à-vis the size of the fund. This ratio is a factor of sector and stage: For example, an early-stage technology fund would have a loss ratio of as much as 50 percent. A later-stage health care fund would be looking at a lower loss ratio. "Anything above 20 percent would make me nervous," says an institutional investor who invested in a venture fund with a loss ratio of 3 percent.

Exhibit 14.6 **Sample Fund Performance: Benchmarked Format.**

Vintage Year	Fund IRR	S&P 500 Return (%)	PME vs S&P 500	Russell 2000 (%)	PME vs. Russell 2000
2010	17.5%	12.85%	1.16	11.68%	1.25

Investors seek all these data points to predict a GP's ability to deliver consistent returns. "We use a number of data points — we start with our own internal notes, look at fund quarterly reports, web research, conferences, and portfolio company meetings — it is multidimensional. This assessment improves our ability to predict a firm's potential to earn the desired return," says Lisa Edgar.

One simple method of showing performance that includes public benchmarks could be as seen in Exhibit 14.6.

Predicting future performance is a harder challenge for any investor, but GPs need to be prepared to address what will make them successful in the current times. "If you don't have credible answers on how you plan to consistently generate returns, don't even bother knocking on any doors," says Gus Long of Stanwich Advisors.

MEASURING REALIZED RETURNS

In the world of VC, the savvy never count their chickens until they are hatched. Or calculate returns until you have moolah in the coolah. But some count those unhatched eggs. And then go a step further — they rank chicken farmers based on their "unhatched" chickens. The conundrum of measuring VC returns can get inane if you start to go down that path. Measuring realized returns is the only way to avoid this madness.

Let's look at unrealized value in Exhibit 14.7. As much as 68–86 percent of the fund value is still on paper. This can change the final outcomes by orders of magnitude. If residual

Exhibit 14.7 **Measuring What Matters.**

Vintage	Fund Size	Distributed Value	Unrealized/ Residual Value	Unrealized Value as % of Total Value	Multiple of Invested Capital	Internal Rate of Return
2009	$ 300m	$ 472m	$301m	38%	2.6X	42%
2010	$ 650m	$439m	$965m	68%	2.3X	25%
2012	$ 1,500m	$329m	$2184m	86%	1.7X	27%

value is high, we should not count these chickens yet. Nor should we declare winners. Distributions occur after as much as 10+ years from launch. VC industry data must be measured/ compared once the funds are fully liquidated. Then and only then can we know for sure who leads the pack. So why do we even measure data/returns when we know the game has just begun? Counting chickens before they are hatched is silly. But starting to compare my unhatched chickens with yours and then declaring winners is even sillier.

While selecting benchmarks, a number of self-selection caveats crop up:

- *Vintage year.* A fund manager may be tempted to assign a vintage year when she started raising the fund as compared to when the final close occurred, or even when they made their first investment.

- *Universe of benchmarks.* The data source matters, as does the selection of benchmarks. Several data providers, including Cambridge Associates, Pitchbook, and Preqin, gather returns data. The universe of benchmarks can get equally large. Clever fund managers could play around and find a category in which they look like heroes. You could position your fund as a shining star in the universe of venture funds. If that doesn't look too good, you could look at early-stage venture funds. Or you could try to slice it by early-stage technology venture funds.

- *Realized versus unrealized value.* The data can become muddier as you try to compare apples and oranges. Unrealized returns often translate to risk: value of shares held in any private companies often swing wildly.

- *Veracity of data/self-reporting.* As this industry calls for self-reporting, the skeptical LPs pointed out that on an industry-wide basis, the bad managers and the best managers never report their data — only the mediocre ones do. Diana Frazier of FLAG Capital management, a fund of funds, says, "The best managers do not bother submitting their data to any databases." Thus, this creates another layer of complexity in trying to assess true performance of the vintage year. "We never used any public database due to the veracity issues. We had built our own internal assessment tools, which would give us some very powerful insights. I believe most LPs have similar internal tools," one LP pointed out, whose firm receives at least 200 PPMs each year. His analysts would key in data from all investments from these 200 firms, building a substantial database, which could be sliced and analyzed in a number of different ways. Rizik suggests intellectual honesty: "Make it simple: show me every investment you have made, along with the cash flows. If we smell any issues, it becomes a nonstarter. GPs should be forthcoming on the history."

SELF-SELECTION BIAS: GIANTS AMONG MIDGETS

Exhibits 14.8 and 14.9 demonstrate the variance between the top and the bottom ends of the spectrum between two separate data sources. A clever fund manager would use a data source to auto-magically show that they are the tallest among the herd. *To position themselves in the top quartile, 77 percent of firms were found to change key data inputs such as the selection of the reference benchmark and the definition of the fund's vintage year.*[6]

Exhibit 14.8 **The Best versus the Worst: IRR Performance Variance in Venture Funds.**

Vintage Year	Best Performer	Median IRR	Worst Performer
1980	50.6 %	16.6 %	5.5 %
1985	40.7 %	13 %	4 %
1990	74.4 %	19 %	−35.9 %
1995	447.4 %	26.3 %	−10.6 %
2000	52.9 %	−1.6 %	−40 %
2005	104.9 %	4.1 %	−55.5 %
2010	51.6 %	12.8 %	−9.8 %
2015	89.5 %	13.2 %	−3 %

Source: Adapted from Preqin Global Alternative Report 2018.

Exhibit 14.9 **IRR Performance Variance in Venture Funds.**

Vintage Year	Top Decile	Top Quartile	Median IRR	Bottom Quartile	Bottom Decile
2000	5.42%	2.29%	−1.50%	−6.24%	−15.20%
2005	15.65%	9.72%	4.40%	1.99%	−8.20%
2010	38.58%	27.20%	13.23%	4.08%	0.85%
2015	41.02%	22.94%	14.49%	9.25%	4.06%

Source: Adapted from Pitchbook Data, Dec 2018.

In this vein, one LP sardonically pointed out, "Sure — any fund can be in the top quartile when you self-select the benchmark and compare with funds that have all exits that occurred on a Monday in the month of October when the full moon was shining at its brightest."

With stellar returns, it is no wonder that VC is an extremely attractive investment — and that investors are looking for the crème de la crème of the universe to maximize returns. David Swensen of Yale University writes, "Selecting top-quartile managers in private markets leads to much greater reward. . . . The first quartile venture capitalist surpasses the median by 30.1 percent per annum, providing a much greater contribution to portfolio results."[7]

But the criteria for establishing performance benchmarks are riddled with inconsistencies and ambiguity, with measurements to identify top-quartile private capital funds varying widely. While public equity fund managers can look to indexes such as the S&P 500, private fund managers do not have the luxury of straightforward benchmarks. LPs point out that *top quartile* can mean different things to different people. Is it net IRR of 25 percent for its latest fund? Or is your "MOIC multiple" in the top quartile? Funds with very attractive rates of return may have inferior multiples, or have no cash distributions. A venture firm may have a range of strong performing funds and one poor fund that, if excluded, can boost the other funds and bring it into the coveted top quartile position. *In fact, omission of certain investments from the historical track record to boost performance indicators is a common tactic practiced among funds.*[8]

With the imperfect state of performance benchmarking in the VC industry, investors cannot always make accurate investment decisions. Assessing performance is as much an art as it is a science.

When the top performers have no motivation to share their performance data, and those at the bottom of the pile hide the data to avoid any further embarrassment, what we have left are data from a pile of mid-level players. Any LP struggles with this conundrum — you could end up with "tallest among the very small." You can sense the challenges in the following excerpt from a fund of funds newsletter:

A serious problem in establishing benchmarks is the sourcing and aggregation of financial data because of the lack of transparency and publicly disclosed information from private companies. Whatever the source, significant biases adversely affect frank attempts to benchmark the data. Sources dependent on accessibility and selective contributions lead to nonrepresentative sampling of the universe of funds.

Finally, incentives to report are also misleading.

Consider the choices top-performing managers have. There is no incentive to contribute fund data to the index, which only serves to raise the benchmark and makes the performance of the fund look less stellar compared to its peers. On the other hand, poorly performing fund managers also have no incentive to disclose data to a third party because they are highly unlikely to raise another fund. As one LP remarked, "Two poorly performing funds, and you are out of the game."

Existing barometers for investors are therefore the best of what's available, but they should be approached with a grain of salt. *Performance evaluation is still important; the key is to be cautious on selection of benchmarks, especially if self-selected by GPs.* LPs dig deeper into manager track records, identify quantitative and qualitative indicators of performance on an absolute and relative level, and monitor the fund diligently beyond static indicators, such as the seemingly inviolable top-quartile benchmark.[9]

When a multibillion-dollar French institutional investor, a financial powerhouse of sorts, came to Silicon Valley eagerly seeking relationships with a top quartile fund, they did not get much love: "After a number of calls, one of the top-tier Sand Hill Road venture funds agreed to meet with us. All they would share is *a statement of net returns*. No details of portfolio companies or the amount invested, nor gross returns. Nor would we get any additional materials for due diligence. This fund was obviously trying to be efficient on the due diligence process as well as hiding the fee income. Their take-it-or-leave-it attitude was indicative of the demand-supply situation."[10] The French investor passed on the opportunity to invest in this top quartile fund. Transparency, authenticity, and how you engage in a potentially long-term relationships matter to LPs. As practitioners, it is our duty to start these relationships with intellectual honesty.

15

Terms of Fund Investment

The Limited Partnership Agreement

A typical fund-offering document, called the private placement memorandum (PPM), includes the fund's investment strategy, the fund manager's background and expertise, and market opportunity. The fund's limited partnership agreement (LPA) is the document that contains legal terms that describe the fund control mechanics, management, investment, and distribution of returns.

"Terms are important but seldom the primary drivers of investment decisions. As they say, terms never make a poor firm look good nor make a good firm unattractive," says Kelly Williams, managing director and head, Customized Fund Investment Group, Credit Suisse Fund of Funds.

KEY TERMS

A short summary of key terms is usually included in the fund documents and is presented here in Exhibit 15.1.

The highly negotiated terms between any investors and fund managers are defined in Exhibit 15.2.

The various financial and governance terms in a fund are structured to meet the goals of both investors and fund managers, as shown in Exhibit 15.3.

Exhibit 15.1 **Key Fund Terms.**

Fund size	$100 million
Commitments	Institutions: $5 million minimum Individuals: $1 million.
Investment size	Approximately $1,000,000 to $2,500,000 per initial investment. Maximum investment per company capped at 10% of the fund or $10,000,000.
Fees	2.5% reducing by 0.5% each year after year 5
Industry focus	Technology (enterprise, consumer, security) and digital health
Investment stage	Seed-stage companies with committed management teams and proven commercial viability.
Geographic focus	Silicon Valley, primarily
Term	10 years. The fund will invest aggressively in the first 3–4 years and seek to realize returns on its portfolio investments in 6–8 years.
Investment structures	Priced equity rounds, capped convertible notes with warrants/discounts.
Investment term	Anticipated year 1 to year 4. Due to the stage of investments, the holding period may be up to 5–7 years or longer.
Portfolio construction and governance	Target portfolio will include a mix of startups with high-risk profiles (30%), medium-risk profiles (40%), and lower-risk profiles (30%). Governance and management of portfolio will be via board seats and active engagement with founders.

Exhibit 15.2 **Most Negotiated Terms in a Fund.**

Term	Definition
Carry	The percentage of profits, or "carried interests," shared by the investors and the fund managers. Typical carried interests are split 80% to the investors and 20% to the fund managers.
Management fees	The annual fees paid by investors to fund managers for operating expenses of the fund. Typical fees are 2.5% per annum of committed capital, paid quarterly.
Waterfall	The process and flow of sharing the returns.
Clawback	The process of recovering excessive profits, if any, from fund managers at the end of the fund life.
Key person	Key persons, or the investment team of the fund managers, are identified. Should these key people leave the fund or are unable to conduct their duties, the investors trigger the right to take action, including stop-making investments.
Indemnification	The fund investors indemnify the fund managers if they lose their capital.
Side letters	Some institutional investors such as pension funds often ask for additional rights via side letters. Because these agreements are drafted on a case-by-case basis, these are called "side letters," as these are aside of the limited partnership agreement (LPA).

Exhibit 15.3 **Financial and Governance Terms.**

Terms	Goals
Fund size, term, management fees, minimum contributions, and GP commitment	Describes the basic financial transactions between LP and GP
Drawdowns, reinvestments, investment limitations, defaults, co-investments	Describes the flow of investment capital between fund and portfolio companies
GP investment committee	Determines how investments are made
Allocation of profits and losses, distributions, GP clawback	Describes the flow of returns from the GP back to the LP
Key person event, investment period termination or suspension, no-fault divorce or GP removal, for-cause termination or GP removal, transfer of LP interests and withdrawal, reports, parallel funds and successor funds, audit, LPAC	Describes the management and governance of the fund
Liability of LPs, indemnification, employee benefit plan regulations, public disclosure issues, tax-exempt investors, non-US investors	Other legal, taxation, and regulatory matters are defined in these terms

FUND FINANCIAL TERMS

All investors seek a balance of financial and control provisions in the fund terms. With respect to financial terms, typical negotiation elements include the following.

Management Fees

- *Percentage.* Management fees are typically 2.0–2.5 percent per annum of committed capital.
- *Duration.* Fees ratchet down each year after the investment period, which is typically five years. Fund managers should establish a minimum floor to make sure there are adequate fees to support the portfolio management, accounting, and tax matters toward the end of the life of the fund.
- *Fees from multiple funds.* Investors insist that fees be reduced when a successor fund is formed. The fees are also typically reduced if the fund managers receive any compensation or fees from portfolio companies. If the

fund managers manage an existing fund, investors often assess the existing fund's investment period, commitments, fees, and impact on the proposed fund's fees. It is typical for fund managers to raise a new fund when an existing fund is about 70 percent invested.

As shown in Exhibit 15.4, the amount of investable capital varies over the life of the fund as the structure and timing of fees vary.

Seth Levine, managing director of the Foundry Group, a leading technology fund based in Colorado, says, "Good GPs [general partners] think of management fee as a loan against carried interest. Carry is paid on the full fund value, not net of fees. Any fees you take out are effectively loans against future performance."[1]

Financial Commitment of the General Partners

The industry standard for GP commitment to the fund is at the minimum 1 percent of the capital. Thus, for a $100 million fund, the managers are expected to invest at least $1million. This ensures that the GP has some skin in the game. However, some managers are bold enough to take bigger bets, proving that they can eat their own cooking by investing as much as 30 percent of the fund.

Exhibit 15.4 **Fund Management Fee Vesting Scenarios.**

	Years 1–5	Year 6	Year 7	Year 8	Year 9	Year 10	Total GP Fees ($M)	Investable Capital ($M)
Scenario 1	2.5	2.5	2.5	2.5	2.5	2.5	**25.00**	75.00
Scenario 2	2.5	2.25	1.75	1.5	1.25	1	**20.25**	79.75
Scenario 3	2.25	1.8	1.44	1.15	0.92	0.73	**17.30**	82.70
Scenario 4	2.5						**12.50**	87.50

In Scenario 1, the fees stay flat at 2.5% of the committed capital. This is unlikely — a GP dream scenario — but is presented for illustration.
In Scenario 2, the fees drop by 10% after year 5, or the investment period.
In Scenario 3, the fees start at 2.25% and drop by 20 percent after year 5.
In Scenario 4, the fees drop to zero after year 5. This example is atypical and is extracted from a single LP fund.

It's Not Always About Your Fees

Some of our VC partners are willing to raise capital at less than a market-clearing price. For example, they can get much better fees and profits with newer LPs, like sovereign wealth funds who are eager to get in the game at Sand Hill Road. But for our VC partners, supporting our foundation is important. Our foundation stands for certain values and plays an important role in the social fabric — the work our VC partners do helps impact our foundation but it has a much bigger impact in the society.

— *Anonymous, investment manager at $10 bn US foundation*

Carried Interests and Performance-Based Triggers

The industry standard for carried interest split is 80/20, where the investors retain 80 percent of the profits and 20 percent profits go to the fund managers. In Tier One funds, where performance has been demonstrated over multiple funds and economic cycles, carried interests can be as high as 30 percent. However, this is rare, and most fund managers stay with the 20 percent structure. Often, emerging managers attempt to drop the carry to 10 percent to lure investors. This seldom impacts the ability to attract investors or hasten the capital raise process. Most institutional investors ignore such overtures and treat these as a deviation from the norm. At times, it is perceived as a sign of weakness.

Venture capital funds typically do NOT offer a preferred rate of return. This is a norm in private equity funds, where a return rate of, say, 8 percent is established. Often called a hurdle rate, this rate factors in the cost of capital over the time period.

More importantly, a cause of heartburn for LPs is the way fund managers calculate carried interest to their advantage. Take, for example, the calculation of carried interest. Carry should be calculated on the basis of net profits, not gross profits, according to the Institutional Limited Partners Association (ILPA) best practices. Put differently, fund managers should treat fees as a loan.

Separately, in a survey of 50 institutional investors, the largest issue for any LP is the calculation of carry: Is it calculated deal by deal or by fund level? Needless to say, LPs prefer fund-level calculation of carry, which allows them to recover their capital first before any carry split.

Several funds have developed a tiered carry structure. For example, the 80/20 split is effective until the investors receive three times the committed capital, over and above which the structure changes to 70/30. Such performance-based triggers are not an industry norm but are seen in hypercompetitive regions such as Silicon Valley or smaller micro-venture capital funds.

Example: Carry Calculation: Net Profits versus Gross Profits

To illustrate the difference between net profits and gross profits, consider the following table:

	Net Profits ($M)	Gross Profits ($M)
Profits	$125	$150
GP carried interest at 20%	$25	$30
GP fees + carry =	$50	$55

Assume fund returns are $150 million. The difference between net profits and gross profits can be substantial. LPs look at the gross profit calculations unfavorably, especially for larger funds.

Waterfall

The waterfall defines how capital will be distributed as exits occur. The industry norm, as seen in the Exhibit 15.5, is to first return the principal amount back to investors (also called "100 percent catch-up") before the fund managers share any profits.

Exhibit 15.5 **Presenting Waterfall to Investors.**

Partial Sale of (Company Name)	Investor LP Pro Rata Share ($m)
Distributable cash	200
Return of capital	100
Pre LP/GP split [A]	100
After LP/GP split [B]	80
Carry paid/(received) [A–B]	20

Typically, distributions are made in the following amounts and order of priority:

1. First, 100 percent to all partners in proportion to their respective capital contributions until the partners have received cumulative distributions equal to the sum of their capital contributions.

2. Thereafter, the balance (a) 20 percent to the general partner (the "carried interest distributions") and (b) 80 percent to the limited partners in proportion to their respective aggregate capital contributions.

Investors are supportive of distributing carried interest to fund managers after the investors receive back their entire committed capital. Certain fund managers allocate carry on a deal-by-deal basis, and profits are distributed after each exit occurs. This creates potential challenges for the future when the final investments are liquidated. If, at a fund level, losses are generated, clawbacks are triggered where the fund managers have to pay back amounts to investors.

Clawbacks

One of the heavily negotiated provisions, clawbacks, occurs when returns need to be paid back by the fund managers to the investors. When carry is distributed early in the life of a fund only to be followed by later losses, clawbacks ensure that investors get their 80 percent profits for the full portfolio at the end of the fund term. It is impossible to predict what the overall portfolio returns and fund profits will be at the end of the term. Overdistribution to fund managers is likely to occur if the early successes are offset by later failures. Thus, an LP can "claw back" the shortfall amounts from fund managers at the final liquidation.

Fund managers must take great care to plan for claw-back possibilities. "I have known of managers that have to sell their houses due to clawbacks," says Kelly DePonte of Probitas Partners. "This is a Damoclean sword that hangs over every GP's head."[2] LPs prefer that an escrow account be established and combined with joint and several personal guarantees from all fund managers/carry recipients. The clawback conditions on taxes are obvious in that LPs shall not seek to claw back the income taxes paid by the GP on the carry earned.

Naturally, neither party looks forward to triggering this clause, but it is a necessary clause for investor protection. An escrow account is often a suitable middle ground, where a portion of distributions are set aside for such situations. With fund managers themselves, suitable agreements need to be established. If clawback liability is joint *and* several among the carry recipients, one partner can be liable for another partner's liabilities.

FUND GOVERNANCE TERMS

Fund governance or control provisions are often governed by a limited partner advisory committee (LPAC). It typically includes three to five larger investors in the fund. A balanced LPAC has representation of various constituents by size of investment or type of constituent (pension funds, endowments, HNWIs, etc.). In designing LPAC, the largest investors in a fund would always look for the interests of the smallest investor. At times, larger LPs insist that the GPs invite at least one representative from the high-net-worth group to participate on the LPAC.

Responsibilities of the LPAC include but are not limited to the following sections.

Investment Limitations

Investors limit the fund manager's ability by percentage of capital, geography, and type of security. For example, managers cannot invest more than 10 or 15 percent of fund commitments in a single company because it's a prudent risk management and mitigation strategy. Other constraints include geographic (e.g., fund managers cannot invest in portfolio companies domiciled outside of the United States or Canada) or types of securities. Fund managers cannot invest in publicly traded securities.

In several investor interviews, strategy drift was brought up as a minor irritant. Strategy drift occurs when GPs claim to make investments in a certain sector and stage but later shift away from the agreed-upon strategy. Though most agreements allow for up to 10 percent of capital to be invested in such "opportunistic" investments, investors start to feel uncomfortable when a larger amount of capital starts to move into other categories. When any market forces cause shifts in strategy, fund managers are better suited in seeking LPAC approvals. When the cleantech sector started to go out of favor and yet funds were bound by the agreements, fund managers started to push the envelope on investments. One institutional investor remarked, "You will be amazed what was being passed off to us as a cleantech opportunity." Another said, "When the best returns for a GP come from the 'other' investment categories and not the primary investment thesis, it makes us wonder."

Conflicts of Interest

Can fund III make an investment in a fund II portfolio company? Under what circumstances will the investment be referred to LPAC for approval? Fund managers often find themselves in situations that may be perceived as self-serving. Some managers may have other sources of income, and may make personal investments in select portfolio companies or in companies outside of the fund. Such potential acts of conflict need to be approved or disclosed.

"Key Person" Provisions

If there are any changes in the core investment team personnel, the investors have the right to suspend the fund's investments or terminate the fund. The fund managers, on the other hand, have an interest in continuing the entity and investment activities. The following list some negotiation elements:

- *Who are the key persons?* What subset of partners is considered more important to execute the strategy? Are the LPs in agreement with the selection? It is critical for investors to identify the key persons and have adequate remedies if they are no longer managing the fund.
- *What is defined as the trigger for such a clause?* Death, disability, and failure to devote appropriate time are often standard trigger conditions. LPs prefer the suspension of investments to be automatic after a triggering event, unless a plan is approved by the LPAC to move forward with alternate personnel.

No-Fault Divorce

Investors can terminate the relationships with the fund without any particular reason or "fault" on either side. This certainly tilts the axis of power. Depending on the terms of the partnership agreement, the fund can thus be dissolved, the investment period can be stalled, and/or the GP can be replaced. While LPs seldom trigger this clause, it creeps up when issues such as GP misconduct or breach may have occurred. Tax/regulatory matters, felonies, bankruptcies, negligence, and breach of agreements by GPs can trigger this clause. "In my experience, a 75 percent to 80 percent LP vote is typical for a no-fault termination of the fund," says Howard Beber, a fund attorney at the law firm of Proskauer Rose.

Indemnification/Standard of Care

This clause eliminates any liabilities for the fund manager for any act or omissions and prevents lawsuits. Exceptions include fraud, good faith, gross negligence, or willful malfeasance.

Confidentiality

Certain investors, such as state pension funds and university endowments, are subject to the US Freedom of Information Act (FOIA) guidelines. FOIA is an information disclosure statute that encourages accountability through transparency. Though FOIA laws vary from state to state, generally, in the venture capital context, certain information reported by a GP to a public plan limited partner can be the subject of an FOIA request. A newspaper reporter could submit an FOIA request to a public plan limited partner and subsequently publish sensitive fund or portfolio company information. To date, many states have modified their laws to protect portfolio company information from public disclosure. GPs also seek to limit details of fund investments in portfolio companies from becoming public, as they could impact future financing and valuations. A variety of remedies exist, including limiting information to such LPs or, in extreme cases, barring such LPs from future participation in funds.

Other terms include the following:

- *Valuation matters.* LPAC adopts guidelines and weighs in on markups or markdowns of portfolio company valuation.
- *Side letters.* All LPs are equal, but some LPs are more equal than others. Side letters provide additional clarity or describe the specific agreement (above and beyond the standard terms) between the GP and the LP. LPs know that side letters are a common theme in the business. To avoid debates regarding the GP fee calculations, one LP proposed an elegant side letter asking, "The auditors have reviewed and ascertained that the GP fees have been calculated correctly."

- *Coinvestments.* LPs may negotiate coinvestment rights to have the ability to cherry-pick investment opportunities and invest more capital in promising companies. In doing so, LPs also gain insights into how the GP chooses the opportunities, structures investments, and adds value as a board member. The process and timing of responses need to be managed effectively by the GP: It is likely that the LP may not have the ability to conduct due diligence, invest in follow-on rounds, or respond within the allocated time frame. However, if an LP can bring some strategic insights to the company, it is often worth the time and effort for both parties. GPs also need to be cautious in that such an investment from an LP, especially a corporate LP with industry knowledge, does not scare off acquirers and impair the exit potential and value.

WHAT INSTITUTIONAL LPs SEEK

The Institutional Limited Partners Association (ILPA) represents 240 organizations that collectively manage over $1 trillion of private equity capital. ILPA has developed best practices for fund managers that focus on alignment of interest, governance, and transparency:[3]

- *Alignment of interest.* The GPs should focus on profit maximization and not merely management fees.
- *Governance.* The fund managers should put controls and adequate checks and balances in place so that investors' interests are primary at all times.
- *Transparency.* The fund managers should share financial performance, fee income, and returns calculations.

These practices are governed by the terms shown in Exhibit 15.6.

EXHIBIT 15.6 **Industry Best Practices: GP–LP Terms Summary.**

Driver	Terms
Alignment of interests between LP investors and GP fund managers:	
Does the GP have skin in the game?	Is the GP commitment significantly above or below industry standards? What is the GP's commitment with respect to his or her net worth?
Are the management fees structured appropriately?	Do the management fees adjust when successor funds are raised? How are the fees adjusted after the investment period?
Are there opportunities where a GP–LP conflict of interest may arise?	Can the GP coinvest its personal capital in select cherry-picked opportunities? Will this create a fundamental conflict in the portfolio? As one LP asks, "Why should a manager have side bets and other businesses?"
Is the GP–LP profit sharing structure designed appropriately?	Waterfall distribution and clawback provisions
Are all the GP management team members motivated to succeed?	Compensation, GP distribution of carry within its team, resources to operate the fund
What is the investment strategy?	Investment limitations by company, sector, pace of drawdowns, reinvestments, investments from multiple funds in same opportunity
Governance and controls of the fund and its management	
Does an LP advisory committee (LPAC) exist? What are the roles and responsibilities of such a committee? Do the LPs receive adequate information from GPs?	LP advisory committee (LPAC) size, responsibilities, and frequency of meetings; reports, annual meetings, valuation guidelines
Standard of care: does the GP allocate substantial time and attention to building and managing the portfolio?	Is the fund a GP's primary activity? Does the GP have other income streams, investments, or interests?
Do the LPs have options to limit the downside or exit the relationship?	No-fault divorce, key person event, key person insurance, termination of investment period, transfer of LP interests, and withdrawal
Transparency of financial information	
Transparency of GP income streams, portfolio quality	Fees and carried interest calculations, valuation, and financial information, other relevant GP information, and protection of proprietary information

As the managing director of private equity for the University of California Regents, Timothy Recker manages a portfolio of venture capital and private equity funds. As the former chair of the ILPA, he worked on a number of issues to ensure that the interests of the two sides are aligned. "The ILPA has diligently worked to address a number of issues that make the

GP–LP relationship stronger," he says.[4] According to industry surveys, as many as 58 percent of LPs choose not to invest in funds that ignore the ILPA guidelines.

OFFERING SWEETENERS TO ATTRACT LPs: A DOUBLE-EDGED SWORD

Several GPs offer sweeteners to make the fund attractive to potential LPs, and some even attempt to create a sense of urgency. Liam, Founding Partner of .406 Ventures offers a good example of a sweetener:

> We pooled our own capital, invested in five companies and offered to contribute this portfolio of five investments to the fund at cost. LPs got a sense of opportunities we can attract and realized that we were serious about getting in the business. We believed that this is a small price to pay. We could demonstrate we understood how to build a portfolio that aligns with our strategy. LPs know that it is easy to write about strategy in an offering document, but having actually "walked the talk" and done it as a first-time fund, that level of thoughtfulness and sophistication allowed us to demonstrate that we can walk the talk.[5]

When one of Liam's portfolio companies, HealthDialog, a health care analytics company, was sold for $775 million, the LPs received 2X in less than seven months.

Examples of sweeteners that have not yielded positive outcomes include offering portfolio companies from previous funds that may not have made any meaningful progress. In one example, fund III offered at least half a dozen companies from fund II to LPs at cost. This can irritate existing fund II LPs who have borne significant risk. Future fund III LPs may also wonder how they might be treated when it comes time to raise fund IV.

MOST NEGOTIATED LP–GP TERMS

For GPs as well as LPs, the primary tension arises around the overall economics — management fees and the management of the fund. In a survey conducted by the Center for Private Equity and Entrepreneurship at Dartmouth's Tuck School of Business, about 100 GPs and LPs were asked to rank the most negotiated terms.[6] As Exhibit 15.7 shows, key person provisions, clawbacks, and management fees were among the top negotiated terms.

Understanding key limited partner agreement (LPA) terms and knowing what to negotiate can help a GP accelerate the fundraising process. Investors seek to ensure the alignment of interests. The fee carry, and other restrictive covenants, safeguard their investments and focus the GP toward long-term profit creation. LPs may have remedies, such as key person provisions, cause or no-fault fund terminations, or fund manager removal provisions. These remedies are rarely exercised yet provide a negotiating leverage and a safety cover.

Selecting an experienced fund attorney to develop an appropriate negotiating plan is equally critical. "Choose your service providers wisely — the wrong choice can damage your prospects," says Kelly Williams of Credit Suisse Fund of Funds. "We have seen some very good first-time funds

Exhibit 15.7 **Most Negotiated Terms in Order of Priority: LPs and GPs Views.**

LPs — Most Negotiated	GPs — Most Negotiated
1. Key person	1. Clawbacks
2. Waterfall	2. Key person
3. Management fees	3. Management fees
4. Clawbacks	4. Carry
5. Side letters	5. Side letters
6. Indemnification	6. Waterfall
7. Carry	7. Indemnification

but their legal counsel behaved poorly and it did not help the cause."[7] A good attorney knows the market trends of the terms, understands the value of attracting an institutional LP, and proceeds to guide the fund managers accordingly. In one example, a $30-plus billion institutional investor complained that a mature venture firm, now raising fund IV, had picked a small-town attorney with very little experience in negotiating LPAs. "We were utterly flummoxed," says this LP, "and wondered — were the GPs trying to save the fees? I mean, this inexperienced attorney created much angst at our end. They used improper terminology, did not know the market standards . . . it reflected very poorly on the GPs. In fact, nowadays, the first thing we look at in an LPA is the name of their legal counsel. If this is an experienced firm, well versed with private equity, it shows that the GP knows what they are doing."[8]

And if needed, a placement agent can (for a generous fee) introduce you to several investors. Often agents are invited to help top-off a fund, which may have reached 70 percent of the target raise. The role of placement agents is addressed in the following chapter. Most industry veterans agree: LPs do not invest in funds based on terms (but they may choose *not* to invest if terms are too GP favorable). Rather, LPs make investment decisions based on the full package — team, strategy, and past performance. As one investor remarked, "Show me an established firm with consistent top quartile returns and I will concede on most terms."

WHY LPs TERMINATE EXISTING RELATIONSHIPS

Catherine Crockett, founder of Grove Street Advisors, a fund of funds with over $6 billion under management, says, "Terminating a relationship is the hardest part." Crockett and her team screen over 500 fund managers and deploy $500 million in any given year.

"It's a swell offer, Brad, and you're a great guy, but I've just got out of a bad limited partnership, and I'm not ready for that kind of commitment yet."

Source: Cartoon Collections.

The primary reasons for terminating a relationship are fund performance, partners' motivations and alignment, and fund size:

- *Fund performance.* When performance falters, the decision is easy. No re-ups; it is an easy good-bye.
- *Partners' motivations and alignment.* As partners become successful, they lose their motivation — bloated senior partners with decreasing appetite should stay on the couch, not feature prominently in the private placement memorandum (PPM). They are not an asset in this business. Ensuring that the rewards are shared with all investment committee and junior members is important. Finally, partners need to stay current with the market and technology developments.

- *Fund size*. Successful funds grow too big too fast. LPs worry that with bloated funds, finding the right investment opportunities and generating returns will be harder. Small is beautiful, indeed. While success breeds success, and as more LPs try to kick down the doors, the smarter LPs quietly exit through the side doors.

In a dynamic world, markets change, and the ability to generate returns changes. "If the three variables, investment team, investment strategy, and the market environment, are static, it is easy to make re-up decisions. But these are in a state of perpetual flux," says Lisa Edgar of Top Tier Capital Partners.

Fundraising is an extremely competitive exercise. Consider the fact that more than 400 funds were seeking aggregate commitments of $80 billion.[9] Only about a third of the population will be able to attract capital. Thus, any fund manager needs to establish strong differentiators.

First-time funds have a limited probability of raising funds with institutional investors, but they are looked on favorably by some funds of funds. History shows that fund managers who started small, raised capital from high-net-worth individuals (HNWIs) and local foundations, and built a track record were able to achieve liftoff. The LP courtship process is a long and slow dance. As most LPs say, introductions are the best way to start. The role of a placement agent can be critical. For new managers, the typical timeline from the first touch to a commitment is about 12 months or as long as three years.

A new fund is always scrutinized to the highest degree. The amount of diligence is an order of magnitude higher: track record, references, and such. Finally, success begets success. Benchmark Fund I generated an envious 92X cash-on-cash (C-on-C) multiple. The fundraising timelines for Benchmark Fund II were probably much shorter as compared to the first fund.

16

The Venture Firm's Ethos, Culture, and Values

The investment firm Goldman Sachs is considered to be one of the best money-making machines on Wall Street. Yet it was once described as "a great vampire squid wrapped around the face of humanity, *relentlessly jamming its blood funnel into anything that smells like money.*" Surely, for any investor, success is measured by the returns you generate. And the more you make, the better it is.

But what gives, along this path to riches? What keeps you from turning into a soulless vampire squid? Defining your ethos, and cementing it in your soul, is a foundational step in building the venture firm.

Besides its ethos, values as well as a firm's value proposition can define its brand identity. Many firms believe that a fancy website, smiling faces, and partner headshots with overstated bios and some logos are sufficient. In an era when entrepreneurs have plenty of choices, the venture firms need to weigh the importance of building and branding their venture firms in a compelling fashion.

The archetype of a firm can take several forms — a tight-knit small partnership (Benchmark and the Foundry Group), a service agency (Andreessen Horowitz, with over 100 team members), or a technology-led community platform (First

Round Capital). Though each of these models have their own nuances, let's start with the ethos of the firm.

ETHOS

What defines the beliefs, values, and character traits of the firm and its partners? How do they treat people — the founders, their LPs, and their service providers? More importantly, how do they interact with those from whom they cannot gain anything? What role can a VC fulfill in society? Are they more than just money-making machines? Pardon my Greek, but Aristotle defined the three categories of ethos as:

1. *phronesis* — wisdom, good judgment, and excellence of character
2. *arete* — excellence, moral virtues, living up to your full potential
3. *eunoia* — benevolence, beautiful thinking, and goodwill

While some firms share their ethos publicly, others may have internalized these. Sequoia Capital, a firm that has succeeded across 50 years of economic cycles and three generational transitions, defines its ethos in a succinct manner.

CULTURE AND VALUES

"Culture is like cement — it firms up quickly" reminds Rob Ward, co-founder and partner at Meritech Capital. Rob is known amongst entrepreneurs for his "little hat; lots of cattle" approach — the inverse of the Texan slam, "All hat, no cattle," which implies lots of talk and no action. Meritech, like Benchmark, has earned respect among the elite founder circles in Silicon Valley for its no-nonsense approach to investments. The partners form a tight-knit team, do all the work themselves,

Defining Your Ethos: The Sequoia Way

Sequoia, 1972 and Beyond

The creative spirits. The underdogs. The resolute. The determined. The outsiders. The defiant. The independent thinkers. The fighters and the true believers.

These are the founders with whom we partner. They're extremely rare. And we're ecstatic when we find them.

We partner early — sometimes when a company is no more than an idea. We know these crucial first decisions can have an exponential influence on the curve of success.

Our style is not for everyone. We push when we see potential. We are direct. Some don't like our approach. Most who know us do.

Our team mirrors the founders with whom we partner: hungry overachievers with a deep-rooted need to win. Many come from humble backgrounds. Many are immigrants. Many formed or built companies of their own before joining Sequoia. Each shares the mindset of an entrepreneur, and knows what it means to walk that path.

We value teamwork over showmanship. Our contribution to a company always comes from several of us working together. We're skittish about the first person singular, and don't care to see our names in the press.

Our team is small. We prefer a few people with diverse strengths focused — some painfully — that are eternal truths. Our network is strong. Our advantage comes from four decades of legendary founders helping each other.

Long ago, we made nonprofits the backbone of our limited partner base. Working for these charities brings intense meaning to what we do. It gives us a heightened sense of responsibility.

We're serious about our work and carefully choose the words to describe it. Terms like *deal* or *exit* are forbidden. And while we're sometimes called investors, that is not our frame of mind. We consider ourselves partners for the long term.

We help the daring build legendary companies, from idea to initial public offering (IPO) and beyond.

and are heavily engaged in the business. No junior partners are slaved to write memos or diligence calls. Even the mundane scheduling activity is managed by partners themselves. "A shared success model has its merit — too much is based on one person in our business, and that often causes challenges. Our culture is built around selflessness — we build/share and care," says Rob.

Hard-nosed investors and left-brained analytical minds find this whole culture and values discussion to be soft and gooey. Dismissing this as unimportant, such investors often dive into the money-making fun parts of the business. That lackadaisical approach to the core tenets of business led to behavior where investors who preyed on women founders, colleagues, and peers. Sexual harassment was rife, especially where men dominate the flow of capital and assume a power stance with founders.

In his book *Flow*, Mihaly Csikszentmihalyi describes a study in which happy and productive professionals were compared with unhappy and unproductive. *The most important factor was alignment with personal values.* If you ask, "What are values?" try to recall a tough situation in which stakes were high and both options looked equally compelling. What tilted the scale for you? Why did you move in one direction when both paths looked the same?

Our values are a set of drivers that propel each of us in different ways, to fulfill our deepest yearnings. Yet values can deviate in circumstances — one person may make choices that the rest may not agree upon. Exhibit 16.1 offers some guidelines.

Exhibit 16.1 **Framework for Values.**

Factor	Values
Behavior and actions	Optimists, risk takers, first movers, independent thinkers, honor the founders' journey, keep your commitments, be responsive, make prompt decisions
Sharing rewards	Did you act as a steward of your LP capital? Did the founders and syndicate investors win? Was this a zero-sum game?
Addressing challenges	Accept responsibility, practice empathy and compassion, fight for the common and greater good

At Base10 Ventures, their values are quite simple — no elaborate, fancy language nor confusing, generic platitudes.

- *Serve the entrepreneur.*
- *Take the long view.*
- *Be humble.*
- *Serve our investors.*

Core Values — New Schools Venture Fund

New Schools Venture Fund defines its core values, which inform the work they do and how they do it.

We are:

Bold. We are optimists who find, fund, and support passionate entrepreneurs with powerful ideas. We take risks on early-stage teams with plans that possess the greatest promise for transformative impact. Our efforts help to create a better future for all students.

Passionate. We bring enthusiasm and humility to our work, along with an unwavering commitment to deliver on our mission. We love what we do and bring our best selves to work every day.

Connected. We build trusting, collaborative, and honest relationships with our partners and one another to accomplish more together. By forging deep connections with our ventures and other education leaders, along with the students and communities they serve, we can deliver on our common goals.

Inclusive. We urgently confront present-day inequality by investing in and amplifying the voices of diverse entrepreneurs so that powerful ideas have a chance to flourish. We nurture a respectful culture that leverages the strength of varied talents and perspectives.

Accountable. We make decisions based on rigorous analysis and are conscientious stewards of the resources entrusted to us. We actively measure our progress toward transforming PK–12 education for all students. We take responsibility for our actions and honor our commitments.

Take the example of the following core values:

- *Communication — We have an obligation to communicate.*
- *Respect — We treat others as we would like to be treated.*
- *Integrity — We work with customers and prospects openly, honestly, and sincerely.*
- *Excellence — We are satisfied with nothing less than the very best in everything we do.*

This company was named "most innovative company in America" by *Fortune* magazine for six years. It had over 25,000 employees and claimed $100 billion in revenues. Yet the CEO landed in prison as the company was declared bankrupt. The highest echelons of the company were unable to put these core values in practice. Any company could claim these values as a part of their own ethos. But as this case of Enron demonstrates, putting values to work, on a daily basis, is the challenge. Writing it down is the easy part — such exercises are often done by a coach, at a fun, off-site location, ideally by the sea where team pictures at sunset are filled with smiles and glee. And then reality hits, once everyone gets back in the grind.

"Values are words — culture is how you actually live those words. Articulating values, living these values day-in and day-out and testing them, and then adapting these as needed requires deliberate effort. At Enron, you had 'respect.' Sounds good, right? But respect can be such a vague word, and it's hard to know if someone is being truly respectful," says Jeff Lawson, founder and CEO of Twilio.[1] "At Twilio we have: Be humble. It's a more specific version of respect, and it's actionable. We all know what humble is, we all know what humble is not. We have a pretty good sense for that." But in a venture firm, which is often a group of type A personalities and cowboys hunting, who will design and enforce the value system becomes a fundamental challenge. As a company CEO, it may be easier to put these in place, but harder in a venture firm. Yet these values need to be monitored and put in practice. Lawson says, "Leading a company means being a conscious custodian of its values. It's a requirement, not a nice-to-have. Because, here's the reality: *Every company has a culture and has values, whether or not you put them into words. You might as well articulate them so that they stay in your sight, and you can guide them.*"

Diversity

Just 11 percent of American venture investors are women, an appalling metric by any standard. Effectively, this is like shutting out 50 percent of the population's views and inputs, and ignoring the market trends and opportunities that come with this diversity. Does increased diversity lead to better firm performances? In a research study, authors Paul Gompers and Sophie Wang looked at a dataset of the gender of venture capital partners' children. They found strong evidence that having a daughter leads to an increased propensity to hire female partners by venture capital firms. Second, improved gender diversity improves deal and fund performances. "Taken together, our findings have profound implications on how the capital markets could function better with improved diversity," the authors wrote.[2] But this study begets a fundamental question — why did male VC partners only become sensitive to gender diversity AFTER they had daughters? Did they not have mothers? Sisters? Spouses? Or were they afraid that the world would treat their daughters in an equitable manner?

Investment professionals need to establish practices to not only increase diversity but also make it safer for all. How can we develop the right methods to identify and respond to perceived workplace harassment in its various forms? The failure to catch and investigate sexual harassment can cause reputational and financial risk. In an anonymous sexual harassment survey conducted by Investment Management Due Diligence Association,[3] the findings were quite appalling. LPs did not care much about harassment either:

- 89 percent of investment allocators do not inquire about sexual harassment in the workplace.

- 82 percent of allocators do not ask follow-up questions about sexual harassment if a manager declines to answer questions.
- 76 percent of allocators would still consider or invest with a fund manager who has had issues with sexual harassment.
- 67 percent of allocators limit background checks to only principals and senior staff.
- 36 percent of allocators do not check social media for red flags (e.g., inappropriate pictures and comments disparaging women), indicating harassment is likely not on their radar.

To address this gap, AllRaise, a diversity nonprofit, was formed to encourage collaboration among women in the VC and startup field. AllRaise seeks to push the number of female venture partners to 18 percent within 10 years and to increase the percentage of funding going to companies with a female founder from 15 to 25 percent within five years. The group holds small gatherings to teach women skills such as how to serve effectively on boards. AllRaise says it has arranged introductions between startups and investors, leading to around 50 checks for startups.

As in any other social challenges, it is important for the ones in majority to ask if they are open to accepting the diversity or afraid of the change. What subconscious biases do the majority follow, that prevents the minority from rising up as equal partners?

Jess Lee, partner at Sequoia Capital says the firm has also gone to great lengths to ensure she succeeds. To bring her on board, two existing partners — Jim Goetz and Roelof Botha — went the extra mile. Like all new partners, she was invited to board meetings at portfolio companies and given an official mentor, to decipher Sequoia's weekly partners meetings and brainstorm ways to help the six portfolio companies on whose boards Lee serves. Sequoia now has four female partners. Pat Grady, partner for over a decade at Sequoia, says that the firm wants to ensure a diverse representation from all segments of the society.

Cosplay in a Café — Sequoia Hires a Partner

Shortly after Yahoo! acquired Polyvore, its CEO, Jess Lee, agreed to meet Jim Goetz, a Sequoia partner, at a café in Silicon Valley. When she showed up, she tried not to stare at two customers at a nearby table dressed head-to-toe as characters from *Toy Story*. After a few minutes, Woody and Buzz Lightyear held up a watercolor of the cowgirl character, Jessie, and other toys from the movie. Words beneath read: "Will you join US on a new VENTURE?" The toys then removed their headpieces: Woody was Goetz; Buzz was Roelof Botha, another Sequoia partner who'd backed Instagram and payment company Square. Lee, a cosplay aficionado, was impressed. "It meant that I could bring my whole self" to work, she says. She accepted the offer.[4] Botha celebrated the successful close with a picture (Exhibit 16.2) and a tweet — "It was a team effort."

Exhibit 16.2 **Sequoia goes the extra mile to recruit a partner.**

Source: Sequoia Capital

The Archetype of the Firm: Its Operating System

Like any startup, the firm needs to build its brand identity. However, many firms believe that a website and some fancy logos are sufficient to create their brand identity. In an era when entrepreneurs have choices, the venture firms need to weigh the importance of branding their venture firm appropriately.

The venture firm can develop into several archetypes, some of which include (a) group of cowboys; (b) a service agency; and (c) a community platform.

The Firm as a Group of Cowboys

"I think of venture capital business as a series of individual personalities, as opposed to a series of firms,"[5] remarked James Bryer of Accel Partners, former chairman, National Venture Capital Association. Most firms operate as a crude aggregation of cowboys: each partner does his or her own thing. Each partner works solo to find opportunities and bring these to the table. On Monday morning, at the partner meetings, each cowboy tries to show other cowboys what a great catch he or she has brought to the table. Often, a fight erupts to establish the hierarchy. The smarter partners often preempt such brouhahas by working behind the scenes, gathering the votes and eliminating any objections. The discussions are often perfunctory and awkward.

At its core, these cowboys need each other to raise money because limited partners invest in teams, not solo performers. So the soloists pretend to be a part of a symphony and raise the fund, and then promptly go back to doing what they do best — being cowboys. Down the road, when these opportunities start to struggle, the other cowboys may have that "I told you so" look on their face. Cowboys are now forced down this lonely path of trying to resurrect the dying opportunities. Others watch, sigh, and move on.

Often, the CEOs of portfolio companies wonder why they do not get much help from the other partners in the firm. In a survey of over 150 CEOs, the differences in the views of the CEOs and those of the venture capitalists (VCs) were indicative of the chasm that exists between the two.[6] CEOs care more about partners than the overall firm and even less about the reputation of a firm's portfolio companies. However, most venture firms tout the past successes — IPOs or acquisitions — on their websites. Partners brag about the string of the investment successes when CEOs don't necessarily care about them.

Limited partners are concerned about succession and the strength of the overall firm. They seek a perpetual money machine generating superior returns, not afflicted by individual egos and limited life spans. But for entrepreneurs, the individual personalities and reputations matter, not succession issues. Entrepreneurs are attracted to the partners as much as the money. A firm's brand impacts their ability to attract the best and brightest founders. But entrepreneurs don't look at a firm's website as much as they consider what their peers and third parties think about the firm. But star power is the beginning: how the entrepreneurs benefit from the firm matters.

The Firm as an Agency

For Andreessen Horowitz, the model of the venture firm is simple: be the change you wish to see in this world. The firm has modeled itself and blended values of three firms, a talent agency — Creative Artists Agency (CAA) — and two financial firms — Allen & Company and JP Morgan.

"We aspire to be like these firms. Allen & Company is a boutique investment bank that, since 1920s, has gone through generations of leadership and strategy but has preserved its culture and value systems — which is remarkable as a Wall Street firm. The original JP Morgan of the 1910–1920, era . . . played a fundamental role in financing the build-out of modern America," says Andreessen.

Setting the Services Standard

We saw the opportunity to create the venture firm we as entrepreneurs would have taken money from, had it existed at the time.[7]

—Marc Andreessen, Andreessen Horowitz

Creative Artists Agency (CAA) is a Hollywood talent agency that is said to be the entertainment industry's most influential organization, managing some 1,400 of the top talents in the acting industry. Their partnership was based on teamwork, with proceeds shared equally. There were no nameplates on doors, no formal titles, no individual agent client lists. Practices followed the company's two "commandments": Be a team player and return phone calls promptly. According to Andreessen, the period of CAA's growth under the leadership of its founder, Michael Ovitz, had an enormous impact on the talent management arena.[8]

Here are some lessons from these firms that have been incorporated into Andreessen Horowitz's operations:

- *Focus on thought leaders and the best talent.* Over the years, CAA has kept its hold on the market by retaining the best clients in Hollywood. It has captured a near monopoly of A-list actors, directors, and writers. CAA is aggressive when it comes to attracting talent, just as Andreessen Horowitz may be when it comes to attracting talented CEOs. At times, if CAA couldn't get the actors they wanted, they would poach the agents who managed them, sometimes tripling their salaries, and got their clients along with them. Similarly, Allen & Company hosts an annual Sun Valley conference, which attracts the thought leaders in media and technology as well as politicians and policy makers.

- *Create a one-stop shop.* CAA's original revenue model was to rely on commissions from clients. As the business started dropping for various reasons, it aggressively expanded to become a one-stop shop for the entertainment industry. Some of their services now include brand management, communications, market research, trend forecasting, and strategic marketing. CAA even helps its celebs to turn into social mavens. Similarly, Andreessen Horowitz aims to serve the portfolio companies in a myriad number of ways. When it comes to helping portfolio companies recruit talent, the firm has 11 recruiting experts on staff. Cofounder Ben Horowitz calls it "HR in a box," and the firm measures success on the "introduction-to-hire rate."[9]

- *No-ego/team spirit.* CAA's corporate culture is a blend of eastern philosophy and team sports. Team members are encouraged to suppress their individual ego for the benefit of the team. Every Monday morning, the 100 agents meet and share their own schedules and industry developments. CAA shuns the media and likes to operate under the radar. Allen & Company, one of the underwriters for the Google and Twitter public offering, does not even have a website.

The Firm as a Community Platform

For larger firms, the ability to deploy resources is easier. For smaller funds, the management fees often constrain the abilities to build a large team. First Round Capital took a different approach to tackling the issues. "We think of ourselves as building a community, not a portfolio. Historically, value-add was primarily delivered by a venture capital partner interacting with a CEO. We think far more value can be delivered by creating a community of founders, where each CEO in our portfolio can help the others, and each CTO, each CFO, each recruiter, each engineer," says Josh Koppelman.[10]

First Round has a team of six people focused full time on building products, events, and services to help connect the companies with one another. "If you are the SEO person at a startup, your job is pretty lonely and you don't have many peers to ask for help and advice. But we have over 30 people focused on SEO in our portfolio, and are building software — including an extremely active online network tool — to help them interact with each other. Now, every time we invest in a company, it actually adds value to our prior investments because there are new smart people who participate in the dialog, rather than subtract," points out Josh Koppelman.

Brett Berson, head of platforms at First Round Capital, manages a team of nine people. He says that such an online peer-to-peer teaching model changes the game. "Instead of knowledge accumulation, we are ensuring disintermediation. Let the best ideas come from the best people," he says. The platform, which includes a Yelp-like system for finding service providers such as accountants and lawyers, is helpful to port-folio companies. Portfolio CEOs, CTOs, and CFOs are all con-nected with one another and post topics for others to chime in on, such as how to motivate a distracted founder, structure a compensation plan, plan for ad optimization online, or assess the benefits of raising venture debt. "As a VC, we are now shift-ing to platform-as-a-service," says Brett. The platform model is catching up. However, the usage in an open arena versus closed loop can be different. Finally, the platform is not a sub-stitute for mentoring, which is often more effective in person.

Until recently, ethos, culture, diversity, and values were not a part of our vocabulary. But the industry is maturing, and we are waking up to the importance of these fundamental build-ing blocks. We can evolve and behave as better human beings. Or we could denigrate into giant vampire squids, sucking all the money we can from every crevice there is.

GOVERNANCE OF THE FIRM

The governance of the firm primarily rests on the shoulders of the head of operations, or, in smaller firms, the cofounders, or the managing directors (see Exhibit 16.3).

Prior to formalizing a partnership, the fund's founders need to agree on the various operational matters, decision-making guidelines for all operational matters, such as the following:

- Firm operations:
  - Employee matters: Compensation, hiring, and fir-ing processes
  - Service provider selection: attorneys, accountants/audit firms, marketing and PR-related activities
  - Budgetary allocations
  - Operations, ethics, and confidentiality matters

Exhibit 16.3 **Operational elements of a well-governed venture firm.**

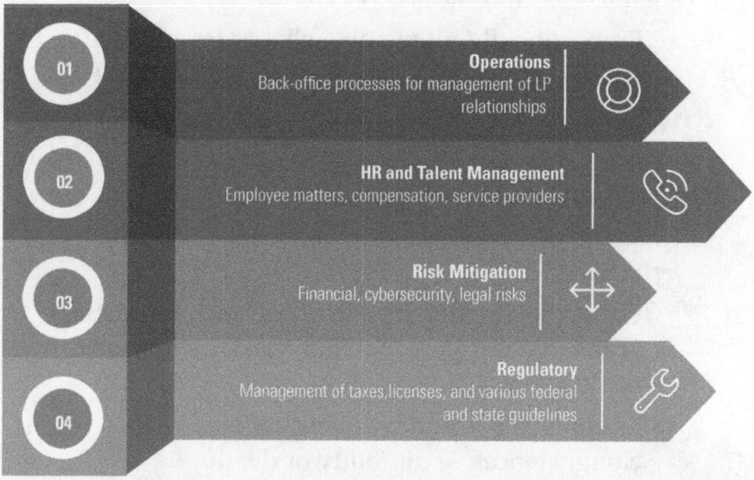

- Investments:
  - Investment committee composition: process of admission and selection of investment committee members
  - Selection of venture partners and entrepreneurs-in-residence
- Board participation:
  - Best-suited member versus one who sourced the opportunity
  - Participation on conflicting company boards
  - Post IPO, public board participation

The Firm's Operational Guidelines

The founding partners establish guidelines that ascertain how the following decisions are made:

- *How are new individuals admitted or terminated from the GP membership?*
  - Majority vote of number of current members.
  - Majority vote by percentage of carry allocation.

- *Upon addition of new members, how will carry or economic interest of existing members be diluted?*
  - Proportionally, all member shares are adjusted.
  - Selectively, a few member shares are adjusted.
- *Will investment decisions require unanimous vote or a majority vote? How does the partnership agree to invest additional amounts in portfolio companies?*
- *Under what conditions can a member withdraw or be terminated?*
  - Cause: negligence, breach of conduct, fraud, SEC or tax matters, personal financial situation, such as bankruptcy.
  - Membership withdrawal in challenging circumstances — disability or death.
- Voluntary withdrawal.

Under each of the conditions above, the withdrawn members' financial interests are reviewed:

- Retain carry interest as it's liable for clawback.
- Retains carry in existing investments, but no new carry is offered.
- Forfeits carry completely.
- Is liable for pro rata share of capital contributions.
- Stays/resigns from portfolio boards.
- Investment committee structure, decision-making criteria, and votes.

Administration and Operations: The Back Office

Back- and middle-office operations are critical to a fund's success. Investors are paying more attention to the details; poor or insufficient back-office administration is often a reason for investors to forgo making an investment in the fund. Georganne Perkins of Fisher Lynch Capital, a fund of funds (FoF), puts it bluntly: "If the GPs are equipped to handle other people's money, it can be a positive." Put another way, any startup with the requisite technical and financial oversight and controls (a CFO) is attractive to any GP, and the same goes for any LP.

"Well-designed back- and middle-office operations provide fund principals and investors with confidence that the data they are receiving is correct — data integrity — and may be used to base decisions on," says Harry Cendrowski, author of *Private Equity: History, Governance and Operations.*[11] Harry is also the founder of Cendrowski Corporate Advisors, a back-office services firm that offers financial services, taxation services, and investor relations to a number of private equity and VC firms. According to Harry, a back office can offer the following:

- *Financial reporting.* Fund and portfolio company financial reporting for limited partners and fund managers, and monitoring of portfolio company performance is provided.

- *Accounting.* Accounting services are a critical component of the back- and middle-office operations. Fund principals rely on the information generated in the accounting system for decision-making (e.g., how much cash should be distributed to investors; what are the cash needs of the fund for future expenses?), inspiring investor confidence (are capital accounts properly stated and communicated timely?), and their own economic interests (are management fees properly calculated; are incentive allocations properly calculated?).

- *General and capital accounting.* Bookkeeping functions, posting journal entries, account reconciliations, preparation of financial statements, management of operating cash, maintenance of the general ledger, including posting of all transactions, is necessary for proper financial and tax reporting.

- Tracking cash intake, basis in entities, maintenance of investor capital accounts, and calculation of distributions is provided:

- Maintenance of investor capital accounts is a critical function, as this is the primary measure that investors rely on in assessing their investment. It represents the investor's economic interest in the fund and is often the key component in determining distributions as well as profit and loss allocations.

- Components of investor capital accounts include the proper computation and documentation of capital calls and distributions. Computation and documentation of capital calls allow the fund to meet its obligations and commitments for fund expenses and portfolio investments. Computation and documentation of distributions is critical to investor confidence by indicating that fund principals are abiding by the terms of the operating agreement. In addition, fund principals need to know how much capital has been committed, how much has been called, and how much has been returned to investors.

- The proper allocation of economic and taxable profits and losses is another reason why proper maintenance of capital accounts is critical. Economic income affects the investors' right to distributions.

- *Business valuation.* A back office interfaces with fund principals with respect to the valuation of portfolio investments. *Generally accepted accounting principles* (GAAP) basis financial statements must reflect investments at their fair value rather than historical cost. The back and middle offices may provide assistance in the valuation process and must ensure that the proper value is recorded in the general ledger. ASC 820-compliant (formerly FAS 157) mark-to-market portfolio company valuations for fund return calculations are essential.

- *Preparation of investor communications.* Fund return calculations, investment reports, and capital call notices are included in communications. Pat Grady of Sequoia Capital says, "At Sequoia, every partner takes turns in writing the LP letter. It's a reminder for us as to who we work for."

- *Audits and taxes.* A back office coordinates the annual financial statement audit of the fund and is the primary contact with auditors. It is the source of all the information the auditors will be assessing in their examination. As such, it is critical that the back office not only is able to provide the necessary information in a timely manner but also is able to provide explanations and answer questions with respect to the information on the auditor's request. The back office is usually involved in the preparation of fund tax returns and investor K–1s. In addition, the back office is responsible for calculating and documenting tax basis — the fund's tax basis in its investments as well as the investors' tax basis in the fund. Some back offices extend their services into offering consultative services in the partners and principals' tax liabilities and goals, develop a plan to minimize their tax liabilities, and/or enhance after-tax return on investment.

Transferring responsibility for these activities to an independent third party reassures limited partners that they are receiving timely and accurate information. Administrative resources at the fund level are freed up, permitting managers to focus on scouting, screening, and harvesting deals. Costs to the firm are further decreased, as these operations are typically borne by the fund, not the general partners. Thus, it is in any GP's interest to establish strong business systems.

While building the firm's brand is critical, establishing the underlying fabric of economics, ownership, and culture requires a diligent approach. For many first-time funds, the fundraising activity often commences prior to formal establishment of structures.

17

Raising Your First Fund

Among the various exotic forms of self-flagellation, raising the debut venture fund is high up on the torture scale. One VC described a fund raise as "crawling on all fours" and then he paused for effect ". . .on a steep uphill crawl" and finally topped it off with ". . .sprinkled with some broken glass." So if you can smile cheerfully, while crawling uphill, on broken glass, and live without a paycheck for two years, while investing your life savings in illiquid high-risk startups — this chapter is for you.

Financially, emotionally, or intellectually, the fundraising journey will test your timbre and mettle in every possible way — it does not get any worse. But if you can make it across the finish line, you can rest for a day. And then start the real work — multiply the capital by 3X in five years. Lindel Eakman manages fund investments for Foundry Group and has been investing in venture funds for 15 years. "My first question to anyone getting ready to raise their first fund is — are you sure you want to do this?" he asks. And my second question is, "Have you made enough money to risk two years of your life without any current income — to withstand this journey?" Indeed, as romantic and cool of a career as it may appear from the outside, the opportunity cost of raising a fund can be very high.

FIRST STEPS

To start with, a fund's investment strategy addresses these basic questions:

1. Where do you see untapped opportunities for investments?
2. Why are you best suited to generate superior returns?
3. Why now?

Untapped opportunities to generate returns can be found across various technology sectors, geographies, and stages of investments. But the other two questions fall harder on most fund managers. Superlatives abound aplenty. Overarching statements like "I have a maniacal focus on generating returns" have been used extensively, much to the chagrin of LPs. It calls for honest self-assessment, combined with intellectual rigor, objectivity, and willingness to accept that you could be fallible. Some entrepreneurs use their business background and relationship networks as a way to establish an edge. Angel investors show their track record to demonstrate their chops, as well as unique views of the market opportunity. Investment bankers bring their analytical views to show how they can find some hidden nuggets in the startup gold rush. There is really no formula or ideal profile that defines a winner.

On the softer side, the ability to build relationships with founders, compete for investment allocations in overheated rounds, take measured risk, understand trade-offs, generate financial returns consistently, and be able to work alongside driven CEOs, those smart type-A personalities, is an essential part of the business. "My goal is to pick an investment team that's aligned with a market opportunity, and has repeatable access to the right entrepreneurs," says Lindel. Chris Rizik is the CEO of Renaissance Venture Capital, a fund of funds with investments in over two dozen venture funds. "We see over 500 fund presentations each year — it is difficult for funds to truly differentiate and stand out in this noise. They all begin to sound the same after a while."

Strategy in venture firms is rarely unique, is ever evolving and opportunistic, and at times is developed to appease investors. We will address fund strategy in greater detail in other parts of this book.

TARGETING LPs

When Don Valentine, founder of Sequoia Capital, started his fundraising journey, he recalled, "We went to see a guy at Salomon Brothers, and he said, 'You know, I've listened to the pitch, but, you know, you didn't go to Harvard Business School.'" Valentine said, "Great observation. True. Guilty as charged. I went to *Fairchild Semiconductor* Business School. Great business school. Startup company. Pioneer in technology. Phenomenal leadership and recognition. I don't need to go to a business school for what I'm gonna do." He was rebuffed by this LP, but Valentine's father was a truck driver, and he had taught his son some tenacity. He did not give up and found his first LP in Southern California. Screening and targeting the right limited partners is no different from a sales process — you have a lead generation engine, qualification process, warm referrals, early adopters, and closing. And you are tenacious.

David Cohen, co-founder of Techstars global accelerator, has gone on to raise four venture funds. He warns, "You have pick the right LPs. If you sell to everyone, you can become overshopped and fatigued."

Two primary questions should drive the selection process: Are we a good fit for this LP? What value can we bring to them?

To screen for the LPs that matter, qualify them along these criteria:

- *Affinity for emerging managers.* While some funds of funds have dedicated emerging manager programs, others seek established managers. An LP who prefers the latter told me, "I don't like to see GPs who are still in kindergarten — they can call me after they cross Roman numeral IV," implying that funds that have a track record of four fund cycles.

- *Typical size of investment.* Institutional investors have no desire to create a large portfolio of small commitments. Each fund commitment requires time and effort to diligently manage the relationship, creating an operational burden for the investor. To improve internal efficiency in managing their portfolios and generate their target returns, LPs often establish an average check size. These checks are typically no more than 15 percent of any fund. A $50 billion pension fund may have to spend a lot of time and resources to invest $10 million. And worse, even if that $10 million investment in your fund were to generate a 3X outcome after 10 years, the $30 million does not move the needle for them. Typical investment size for such a pension fund would be $50 million or higher. Further, LPs often have a ceiling of, say, 15–20 percent commitment of the total fund size. If a $50 million fund were to approach a large pension fund, the 20 percent commitment threshold caps them at $10 million, which is too small a check for the pension fund. It's a classic Catch-22 situation, best avoided. The starting qualifier ought to be — what is the average check size of your commitment? If it's more than 20 percent of your fund size, it's not a good fit. Kimon G. Pandapas, member of the Global Investment Team at MIT Investment Management Company, says, "It's not possible to time venture or size in and out of venture firms. Demand to be in the best firms, like Sequoia, is high, so if you pass on a fund, you're unlikely to get back in. Investing through cycles is part of it. We are playing the long game."

- *Affinity for sector and stage of investments.* Does this LP typically invest in sector/stage/geography of your fund? Some LPs have found middle-market buyout to be a suitable strategy; conversely, others have found early-stage venture to be appropriate. Is the LP looking to build a portfolio of technology funds? Or are they in a maintenance mode?

- *Timing*. Are they investing in VC funds currently? Do they have an allocation available? When do they plan for their yearly allocations? GPs are often surprised to hear that most LPs plan their annual allocations at least six to nine months in advance. The sales cycles are long and opaque. A beleaguered LP told me, "We have many GPs who expect to walk out with a check after one meeting. My response to them is a polite version of — not tonight darling, I have a headache."

- *Current portfolio*. Are they planning on re-upping with existing funds? Or bring on new funds in their portfolio? This is another area most GPs ignore — adding a new relationship means a lot of work for LPs, not to mention additional risk. Re-upping in an existing relationship in a high-performing fund is a lot easier for any LP.

- *Past investment activity*. Has the target LP invested in similar funds? What are the average amounts? If an LP has not invested in this asset class, be prepared to spend inordinate amount of time in a long education process. And frequently, after you educate the potential LP, you might find that this LP has decided against investing in this VC asset class—or worse, to invest in another, likely better-performing fund.

- *Process*. Investment committees, votes, memos, diligence, reference calls to CEOs, co-investors, background checks . . . why do LPs take so long? Can't they just wire me the money after one meeting?

- *Decision timelines*. For some LPs, it is a few weeks — for others, it's a few years. One LP told me that they watch a fund manager complete an entire cycle (raising a fund, building a portfolio, exiting, and performance review), — that's a five-year dance. Are you prepared to date for a long, long time, only to hear a possible no?

- *Expectations*. What does the LP expect from this relationship? What constitutes a good partnership for them? How do they define success? Do they prefer co-investing? Ask them. Please.

If you are a new fund with no brand, limited track record and past performance, and raising in tough market conditions, the process can take up to 18 months.

In Exhibit 17.1 the LP outlay variation can be seen by size of funds. In any smaller, early-stage fund, the population of family offices and high-net-worth individuals is significantly large.

When it comes to fundraising, the top-quartile established venture firms have no problem raising money — they have a first-world problem of cutting down the demand for LPs to meaningful allocations. In the brief fundraising window, the problem of excessive LP demand prevails — how to choose from all those LPs kicking down the doors and ensure that an appropriate share is allocated to each LP, when everyone wants more. This is the classic first-world problem every GP dreams of.

Recall that larger LPs, who typically have billions in assets under management, would be underwhelmed with a tiny share of a top-quartile fund. Even if the top-quartile fund doubles its invested capital in 10 years, the overall impact on the pension fund returns would be minimal. A drop in the bucket doubles to two drops — still a minor trickle in a large pool.

Exhibit 17.1 **LP outlay varies by type of fund.**

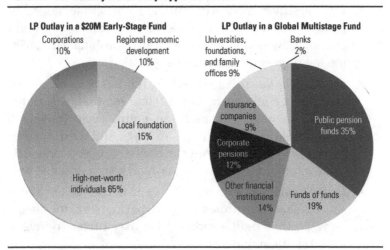

LP Outlay in a $20M Early-Stage Fund

- Corporations 10%
- Regional economic development 10%
- Local foundation 15%
- High-net-worth individuals 65%

LP Outlay in a Global Multistage Fund

- Universities, foundations, and family offices 9%
- Banks 2%
- Insurance companies 9%
- Corporate pensions 12%
- Public pension funds 35%
- Other financial institutions 14%
- Funds of funds 19%

When funds reach that top-quartile hot fund stature, the fund-raising cycles become shorter and shorter as existing LPs tend to stay put and the new LPs compete to get in. Leading funds have no LP churn. On the other hand, several subpar or below-average firms are able to sucker in newer LPs at every fund-raising cycle.

MARKET TIMING

Institutional investors are often wary of new market opportunities and move slowly and cautiously. Market timing is critical when it comes to fundraising. Investors are quick to point out that "Why should I invest in your fund?" is not a question that is as important as "Why should I invest in your fund *now*? How is your investment strategy relevant in the present market conditions?"

"LPs often adopt a market-driven and opportunistic approach within their portfolio architecture,"[1] remarks Christophe Nicolas, executive director, Morgan Stanley Alternative Investment Partners, a fund of funds. Exhibit 17.2 shows how various sub-asset classes within private equity compete for investor capital.

If the institutional investors seek to rebalance their portfolios or reduce their commitments, it is likely that a fund manager may not have much traction in fundraising discussions. "We have exited our relationships on several occasions when we are overweighted in certain categories. At times, we find that the number of relationships cannot be monitored effectively," says Kenneth Van Heel. On other occasions, fund managers tend to be highly opportunistic in timing the raise of a new fund. "I get a chuckle when I receive new fund documents right after a big exit has occurred. The performance looks fantastic, but most of us look past the short-term good news," quips one institutional investor.

For any fund manager getting ready to raise his or her next fund, market timing is important but the amplitude of these shifts

Exhibit 17.2 **What's hot and what's not — LP view of opportunities.**

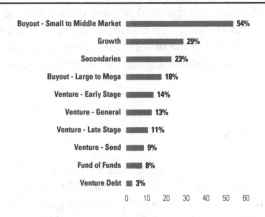

Source: Adapted from, PREQIN INVESTOR OUTLOOK: ALTERNATIVE ASSETS, H1 2019.

must be closely timed with LP sentiment. Successful fundraising is tied to performance as well as macro market conditions.

FIT WITHIN THE LP's CURRENT PORTFOLIO

Any institutional investor manages a number of portfolio relationships. Capital is allocated in various asset classes to balance risk and returns. In *Beyond the J Curve: Managing a Portfolio of Venture Capital and Private Equity Funds*, authors Thomas Meyer and Pierre-Yves Mathonet point out that institutional LPs typically follow a top-down or a bottom-up approach, or a combination of the two.[2] In a top-down approach, an LP would start with picking a sector (technology or life sciences), geographic region (Silicon Valley, Beijing, Israel), and stage (early, growth, multistage).

A bottom-up approach is opportunistic and starts with identifying suitable funds, conducting a thorough analysis, performing due diligence, and completing the investment.

Most LPs tend to blend these two approaches. "We look at every prospective deal in two ways: first in isolation, to see that it stands on its own merits; and second, we see how the deal fits in the context of our existing portfolio. We obviously do not want to load the portfolio with a lot of [GPs] pursuing the same strategy, but there are areas where we are actively seeking greater levels of exposure," says Peter Keehn, head of alternative investments, Allstate Investments, managing $120 billion in assets.[3]

The chain of relationships is vast and intricate, as seen in Exhibit 17.3; thus, any GP ought to qualify a target LP vis-à-vis his or her current portfolio. While no LP publicly discloses a portfolio, one LP suggests a simple approach: "We are trying to build our relationships, like everyone else. If I get an email asking whether we are looking to invest in early-stage technology funds, I would have little hesitation in responding with candor."

A $50 billion state pension fund manager confessed that for the right fund manager, we can always make room. "We design our portfolio, but in general, we have always found room to accommodate a good opportunity. We have a top-down

Exhibit 17.3 **LP portfolio — much more than VC.**

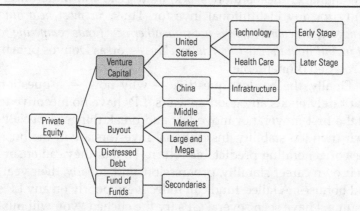

approach with subgroups within private equity such as venture, buyout, mezzanine, distressed debt, and growth equity.
When we add a new fund, my allocation moves from 9 percent
to 10 percent, so it does not make a significant difference. But if
we are overweighed in a sector, say, I have eight biotech funds,
we are not going to go for the ninth, obviously. We do watch
allocations within each subgroup to ensure we are balanced."

Chris Douvos uses a dinner table analog to help new
entrants understand the dynamics in any LP's portfolio: "All
my GPs are like my children: I love them all, but they all
keep me up at night for different reasons. But I have a limited
amount of money. At my dinner table, I can ladle out only so
much soup. If you want to come for dinner, I have to send one
kid off to college or juvenile hall — my table is a crowded one.
If you are doing the same old same old thing, it's not compelling. What is it about your voodoo that would make me send
one of my kids packing?"

Any institution invests a considerable amount of time in
building a portfolio of relationships.

"Investors have invested the effort, completed the due diligence, and committed to the marriage," says placement agent
Gus Long. The easier thing for any investor is to commit additional capital to an existing relationship, often called a re-up. A
new manager means more work, more risk, and more uncertainty for any institutional investor. Thus, *for most new fund
managers, the competition is not from other new funds competing to
get in, but from the existing relationships* — or, as Douvos puts it,
a crowded dinner table.

Finally, the hardest question — why now — a question
that rarely elicits any good answers. LPs have no incentive to
be the first-mover, nor move fast and break things, especially
their own job stability. Institutional investors are in the business of generating predictable returns so that they can ensure
their own career stability, progression, and, ideally, their year-
end bonuses. A failed fund can reflect very poorly on any LP's
resume. I have seen several GPs try the clichéd "you will miss
the train" pitch to create a rush and a sense of urgency, but
that's a flawed approach. No LP has ever jumped in, and many

have likely been turned off. For most LPs, there are plenty of fish in the sea. As one fund-of-funds manager told me, "Most GPs walk in thinking they are a special snowflake. They rarely do the homework to understand the competitive pool of managers, and their performance."

What should your LP universe look like? A healthy practice is often to target certain kinds of LPs because of the inherent advantages they offer. A healthy mix of fund of funds, foundations, family offices, and pension funds is ideal.

18

The Fundraising Roadshow

Roadshows — that humbling time for most VCs when they are not quite in charge, their ego is tamer, and no one feels omnipotent for those 12–18 months. For some, it's a walk in the park — though past performance may not guarantee future returns, it sure does guarantee short fundraising cycles. For the less fortunate ones, the roadshow turns out to be worse, a "shitshow," as one GP woefully described it.

OVERVIEW: THE FUNDRAISING PROCESS

The process begins with researching LP targets, developing a short list, kicking off the roadshow, and correcting course, as needed. See Exhibit 18.1.

Having a data room ready, with all the relevant fund documents (see Exhibit 18.2), can accelerate the fundraising process. Build a target list of investors, screen for a suitable fit, and get going. The journey is long and hard, and, unfortunately, the world of LPs has very few innovative and entrepreneurial thinkers who can take meaningful risks on emerging fund managers.

GETTING IN THE LP DOOR

Most institutional investors typically see anywhere from 200 to 600 funds each year. With such a high volume, the best way

Exhibit 18.1 **Fundraising process.**

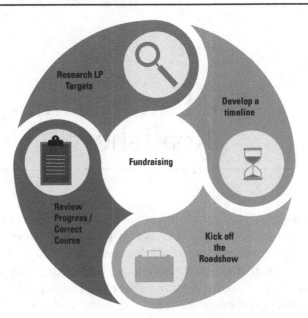

Exhibit 18.2 **Sample Data Room Folders.**

Topic	Remarks
Investor presentation	Fund pitch deck, which outlines the fund strategy, team, portfolio construction, and past performance
Team biographies	Include detailed resumes of each member of the investment team, advisory board members, operations (legal and finance)
Track record	Spreadsheets detailing investments, returns and cash flows, including returns (IRR, MOIC, TVPI, and DVPI)
Investment memos	Sample investment memo for any portfolio company, showcasing the analytical rigor, diligence, and return projections
References	List of (a) founders, (b) investors, and (c) industry thought leaders who can speak to the investment acumen of the team
Due diligence questionnaire	A detailed questionnaire (see Appendix for template) that addresses all relevant details of the fund in narrative form. Details that are included in the investor presentation are often presented here with more detail.
Legal documents	Limited partner agreement (LPA) and private placement memorandum (PPM), including summary of investment terms, fees, carried structure, waterfall, and key-man risks
Operations/Policies	Details relating to administration, tax, accounting, auditors, insurance, back-office systems Policies reacted to firm's approach on (a) valuation, (b) conflicts of interests, (c) insider trading, (d) diversity, (e) establishing healthy cybersecurity practices

to stand above the ambient noise is to begin a relationship through an introduction. Without a warm introduction, fund documents that come in the door often head for the trashcan. Institutional investors often like to take it slow and warm up to a new fund manager over time, cautiously observing the fund's evolution and performance. G. Thomas Doyal, managing director of global private equity investments for a family office, says, "We watch managers over several years and multiple investment cycles before we are ready to engage." Doyal, who sees about 50 fund documents each year, says, "It is very unusual for us to look at anything cold."[1]

To pave the way into a LP's door, a trusted relationship, ideally another peer-level investor, an existing GP within the LPs current portfolio, or an attorney with proven credentials can make this entry path much easier. An inappropriate starting point could blow up this process very quickly. State pension fund managers often get calls from politicians, including the governor's office, gently suggesting to look at a fund. Such pressure tactics, despite stellar performance, are unlikely to yield a positive outcome, and such managers often start with a deficit.

Getting in the door is the hard part, but the process from screening, to diligence and final decisions often takes up to six months, possibly longer. Once you get in, make sure the presentation is executed flawlessly. GPs should start the meetings by asking how the LP would like to best use the allotted time. Rarely do LPs want to sit through a monologue. Let the LPs review the deck ahead of time, and make it a conversation.

"A GP should approach the LP exactly the same way they want an entrepreneur to approach them. I have been surprised how few GPs can actually eat their own cooking when it comes to making presentations," says Chris Rizik. GPs should consider approaching LPs from a customer-centric view: the LPs should clearly see the benefit in investing in you. He laments, "VCs demand superior pitch skills of their portfolio CEOs but GPs seldom approach LPs with a clear fund value proposition. If a GP can make it in the interest of that LP, they may actually want to invest in the fund. This simple perspective seems to be lost on a fair number of GPs," says Rizik, who raised two venture funds as a GP and now manages Renaissance Venture Capital Fund, a fund of funds.

Really, that is your elevator pitch! That is a common reaction after LPs have suffered lengthy, boring presentations where GPs get into self-aggrandizing mode. Slide after slide of ennui where GPs get into "and let me tell you about this company . . ." mode has caused many LPs to wring their hands.

LP Pitch Guidelines: Don't Fall Asleep or Appear Bored

LPs shared top-10 Dos/Don'ts for fund managers when meeting with potential investors. Make sure you follow these:

- Don't stretch a meeting to longer than 90 minutes. The sale is not made in the first meeting.
- Don't use superlatives in self-description.
- Don't just address the older members of your audience.
- Don't direct the first female in the room to "get you a cup of coffee with milk and sugar." That female could be the decision maker.
- Don't be late.
- Do make sure that no one on your team falls asleep or appears bored during the presentation.
- Do be as transparent as possible about your successes and nonsuccesses (aka failures). Take appropriate credit for both sides of the equation.
- Do exhibit a sincere passion for what you do. Make it seem like you'd still come into work every day, even if you didn't have carry.
- Do ask about the LP's investment program and approach. And appear interested in it.
- Do be clear about what you won't invest in and why. It's okay to have skepticism/self-regulation about areas outside your expertise.[2]

If given a chance to present your pitch, drink your own Kool-Aid. Remember when you chastised entrepreneurs about their presentations being long-winded and off point? Your pitch should be no more than a dozen slides and 15 minutes. This is so basic, but rarely happens.

A lengthy 40-slide presentation, macro trends, and off-point information will not further your cause. Having lived the life on the other side as a VC, Chris is sympathetic about the challenges faced by any GP. Some pitch decks are as lengthy as 60 pages, which make LPs "want to get out of this meeting." Firms shouldn't just stick to the pitchbook during meetings, he says. "Try to get off the scripted stories and the pitchbook. I love that."[3]

Igor Rozenblit adds, "The goal of the meeting is for the LP to collect information from the GP. The GPs should not spend time telling us about their value-add to the portfolio. *In my opinion, most LPs do not believe that GPs add any value; thus, GPs are better off focusing the time on answering LP questions during the meeting.*"

Do You Need Placement Agents?

Placement agents not only advise venture capital funds seeking to raise a new fund but also broker much of the crucial interaction with institutional investors and key players in the private equity community. Expanding the investor base and accelerating fundraising efforts, placement agents often act as advisors and sounding board. Emerging managers as well as more established firms look to placement agents to gain access to new institutional investors and to streamline the logistics of the fund-raising operations. Beyond opening new doors for funds, agents also influence fund terms and offer advice on market terms and conditions.

According to Preqin surveys, as many as 77 percent of funds utilize the services of a placement agent, 63 percent of which have exceeded their original target size.[4] Even though the best funds don't need placement agents, across the board, institutional investors prefer to interact with placement agents.

A few reputed agents are able to build a matrix of institutional investor relationships and reduce the friction in the process as well. Igor Rozenblit, who led fund investments on behalf of a $2.5 billion European financial services company, says, "Many venture fund managers would not bother to do a primary assessment of our investment criteria and send us completely irrelevant fund memorandums. These would land in the dustbin quickly." Other institutional investors agreed. Edgar adds, "We get fund memorandums from all over the world — China, India, Brazil — and a lot of these are not even relevant, nor fit within our strategy."

Several institutional investors highlighted the role of a placement agent as being critical in the sourcing process. A placement agent brings expertise and a set of relationships, along with knowledge of market trends. These minimize the friction any fund manager may face while raising a fund.

Good placement agents are inundated with solicitations and are highly selective of engagements. For the right fund, placement agents will risk their reputation and invest significant time with the expectation of getting paid after the fund is closed. Kelly DePonte, partner with Probitas Partners, a leading placement agency, says, "I review 600-plus placement memorandums in any given year, and barely a handful will make the cut." DePonte's perspective comes from his interactions with leading institutional investors across the world who make multibillion-dollar decisions. Augustine "Gus" Long, partner at Stanwich Advisors, points out that a good placement agent functions as a proxy institutional investor. "If we cannot gather enough confidence and comfort in the fund manager, we do not engage," remarks Long, who managed a $1 billion fund of funds (FoF) prior to joining Stanwich Advisors. Rozenblit concurs that a good agent can make a significant impact for the right firm: "The top venture firms do not need agents, and on the other end of the spectrum, there are firms that are so bad that even a placement agent will refuse to touch them. There can be a few good venture firms in the middle who can benefit from placement agents." Thus, emerging managers with some demonstrated track record, and a compelling strategy, ought to consider whether a Kelly or a Gus can make the uphill task easier.

Investment banks like Credit Suisse and UBS have divisions that offer placement agent services. These global entities, operating from many offices with dedicated staff handling multiple accounts for their private equity customers, can access a larger pool of investors quickly. In addition to investment banks, there are also other global investment placement and advisory firms that focus on providing placement agent service. Unlike investment banks, however, these large independent entities often work exclusively as placement agents. Smaller boutique independent firms also provide placement services, often focusing on a sector or geographical niche (e.g., the Middle East) or a select circle of investors. They may also specialize in specific types of funds (e.g., funds of funds and venture capital funds). "The big houses like Credit Suisse or UBS typically send institutional investors a book of deals in the market. You can pick a few and ask for more details. The good placement agents research extensively and listen carefully. More so, even before they sign up a client, they know who they will market it to," says an investment fund manager, working with a $50 billion pension fund.

The right placement agent can make a significant impact during the fund raising process by providing insights in market trends, identifying key relationships in institutional investor universe, and refining the strategy/pitch materials. Gus said, "We spend a tremendous amount of time getting fund materials ready, presentations and rehearsals to ensure consistency of communication. Getting an hour with a leading institutional investor is difficult, but when you do get it, we make sure that the fund manager can make the best use of it."

Kelly DePonte points out the critical roles that a placement agent plays in supporting venture capital funds:

- *Market intelligence and social capital.* Placement agents offer connections and a solid base of contacts for their clients, but they are much more than a glorified Rolodex or phone book of investors. Rather than serving as a static database of names for private equity funds, the best placement agents are aggressive trackers, watching the shifts in personnel, sniffing out sector trends, and monitoring investment appetite in the allocations of private equity. In hiring placement agents, funds gain more efficiency in their fundraising efforts by benefiting from the agents' targeted approach rather than by relying on shallow leads and marketing plans.[5] Agents keep a constant check on the pulse of the market, honing long-term insight and an instinctual know-how on what relationships work or don't work. Placement agents also provide access to new investors and sources of capital. As one fund manager pointed out, when trying to raise a larger fund, you have to talk to new investors — strangers — and a placement agent can simplify this process.

- *A guide on fund terms and trends.* Finally, placement agents offer value to venture capital firms by keeping fund managers informed about fund terms and conditions before going to market. Agents are aware of institutional investor demands on economic and legal trends such as distribution waterfalls, no-fault divorce, clawback provisions, and more. From their interactions with investors, placement agents can predict how the investment market will react to fund terms and conditions, as well as adapt to shifting economic and governance provisions. Venture capital fund managers should look for placement agents who can appropriately address the market to your fund type. Agents focusing on international funds can seldom assist a seed-stage fund. Besides possessing insights of the LP community, agents often share their expertise in due diligence. On the other side of the coin, as institutional investors become increasingly selective about the funds they invest in, the placement agent's role becomes more critical than ever in smoothing communication and managing process between general and limited partners, particularly for emerging funds. Though many limited partners want to invest in safe bets and brand-name

Let Me Help You Help Yourself

Placement agents allow fund managers to "focus on [their] core competency — deal making." Placement agents save a fund from being distracted on the lengthy and painful process of fundraising — a necessary but often periodic step. "You only raise funds every four, five, six years, [so] you can't do it as well as a professional," said Doug Newhouse, whose fund was oversubscribed.

Placement agents are key strategists in determining the details of a fundraising campaign, such as a target fund size, investor expectations on staffing and professional backgrounds, selection of the right legal team, and other launch details that might be overlooked, even by more experienced fund managers or fund managers overseeing multiple funds. They also play an indomitable role in marketing, giving advice on putting together a scalable mix of investors who not only are willing to commit but also have the resources to do so given a difficult market. With their close contacts, they often have a better sense of the investor market than does a venture capital fund manager. Also, in taking a lead negotiator role in interfacing with investors, placement agents can advise on the right timing for a launch by gauging the strengths and handicaps of investors. More importantly, placement agents can sustain the momentum in a marketing or fundraising campaign. By moving swiftly in these areas, a fund is brought to a close much faster and avoids languishing and being dubbed unimportant or irrelevant by investors faced with a wide range of opportunities.

Gus Long said, "The fund-raise process is a step function — the objective of the first meeting is not to get signed subscription documents — the objective is to get to the next step, which is on site for due diligence. For some institutional investors, it's three steps, and for some it's 20 steps — but you have to be ready at every step. A qualified team without the right form and delivery can kill the investment. There are groups that should get funded but do not because they cannot communicate their story effectively . . . that part of our preparation process is often painful, but that's where we make the biggest impact."[6]

funds, they are also willing to invest in new funds if an accomplished placement agent brokers the deal. Placement agents are particularly supportive of new venture capital funds run by managers with a strong track record. Igor Rozenblit, who represented a $2.5 billion European financial services company seeking investments in venture capital and private equity funds, would frequently interact with some of the top placement agents such as UBS, Credit Suisse, Lazard, and Park Hill. He says: *"Some fund managers may not be good at exaggeration, but the placement agents are gifted at it.* Placement agents would usually puff things up — and the top worn-out clichés of placement agents ignored by most institutions include statements like, *'We have soft-circled about two-thirds of the fund . . .* or *this is the hottest fund to date'* . . . and the best one *'It's going to be oversubscribed — we are closing tomorrow.'"* Rozenblit quipped that agents who are too slick can hurt the fund, or lose credibility for both parties. "In one case, we closed one month after *the final close* — the agent was not happy."

LOCKING YOUR ANCHOR INVESTOR

A good lead (or an anchor) investor can act as a source of other introductions, be a powerful reference, and greatly improve your chances of raising the fund. GPs should focus their early efforts on attracting such a kingmaker. But finding someone who will take a leap of faith is not easy.

Once a lead investor has committed, the GPs ought to continue to attract those fast followers, and finally those laggards, who will come in days before the final close. The only proven way to attract these is to communicate effectively.

Consider ARCH Venture Partners' ability to find a lead investor for their Fund I. On a Saturday afternoon, Steve Lazarus, founder of ARCH, was able to pitch a vice chairman of an insurance company. This potential LP took a break during his tennis game and committed $4 million by the end of the hour-long meeting. "I had my nut, and from that point the money rolled in," Lazarus would say.[7] ARCH raised $9 million for its Fund I. Newer funds are better suited in targeting a larger number of smaller investors, such as high-net-worth individuals and family offices.

Look for an anchor investor — an entity that will commit at least 10% of the total fund, possibly even 20% — and be the first mover. In the world of institutional investors, every entity is competing to be a fast follower. The first mover has to do some serious heavy lifting, similar to a lead investor in a startup. The diligence process often takes four to six months, depending on the complexity.

Snagging That Lead Investor: Lessons from Dick Kramlich, Founder of New Enterprise Associates (NEA)

LP: "So, let me get this straight. You're talking about us putting up a million dollars, right?"
Kramlich: "Yes, sir."
LP: "You're talking about not telling us how you're going to invest it, is that right?"
Kramlich: "Yes, sir, that's correct."
LP: "And you're telling me this money is going to be illiquid for 12 years, is that right?"
Kramlich: "That's correct."
LP: "You're telling me, you all, as a group, have no track record, and you're not promising any rate of return, is that right?"
Kramlich: "Yes, sir, that's right."

"So finally, this LP says, "Well, if you all feel comfortable taking the risk, I'll support you."

This LP invested $1 million in NEA Fund I, which was ~$16 million in size.[8]

SELL, SELL, SELL

A good VC is a salesman at heart. First you sell your vision for your fund to potential limited partners. Once you raise a fund, you have to then sell your intangible value-creation skills to an entrepreneur, so that they take your money over other competitive investors. And then, after you invest in portfolio companies, you have to sell those companies to customers, potential employees, and acquirers. A salesman is often misconstrued to be the likes of a used-car peddler — slick, fast-talking, and nimble-fingered, leaving you stuck with a product you never wanted. A VC as a salesman is more intellectually driven, uses data, market knowledge, and competitive dynamics to understand the landscape. Having strong persuasive skills is a must, so is tenacity and a never-give-up attitude. A good VC can push appropriately, understand the decision-making process, timelines, and find all the touchpoints and triggers that would lead to a favorable decision. At the same time, be willing to walk away from anyone that is spinning you around in infinite loops without any clarity or confidence.

The process of managing multiple LP relationships effectively and leading these to a close is fraught with uncertainties and challenges. GPs who were successful pointed out that they followed some simple guidelines:

- *Communicate.* Any potential investors with whom you met would like to know how you are progressing with your fundraising efforts. A steady flow of meaningful communication, timely but not excessive overload, can help a GP to gain ongoing mindshare with LPs.

- *Create momentum.* The ability to create momentum with LPs is an art form, akin to rolling a snowball downhill and making sure that it arrives at its destination in one piece. Tying momentum and communication together, an example could be, "In the past 90 days, we have added commitments of an additional $10 million, raising our total commitments to $25 million. These commitments include a family office, several HNWIs, and a strategic corporate investor."

When Liam Donohue, co-founder and managing director of .406 Ventures, was raising Fund I, he successfully attracted $167 million in the tough economic environment. "About 90 percent of our fund was raised from institutions. It took one year to get it done from first close, 18 months from start to finish. LPs tested us at every step. We were politely persistent and created momentum. It is a lot of work and not for the faint of heart," he says. After 10 years, .406 Ventures has raised four funds and has over $650 million under management.

Maybe You Are Just Not Ready for Venture Capital . . .

When a potential LP is indecisive, drags their feet, and is firmly perched on a fence, how do you convince them to take the leap? "Maybe you're just not ready for venture capital," William Draper III told a potential LP, debating over a $10 million commitment.

"Oh, no, no, no," the LP said. So all of a sudden, the cards turned and he signed it.

The LP committed, although Draper Gaither Anderson did not ever invest the entire $10 million. They invested $6 million and returned ~$750 million to their happy investors.[9]

LPs often struggle with the same challenges that most VCs do — speed, decision-making, communication, and responsiveness. In Exhibit 18.3, we list some common challenges that GPs encounter in fundraising.

GPs cannot do much in managing LP behavioral challenges except grin and bear it. Some move on. Others endure the nausea-inducing roller coaster ride.

Exhibit 18.3 **GPs view of LP Behavioral Challenges.**

Challenge	Manifestation
Engagement	Lack of responsiveness to emails and calls. Unclear if they are open for business, interested, busy, or just lazy. No clarity on fit or timing. GPs are often shooting in the dark.
Process	Diligence can be formulaic, cumbersome, and heavy. One solo GP pointed out that his previous fund was $5m, and I was raising a small $25m fund, but got "*a 60-fucking-page-long due diligence questionnaire*". "They asked for a PPM when all I had was a deck. I mean, they could have just told me to go away instead". Diligence might be initiated but drags on forever. No clarity on next steps, timing, and decision-making process. As one fund manager pointed out, "After six months of diligence, the LP vanished. We cannot do anything but grin and bear it, as we may need them in our next fund."
Decision-Making	"No sense of urgency. Slowed down closing just because they could. Did not respect our timelines." "One of our existing LPs took six months to let us know they would not come in for our next fund. It hurt us significantly and drastically slowed down our close timing. LPs have no accountability and behave carelessly when it comes to treating GPs." – GP on Fund III
Overall	"LPs lack creativity, speed, and decisiveness. They are worried about career risk and capital/self-preservation. We seek the very opposite qualities in our founders. As a GP, sitting between these two sides is schizophrenic, and has been my biggest challenge in the VC business" — anonymous GP

SHOULD YOU WAREHOUSE PORTFOLIO COMPANIES?

Chris Douvos, managing director of Ahoy Capital, a Silicon Valley–based fund of funds, has been investing in venture funds for two decades. One of the pioneers of the micro VC movements, Douvos is a rare LP who can quote Walt Whitman, Shakespeare, and Heraclitus while discussing IRR, MOIC, and TVPI. "Having a strategy is a good start, and a team that aligns with the strategy is even better. But what I'd love to see is your strategy in action," he says. There is no other "proof of concept," indeed, than to put your money where your mouth is, and show a portfolio in creation. Building an initial portfolio demonstrates:

- Sourcing abilities — you can find the right companies.
- Ability to structure the right transaction — did you pay the right price?

- Your ability to win — not only can you find good companies, but you can get a seat at a crowded cap table and win an entry into a hot company. If the hot company has brand-name co-investors, it often acts as an advantage and (superficially) validates your picking abilities. I have seen fund managers warehouse as many as four to six companies as they start their fund raise. It is not important to write significantly large checks (by all means, do so if you can), but it's more so a demonstration of your ability to put the strategy in motion.

Finally, one of the subtle advantages of a warehoused portfolio is that, as you continue your fund raise, some of these companies are likely to step up in value. Some bargain hunters can get enticed to invest in your fund, as they will appreciate an "immediate" step up in value, albeit on paper.

YOUR BIGGEST FUNDRAISING RISKS, AND HOW TO MANAGE THEM

For every fund that crosses the finish line, there are three that die along the way. The story goes like this — a group of spectacularly accomplished individuals facing mid-life crisis, boredom, unexpected large inflows of free cash flows, or other first-world challenges team up and decide to dabble. After all, venture capital has all the right ingredients to bring about the enviable level of attention at a wine gathering. Its social cachet is strong. Funds that get started off with a whiff of boredom rarely make it — the ones that get started by hungry, driven individuals who have a chip on their shoulder often make it past the finish line. They are out to prove their chops in this world and are the unstoppable ones. Funds die due to many reasons, but the most frequent reasons are listed in Exhibit 18.4.

Of the many funds that have struggled, some have gone out in epic flameouts, complete with trumpets blaring. Others have recovered to find a new day.

Exhibit 18.4 **Key Risks in Fund Raise.**

Risk	Remarks
Team falls apart	Most partnerships disintegrate due to lack of endurance, alignment, or emotional compatibility. Cohesion of team is one of the biggest challenges in the 18- to 24-month fund-raise journey. An investment team member may decide to shift gears and chase a lucrative current income opportunity. Or members could be misaligned in their distribution of roles, responsibilities, and share of carried interests. Often, strong personalities are unable to build a mutually respectable working relationship, due to constant bickering and political drama.
Unproven team	Investment team members do not have an enviable track record, showing superior returns.
No anchor investor	A number of small commitments keep trickling in, but there is no significant commitment to make it across the finish line.
Inadequate financial buffer	Besides living without a paycheck for two years, managers often have to self-fund the warehoused portfolio companies, operating, legal, and travel expenses.
Market timing	The markets are driven by LPs' focus areas. If they choose to get excited by "middle-market buyout funds" or if macro events freeze LP allocations, not much can be done.
Fund strategy	Undifferentiated strategy follows me-too approach to investments. Lacks sourcing advantages. In some cases, fund size in not correlated with stage of investments.
Lack of focus	Fund managers try to do too many supplemental activities to stay afloat while fund raising. Several funds have fallen apart because managers consulted on the side, or even acted as investment-bankers in a few cases. Fundraising demands 110% from you, and LPs can smell your conviction, or lack thereof.

Social Capital lost its investment team due to differing views on strategy. The two partners at XFund, a $100 million fund, got into a messy legal fight, calling each other names like "spiteful moron," leading to one founder being banished from USA. At Rothenberg Ventures, its founder Mike Rothenberg, who boasted of the twitter handle @VirtualGatsby was accused by SEC of defrauding his limited partners upward of $7 million by throwing lavish parties. The SEC also came knocking at Burrill Life Sciences, where over $4.5 million was spent on family vacations to nice summer resorts at St. Bart's and Paris.

19

Why LPs Seek First-Time Funds

"Our best investment ever was in a first-time fund." This remark by Sergey Sheshuryak of Adams Street Partners, a fund of funds, could well be the saving grace and sales pitch for every first-time fund manager. For most institutional investors and limited partners, an emerging manager — or a practitioner who has yet to demonstrate superior returns in a consistent fashion — is a huge risk. But for others, it is a great opportunity. Take the example of Steven Lazarus, founder of ARCH Venture Partners. When Lazarus started to raise ARCH Venture Partners Fund I, investors would say, "Your track record is all ahead of you."[1] Those investors threw Lazarus in the emerging manager box and dismissed him. ARCH Fund I celebrated four IPOs as well as four acquisitions and generated 22 percent internal rate of return (IRR).[2]

The changing industry offers new opportunities for investors to access investments outside the mainstream venture capital universe. For institutional investors, striking a balance between established fund managers and tilting (even slightly) in favor of emerging managers is increasingly becoming the norm. In building more mixed portfolios with funds managed by premier names, as well as funds managed by emerging managers, investors can build dynamic and diversified portfolios and ensure risk-adjusted returns over the long run. Eric Doppstadt, VP and CIO at Ford Foundation, says, "We rarely backed those who did not have a realized track record.

Today, we have to look at this universe with a somewhat different lens. We often ask, 'Why do founders want this investor on their board?' and, 'Do the best founders want this investor on their board?'" Kimon G. Pandapas, member of the Global Investment Team at MIT Investment Management Company, says, "We back firms with strong brands because brand drives deal flow. Top-tier firms like Sequoia Capital and Greylock have massive brands, which puts them on most founders' top five list. But the industry is constantly evolving, so we try to stay alert to emerging firms with distinct competitive advantages and the potential to develop dominant brands."

Several criteria are often used in identifying emerging managers. At one end of the spectrum, they may be "first-time fund, first-time investors" — a group of professionals who lack significant investment experience. They may also be a group of individuals who have experience but no track record working as a cohesive team. There could also be spin-offs of existing, more established funds. Partners who have raised money on a deal-by-deal basis and built their track records would be appropriate candidates for raising funds.

But limited partners (LPs) prefer experienced investors who have played the game well, or who bring some unique chops to the game. Christy Richardson, director of Private Investments at Hewlett Foundation, says, "We reach out to 50 fund managers each year and narrow down the funnel, adding one new manager every two years or so. The odds are steep. The one big criterion for us is, "Does the GP have access to the best deal flow? It's a ground war out there — can you win the best deals?"

As Gus Long of Stanwich Advisors points out, "First-time fund is acceptable, but not a first-time investor." As venture firms grow, partners who perform well run into incentive sharing and succession issues.[3] These issues may cause the stronger partners to split and form new firms, where they are in better control of their destiny, the brand, and the economics. Such investors are often well received due to their existing network and investment experience.

Finally, women or minorities who have been traditionally underrepresented are often dubbed as emerging. Emerging managers compensate for their perceived shortcomings in many ways, offering a unique edge for investors.

CREATIVITY, HUNGER, AND PERFORMANCE

Kelvin Liu of Invesco Private Capital, a fund of funds, writes that "since they do not have historic challenges of poor performance, they are able to pursue unique investment strategies."[4] As mavericks in the capital markets, they often have stronger motivations.

According to Hany Nada, cofounder of GGV, "When we started GGV-I, it was the aftermath of the dot-com crash in 2001 — one of the toughest periods to launch a new fund. Our compelling investment strategy was an important factor, but the only reason we made it during the tough economic times was because we were 'all-in' — a 110 percent commitment in making this fund successful. We had burnt all boats and there was no plan B. The LPs could sense this commitment."

As a result, they are more fiercely driven toward achieving high performance and results right out of the starting gate and evolve to be nimble in their decision-making. With entrepreneurial sensibilities, they often seize the market opportunities that their more established colleagues would balk at. In many ways, they run faster and have less to lose and more to gain from investing smarter than the bigger players.

Underdogs looking to prove themselves, they are often more flexible in working with investors, resulting in a greater alignment with investor interest. LPs and investors often take bigger percentage shares in their funds — larger than the typical 10 percent cap. Empowered, investors can then wield influence on decisions, terms, and fees.[5] "We don't mind being a disproportional part of the fund — in some cases we invested, say $5 million in a $40 million fund, and in others, we have about $19 million in a $50 million fund," says John Coelho of StepStone Group.[6]

Often, emerging managers integrate a different cultural mind set. Much more open, some share their views in blogs and live a transparent life. Their way of doing business makes their more established counterparts look downright prosaic and even backward.

The general misperception of emerging managers is that they lack the experience and track record. Within the institutional LP community, the perceived risks in investing in emerging managers are high, because these are perceived as ill-equipped, untested, and unseasoned neophytes. In essence, they were dismissed as minor league players in the world dominated by juggernauts.

All these qualities — smaller fund size, a taste for nontraditional investment strategy, drive, and innovation — are elevating emerging managers among those investors looking for a different path toward success.

RANKING EMERGING MANAGERS

Rarely does an LP make an investment decision solely on the fact that a general partner (GP) is emerging — it may get a GP's foot in the door, which is a good start. A pecking order, as seen in Exhibit 19.1, establishes the probability of raising an institutional fund.

The primary risk that any LP faces with emerging managers is career risk. After all, why would LPs risk the embarrassment of losing their capital (and their job) with an unproven manager? "It's a lot safer to invest in Fund V," says John Coelho of StepStone Group.[7] Factors that impact LP decisions include the following:

- Ability to distinguish between market hype and market reality
- Strong knowledge base/domain awareness
- Differentiators of the fund strategy
- Sustained differentiation: Barriers to entry from other competitive investors
- Team dynamics and cohesion

Exhibit 19.1 **Emerging managers — a pecking order.**

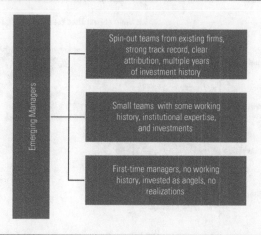

And the signal-to-noise ratio in this category is significant. "Over the past eight years, we have seen 1,100 emerging manager funds and have invested only in 36," says Amit Tiwari, director at Invesco Private Capital.[8] Some managers deliberately slot themselves in this "emerging" category to gain attention from LPs, a ploy that is not necessarily advantageous. After being hounded by one firm for too long, an LP acerbically commented: "You have been emerging for too long — just call me back when you have actually *emerged*!"

Emerging managers tend to be sought out by high-networth individuals (HNWIs) and family offices rather than by established institutional investors.[9]

Amidst the LP universe, funds of funds are more open to emerging managers and have specific mandates (see Exhibit 19.2). Major institutional investors, such as California Public Employees' Retirement System (CalPERS) and California State Teachers' Retirement System (CalSTRS) actively invest in emerging manager-led funds. The effort is dubbed as "building investment portfolios that tap into the changing demographics and talent emerging in California and the nation."[10] For investment authorities at CalPERS and CalSTRS, the decision enables beneficiaries to access an untapped and

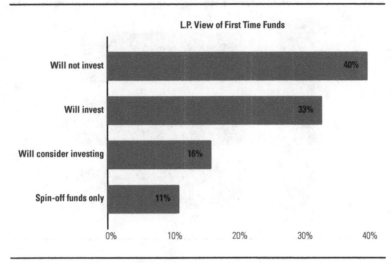

Exhibit 19.2 **LPs' preference for investing in first-time funds.**

Source: Adapted from, Private Equity & Venture Capital Spotlight, February 2017. Preqin Ltd.

dynamic market. A chief investment officer for CALPERS once noted that "it's easy to miss emerging firms that are still struggling to raise capital. . . . Most large firms started at the small end of the market and we want to find them on the small end of their asset class. Then we won't have to stand in line for their services on the big end later."[11]

In LP surveys, 42 percent of the world's top 100 LPs were open to considering first-time funds. In partnering with emerging managers, investors have touted many benefits — early access to industry leaders, gains from better returns, higher rates of proprietary deal flow, and a management focus on maximizing profits rather than on increasing assets under management.[12]

A FUTURES OPTION

Kenneth Smith, of Park Street Capital, says, "My primary approach to emerging managers is to identify those super-performers who will be hard to access in later funds."[13] Often hungrier, they have a passion for investing in new platforms or in emerging markets such as Brazil and China. Grove Street Advisors, a fund of funds (FoF), has developed a simple yet effective technique to build an emerging manager portfolio (see Exhibits 19.3 and 19.4): make small commitments and build up the position as the performance improves.

Exhibit 19.3 **Fund-of-funds allocation for an emerging manager portfolio.**

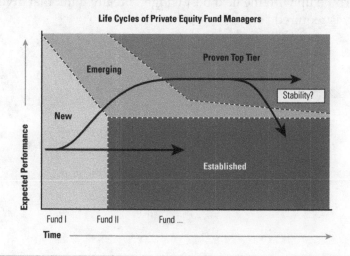

Source: Grove Street Advisors, "Case Study 1," May 10, 2001, accessed February 20, 2011, www.grovestreetadvisors.com/news/gsa_case_study_01.pdf.

Exhibit 19.4 **Concentrating capital with top performers.**

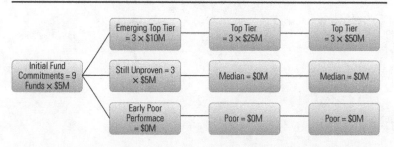

Source: Grove Street Advisors, "Case Study 1," May 10, 2001, accessed February 20, 2011, www.grovestreetadvisors.com/news/gsa_case_study_01.pdf.

Pension programs have demonstrated staunch support for minority representation among their emerging funds. Thus, the definition of emerging has expanded to include demographic factors as well as performance. CalPERS's alternative investment management (AIM) program explicitly states that its goal is to invest in women-owned or minority-owned funds. Kristine Brandt, director and CEO of Invesco Private Capital, said, "The economy is global, so you have to have a global mind set. . . . In order to build better companies, in order to come up with the next best widget, I really think that diversity is required."[14]

20

Sourcing Investment Opportunities

OVERVIEW: THE SOURCING PROCESS

"I give a lot more importance to sourcing, even more than the value-add claims of VCs," says Erik Lundberg, chief investment officer of University of Michigan Endowment.[1] While typical sources of investment opportunities lie embedded within the network for founders — the social fabric woven over time that yields consistent quality referrals — the future, as they say, is in data-driven sourcing.

Venture firm SignalFire has raised over $300 million as it built its investment thesis as a data-driven fund. It has developed a data platform, called Beacon, which tracks more than half a trillion data points. SignalFire is different from the average venture fund, says one of its LPs, Lance Cottrill, a partner with Horsley Bridge Partners. As an LP in venture firms such as Index Ventures, Benchmark, and Andreessen Horowitz, fund of funds Horsley Bridge has seen various investment strategies. It invested in SignalFire's maiden $50 million fund alongside 50 other tech and venture professionals. "It piqued our interest. This is software eating the venture model," Cottrill remarked.[2]

Chris Farmer, founder of SignalFire, who spent his early years at General Catalyst and Bessemer Securities, interviewed

500 founders and over 150 funds about the strengths and weaknesses of venture capital. As their platform, Beacon tracks more than 4 million companies, over 8.5 million engineers, and billions of anonymized US consumer financial tractions, SignalFire is able to bring unique insights in growth, hiring, and consumption patterns to their portfolio companies. Farmer says that the future of venture capital will be determined by data — the new oil in the venture landscape. "Most firms are not designed to, nor will be able to scale — or cross the chasm — the way we could. We are like an Uber when other firms are trying to be good taxi companies. Or think of how cloud computing changed the way we consumed technology at scale, antiquating the client-server model."

Similarly, Thomas Laffont, co-founder of Coatue Venture, who came into Venture from the hedge fund world, says, "Data are the future of business. It's an architectural divide, and you have to be on the right side."[3] Coatue has raised a $700 million early stage fund and spends more than $30 million a year buying data to feed its algorithms. It employs 40 data scientists and engineers — about half the team that works on investments. Though the investment universe gets hypercompetitive, it demands creativity in sourcing, hustle, and youthful vigor.

Investing without a data-driven proactive approach is inefficient, like shooting in the dark — you might see the target outlines, but you can miss the bull's-eye.

Google's venture capital arm has also been down this data driven path — it collects, collates, and analyzes data such as timing of launch of the venture, past success record of founders, and location of the venture, say, in tech hubs such as the San Francisco Bay Area. "If you can't measure and quantify it, how can you hope to start working on a solution?" asked Bill Maris, the former managing partner of Google Ventures. "We have access to the world's largest data sets you can imagine. It would be foolish to just go out and make gut investments." Intuition still plays a role in the investment decision and can sometimes overrule results suggested by data in such situations. "We would never make an investment in a founder we thought was a jerk, even if all the data said this is an investment you should make," says Bill. "We would make an investment in a founder we really believed in, even if all the data said we're making a mistake. But it would give us pause."[4]

The existing sourcing model, of working with entrepreneurs or trusted peer investors, brings about a steady stream of qualitative and reliable opportunities. But it has restrictions, say, to a geography or the size of your active network. Worse, such approaches can be reactive, and you could land on the opportunity when the round is almost done and be too late to the game. Chris Farmer says that you not only have to see the best opportunities but also win those effectively.

Other sources include incubators and accelerators, attorneys, angel networks, banks and nonbank financial institutions, and technology transfer offices. Exhibit 20.1 depicts the overall investment process, which commences with sourcing. Exhibit 20.1 outlines these options in more detail.

Any top-tier firm sees anywhere from 2,000 to 10,000 opportunities each year, and after sifting through this enormous pile, will invest in 10–15 companies. Studies conducted by academic researchers show typical sourcing statistics (Exhibits 20.2 and 20.3).[5] Note that as many as 51 percent of opportunities come from a mix of personal network and referrals.

Exhibit 20.1 **A venture fund's investment process.**

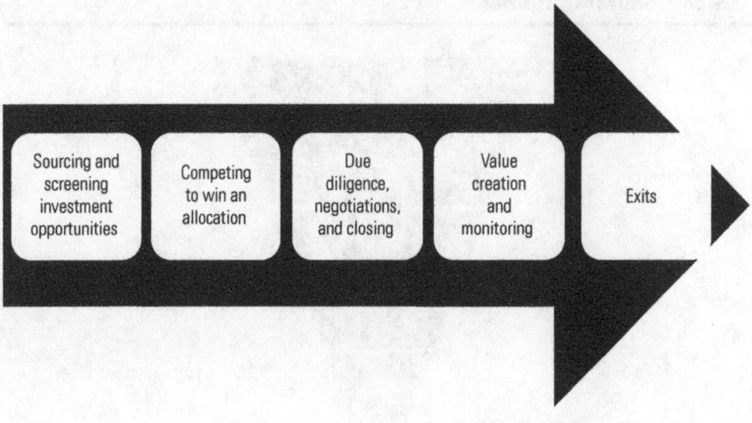

| Sourcing and screening investment opportunities | Competing to win an allocation | Due diligence, negotiations, and closing | Value creation and monitoring | Exits |

Exhibit 20.2 **Sources of investment opportunity.**

Source	Advantages	Disadvantages
Data-driven/ Proactive Sourcing	Preselected, highly targeted opportunity set.	Timing of capital raise may be off, not all data are publicly available so some signals may get lost, or overstated.
Network/Peer investors	Speedier due diligence in trusted relationships.	*Caveat emptor* — struggling opportunities can be upsold.
Accelerators and incubators/demo-days	Large volume of vetted opportunities. Best suited for seed and early stage investors.	Overcrowding — the best startups are funded prior to demo-days. For some startups, valuation can get inflated very quickly.
Serial entrepreneurs	Well-vetted ideas, better understanding of investor mind-set, recognition of challenges.	May not have any skin in the game.
Business plan competitions and venture forums	Prescreened and vetted, this may be a good source of opportunities for early-stage investors.	Nonexclusive; watch for overshopped companies.
University tech transfer offices, federal research labs	Diamond in the rough! May need to invest time to build the business strategy and team.	Watch for technology in search of an application, or a hammer in search of a nail.
Corporate spinouts	Potential for joint development, co-investments	Market size may be limited. Patents may have limited shelf life.
Attorneys, accountants, and consultants	Can provide some level of prescreening based on fund criteria and fit.	Lack of technical of business depth.
Banks/venture debt providers	Can mitigate risk; may have skin in the game.	Senior lenders have first lien on assets.

Exhibit 20.3 **Sourcing funnel.**

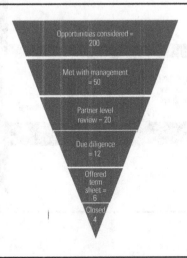

Exhibit 20.4 **Sourcing channels.**

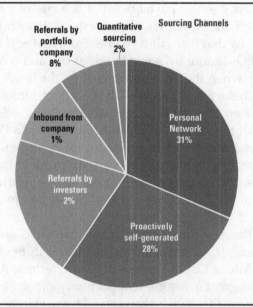

Source: Data from Gompers, Paul A., William Gornall, Steven N. Kaplan, and Ilya A. Strebulaev. "How Do Venture Capitalists Make Decisions?" NBER Working Paper Series, No. 22587, September 2016.

PROACTIVE SOURCING

Though cold calling might be the most painful part of any analyst's job, it is now an essential mechanism to source opportunities in hypercompetitive markets. "I had barely started, but we were expected to cold call and source at least 25 opportunities each month," says an analyst at a leading Silicon Valley multistage venture fund. Though some firms have found cold calling to be tactically advantageous, others have relied primarily upon their networks.

Though Exhibit 20.4 shows as many as 28 percent of opportunities are proactively self-generated, most practitioners I talked to did not share stellar examples of opportunities sourced as a result of cold calls. I'm sure there are a few winners here and there. Some complained that the process is riddled with inefficiencies. In fact, many shrugged their shoulders, and one muttered, "I just need to make my quota of calls . . . my senior partners say it is a rite of passage and builds my character, but it's just a waste of time and hurts our brand. I know that if anything comes from it, it will be a stroke of luck. CEOs ignore us, some laugh us off, and others ask us to call back when the senior partner is on the line." Not much difference in the past 50 years — in 1962, Pitch Johnson and Bill Draper put up all their personal savings, launched a partnership, and hit the streets. "Pitch and I each leased a Pontiac and went around and knocked on doors. And if it sounded like ABC Electronics, then we'd go in, ask the president to sit down and tell us, 'What do you do?' And they would ask, 'Well, what do you do?' 'Well, we are venture capital investors,' we would say."[6]

But at times, a proactive approach can yield serious gold. Kevin Efrusy of Accel Partners was ranked in the top five of the *Forbes* Midas List of venture capital investors. After all, he sourced this great investment opportunity called Facebook for Accel Partners. Efrusy, who had served two separate stints as an entrepreneur-in-residence at Kleiner Perkins Caufield & Byers (KPCB), had joined Accel with the primary directive — find the next big thing in social startups. While Efrusy was on the hunt, he found his target two years into his career at Accel. Chi-Hua Chien, a graduate student doing research for Accel, pointed out this opportunity called Facebook to Efrusy, who never gave up until he trapped this elusive beast. "Social networks had this dirty name," he said in *The Facebook Effect*.[7] Facebook had over 20 competitors when it was launched. Efrusy called and e-mailed the startup relentlessly — and was stonewalled or turned down. "We will move heaven and earth to make this a successful company," Efrusy once told Mark Zuckerberg. But Facebook was not interested in talking to venture capitalists. "He was hounding us," one Facebook executive would recall. Finally, Efrusy decided to walk over to Facebook's offices and entered a chaotic scene, where remnants of the previous night's liquor party were strewn all over. One person, struggling to assemble a do-it-yourself (DIY) table, had blood oozing from his forehead. Efrusy promised Zuckerberg, who was nibbling on a burrito, "Come to our partners' meeting on Monday. We'll give you a term sheet by the end of the day, or you'll never hear from us again." Over the weekend, Efrusy did some intense calling around to find out more about the Facebook phenomenon. On Monday morning at 10 a.m., Zuckerberg, wearing his flip-flops, shorts, and a T-shirt, showed up at Accel's offices with two cohorts. They didn't bother bringing any slides. Five days later, after much song and dance and pleading, Accel had closed on a $12.7 million investment at a $100 million pre-money valuation, owning a 15 percent stake in Facebook. Efrusy did not get a board seat. "It hurt my feelings," he would say, "But I understand."

Efrusy displays all attributes essential to source a good investment opportunity: rapid assessment, proactive contact, and a hunter-like tenacity. But it is not just Efrusy's qualities that count — the brand of the venture firm matters. James R. Swartz, founder of Accel Partners, speaking prophetically of investing in new technological waves, once said, "The older generation . . . better just get the heck outta the way, or if you want to stay in the game, get a kid and let him do his thing."[8] Little did Swartz know that this Efrusy kid was already at work, sourcing the next big thing for Accel. Hany Nada, cofounder of GGV, a venture fund boasting of investments in Chinese giants like Alibaba, agrees. "I find that it is better to bring in the newer generation — they understand emerging technology trends better than I do."

Sourcing requires hustle, especially in the ever-competitive investment world. But what if you find a good company and the round is closed? How can you creatively get in? When Kevin Rose found out that mobile payments company Square was raising a round, he reached out to Jack Dorsey, cofounder of Square and Twitter. But the investment round was full, and Jack politely declined, saying Square didn't need any more investors. Kevin noticed that Square did not have a video demonstration of the product and quickly put together a video and showed it to Jack. Impressed, Jack turned around and opened up the supposedly full Series A round.[9]

Catch 'em Young — Dorm Room Fund

Facebook, Google, Microsoft, Dell, Napster — what do the founders of these companies have in common? They all started in a dorm room, their founders absconding from their classrooms. And how do you source these opportunities? Enter the Dorm Room Fund, a venture fund backed by First Round Capital, which is run by students for students. The fund provides student entrepreneurs with seed capital and mentorship right on their own campuses.

The Dorm Room Fund aims to be the first choice for student entrepreneurs who need capital. Started in Philadelphia, the fund is now present in eight US-based universities including Stanford, Massachusetts Institute of Technology (MIT), and Princeton.

Some VCs are proactively tapping into online founder-investor matchmaking portals such as AngelList and Funders-Club (which brands itself as an online VC). Such online marketplaces are gaining traction and will change the landscape of investments eventually, but in the short run, online portals offer insights to a decent pool of opportunities.

NETWORK-BASED SOURCING

In any business, it's primarily relationships that matter. But in the venture business, relationships can make or break a practitioner. For the handful of venture firms that have established brands, opportunities may arrive from a vast matrix of relationships: serial entrepreneurs, peer venture investors, attorneys, investment bankers, and service providers. Brad Feld of the Foundry Group had a 15-year relationship with Mark Pincus, the founder of Zynga. Feld and Union Square Ventures led the first round of investment in this startup, and in four years the company's valuation was well over $5 billion. Or consider Pierre Omidyar, founder of eBay. While seeking the first round of capital, Omidyar had a term sheet that offered at least 2.5 times higher valuation, but he still chose to go with lower valuation offered by Benchmark Capital. Pierre knew Bruce Dunlieve, a general partner (GP) at Benchmark who had invested in his prior company, and he trusted the relationship. Thanks to the relationship advantage and gravitas, Benchmark netted $2.5 billion on its $5 million eBay investment.[10]

Networks function well within certain geographies. "Northern California is very network-centric, and it's relatively uncommon to find really high-quality investment opportunities in the straightforward way of going to conferences and having people submit things on your website. The really good deals go through a network because it's an extremely well-connected, low-friction community," says William Elkus, managing partner of Clearstone Venture Partners.

When Opportunity Meets the Prepared Mind

One evening, Donald T. Valentine, founder of Sequoia Capital, was dining at a restaurant when he saw Steve Jobs and Mike Markkula together and sensed what was being discussed. He dispatched a bottle of wine with a note: "Don't lose sight of the fact that I'm planning on investing in Apple."

Valentine, who had introduced the two of them, invested $150,000 shortly thereafter in Apple at a $3 million valuation.[11]

For the rest of venture practitioners, the sourcing process is a lot of shoe-leather grunt work, often delegated to junior analysts: attending industry conferences, reading various publications, and initiating contact with company executives to build trust and initiate due diligence. One venture capitalist (VC) had a picture on the wall, which bemoaned, "O, but how many frogs should I kiss?"

Brent Ahrens of Canaan Partners summarizes: "This business is about deal flow and cash flow — if you can generate quality deal flow or raise cash from limited partners, you are good."[12]

The business calls for the perpetual development of the art of honing sourcing abilities. Regional venture conferences blend company presentations with the wisdom of reputed venture practitioners. Though it is rare to find truly novel and groundbreaking opportunities at such events, this is fertile ground for most venture practitioners. However, LPs are seldom impressed to hear that your firm's sourcing strategy consists primarily of attending conferences. LPs often wish to know whether you have any unfair advantage or competitive threats in sourcing opportunities. Chris Douvos, who has been a limited partner for over a decade, says, "Some of the brand-name funds have a deep network, which is very hard for new GPs to replicate. This network can be a significant advantage — you can validate ideas, launch products, and even engineer exits at the right time."[13]

Sourcing Advantage: Treat Every Entrepreneur with Respect

My best opportunity ever in my 30 years of investing experience came from an entrepreneur I had turned down. He referred another entrepreneur to our fund, and we made an investment that turned out to be our best performer ever. I guess when we said no, we must have done it in a thoughtful way.

— Jack Ahrens, TGap Ventures

When a successful entrepreneur reaches out to you and asks you to participate in his next big thing, you have arrived. That sourcing advantage can be immense. As Chris Rizik says, "What is it about you that acts as a magnet to entrepreneurs? Dumb money is found aplenty, everywhere."[14] As much as the network matters in sourcing, networks take time to get established. And there are disadvantages of relying too much on others: the best opportunities are rarely shared. For those starting fresh, often the best way to source a good opportunity is get out there and start hunting. Accelerators, demo-days, and angel networks are some good starting points to source opportunities.

ACCELERATORS

Accelerators have sprung up in every corner of the world, and they bring in mentorship, seed capital, networking opportunities, and access to future funding.

Two examples that stand out from the hundreds that operate out there are Silicon Valley-based Y Combinator (YC) and global network Techstars. "About 11% of all Series A opportunities come from accelerators," says David Cohen, co-founder of Techstars accelerator network. Techstars, launched by David Cohen and VC Brad Feld in Boulder, Colorado, has expanded globally (see Exhibit 20.5). Cohen, who has gone on to raise four venture funds to invest in Techstars portfolio companies, says, "We see so much that we have very strong pattern recognition compared to any other VC."

Exhibit 20.5 **The Exponential Growth of Techstars.**

	2014	2016	2018
Number of annual programs	14	21	38
Total companies	505	921	1628
Capital raised by companies	$1.2 bn	$3.0 bn	$6.4 bn
Portfolio market capitalization	$5.1 bn	$9.6 bn	$18.9 bn

Techstars Accelerator — from a Concept to a Global Network in a Decade

- Global Accelerator — started in 2007, and a decade later it hosts 50 accelerator programs annually, each funding 10 companies, in 32 cities in 16 countries.
- 2,000 portfolio companies, adding 500 each year.
- 1,000 startup weekends annually in 120 countries.
- $8 bn raised by the portfolio since inception. In 2019, over $2 bn will be raised by the portfolio companies, up from $1.5 bn in the previous year.
- 80 percent companies are active, 10 percent were acquired (>200 companies), and 10 percent failed.

ANGEL NETWORKS

Fertile territories for opportunities for venture investors, angel funds, and affiliated forms of seed capital provide an early access to investment opportunities. Over 500 angel groups exist worldwide,[15] nearly 300 of which are based in the United States.[16] Angel investor groups are composed of wealthy individuals or high-net-worth individuals who pool resources and investment expertise. Angels typically target early-stage entrepreneurs who need $100,000 to $1 million in equity financing. Angel groups have limited cash resources for administration and management. Before you build inroads to any angel investor network, consider the following:

- *Understand the overall process and the strength of the network.*
  - Does the network have good opportunities in the pipeline?
  - How is the prescreening conducted? Who conducts the due diligence?
  - Does each angel invest one off on his or her own, or are the investments pooled and negotiated as a group?[17]
  - Are there standard terms of investment? What, if any, sectors are preferred over others? Have the angels made any follow-on investments?
  - Have there been any up-rounds or syndications with venture capitalists? Any exits?
- *Limited bandwidth.* Angels have limited resources to invest, and an angel can lose interest fast after a few investments turn into tax write-offs. A measure of activity is the number of investments made in the past 12 months.
- *Limited sector expertise.* If an angel has expertise within a certain sector, that's a good start. Make sure you spend time with those who have domain knowledge and can share their experiences.
- *Get to know the big dog.* Every angel group has a big dog — the center of this universe or the smartest guy with the deepest pockets. The big dog is essential to the

longevity and cohesion of a group: Many angels typically follow the investment rationale of a big dog. Big dogs make a lot of investments and are astute in managing their portfolios and risks. By the same token, be wary of passive angels and tire kickers: many angels sign up as members but are rarely active. For example, 65 percent of the memberships in angel groups are latent angels, individuals who have the necessary net worth yet have not made an investment. Either they are too busy or just not interested or they are tire kickers, entertaining themselves at the cost of entrepreneurs. Avoid these unconscionable devils at all costs.

- *Standardized terms*. Angel investment terms can be nonstandard. *In one survey, 78 percent of VCs said the number one reason that makes an angel-backed company unattractive to VCs is overly high, unrealistic valuations.* 58 percent of the respondents said angels' involvement had made a company unattractive. Angels also complicate negotiations and are viewed by venture capitalists as generally unsophisticated.[18] Opportunistic angels can stick an entrepreneur with investment terms that hurt both parties in the long run. In another study, it was evident that angel funding was helpful in survival of a company per se but was not central in whether a company obtained follow-on financing.[19] Despite this, at least 49 percent of the venture capitalists coinvest with angels on most opportunities.[20]

- *Quality of the portfolio:* Are the investments progressing toward an exit? The ultimate test of any investment activity is future rounds from venture investors or, better still, exits. Only 45 percent of angel groups had a co-investment with venture capital firms.

COMMERCIALIZING UNIVERSITY RESEARCH

According to the Association of University Technology Managers (AUTM), academic technology transfer has created about 11,000 startups.[21] When it comes to mining universities, Robert

"Bob" Nelsen of ARCH Venture Partners may have mastered the art of sourcing opportunities within university labs. When Bob met Mark Roth, a cellular biologist at the Fred Hutchinson Cancer Research Center, Mark was working on suspended animation — a technique to induce a hibernation-like state in animals by cutting off their oxygen supply. Most venture capitalists would flee such a discussion. Not Bob, who worked with Mark patiently for five years. Steven Lazarus, founder of ARCH and now its managing director emeritus, would say of ARCH's investment strategy, "This was not seed capital. In our case, we were identifying science literally at the site of inception, assessing whether it had commercial potential and then erecting a commercial entity around it — it was virtually [starting] from scratch."[22] As a result, Ikaria was formed with an initial investment from ARCH, Venrock, and 5AM Ventures. And Mark Roth, the scientist who could have easily been passed off as a mad scientist, went on to win the MacArthur Genius Award after the company was launched.

Sourcing Advantage: How to Monetize University Startups

Osage University Partners has partnered with over 50 universities, essentially acquiring each university's investment participation rights. Universities often take anywhere from 2 percent to 10 percent equity in a startup. While a university can maintain its participation rights by investing additional capital at future rounds, it's rare that technology transfer offices actually exercise these rights. Quite simply, these are not investment entities but rather are focused on commercialization. Enter Osage. The partners at Osage built an index of startups from 50 top-flight universities that had licensed their technology to those startups but had not invested in them. What they discovered startled them: There was a very respectable 33 percent rate of return, which is better than most VC funds have generated.[23]

It is seldom the science that translates to opportunities — the business talent is a critical component of the mix. Many university startups flounder when founding teams lack a healthy balance of business acumen, as well as a sense of urgency.

Universities as a source of entrepreneurial talent are much more fertile ground. When angel investor K. Ram Shriram bumped into two young kids called Sergey and Larry in an elevator at Stanford University, it was a chance meeting. Yet, he went on to be the first one to invest $500,000, and the term, "elevator pitch" was born. Sergey and Larry's startup, Google, catapulted K. Ram Shriram onto the list of *Forbes* billionaires.

CORPORATE RESEARCH

Research and development (R&D) spending by US companies is at least four times that of university expenditures. In the United States, the annual corporate annual R&D investments are well above $300 billion. According to Booz & Company, a consulting firm, the top 1,000 companies invest $500 billion each year globally.[24]

While these territories may seem fertile, most R&D investments occur to further productivity and profitability. Corporations have little expertise or motivation in spinning startups that eventually become venture backed. As such, corporations have a reason to be threatened by startups. Rather than promote startups, corporations tend to relinquish rights to a valuable IP.

Xerox is one example that comes up often, in view of missing the opportunity on the graphical user interface (GUI), which was monetized by Apple. To that point, it was Bill Gates, founder of Microsoft, who once famously called on Steve Jobs, "Hey Steve, just because you broke into Xerox's store before I did and took the TV doesn't mean I can't go in later and steal the stereo."[25]

A similar example of a missed opportunity originates from the merger of Pharmacia and Upjohn, two pharmaceutical giants. After the merger of Pharmacia and Upjohn, David Scheer, an entrepreneur and investor who blended his knowledge of science and venture capital, was hired to scour some back-burner projects for potential development or divestiture. A compound caught David's attention. "Apo-I Milano protein was the most interesting," Scheer recalls. "We had vision that this project deserved a platform as the next frontier in the cardiovascular arena."[26] Scheer partnered with Roger Newton, the co-discoverer of Lipitor, the world's most successful cardiovascular drug, and launched Esperion Therapeutics. Esperion went public in five years and was acquired by Pfizer for $1.3 billion. In the biotech sector, spinout activities have occurred more frequently as compared to other sectors. While larger companies are sources of talent and know-how, limited startup and venture activity of merit has evolved from larger companies. In select cases, and especially in the pharmaceutical sector, corporations can be a rich source of opportunities.

TRADE CONFERENCES

Trade conferences, where the cutting edge of developments can be seen, are often rich sources of opportunities for seeking investments. Trade shows can be an ideal place to seek investments. Investors often go to a conference and engage with business unit heads and the geeks to gather data and information. Such shows act as a fabric between the worlds of investors, entrepreneurs, and large company executives. Arthur Rock, one of the early investors in Apple, once went to a computer show in San Jose when nobody really had a computer to show, but rather had parts of computers. And while other booths were empty, there was a long line at the Apple booth. Arthur, who invested in Apple subsequently would recall, "Jesus, there's got to be something here."[27]

Leading investors walk the halls of trade shows to assess industry trends and direction, meet with the technical thought leaders, and explore investment opportunities. Startups that may have achieved a certain stature or size are often exhibiting their wares at industry trade shows.

At times, it may just be a serial entrepreneur wandering these halls, looking for his next new thing. That's how William Draper III came across LSI Logic, a semiconductor company. Wilfred Corrigan, then CEO of Fairchild Semiconductor, was itching to do something new. He met with Draper at a convention and expressed his desire to start a new company. Draper invested, and LSI Logic went public two years later. At the time, NASDAQ billed it as the largest technology IPO.[28]

"A combination of factors is at play — attending conferences, listening to the keynote speakers present new ideas, and looking at the new products helps us to understand the problems these smart people are trying to solve. We take that into consideration and try to define what really makes sense for us to invest in," says Lip-Bu Tan of Walden International. "Ideally, for a new market, there are no conferences. We find many of our most interesting opportunities in tiny conferences, where there are 30 or 40 vendors, and we're the only VC firm that's at the conference," says one Sand Hill Road investor.[29]

But while attending conferences is one way of seeking opportunities, Tim O'Reilly, who organized such conferences frequently, had a head start in sourcing when he partnered with Bryce Roberts to raise a venture fund. "Tim is one of those rare businesspeople who not only takes the longest and broadest possible view," the *Linux Journal* wrote of Tim O'Reilly, who launched a series of publications and conferences around technology and innovation.[30] After hosting O'Reilly Media's first Open Source event, O'Reilly garnered national publicity and since has held summits on peer-to-peer technology, web services, geek volunteerism, and Ajax. These summits forge new ties between industry leaders, raise awareness of technology issues, and crystallize the critical issues around emerging technologies. And of course, they are a fertile ground for investment opportunities. O'Reilly Media describes itself as "a chronicler and catalyst of leading-edge development, homing in on the technology trends that really matter and galvanizing their adoption by amplifying 'faint signals' from the alpha geeks who are creating the future."[31] LP Chris Douvos says, "Tim is the Obi-Wan Kenobi of the tech space . . . a great ecosystem exists around him and entrepreneurs are attracted to this guru and the ecosystem."[32] So when Tim and Bryce Roberts decided to raise a fund, O'Reilly Alphatec Ventures (OATV), Chris jumped in with both feet and invested. OATV has a significant sourcing advantage, a first look at many new opportunities even before they become opportunities.

Practitioners can benefit from conferences primarily via gathering industry trends and interacting with thought leaders. Consider these as educational sessions. Every now and then, an opportunity might pop up that will merit an investment.

INVESTOR PITCH SESSIONS

Equivalent to a beauty pageant, entrepreneurs walk the ramp in 10 minutes or less, the VCs show the scorecard of a 5 or an 8 ("Never a 10, one VC told me — that would mean I would be hounded by the entrepreneur"), and the audience claps and moves on to the next pitch. As the pitches roll by, the VCs offer their feedback. "Sounds like a Swiss knife," they say to one idea. A Swiss knife is a technology with 23 or more features, very difficult to manufacture, and in VC jargon translates to "you are trying to do too much — let's get focused here." Entrepreneurs who could barely scratch the surface in two minutes, protest, "I have a lot more to say here . . ." but are gently ushered along into the Q-and-A session. "I applaud you for trying to change the world," says one VC. Ninety minutes later, the VC panel having shared its observations, the entrepreneurs leave the room with lots of advice and no cash. But for practitioners across the country, such events are a tactical mechanism of looking at opportunities. For entrepreneurs, this presents an opportunity to meet and pitch a VC, albeit under pressure. Any practitioner worth his or her expertise or money is invited to participate on such panels, where entrepreneurs seek attention and capital, not necessarily in equal parts. And then there are entrepreneurs who will stop at nothing at such events to get a VC's attention. "Someone started to whisper in my ear at a urinal — bad idea!" says Rick Heitzmann of First-Mark Capital.[33]

These events offer prescreened opportunities to investors who may choose to follow up after these events and dig deeper into the investment thesis. Ask Rajeev Batra of the Mayfield Fund, who was featured on a panel called "Hand us the next killer Cloud app, and we will hand you $100,000." Forty companies were invited to present to a VC panel, with leading practitioners from firms like Sequoia Capital and Bessemer Venture Partners. Such pitch sessions are ideal opportunities to screen and possibly land the next big thing.

For business school students across the country, participating in and winning a business plan competition is a badge of honor. Some students have found these to help make some pocket change on the side. Several startups have been funded and launched successfully — thanks to such competitions.

When Jayant Kulkarni and Adam Regelman started Quartzy, a company dedicated to solving inventory management solutions for scientific laboratories, they participated in the Olin Cup — a business plan competition at Washington University at St. Louis. After winning the competition, they attracted two term sheets and closed a seed round shortly thereafter. Quartzy went on to win another business plan competition in New York City, and was accepted at Y Combinator. The company closed its Series A investment, led by Keith Rabois of Khosla Ventures.

For Scott Hanson, founder and CEO of Ambiq Micro, winning the DFJ-Cisco business plan competition was a pleasant surprise. Scott had just beaten 16 teams from around the world to win a $250,000 seed investment. Six months after the award was announced, Ambiq raised a $2.4 million round led by DFJ Mercury to develop the next generation of energy-efficient microcontrollers. Reducing energy consumption in phones, computers, and other computing devices by a factor of 5–10 times tipped the scale in his favor. Todd Dagres of Spark Capital found his Akamai — an IPO opportunity when he was mentoring a team at the MIT competition. Dagres, who was then at Battery Ventures, invested in Akamai, which subsequently went public.

THE AGONY OF MISSED OPPORTUNITIES

As successful as some of these venture capitalists may be, every investor misses a few good opportunities. Menlo Ventures invested in Uber but missed Facebook. Venky Ganesan of Menlo Ventures recalls, "When Sean Parker said, 'Venky I'm going to Boston to meet this young college student who wants to start a site focused on connecting college students with each other. It's called The Facebook. Would you like to meet the guy?' I said, 'Wait, college student . . . dropped out of Harvard . . . site aimed at college students, that thing is never going to make money.' I remember that moment every day."[34]

First Round Capital Loses Some and Gains Some: Twitter and Square

Evan Williams (co-founder of Twitter) was working on this thing, T-w-t-t-r. He could not afford the domain with the vowels! We offered them a term sheet — $500,000 at a $5 million premoney valuation, meaning his firm would hold a 10 percent stake in the company. Evan continued to fund it, and three months later, Union Square Ventures led the round at a $20 million valuation. It was four times the price First Round had offered. We could have participated but passed.

That led to one of spectacular success. Jack Dorsey was starting Square, and I told him "Dude you got to let me redeem myself," and over dinner Jack said, "You thought that was expensive?" Josh agreed to the valuation promptly this time, a number much more higher than $20 million. "No problem, we are in," and Square turned out to be a spectacular success for First Round Capital.[35]

—Josh Koppelman, First Round Capital

Bessemer Venture Partners has created the anti-portfolio showcasing their missed opportunities. The Bessemer anti-portfolio lists the investment opportunities that the firm missed — one of the few venture firms to make light of its opportunities lost, which include Google, Apple, and other legendary barn-burner investment opportunities.[36]

OVP Venture Partners, a venture firm based in Portland, Oregon, missed its opportunity to invest in Amazon.com. "If you are in this business long enough, you'll see some great deals walk through your door. If you are in this business long enough, you'll show some great deals the door. We try to limit our self-flagellation to one deal per fund."[37] OVP's Gerry Langeler suggests that "it takes a certain personality, one that many venture firms lack, to publicize your fallibility. . . . It indicates you're not some stuffy, highfalutin' group that's going to lord over your entrepreneurs," Langeler writes. "Business is fun. . . . you may not be able to laugh on most days, but if you can't laugh, find another line of work." And for the limited partners who invest in OVP, such acts build "credibility that comes from candor and self-disclosure."[38]

Legendary investor Warren Buffett admired Bob Noyce, co-founder of Fairchild Semiconductor and Intel. Buffett passed on Intel, one of the greatest investing opportunities of his life as he seemed "comfortably antiquated" when it came to new technology companies and had a long-standing bias against technology investments.[39]

Peter O. Crisp of Venrock missed one, too. One "small company in Rochester, New York, came to us, and one of our junior guys saw no future [for] this product . . . that company, Haloid, became Xerox." Venrock also passed on Tandem Computers, Compaq, and Amgen.[40] ARCH Venture Partners missed Netscape — that little project Marc Andreessen started at the University of Chicago. An opportunity that, according to Steven Lazarus, would have been worth billions! "We just never knocked at the right door," he would say. Eventually, ARCH decided to hire a full-time person to just keep tabs on technology coming out of the universities to "make certain we don't miss that door next time."[41]

KPCB missed an opportunity to invest in VMWare[42] because the valuation was too high: a mistake, according to John Doerr. Draper Fisher Jurvetson (DFJ) was initially willing but eventually passed on Facebook, as the firm believed the valuation was too high at $100 million pre-money.[43] KPCB, not wanting to be left out of a hot opportunity like Facebook, invested $38 million at a $52 billion valuation.[44]

Tim Draper of DFJ, who earned his stripes with opportunities like Baidu (the Chinese version of Google), turned down Google "because we already had six search engines in our portfolio." Several leading valley firms like NEA and KPCB invested in Fisker Automotive, which consumed over $1 billion and teetered on bankruptcy. DFJ backed its competitor Tesla Motors, which did spectacularly well. DFJ missed Facebook but made it nicely on Tesla.

Angel investor K. Ram Shriram almost missed his opportunity to invest in Google when he turned the founders away. "I told Sergey and Larry that the time for search engines has come and gone. But I am happy to introduce you to all the others who may want to buy your technology."[45] But six months later, noticing an interesting pattern, Ram K. Shriram invested $500,000 as one of its first angel investors.

Steve Jobs used to work at Atari before he started Apple, and he made an offer to Nolan Bushnell (founder of Atari). Bushnell would recall *"I turned down one-third of Apple Computer for $50,000."*[46] Tom Perkins of Kleiner Perkins Caufield & Byers (KPCB) would have the same grief, "We turned down Apple Computer. No — We didn't. We didn't even turn it down. We didn't agree to meet with Jobs and Steve Wozniak." Bill Draper too missed investing in Apple. "I sent my partner down to look at Apple. He came back and he said, "Guy kept me waiting for an hour, and he's very arrogant." And, of course, that's Steve Jobs! I said, "Well, let's let it go." That was a big mistake. But Donald T. Valentine of Sequoia Capital snagged Apple, "I went to Steve's house. And we talked, and I was convinced it was a big market . . . just embryonic in the beginning. Steve was in his Fu Manchu look, and his question for me was, 'Tell me what I have to do to have you finance me.'"

Valentine responded, "We have to have someone in the company who has some sense of management and marketing and channels of distribution. Jobs said "'Fine. Send me three people.' So I sent him three candidates. One he didn't like. One didn't like him. And the third one was Mike Markkula," recalls Valentine.[47] Markkula ended up investing in Apple and working alongside Steve Jobs. Valentine had added value to the fledgling company even before he invested.

Be in this game long enough and you will have your own share of misses. But it's the hits that matter, and sourcing is a critical component of that hit–miss ratio. LPs are eager to find out if you have any unfair advantage in sourcing opportunities. When capital is available aplenty everywhere, why would entrepreneurs call you?

Target the right sourcing arenas. If you are not fishing in the right pond, as Warren Buffett says, you could end up with a lot of frogs in your portfolio. Any GP needs to ask, "Can I find an opportunity that can grow or generate 10X within my investment horizon?"

If your networks are thin, you will attract subpar opportunities. "The ability to attract the best opportunities is closely tied to a brand — the aura of the venture firm, which is a byproduct of historic performance. You originate deals based upon the reputation of the firm — that's recursive. The better deals you've done, the better your reputation and the easier it is to find people willing to approach you. The reputation of your firm depends upon your success in marketing, but more important, it fundamentally depends upon the quality of the people. It's a complex set of dynamic variables," says William Elkus of Clearstone Venture Partners.

Proprietary relationships is a tired and overused term found in every fund document. LPs abhor it. Use it at your own risk.

Good practitioners track sources of good opportunities systematically. This effort seems painful at first, yet can be rewarding in the long run. A sourcing pipeline is not substantially different from any sales pipeline — if it is thin, you will be in trouble, sooner or later. Tracking tools also help to periodically assess the forest, the patterns of missed opportunities, strong sources, relationship dynamics. and more. In the world where data and analytics are at the core of decision-making, such a tool becomes imperative.

The opportunities you attract are an indicator of your brand, network, and strategy. Building your personal brand is equally important as is that of the venture firm. As Goldman Sachs's eighth commandment goes, "Important people like to deal with other important people. Are you one?"[48]

As we will see in the following chapters, sourcing is only a small part of the puzzle. Negotiating terms and closing in on the investment are equally important. As one GP quipped, "If sourcing was like dating, closing the investment is like a marriage — it is a commitment."

Part Three
Building Your Portfolio

And now begins the fun part — investing.

One newly minted VC told me that he felt like a kid in a candy shop of quantum computing, the decentralization of power and blockchains, the brave new world of AI, the longevity with CRISPR and gene editing, space travel, mars colonization, the gig economy . . . . these waves keep coming at you. The same VC broke his tibia — the longest bone in your body that connects the knee to the ankle — while trying to romp on the beaches of Hawaii. So how do you avoid breaking your bones while being in a state of rapture of technology waves coming at you?

This section looks at the nuances of sourcing opportunities — which is much harder for newcomers and an embarrassment of riches for the established firms. We are paid to be good stock pickers, so building a portfolio calls for the hunter's mind-set — first find the best ones. There is some degree of luck involved here, so stay open and loose — be kind; welcome them all. Any portfolio is a mix of proactive and reactive — what you hunt for, and what comes in the door.

Once you engage, it's the swift skill of analysis — how will this opportunity change the world, and shape your returns? Does this management team exhibit business, technology, and strategic thinking — a winner's mind-set, charm to attract resources, tenacity to cross chasms and slay dragons? And then, the closing — this is where you agree on terms, shake hands, and open that bottle of vino at the closing dinner. In this competitive world of select opportunities, you will win some and lose some. But that's the nature of the game. The bigger questions remain — do you overpay to win? How do you know which ones will play out in the long run?

How can you diligence the spirit of a man? Who wins — who fails and what breaks one down and makes them back up. And are people merely to be treated as "money-making machines" or something more? If founders fail, do you abandon them? Or do you attend to them? Let me leave you with a line from poet Gwendolyn Brooks:

"We are each other's harvest;
we are each other's business;
we are each other's magnitude and bond."

21

Due Diligence
Cheat Sheet

The only measure of venture capital success is performance. The ability to pick the right companies that generate superior returns is paramount to any professional's success in this business.

The investment process — sourcing, due diligence, negotiation of investment terms, board roles, and supporting entrepreneurs — is important, yet secondary. Investors primarily care about strong financial returns. While sourcing investment opportunities is a function of the firm's team expertise and relationships, the venture firm's brand as being entrepreneur friendly has also become an important factor. Investors, who are independent and act decisively, are responsive and treat entrepreneurs as equals attract strong opportunities. Eventually, a strong brand is built on this foundation.

When it comes to due diligence, seasoned investors are students of the market; they make quick decisions and actively invest in opportunities that serve the market needs. Management team, product, features, and competition are important attributes, yet the best investors rarely overthink and are comfortable in ambiguity.

These five general criteria determine investment decisions:

1. Does the management team demonstrate integrity, a sense of urgency, knowledge, and agility?
2. Is a clear market pain point identified? Has a value proposition been established?

Exhibit 21.1 **Due Diligence — Key Criteria.**

Criteria	Definition	Remarks
Management Team Criteria		
Management team	Stage-ready and well-rounded team, committed and coachable.	Company should have attracted a strong team with clarity on skills for sales and marketing and product development. Though each company has specific needs for talent, look for the individuals, their backgrounds, and a fit with their roles.
Operational systems	Financial, sales, and operations systems are documented and managed effectively.	Company should demonstrate adequate internal systems such as (a) financial reporting, controls, and decision-making, (b) sales and marketing systems, (c) product development road maps.
Overall milestones	On plan to meet its milestones. No material change in its business strategy or direction.	Review company's product road maps and assess with the quarterly reports and actual progress. Though deviations are a norm, ensure that the company is on or ahead of plan prior to considering follow-on funding.
Reporting and communication with investors	Monthly, quarterly reports are provided in a timely manner. Verbal updates or meetings are frequent.	Company's ability to keep investors updated on key developments via reports, communications, and updates is important.
Financials		
Revenues	On plan or exceeding plan.	Review financial milestones of revenues and gross margins. Stability of margins will be reviewed. These will be assessed in conjunction with other balance sheet- and cash flow-related matters to ensure the financial stability of the company.
Other	No significant debt or receivables; cash flows are sufficient.	
Investment Terms		
Size of round	Sufficient to help company reach the next milestone	Investment will be syndicated as a part of a larger round. Is this capital sufficient for meeting the stated milestones?
Position	Co-investor or follower	Syndicate follow-on investments with external investors as a mechanism to validate risk mitigation.
Terms of investment	Case-by-case basis	Ensure that current terms of investment are suitable to ensure target returns.
Additional capital needs	Future capital needs and path to break-even are clear	Investment may be ideally suited in situations where companies demonstrate capital efficiency. If companies need substantial follow-on rounds, these would elevate the risk.
Risk Mitigation		
Syndicate investors	Additional investments from current investors or new investors.	Assess various factors of risk mitigation such as (a) professional investment from venture funds at up-rounds, (b) growing demand of products/ pipeline of orders, (c) diversity of customer base.
Purchase order pipeline	A meaningful pipeline of orders is at hand.	

3. What are key risks and a plan for mitigation?

4. Are capital needs, efficiency, and break-even taken into account?

5. Can this investment generate target returns within the desired time frame?

Exhibit 21.1 describes the various criteria in greater detail for investment consideration. Not all of these criteria are applicable to early-stage companies.

While conducting diligence, good practitioners are weary of time and do not overthink a good opportunity or analyze it to death. This is especially important at the seed stage. Mike Maples of Floodgate Fund has invested in some of the leading technology startups in Silicon Valley. He says, "The best deals we have done are the ones where we decided the quickest — which is counterintuitive to me. Ten minutes into a meeting with an entrepreneur, I stopped the presentation, raised my hand, and said I want to invest. The company had momentum, an authentic entrepreneur, and an awesome market."[1]

22

Diligence

Due diligence is the art of sizing up an investment opportunity — its potential outcomes and major risk factors. A good opportunity tests the limits of our observations and experiences, even the limits of our networks and imagination.

Identifying the potential for value creation and estimating its sustained advantage is the heart of any due diligence activity. Mitch Lasky of Benchmark Capital says, "I almost hesitate to use the word *due diligence* because it implies a certain methodical rigor — rather we ask, what are attributes of successful venture investments." Investors primarily focus on the two primary attributes:

- *Management*. Do the CEO and the leadership team have a sparkle, a sense of enthusiasm, penetrating intelligence, and courage? Even if they have not done it before, these qualities are essential. Is there a glimmer of greatness?
- *Market*. Does this opportunity have the potential for creating outsized returns? Is the market ready for this product?

Early-stage investors seldom start with valuation or financial projections. Though it is important to understand financial budgets and capital needed to accomplish major milestones in the next two years, far-out, "five-year" projections or exit multiples are useless artifacts. The two major criteria — management and markets — trump the rest of the diligence criteria by orders of magnitude. Warren Buffett summarizes his due diligence process with four simple criteria:[1]

1. *Can I understand it? Buffett defines "understanding a business" as "having a reasonable probability of being able to assess where the company will be in 10 years."*[2]
2. *Does it look like it has some kind of sustainable competitive advantage?*
3. *Is the management composed of able and honest people?*
4. *Is the price right?*

If it passes all four filters, Buffett writes a check.

Peter Thiel says, "Great companies do three things. First, they create value. Second, they are lasting or permanent in a meaningful way. Finally, they capture at least some of the value they create."[3] According to Thiel, durable startups create something new, or *go from 0 to 1*, instead of replicating an existing model, or *going from 1 to n*. His views on playing in markets where no competition exists are well documented in his book *Zero to One* where he asks critical questions: Have you identified a unique opportunity that others don't see? Do you have a way to not just create but deliver your product?

Once a novel idea has been launched, the goal is to monopolize quickly and, eventually, spread that monopoly into other parallel domains. In Exhibit 22.1, we see the results of a survey showing various criteria that come into effect when selecting investments. The quality of the management team is often the number one criteria in making investment decisions.

Exhibit 22.1 **Most important factors for selecting investments.**

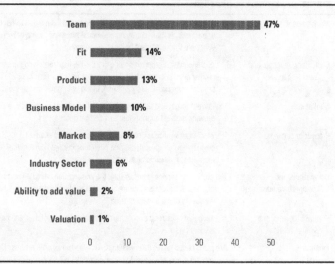

Team	47%
Fit	14%
Product	13%
Business Model	10%
Market	8%
Industry Sector	6%
Ability to add value	2%
Valuation	1%

Source: Data from Gompers, Paul A., William Gornall, Steven N. Kaplan, and Ilya A. Strebulaev. "How Do Venture Capitalists Make Decisions?" NBER Working Paper Series, No. 22587.

THE CHECKLIST MANIFESTO

"Every man takes the limits of his own field of vision for the limits of the world," wrote Arthur Schopenhauer. And often, we find that our own limits can bring about financial failures, or missed opportunities.

A diligence checklist ensures that critical diligence areas are addressed efficiently, in times when transaction speed is critical. (See Exhibit 22.2 for sample diligence checklist.) Prior to take-off, airline pilots are expected to follow a methodical check-list. Boeing Corporation introduced checklists in 1935, after a prototype plane crashed, killing two pilots who had forgotten to disengage a critical lock. In a parked aircraft, wind gusts can damage control components. A "gust lock" is engaged to prevent movement of various parts, such as ailerons and tail fins. The fatal crash introduced the concept of preflight check-lists — a procedure to ensure such errors do not occur.

Exhibit 22.2 **Due Diligence Checklist.**

Criteria	Description
Management	The key team member(s) have the expertise and skills needed to run this type of business. Is there clarity on additional hires and timing of recruitment? What are the significant holes in the team?
Customers, revenue, and business model	The customer value proposition is quantifiable, high, and recognizable. The market need is established, and the customer has an urgency to act. The product price points are identified, along with gross margins and costs.
Market size	The current target and addressable market size is estimated. It is a large and growing market, quantifiable to a certain degree.
Product or service	The product or service is described succinctly as the stage of development — prototype, first customer, multiple customers — is identified. A development road map is included.
Competitors and competitive advantage	The product or service is better than the competition based on features and/or price. Is current and future competition identified and evaluated for weakness or significant barriers?
Capital efficiency and value creation	A reasonable milestone event chart with value drivers, dates, and capital needs is identified.
Financials	Are plans based on realistic assumptions with reasonable returns? Does it contain reasonable, justifiable projections for two to three years with assumptions explained?
Exit assumptions	Is there a reasonable exit time frame? Is there some clarity on the target universe of buyers?

Importance of Checklists: Specialized Ability and Group Collaboration

The volume and complexity of what we know has exceeded our individual ability to deliver its benefits correctly, safely, or reliably, writes surgeon and author Atul Gawande.

The checklist routine "requires balancing a number of virtues: freedom and discipline, craft and protocol, specialized ability and group collaboration. And for checklists to help achieve that balance, they have to take two almost opposing forms. They supply a set of checks to ensure the stupid but critical stuff is not overlooked, and they supply another set of checks to ensure people talk and coordinate and accept responsibility while nonetheless being left the power to manage the nuances and unpredictabilities . . . ."

— *The Checklist Manifesto, by Atul Gawande*

TAILORING DILIGENCE BY STAGE

As stage and sectors of companies evolve, diligence needs to be tailored accordingly.

As seen in Exhibit 22.3, practitioners can focus on the most important criteria of due diligence by stage of the investment opportunity. It is pointless dissecting detailed financials for a seed stage company. Investor and author Nassim Nicholas Taleb reminds us that intelligence is *not about noticing things that are relevant (detecting patterns); but "in a complex world, intelligence consists in ignoring things that are irrelevant (avoiding false patterns)."*[4]

Exhibit 22.3 **Key Due Diligence Questions for Consideration by Stage.**

	Seed Stage	Early Stage	Growth Stage
Management	What is the founder's expertise and understanding of the market pain? Does management have the ability to let go and attract smarter people at the right time?	Based on market needs, can the management team take a prototype and develop a commercial product? Technology development? Sales? Financial?	Can the team achieve high growth, high margins? Explore geographic expansion? Manage resources — people and cash — effectively? What are the board dynamics?
Market	Is there a need in the market? Is it a growing market? Will the market expand to accommodate breakthrough products?	Gauge the ability to cross the chasm from early adopters to mainstream market.	Competitive pressures.
Technology	IP assessment. Freedom to operate. Laboratory scale data. Can you make it once?	What are the features and alignment with market needs? What are the market/customer level data? Can you make it many times?	Look at deployment and operational efficiencies. Can you make it consistently, with high quality, while maintaining costs?
Financials	12- to 24-month milestones and capital needed to reach value creation.	What is the test pricing and what are the revenue assumptions, growth rates projected, and gross margins?	Sustained revenue growth, margin stability/erosion. Ability to improve gross margins is often over-emphasized. Detailed financial analysis of past (1) income statement, (2) balance sheet, and (3) cash flows.

Elements of Enduring Companies: Sequoia Capital's View

Starting a business is rough. Most startups fail. A founder's best chance to thrive is to find the right community, the right partners, and the right network of support from the very beginning. We love nothing more than meeting promising founders during their first days starting a company.

The tech giants of today started as one- or two-person ideas not long ago. We've met many young companies and noticed that startups with the following characteristics have the best shot of becoming enduring companies:

Clarity of purpose. Summarize the company's business on the back of a business card.

Large markets. Address existing markets poised for rapid growth or change. A market on the path to a $1B potential allows for error and time for real margins to develop.

Rich customers. Target customers who will move fast and pay a premium for a unique offering.

Focus. Customers will only buy a simple product with a singular value proposition.

Pain killers. Pick the one thing that is of burning importance to the customer, then delight them with a compelling solution.

Thinking differently. Constantly challenge conventional wisdom. Take the contrarian route. Create novel solutions. Outwit the competition.

Team DNA. A company's DNA is set in the first 90 days. Choose your first few hires wisely.

Agility. Stealth and speed can beat slow incumbents.

Resilience. Hone your ability to bounce back and keep trying.

Frugality. Focus spending on what's critical. Spend only on the priorities and maximize profitability.

Inferno. Start with only a little money. It forces discipline and focus. A huge market with customers yearning for a product developed by great engineers requires very little firepower.

Besides tailored diligence, the process matters as well. An investor needs to conduct diligence in a timely, efficient, and respectful manner. Most indecisive VCs drag the process along, often trying to justify their own lack of conviction. Spinning the founders in a perpetual orbit cannot "diligence the risk out." Igor Taber spent 10 years as an investor with Intel Capital before he switched over to the operating side, "I did not recognize how I was interpreted as an investor. The intent and the communication can be misinterpreted easily. I am a hundred times more cautious in the way I engage now," he says. "This operating role has brought in a deeper empathy for founders."

CHECKLISTS — USEFUL BUT SELDOM USED

As much as the importance of checklists can be emphasized, it is harder to put it in practice. Laziness, bias, and inflated self-confidence often play in our business. The first airplane crash fatality occurred in 1935, and despite putting checklists in place, at least six similar aircraft accidents have occurred since — the most recent almost 80 years later in 2014. Following the most recent crash, the US National Transportation Safety Board (NTSB) urged a study. The study, conducted by the National Business Aviation Association (NBAA), revealed that over a three-year period, about 25,876 business aviation flights (or 18 percent) failed to conduct a complete pre-take-off check of flight controls. As many as 2,875 flights began without a full, valid check[5]. If you are a successful VC, you might fly private (or at least have a NetJets subscription), so bear these statistics in mind. Pilots do not follow checklists consistently, and people die. So how unlikely is it that VCs will follow diligence checklists consistently? After all, it's only LPs' money — it's not like people die when an investment fails. Yet the eternal optimist in me hopes that such checklists can become the norm and save us from our foibles.

Though checklists can bring rigor and discipline, some investors tend to follow these formulaic approaches somewhat mindlessly, checking boxes and overloading founders with inane requests for irrelevant information. Some due diligence meetings are akin to VC overlords in a "power-play" mode grilling entrepreneurs with all and sundry.

The Socratic Method of Conducting Due Diligence

How would the Greek philosopher Socrates conduct due diligence?

Using the Socratic method, the process of diligence is not a prescribed format: It's a shared dialogue between the investor and the cofounders, and both are responsible for agreeing on the key challenges, opportunities, and milestones. Venture capitalists (VCs) often ask probing questions to expose the risks and identify the assumptions that frame the thoughts of the cofounders. Yet, good VCs allow the cofounders to ask questions, as well. The process of excavating risks progresses interactively, and the conversation is open-ended. PowerPoint slides are a deterrent, and there is an immense premium in being in the flow of inquiry rather than using defensive arguments or ideological posturing.

Both parties account for their thoughts and beliefs. While knowing facts is important, how the two sides assess these facts is more important.

The stakes are high. Socratic diligence results in a productive discomfort.

Both sides acknowledge that there is ambiguity and uncertainty; the process does not yield clarity as much as agreement that we are surrounded by darkness. "I don't know" is a refreshingly welcome position, that, if followed through, may yield to surprising outcomes.

Above all, the method aims to keep both parties on a level playing field. The VC knows as much or as little as the entrepreneur. Yet VCs pretend, and most entrepreneurs assume, that VCs have all the answers. It's up to the VCs to change this dynamic and create a balanced mutually respectful learning dynamic.

The art of conducting due diligence is to know what to ask, whom to ask, and, more importantly, how to ask. If the Greek philosopher Socrates would have done due diligence, every company would open up to new worlds of possibilities.

Nobel Prize–winning author Sinclair Lewis, in his 1922 book *Babbit*, describes a fictional character, Conrad Lyte, who was "a nervous speculator . . . before he gambled, he consulted bankers, lawyers, architects, contracting builders and all of their clerks and stenographers who were willing to be cornered and give him advice. He desired nothing more than complete safety in his investments, freedom from attention to details and the thirty to forty percent profit, which according to all authorities, a pioneer deserves for his risks and foresight . . . ."

Not much has changed — due diligence often includes consulting and cornering people, while aiming for complete safety in investments and without much attention to detail. After all, a pioneering VC should make 30–40 percent profit, a well-deserved return for their risks and foresight.

23

Management Team Diligence: Assessing the Intangible

OVERVIEW

In the all-time great movie *Moneyball,* a mediocre baseball team uses a statistical data-driven approach to go on and win 19 consecutive baseball games. At the heart of the movie lies the ability to pick the right team — those baseball players that would have the grit to win. The classical way of picking players involved subjective discussions around their good looks and self-confidence. Their selection criteria included observations like *"clean cut, good face, good jaw. . . he has got the looks — just needs some time."* One player has an *ugly girlfriend "means no self-confidence"* while another player is so self-confident that "his dick gets in the room two minutes before does." Committee members were prone to biases and power dynamics within their own selection committee. As one member kicks off the voting by saying, "I like Geronimo," others quickly agree willingly. "Top of my list" says one. "Real deal," says another. I am pretty sure this dynamic plays out in most venture firms where the leading partner's views influence the weaker voices in the room.

However, once the teams adopt a statistical approach to picking players, the decision biases become clearer and the winning streak can begin. Such a decision-making process is ideal. "At Foundation Capital, we record the minutes of every opportunity being debated, who raised the risks and challenges — the goal is to see how our decisions pan out, as well as who has the clarity of thinking," says partner Sid Trivedi. Investors discuss, debate, and oversell their own data-driven "Moneyball" approach to venture investing. But can it be applied to measuring strengths of management teams in the business environment?

The art of diligence of the management team involves assessing the intangibles — sizing up human potential, strengths, and weaknesses — all within a few meetings. The attributes of strong management teams and the chief executive, the proverbial jockey, are difficult, even nearly impossible to assess in a few meetings. How can we measure the integrity of a CEO, their strategic thinking, ability to share a compelling vision, their salesmanship, attracting investments and a team of high performers? A lot of the startup CEOs are unproven rookies, and you have very little relevant data to make a judgment call. Like Don Valentine says, if you have figured it out, they ought to build a statue to you.

VALUES AND INTEGRITY

"In looking for people to hire, you look for three qualities: integrity, intelligence, and energy. And if they don't have the first, the other two will kill you. Think about it; it's true. If you hire somebody without the first, you really want them to be dumb and lazy."[1] Warren Buffett reminds us that those who do not have integrity but have intelligence can not only take advantage of you, but even kill you. When assessing the management team, integrity ranks first. Integrity boils down to the sum total of honesty in words and actions, an ethos that defines any individual. But there is no easy way to assess this attribute.

Investors spend an extraordinary amount of time investigating business skills and technical expertise of entrepreneurs. The process is imprecise and involves referencing — multiple discussions with people who have former interactions. One practitioner described this as "looking in the rear-view mirror" — an approach of predicting the future based on past behavior. To truly understand the personality

This Is How We Change the World

There are numerous cases of fraud in the startup world—none as significant as Theranos — a Silicon Valley–based health care startup. The company claimed a breakthrough in blood-testing procedures and raised over $500 million. It was valued at $10 billion when a journalist questioned the validity of the technology. Soon thereafter, the house of cards came tumbling down revealing an elaborate charade of fraud and deception. The founder and CEO, Elizabeth Holmes, at one time stated, "We've got an incredible opportunity to try to uphold a legacy in Silicon Valley of changing the world." One investor I spoke with quoted Leo Tolstoy: "What a strange illusion it is to suppose that beauty is goodness." A documentary based on this saga, *The Inventor: Out for Blood in Silicon Valley,* is not discussed by VCs as often as *Moneyball.*

The scale of fraud at Entellium, a Seattle–based developer of customer relationship management (CRM) tools, was not as significant as Theranos, but left enough scars for its investors. The company was recognized as a leader by Forrester Research, and the *CRM magazine* touted it as "market leader" for three consecutive years. But the CEO and CFO were cooking the books much faster than they could raise capital. They overstated revenues by as much as three times for three consecutive years. An employee stumbled on the actual revenue data while cleaning out a former employee's desk and discovered the fraud. Forty people lost their jobs, and the CEO and CFO were arrested. The lead venture fund wrote off $19 million as the company was sold in bankruptcy.

and the mind-set of any entrepreneur, when everyone is in a rush to close the investment is the biggest challenge of the venture business. Those who manage to stay above the law but play games, rush investors to close without sharing relevant information, or hide beneath a web of lies and inconsistent behavior are the ones who always get you!

In management diligence, we often see the obvious — this team is hungry, has solid technical expertise, or has strong business acumen. Integrity and honesty — fundamental qualities of any management team — are much harder to assess. Not everyone can avoid a fraud. But can we try to watch for the subtle warning signals? If we spot any shades of gray, how can we avoid the impulse of rushing in or find ways to justify the investment? Knowing what questions to ask and the willingness to walk away from a "hot opportunity" when sufficient information is not available can save investors from embarrassment and losses. Pete Farner of TGap Ventures says, "I use a simple test in assessing potential CEOs — would I trust them enough to look after my own kids?" Such a high bar would eliminate the vast majority of riffraff quickly.

CAN THE COMPANY ATTRACT GIANTS?

Besides integrity, what are the other qualities to look for in any management team? Can the CEO attract a team of giants — a team that has experience and can scale the company — to help build an enduring company? Can she be comfortable working with people who are more accomplished, smarter, or legends in their own domains? Or do they hire mediocre midgets who can barely conduct baseline operations?

Consider William Shockley, who won the Nobel Prize for co-inventing the transistor. Despite being a brilliant physicist, Shockley had no people skills and successfully alienated his two co-inventors, thanks to his brash and abrasive style. His staff was subjected to lie detector tests, and he publicly posted their salaries. He was even passed over for promotion at Bell Labs. When he died, he was completely estranged from most of his friends and family — his children read about his death in the newspapers.[2]

When eight of Shockley's researchers, termed as the Traitorous Eight, resigned to start Fairchild Semiconductor, all he did was write, *"Wed 18 Sept — Group Resigns"* in his diary.[3] Besides being a poor manager, Shockley's presentation skills were terrible. He read all his speeches in a monotone, was a poor writer, and "flogged metaphors" mercilessly. Larry L. King wrote of Shockley that he "made such an inept presentation that he could not have instructed us how to catch a bus."[4]

In Shockley's biography, the importance of management skills is highlighted, "If Shockley had been a better manager, he'd be one of the richest people in the world today. He is the father of Silicon Valley; he knew more than anybody in the world the importance of these machines, these transistors; he knew that he was revolutionizing the world; he knew that if his company could control the direction that the transistor should go toward, that he would be very rich. Unfortunately, he was a terrible manager and he never had the chance."[5] Despite being a brilliant technologist and a Nobel Laureate, Shockley was his own worst enemy, unable to get over his fear and insecurities.

Compare that with Steve Jobs. One of the early investors in Apple, Arthur Rock, recalls his first meeting with Steve Jobs and Steve Wozniak:

> Jobs came into the office, as he *does now, dressed in Levi's*, but at that time that wasn't quite the thing to do. And I believe he had a goatee and a moustache and long hair — and he had just come back from six months in India with a guru, *learning* about life. I'm not sure, but it may have been a while since he had a bath. . . . And he was very, very thin — he really belonged somewhere else. Steve Wozniak, on the other hand, had a full beard, and he's just not the kind of a person you'd give a lot of money to.[6]

Nevertheless, Rock invested in Apple because Jobs was articulate.

Andreessen Horowitz on the Art of CEO Selection

The art of CEO selection, according to Ben Horowitz, of the venture firm Andreessen Horowitz, can be summarized in three words: direction, execution, and results.

Direction: Does the CEO know what to do?

Strategy and decision-making: Does the CEO know what to do in all matters all of the time? Can the CEO tie the strategy to a story — how is the world a better place, thanks to this company? A CEO can most accurately be measured by the speed and quality of her decisions. Great decisions come from CEOs who display an elite combination of intelligence, logic, and courage.

Execution: Can the CEO get the company to do what he or she knows?

Execution and team building: Once a vision is set, does the CEO have the capacity, and can the CEO execute? Horowitz points out that capacity translates to having world-class, motivated talent. Building a world-class team and ensuring the quality of the team stays strong is important.

Effectively run the company: Very few CEOs get an A and fail to scale because the skills required to manage a well-run organization are wide-ranging, from organizational design to performance management, incentives, communication, the whole gamut. The key question to ask is, "Is it easy for the employees to get their job done?"

Results: Did the CEO achieve the desired results against an appropriate set of objectives?

Were appropriate objectives established? Too low or too high? Horowitz warns against setting objectives for early-stage companies, as no one really knows the size of the opportunity. Finally, the size and the nature of opportunities vary across types of companies: some are capital intensive, while others have measured growth and market adoption. CEOs will perform better on a test if they know the questions ahead of time.[7]

CAN THE CEO EXECUTE? LAMBS VERSUS CHEETAHS

Defined as the fine art of getting things done, execution abilities are one of the top criteria of management assessment. In an early-stage company, execution would be quite simply "the ability to define and meet value creation milestones using optimum resources." In his *New York Times* best-selling book *Who: The A Method for Hiring*, author Geoff Smart asks, "What types of CEOs make money for investors?"[8] Smart, who has frequently interacted with the VC world, grew up in a family in which psychology was discussed at the breakfast table. "My father was an industrial psychologist. So when I interned at a VC firm, I asked the partners what it takes to be a successful venture capitalist. And they said, it's all about management." But Geoff found that despite all the emphasis on management, there was no clear methodology of assessing people. "If people are so important, why is it that we spend all of this time doing Excel models or market analysis?" he would ask. He was told that the people part is intuitive and that there is no way you can evaluate people accurately. "Had I not had the contextual background of psychology, I would have taken everything that venture capitalists told me at face value."[9]

To assess CEO traits, Geoff teamed up with Steven N. Kaplan, a noted scholar on entrepreneurship and finance at the University of Chicago. The team went on to conduct the largest study of CEO traits and financial performance. The results were both compelling and controversial. Data from over 300 CEO interviews was compared with the CEO assessments and actual financial performance. Investors often have a tendency to invest in CEOs who demonstrated openness to feedback, possess great listening skills, and treat people with respect. "I call them 'Lambs' because these CEOs tend to graze in circles, feeding on the feedback and direction of others," he says. And he concludes that investors love Lambs because they are easy to work with and were successful for 57 percent of the time.

But Geoff found that the desirable CEOs are the ones who move quickly, act aggressively, work hard, demonstrate persistence, and set high standards and hold people accountable to them. He called them "Cheetahs" because they are fast and focused: "Cheetahs in our study were successful 100 percent of the time. This is not a rounding error. *Every single one of them* created significant value for their investors."[10] "Emotional intelligence is important, *but only when matched with the propensity to get things done.*"[11]

Separately, Steven N. Kaplan's research leads to the same conclusion. In the study "Which CEO Characteristics and Abilities Matter?" the authors assess more than 30 individual characteristics, skills, and abilities.[12] Surprisingly, the study showed that success was not linked to team-related skills and that such skills are overweighed in hiring decisions. *Success mattered only with CEOs with execution-related skills.* The study asserted Jim Collins's "Good to Great" description of Level 5 CEOs — they have unwavering resolve and are fanatically driven. The essential lesson we derive from Shockley's example is that while technical expertise is important, marrying technical skills with short-term milestones and rapid execution is critical. As Peter Drucker says, effective executives "get the right things done"[13] — at the right time.

SERIAL ENTREPRENEURS VERSUS FIRST-TIME ENTREPRENEURS

All things equal, a VC-backed entrepreneur who has taken a company public has a 30 percent chance of succeeding in his or her next venture.[14] A failed entrepreneur is next in the pecking order, with a 20 percent chance of success, and a first-time entrepreneur has an 18 percent chance. Researchers assessed the cause of success and point out that successful entrepreneurs know how to launch companies at the right time — before the markets get crowded. Market timing skill

Leonardo Da Vinci Pitches the Ruler of Milan, Circa 1480

(With no formal academic training, Da Vinci is recognized as a Universal Genius and a Renaissance Man, who conceptualized armored vehicles, solar power, flying machines, parachutes. And yes, after all that, he painted some of the most famous works like the "Mona Lisa" and "The Last Supper.")

My Most Illustrious Lord,

Having now sufficiently seen and considered the achievements of all those who count themselves masters and artificers of instruments of war, and having noted that the invention and performance of the said instruments is in no way different from that in common usage, I shall endeavor, while intending no discredit to anyone else, to make myself understood to Your Excellency for the purpose of unfolding to you my secrets, and thereafter offering them at your complete disposal, and when the time is right, bringing into effective operation all those things which are in part briefly listed below:

1. I have plans for very light, strong and easily portable bridges with which to pursue and, on some occasions, flee the enemy, and others, sturdy and indestructible either by fire or in battle, easy and convenient to lift and place in position. Also means of burning and destroying those of the enemy.

2. I know how, in the course of the siege of a terrain, to remove water from the moats and how to make an infinite number of bridges, mantlets and scaling ladders and other instruments necessary to such an enterprise.

3. Also, if one cannot, when besieging a terrain, proceed by bombardment either because of the height of the glacis or the strength of its situation and location, I have methods for destroying every fortress or other stronghold unless it has been founded upon a rock or so forth.

4. I have also types of cannon, most convenient and easily portable, with which to hurl small stones almost like a hailstorm; and the smoke from the cannon will instill a great fear in the enemy on account of the grave damage and confusion.

5. Also, I have means of arriving at a designated spot through mines and secret winding passages constructed completely

(continued)

(continued)

without noise, even if it should be necessary to pass underneath moats or any river.

6. Also, I will make covered vehicles, safe and unassailable, which will penetrate the enemy and their artillery, and there is no host of armed men so great that they would not break through it. And behind these, the infantry will be able to follow, quite uninjured and unimpeded.

7. Also, should the need arise, I will make cannon, mortar, and light ordnance of very beautiful and functional design that are quite out of the ordinary.

8. Where the use of cannon is impracticable, I will assemble catapults, mangonels, trebuchets, and other instruments of wonderful efficiency not in general use. In short, as the variety of circumstances dictate, I will make an infinite number of items for attack and defence.

9. And should a sea battle be occasioned, I have examples of many instruments which are highly suitable either in attack or defense, and craft which will resist the fire of all the heaviest cannon and powder and smoke.

10. In time of peace I believe I can give as complete satisfaction as any other in the field of architecture, and the construction of both public and private buildings, and in conducting water from one place to another.

Also I can execute sculpture in marble, bronze, and clay. Likewise in painting, I can do everything possible as well as any other, whosoever he may be.

Moreover, work could be undertaken on the bronze horse which will be to the immortal glory and eternal honour of the auspicious memory of His Lordship your father, and of the illustrious house of Sforza.

And if any of the above-mentioned things seem impossible or impracticable to anyone, I am most readily disposed to demonstrate them in your park or in whatsoever place shall please Your Excellency, to whom I commend myself with all possible humility.

is more important than the novelty of the technology. Interestingly, the entrepreneurs who were able to time the market during their first startup were also able to time the market in their next startup, as well. Those who can time market cycles several times are indeed smart: Luck is no longer a factor for such entrepreneurs. However, with successful entrepreneurs, the hunger level may drop with success or age. Or worse, arrogance may set in.

Most management teams will be replaced, either by choice or by sheer exhaustion, in the travails of the startup journey. A simple question to consider is: Is this person honest and bold enough to replace themselves at the right time, even make themselves redundant?

BIAS AT WORK: SEEKING ATTRACTIVE MEN

VCs would not like to think of themselves as biased, but a Harvard Business School study found male entrepreneurs were 60 percent more likely to succeed in pitch competition as compared to female entrepreneurs. And attractive men were 36 percent more likely to achieve success than their average-looking counterparts. 68 percent of participants chose to fund the ventures pitched by a male voice, and only 32 percent of participants chose to fund the ventures pitched by a female voice.[15]

Another study conducted by two MIT researchers predicted, without looking at the business pitches, who would win a business plan competition with 87 percent accuracy.[16] Neither of the researchers had read the plans or heard their pitches. So how did they predict with such high accuracy? From "honest signals" exhibited by the presenters. Honest signals are defined as nonverbal cues — gestures, expressions, and tone. In an interview with *Harvard Business Review*, the researcher Pentland said, "The more successful people are energetic. They talk more, but they also listen more. . . . It's not just what they

Betting on the Last One — The First-Mover Disadvantage

Ajay Royan, co-founder of Mithril Capital, elegantly debunked the first-mover advantage in startup investing. "PayPal, Facebook, Google, Airbnb, Uber — none of these companies were first movers. Rather, these companies did one thing really well — they shut the door behind them. The rest is history."

Facebook had over 20 competitors when it launched. Orkut, another social networking rival, relaunched its service three months before Facebook's launch. Orkut was backed by search giant Google. And six months after Facebook's launch, MySpace boasted nearly 5 million users. Social networks had clearly seen a deluge of startups.

With search engines, the story is not too different. Google was the 18th search engine born five years after the first search engine was launched. The market was a noisy mess. You had Infoseek, Lycos, AltaVista, AskJeeves, Excite, to name a few. (One search engine was even called Dogpile.) And prior to AirBnb, there was VRBO. In the ridesharing world, before Uber came SideCar and Lyft.

So if VCs are to look at something beyond the first mover advantage, what is it? "Look at the market — can this market withstand an A-minus founder?" asks Royan. "We should choose the correct markets — and then ask, not only are these addressable but are these ownable?"

"A lot of investors are driven by momentum, with a speculative mindset. You have to be deterministic," says Royan. In mathematics, a deterministic system is a system in which no randomness is involved in the development of future states.

The business of venture capital is messy, unpredictable, and has far too many variables that come into play.

But now we know for sure that the first-mover advantage is not a determinant of success. Instead of agonizing if this is an A+ team, flip the logic over its head.

Ask if the market can withstand an A-minus team.

And once you make an investment, figure out if this team can shut the door behind them! And own the market.

project that makes them charismatic; it's what they elicit. The more of these energetic, positive people you put on a team, the better the team's performance."[17] Pentland's research did not indicate which pitch will be best — it just indicated who will win, irrespective of the quality of the idea or the pitch. Venture capitalists look for buzz and enthusiasm, "but they also need to understand the substance of the pitch and not be swayed by charisma alone," he added.

BACKGROUND CHECKS: FALSE MBAS AND CRIMINAL HISTORIES

Studies indicate that roughly 50 percent of job candidates misrepresent their job credentials although the level and degree of misrepresentation varies widely.[18] Furthermore, misrepresentations are made by candidates applying for jobs at all levels of an organization's hierarchy, including its board of directors.

Background checks of key portfolio company personnel are often a component of this due diligence analysis. However, while background checks will detect some issues with potential portfolio company managers, an in-depth background investigation, performed by an experienced professional, will yield a more detailed analysis of potential portfolio company managers and serve to verify the assertions and representations these individuals have made to the VC funds.

Background investigations include significantly detailed analyses of potential portfolio company managers. These investigations examine individuals' work history, board service, educational background, community involvement, criminal background, and, in some instances, assets. While this level of information may seem excessive, it is a necessary component of the due diligence process and serves to mitigate future issues a VC fund may encounter with an executive at a later date. Moreover, the reasons for conducting an in-depth background investigation as opposed to a cursory

But You Are Eight Months Pregnant. . . .

When I started my first company, I met a senior investment partner who politely said, "I don't see how I can fund
you. You are eight months pregnant" — that was a fair statement. Three months later, Sequoia funded me, and we were
off to a good start. But the fun began after we closed the
round. Sequoia challenged me, stretched my thinking and
held me to a high standard. At one board meeting, I had to
take a break, hide in the restroom, and cry. They treated me
fairly at every step. When I started my second company, my
first call was to Sequoia and we did it all over again.
— *Vani Kola, two-time entrepreneur and founder, Kalaari Capital*

background check of a potential portfolio company manager
are myriad.

Background investigations cannot only verify information presented by job candidates but also provide financial
and legal matters. For example, they may potentially reveal a
candidate has been a party to numerous lawsuits, a corporate
or personal bankruptcy, or a personal drug habit. While some
information revealed in the background investigation may be
of a highly personal nature, such issues may soon impinge on
a candidate's ability to successfully perform their job, thus putting a portfolio company at risk.

In one episode, several venture partners interviewed a
potential CEO over a period of 10 weeks. Immediately prior to
presenting a final letter of employment, a background investigation was conducted. This investigation revealed that the
CEO did not have the Harvard MBA he claimed to possess.
The VC fund had to restart the process of interviewing CEO
candidates; 10 weeks of work could have been saved had the
background investigation been conducted at the start of the
interviewing process.

In addition to conducting a preliminary background investigation, experienced investigators state not only that should
PE and VC funds perform investigations prior to hiring an

Would You Like Some Fries with Your Coke?

Tom Perkins, the late managing partner of Kleiner Perkins venture firm, experienced "one of the most bizarre episodes" of his career. After a successful tenure, a portfolio CEO started to demonstrate paranoia, claiming his office was bugged and that he was being followed. Perkins discovered the CEO had a cocaine habit, and the executive was removed. However, by the time of his removal, the CEO had already exacted significant damage on the portfolio company. It soon failed and was shut down.[19]

individual but also that investigations should be conducted periodically throughout the individual's career. Periodic investigations maximize the possibility of detecting issues that may arise after an individual is hired and help minimize potential damage caused by an unscrupulous employee.

For instance, one experienced investigator discovered Interpol was chasing a number of shareholders of a tiny startup, as they were the target of a fraud investigation overseas. In another situation, the investigator uncovered that a company founder had conveniently transferred assets to his business partner's spouse to avoid paying federal taxes. Numerous tax liens were levied against him.[20]

But Nobody Asked Me If I Was a Criminal

Smith & Wesson Holding Corporation chairman James J. Minder resigned when a newspaper report revealed he spent up to 15 years in prison for various armed robberies and a bank heist. Minder maintained he did not cover up his past. Instead, he stated that no one on Smith & Wesson's board asked about his criminal record. A background investigation of Minder could have prevented the embarrassing revelation and allowed the company to better evaluate Minder as a job candidate.[21]

Detailed background investigations are an essential component of the due-diligence process. Though they are more costly than a simple background check, an investigation might yield a significant piece of information that may prevent future embarrassment.

VARIOUS APPROACHES TO MANAGEMENT DILIGENCE

Management due diligence is easy; just be prepared to invest, say, 200 to 300 hours in the process. In conducting CEO due diligence, investors from storied venture firms such as Accel Partners, Bessemer, KPCB, Greylock, New Enterprise Associates (NEA), Sequoia, and Mayfield Fund shared information on how they assessed management teams of over 80 portfolio companies.[22]

Some investors conducted interviews for over 300 hours over six months, interviewing as many as nine categories of references leading to detailed assessments of the team. This approach is compared to the "airline captain approach," one in which the pilot checks every parameter to ensure that a plane is safe to fly. Though the approach is common sense, fewer than 15 percent of venture capitalists actually use this approach. Another survey respondent from Accel Partners said, "Evaluating the management team properly and backing the right people is the difference between success and failure in this [venture capital] business."[23] Some investors spent over a hundred hours on human capital valuation, spread systematically across various methods, and reference discussions with people from 11 different categories of references. This was the highest number of categories of all venture capitalists in the study, leading to a data-driven decision and less gut-based reactions.[24]

Various styles of assessing human capital include the airline captain approach, the art critic, the sponge, and the prosecutor, as developed by Geoff Smart — author of the best-selling book *Who: The A Method for Hiring*. Exhibit 23.1 highlights these four — of which the airline captain approach yielded a median internal rate of return of 80 percent. A high level of systematic and disciplined data collection and analysis of the management team members characterize this approach. In contrast, the three primary alternative approaches achieved internal rates of return under 30 percent. Though airline captains tend to achieve close to 90 percent accuracy in human capital valuations, art critics are lucky if they hit 50 percent. If you're an art critic, one of two CEOs will crash and burn.

Recall Don Valentine, founder of Sequoia Capital, once remarked that if you can select people correctly 52 percent of the time, they ought to have a statue built for you. The moral of the story is that gut checks are good, but a checklist approach will avoid the plane crash.

Exhibit 23.1 **Due-Diligence Approaches.**

Approach	Description
Airline Captain	This "checklist approach" of assessing CEO candidates "resembles the way an airline captain assesses his or her plane prior to takeoff to decide whether it is safe to fly." It is the most effective method for yielding top results, but it is also the most time-consuming and intense.
Art Critic	An art critic glances at a painting and within a few minutes can offer "an accurate appraisal of the value of the work." But art critics in venture capital can be ineffective, especially when trying to value human capital. They "think that their years of business experience equip them to achieve an accurate assessment of people in a very short amount of time — that a person's human capital is as visible in its entirety as a painting on the wall. Art critics talk a lot about intuition, gut feel, and "shooting from the hip." Unfortunately, they also talk a lot about inaccurate human capital valuations and deals in which they lost 100 percent of their investment.
Sponge	"Sponges are like art critics who need a little more data before making an assessment. Sponges do not perform a human capital needs analysis, but 'soak up' data through multiple methods of human capital valuation — and then synthesize the information in their gut. As one sponge said, he does 'due diligence by mucking around.'" The sponge is proven as effective as an art critic.
Prosecutor	"Prosecutors act like prosecuting attorneys." As they walk into the room to conduct an interview, they will indulge in theatrics, such as slamming a fist on the table, pointing a finger, and waving their arms. According to the study, "They aggressively question managers and attempt to 'pull the truth out of them.'. . . . Prosecutors talk about 'testing' management on what they know. The problem with this method is that prosecutors only collect data on present behaviors — how managers respond to questions in the present, live, right now. In comparison, past behaviors are more indicative of future behaviors," concluded Smart. One of the least effective methods for CEO selection, this method is best used for interrogations of prison cell mates.

Source: Geoff Smart, *Who: The A Method for Hiring* (New York: Ballantine Books, 2008).

In these direct interactions, venture capitalists quiz the management team on various issues related to the business. They are called work samples because they allow the venture capitalist to view samples of how the managers think and work firsthand. The time that venture capitalists spent in work samples was positively related to the accuracy of the human capital valuation in early-stage deals but negatively related to accuracy in later-stage deals. Why the difference? In early-stage deals, these discussions are more probing and often personal. In later-stage deals, formal presentations by managers coached by investment bankers can be as misleading as they are informative. The evidence suggests that work samples are not sufficient for achieving accurate human capital valuations.

- *Reference interviewing.* "Reference interviews are discussions with people who have observed the behavior of the target managers. There are several possible sources of reference interviews: personal references, supervisors, coworkers, industry players, current employees, suppliers, customers, lawyers, accountants, bankers, or other investors."

- *Past-oriented interviewing.* "Whereas the work sample relies on present or 'hypothetical' behavior, past-oriented interviews rely on *past* behavior." "This method," branded by Smart as the top-graded interview, "is based on the notion that past behavior is the best predictor of future behavior. Therefore, during past-oriented interviews, venture capitalists talk chronologically with individual managers about their entire career histories. This interviewing format has emerged as the most effective personnel assessment method in industrial psychology within the last five years."

- While these techniques of diligence have been practiced, here are the top three lessons any practitioner should watch for.

Top Three Reasons Given by Venture Capitalists for Bad Hiring Decisions

1. **Speed.** Sign that term sheet quickly and get the deal done. Pressure to invest is due to competition or co-investors.

2. **Halo effect.** What a rock star — great past performance or great technology! We just ought to be grateful to be a part of this investment.

3. **Too many cooks.** A number of syndicate partners, other team members, and no head chef.[25]

As venture practitioners, there is seldom enough time to understand the abilities and creative elements of any candidate. The biggest challenge is assessing the intangibles in a very short time.

Some practitioners have started to bring in shrinks and personal coaches to engage with CEOs. The process has its own challenges[26] and results are unclear. A number of other personality tests exist, such as the Myers-Briggs Type Indicator (MBTI), where a varied set of multiple-choice questions can help establish a window into a person's emotional and intellectual construct. The MBTI is a Jungian personality test that qualifies people into 1 of 16 types based on how they focus their attention, analyze information, make decisions, and orient themselves into the external world.

For example, ESTJ, for extraversion (E), sensing (S), thinking (T), judgment (J), people would be defined as follows: "practical, realistic, matter-of-fact. Decisive, quickly moves to implement decisions. Organizes projects and people to get things done, focuses on getting results in the most efficient way possible. Has a clear set of logical standards, systematically follows them. Forceful in implementing their plans."[27] While the MBTI output paints a picture, it doesn't offer clarity as to whether an ESTJ is suited to be a venture capitalist.

Some investors use a behavioral test for almost all hiring decisions. Equating a person's interest with a person's ability is a flawed approach. You have a lot of wannabe CEOs, but do they have the requisite abilities? Most tests are also easily faked. Obviously, if you ask the true-false question "I am a responsible person," the probability that anyone would select false is near zero. But well-designed tests are structured to eliminate these challenges. Furthermore, desirable qualities for certain positions may be handicaps for others: for example, impulsiveness and originality can be ideal in creative zones but can be seen as evidence of weakness or instability in financial and accounting realms. Keeping the perspective of the person as a whole and not relying on past experience as a prime qualification are two essential ingredients of a good test design, but the ability to match the person to a role is critical. A person's ability to influence, build relationships, solve problems, make decisions, and organize can be aligned with specific job functions that determine whether the best match can be crafted. For example, a manager and a salesperson need varying degrees of certain skills: the ability to persuade others and gain satisfaction from the successful persuasion, the degree of self-respect, the ability to keep pushing when everyone says no with strong sense of self. A CEO has a healthy ego when he or she can take no for an answer yet keep moving in the right direction without flinching.

Once Tim Draper, founder of Draper Fisher Jurvetson venture firm, asked an entrepreneur, "And what will you do if the idea does not take off?" The young entrepreneur said, "I will try something else — maybe find a job." At which point, Tim said, "Entrepreneurs never give up." Such events do not destroy the self-image but rather, drive hunger for the next opportunity. This is the key to resilience. People who take rejections personally lose steam very quickly: They escape — find that it's better to not make the next call. They invite rejection, or worse, potential conflicts. On the other hand, the *ability to persuade* coupled with the intense *need to persuade* can yield a highly productive leader.

But in most venture-backed startups, while attracting top-level talent may be important, the stability of teams is entirely unpredictable. Churn of top-level talent occurs due to a number of reasons — the pace, the pressures, low cash positions, missed milestones — and thus, practitioners need to realize that while management teams are important, no one can predict when teams run out of steam and hit the bottom — or give up!

Professor Steven N. Kaplan of the University of Chicago Graduate School of Business studied 50 venture-backed companies that evolved from business plan to IPO and found that management turnover is substantial. Kaplan concludes that investors in startups should place more weight on the horse, as in the business, and not the jockey. And all the hoo-ha about quality of management may be important in the early stages, but it declines rapidly: only 16 percent of the companies stress the importance of management expertise at the time of the IPO. Founders get slayed quickly along the way: Only 49 percent of the venture capital–backed founders stayed until the IPO.

Kaplan concludes: "Human capital is important, but the specific person appears less so. A business with strong non-people assets is enduring."[28] "The glue holding the firm together at a very early stage is composed of the patents, the stores, and the processes. Except, perhaps, for raw startups, VCs should bet on the horse. We see the jockeys changing, but we don't see the horse changing."[29]

Don Valentine of Sequoia Capital summarized it succinctly: "I think choosing great people is much more difficult than picking great markets because we have always understood the technology and understood the markets."[30]

But maybe technology can solve this problem. Personalities are influenced by genes, and while venture capitalists have not yet launched genetics-based tests as a part of management due diligence, those days may not be too far away. Business leaders tend to be unconscientious, introverted, and disagreeable. Think Steve Jobs. Genes that trigger such

Fast Electric Cars, Rocket Ships, and Mars Colonization — Would You Invest in This Pot-Smoking Entrepreneur?

Born in South Africa, and a self-taught computer programmer, Elon Musk sold his first software at the age of 12, a space game called Blast Star, for about $500. He enrolled at Stanford to get a PhD in applied physics but dropped out after two days to fulfill his entrepreneurial dreams.

His first venture was Zip2, an online publishing platform for the media industry. Things were pretty tough in the beginning, and he didn't have enough money. He sold Zip2 to Compaq for $307 million, in which he made approximately $22 million. He cofounded X.com, offering online financial services and email payments, which eventually went on to become PayPal. eBay acquired PayPal for $1.5 billion, and at the time of sale Musk was the largest shareholder, owning 11.7 percent.

For his final frontier, Musk founded his third company, SpaceX or Space Exploration Technologies, a designer and manufacturer of advanced rockets and spacecraft, with $100 million of his own moolah. The ultimate goal of SpaceX is to enable people to live on other planets. In six years, SpaceX launched its first rocket, *Falcon 1*, into orbit at a cost of roughly $7 million, which was a reduction by a factor of 10 over the prevailing costs.

Ken Howery of Founder's Fund, an investor in SpaceX, points out that "Elon plans on running SpaceX for the rest of his life. It will take him ten to twenty years to get a man on Mars. Potential investors thought we were crazy to back this rocket company, but we had followed it for six years. Elon had taken much risk out of it and even invested $100 million of his own. We won't see much competition anytime soon in this category."[31]

Musk is also the CEO of Tesla Motors, a publicly traded company manufacturing electric cars. Musk has unveiled a prototype for a "hyperloop," or a supersonic air travel machine to carry people from San Francisco to Los Angeles in 35 minutes. The proposed speed of up to 800 miles per hour is faster than most commercial airliners. This concept is aimed to make long-distance travel cheaper than any other means of transportation. So there you have it — a founder with 3 businesses each of which has broken the conventional VC model.

behavior include DRD2 variant, which causes impulsiveness, and DRD4, which makes a person novelty seeking. COMT is called the worrier gene variation that facilitates risk-taking tendencies. HTR2A causes persistence, and MAOA variation is anti-social, causing others to follow them by offering a vision of the future. Finally, the FAAH variation reduces fear and increases reaction to money making.[32] Next time you want to pick a solid founder, go ahead and send them a gene-testing kit as a part of your diligence. Ensure that DRD2, COMT, MAOA, and FAAH markers are present. Let me know how it goes.

24

Market, Product, and Business Model Analysis

The graveyard of startup land is littered with technologies in search of markets, a hammer in search of a nail. To identify the direction and timing of a market is a dark art, but to pick the winning company in an evolving opaque new market is a compounded challenge.

"The information required to make decisive investments in disruptive technology simply does not exist . . . it needs to be created through fast, inexpensive and flexible forays into the market," wrote Clayton Christensen in *The Innovator's Dilemma*. As an investor, how best should we prepare to make fast forays in the market? How best should we understand market risk?

- Is there an unmet need, a pent-up demand, a potential market pull for the products? Customers rarely know what they want and market adoption rates differ for various technologies.
- Is the market demand emerging, mature, or fragmented?
- What is the growth potential? Can the given opportunity grab a large market share quickly?
- What is the competitive advantage of the opportunity? Is it sustainable? How does it fit within the current state of competition?

- Are there any existing barriers to entry? Is there free-dom to operate? Is there an existing structure of market players? Warren Buffett says, "It's no fun being a horse when a tractor comes along. Or the blacksmith when the car comes along."
- Who is going to suffer the maximum pain when this product arrives in the market?

"We go to great lengths to be tuned into market trends, speaking to people in the industry, understanding the currents and identifying interesting opportunities. If you don't understand the problem firsthand, you don't have an insight into creating a solution," says Roelof Botha of Sequoia Capital.[1]

Market readiness is a quaint term that almost killed PayPal in its early years. Prior to joining Sequoia, Roelof Botha was the CFO of this startup, and its goal was to develop cryptography software for handheld devices. Co-founder Max Levchin, partnered with Peter Thiel, then a hedge fund manager. Thiel invested initial capital in PayPal and complemented Levchin's technical acumen. Peter bought into the premise that there is demand for cryptography and that it is a relatively untapped and poorly understood market.

"The assumption was that the enterprises were all going to go to handheld devices . . . as a primary means of communication. Every corporate dog in America will hang around with some kind of device. These assumptions were accurate, except that the timing was wrong — too early by about a decade. Any minute now, there'll be millions of people begging for security on their handheld devices," Levchin would recall. But those millions never came. Pretty soon, they realized that the market was not ready. It was a nightmare that every investor dreads — a technology in search of a market. "It's really cool, it's mathematically complex, it's very secure, but no one really needed it," Levchin would say. The company went through as many as six pivots before it found its groove. Four years from its inception, PayPal was acquired by eBay for $1.5 billion.

Compare this example with Twitter, a company that succeeded despite all its management challenges. "When the Twitter site went down for three hours, ardent fans sent homemade cookies to the engineers at the office with a note, 'We know you guys are working hard to get the site up. Thanks for everything you do,'" Bijan Sabet, Spark Capital, early investor in Twitter, would recall.[2] Mike Maples of Floodgate Fund would say, "People wondered how we could invest in something as frivolous as Twitter. If you would have gone into a VC partnership and said, I do not know how it is going to make me money, but the founder is a stud, people would look at you like, 'But it's still 140 characters or less! Huh?'"[3] According to Todd Dagres of Spark Capital, the rationale to invest in Twitter was clear: "When we invested, the traction was largely among early, techie adopters. We thought the appeal would spread from the tech community to the general population so we invested. *We were not obsessed with monetization when we invested.* [Italics added.] We felt comfortable that monetization would follow if Twitter could build a large and engaged community,"[4] he remarked.

Market readiness, or the buyer's willingness to trigger a purchase of their accord, can be an ongoing challenge for investors. Exhibit 24.1 shows various technologies and their speed of adoption. The rate of adoption in the post-Internet era is remarkably fast and steep. Companies can achieve global growth and adoption very quickly. But at the same time, the noise on the web is significant. A ready buyer, willing to move fast, can spark a startup's product-market fit — that magical moment when the sales motions generate repetitive and predictable outcomes. Adrian Fortino of Mercury Fund says that the biggest pain for an investor is working through this phase of uncertainty. "An investor (and even the startups) *can't will, or push the market to adopt a product.* The companies need to learn and iterate until they get to an adoption acceleration point that signals this fit. But it can be a very painful process for everyone involved before that point."

When it comes to trends, investor Peter Thiel warns, "Once you have a trend, you have many people doing it. And once

Exhibit 24.1 **Diffusion of innovation.**

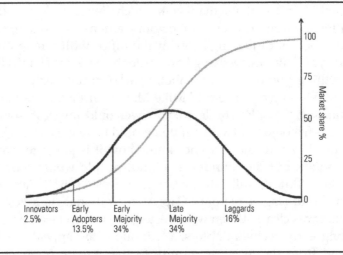

you have many people doing something, you have lots of competition and little differentiation. You do not want to be the twelfth thin-panel solar company or the Nth company of any particular trend. Trends should be avoided. What I prefer over trends is a sense of mission. That you are working on a unique problem that people are not solving elsewhere."[5]

EVALUATING THE PRODUCT

While conducting due diligence for products or technology, look for what pain points this product solves, and whether anyone will pay for it:

- *Primary value proposition.* Quite simply put, does the stated solution offer a significant advantage — a significantly quantifiable improvement over the current solution? Is it faster, better, or cheaper? Terry McGuire of Polaris Ventures says, "Early on in my career, I found every technology fascinating — my reaction would be,

'You can do that, really!' — but over time, I found that you need healthy skepticism. Believe that the world can be changed, but ask all the right questions."[6]

- *Development stage.* Where is the idea in development? Is it a mere idea on a napkin, is it in the beta stage, is it already shipping, or are the first customers at hand?

- *Can it be protected?* How easy is it for another entrant to jump in? Is this an execution play, where better execution could lead to more market share? Or is it a secret sauce, where the patents, processes, or intellectual property can be used to build a moat around the business?

- *Market acceptance and adoption rate.* Several points of friction may come into play as the new technology/product tries to penetrate the market. While this is harder to analyze, the challenge is to ascertain the market pain and reasons for adoption. Are the needs of early adopters — the first customers — and the mass market aligned?

There Must Be Something Here. . . . How an Angel Investor Spots Google

Entrepreneur and investor K. Ram Shriram recounted his initial meeting with Sergey and Larry, co-founders of Google. Ram told them that the time for search engines had come and gone. They should sell their technology to some existing search engine companies. Sergey and Larry followed his advice and shopped around their search engine technology to several existing companies, but nobody wanted to buy the technology. They called Ram Shriram. "No one wants to buy us. . . . our search engine is too fast and brutally efficient . . . it would hurt their current businesses and cut their banner-ad revenues by half. . . ." Sensing the opportunity, Shriram promptly wrote a check that led to the first $500,000 angel round in Google. While making this investment, he was skeptical. "I still did not believe that this would succeed," Ram would recall.

- *Growth potential.* What percentage of growth can be achieved in the first five years, and how does that compare with the size of the overall market? What is the effective mechanism to reach such potential? What are the points of friction in growth? Is the sales cycle long? What distribution channels exist?

Intellectual property (IP) due diligence often focuses on:

- Are the ownership, title, assignments, and license agreements in place?
- What are the claims and scope of protection (technical and geographic)?
- Noninfringement — does the core IP address the company's primary products? Does the company have freedom to operate? Are there any blocking patents?
- Can the IP be invalidated in a litigious environment? Is any threatened or pending litigation foreseen?

It is important to consider the product in conjunction with the timbre of the entrepreneur. In a study, Saras Sarasvathy finds that *"starting with exactly the same product, the entrepreneurs ended up creating companies in 18 completely disparate industries!"*[7]

As the French writer Antoine de Saint Exupéry wrote, "A rock pile ceases to be a rock pile the moment a single man contemplates it, bearing within him the image of a cathedral."[8] Sarasvathy builds a theory of effectuation whereby given means can lead to several imagined end points. The means in any entrepreneurial environment are meager: personal traits, expertise, and social networks. There is no elaborate planning — to the contrary, the plans are made and unmade, recast on a daily basis as entrepreneurs uncover new information. Seasoned entrepreneurs know surprises are no deviations from the path but are the norm from which one learns how to forge a path.

Ethics and Diligence: Avoid This Move

David Cohen, cofounder of Techstars accelerator network, writes, "A VC Asshat Move is when a VC initiates a meeting with a startup that competes directly with another startup that they are planning to fund."[9] In this "asshat" move, the VC reaches out (usually through an associate or principal) and says they heard about your awesome business. They're interested in the space and wondering if the founder can come in for a meeting. A founder goes in so that the asshat (or possibly unwitting) associate/partner VC can assess you against the company they're about to fund.

To the startup, this all feels as if the VC is just interested in startup. The VC has brains. It feels good to the founder. Then they say no. Then 30 days later, they fund a competitor. A founder can be bummed that the VC picked a competitor. However, maybe it's more devious than that. Maybe they already picked them, before they even met with the founder! *They got the founder to come in and tell them all your secrets, and now they're invested in the other company. It happens all the time.*

So avoid being an asshat VC, and treat the founder the way you would like to be treated — with transparency and respect. Try, "We are looking at various companies in this space and are nowhere close to investing in any of them. Can we talk or meet so that we can understand this market better?"

ASSESSING THE BUSINESS MODEL

A business model defines how value is created and monetized. It succinctly addresses *the who* (target customer), *the how* (distribution strategy), leading to *how much* (gross margins), and *how fast* (revenue growth).

The set of choices any company makes differentiates their business and establishes its costs and gross margins. Examples

Pricing Power

The single-most important decision in evaluating a business is pricing power. If you've got the power to raise prices without losing business to a competitor, you've got a very good business. And if you have to have a prayer session before raising the price by a tenth of a cent, then you've got a terrible business. I've been in both, and I know the difference.

— Warren Buffett

of business model jargon include "bricks and mortar" model, "razor blade" model, and "freemium" model, to name a few. The business model determines the efficiencies of meeting the customer needs and ergo impacts the margins and costs for operating. However, at the very early stages of any company, the business model may not be clear. Many investors have passed on opportunities at this stage.

In an interview with NBC, Eric Schmidt, former CEO of Google, recalls his first meeting with Larry and Sergey, and subsequently, his challenges with the Google business model.

"Larry and Sergey were sitting there . . . they looked like children to me. I certainly did not see the success of the company and thought it was a terrible risk. I did not understand the advertising business at all and thought it was a joke. I thought there was something wrong in the cash position . . . they could never be making so much money as they claimed. My first act was to investigate the books to make sure this was legit. . . . I asked to see the money was coming in to prove that the people were actually paying for these adwords. . . . I overheard that a customer who was not getting their reports was screaming at one of the sales executives! I asked our Google sales executive, why is he screaming at you and she said, 'You don't understand Eric, their business needs cash every day and *we* are their business.' And then all of a sudden, I got it!" he recalled.[10]

Schmidt joined Google and took the company public three years later, valuing the company at $23 billion. At the time of his departure, Google's market capitalization was over $180 billion.

What Business Model? We Are Just a Bunch of Kids Farting Around . . .

Speaking with *Wall Street Journal*, Marc Andreessen describes the kabuki-dancers who play clueless when asked about their business model. "Everybody thinks they don't know how they're going to make money but they actually know" he points out. But he also warns not too take all what you see at face value. "Some of the founders will do this *Kabuki dance..* pretending that *we're just a bunch of kids farting around* and don't know how we're going to make money. It's an act. They don't let anyone else realize they have it figured out because that would just draw competition." Examples like Facebook and LinkedIn fall into this category. But then he warns us not to dismiss the ones that do not know how the business model will evolve. "You need to be very cautious on these things because one of the companies that had no idea how it was going to make money when it first started was Google."[11]

At the very early stages of venture investment, practitioners rarely debate the financial projections. Rather, shrewd venture practitioners test the assumptions and capital required to achieve value inflection. "What are the milestones that this financing will achieve? As the company progresses to maturation with Series B or Series C rounds and starts to generate some revenues, the financial projections are analyzed in greater detail. Financial budgets are essential in early stages. Investors and management teams need to agree upon the major spend areas and what value such spending would create. Practitioners do not put much emphasis on detailed projections in early stages, but rather use them effectively to understand aspects of the business.

Arthur Rock, who raised the first round of capital for Intel, recalls, "I wrote the business plan myself, just two-and-a-half pages, double-spaced, which said nothing! . . . Normally I don't write business plans — the companies write a business plan. But in this case, I just felt that the investors were already there and all we needed to do was give them a little sheet of paper they could put in their files."[12] In an interesting study of over a hundred ventures, researchers concluded there was "no difference between the performance of new businesses launched with or without a written business plan."

Aristotle once remarked, "For it is the mark of an educated man to *look for precision in each class of things just so far as the nature of the subject admits*; it is evidently equally foolish to accept probable reasoning from a mathematician and to demand from a rhetorician, scientific proofs."[13] In short, seek precision where it matters. Market pain, pull and growth have often forgiven the wrongs of financial projections.

25

Terms and Conditions Apply

The Art of Structuring Investment Transactions

"Reading a term sheet is no more interesting than reading the latest volume of the Federal Register. And most lawyers will tell you what the terms mean but not how they can be used to screw you, how to negotiate them, and what is the norm," writes Mark Suster of Upfront Ventures.

Term sheets are dense with legalese, filled with jargon designed to protect, but very hard to understand. Most of terms don't apply to a large number of transactions, but they are there because someone got screwed in one situation and that led to the addition of a new term. Before you know it, it has ballooned into a big hairy lump, hard to entangle. You hire attorneys to take this pain away, but if you do not understand the structural elements, it can come back and bite you.

Much has been written about term sheets, including line-by-line explanations and analysis, but it is akin to looking at minutiae — the trees — when the perspective of the forest is critical. The goal of this chapter is to simplify, prioritize, and focus on the forest — or the key terms that help complete a transaction. In the end, it's only a handful of terms that matter.

THE SPIRIT OF THE TERM SHEET

After due diligence, investors propose a set of investment terms that define the transaction. At the heart of it, both the entrepreneurs and investors agree on the following underlying spirit of the term sheet:

- The investment opportunity and market conditions are ripe for rapid growth.
- Both parties bring a unique set of elements — entrepreneurial passion and capital — and together, these elements can help catalyze and create value faster.
- Both parties agree to collaborate for a meaningful period of time, ideally until "exit do us part."
- Both parties understand that financial success is critical for both parties, as is the timing of returns.

While this credo can be established, there can be several points of creative tension or stress between the two parties.

NEGOTIATION STRESS POINTS

The potential stress points in any negotiation — between the buyer (the VC) and seller (the company) — can occur around the economic or control factors. Exhibit 25.1 identifies these stress points and the relevant terms that can be dialed up or down.

The two major types of investment structures are convertible loans and preferred stock. The simplest form of investment, a debt would be governed by some basic parameters, such as the principal, interest rate, collateral, and schedule of payments. Debt may be secured by collateral such as assets and/or receivables, or it may be unsecured. An unsecured debt acts as a quasi-security. In this chapter, convertible note — a debt that converts to equity under given circumstances — and preferred stock structures are presented. The preferred stock

Exhibit 25.1 **Differing Goals of Entrepreneur and Investor.**

	Entrepreneurs Want	Venture Capitalists Want	Relevant Terms That Come into Play
At point of making an investment	Maximize valuation	Lower valuation; potential for up rounds and target returns	Price per share and amount of investment leading to valuation
	Adequate capital to meet and exceed milestones	Capital efficiency; reach break-even/financial independence rapidly	Total round size, use of proceeds
	Avoid loss of control	Exert control if the milestones start to slip. Ensure that the team, strategy, and vision are aligned.	Employment agreements, vesting of founders' stock, structure of board and voting rights, independent board seat choices
Between investment and exit	Freedom to operate their businesses. No micromanagement	Ensure that execution is per predetermined milestones.	Board and governance matters; milestone-based financing
	As needed, investors should assist with future financings, strategy, and customer connections.	If opportunity grows rapidly, maintain pro rata ownership, or increase ownership.	Preemptive rights or right of first refusal
	Stay in control and experiment despite inefficiencies.	If it doesn't grow as well and ends up in the "living dead" category, VCs should have the ability to liquidate their holdings.	Antidilution, redemption, or liquidation, drag-along rights, and tagalong rights
At point of exit	May choose an early exit to accomplish personal financial goals, or delay/avoid an exit to achieve ego-driven needs (like world domination).	Speed to exit and maximized value is critical.	Redemption, dividends, liquidation preferences, and registration rights

is the most commonly used investment structure in venture capital investments. At the heart of it, investment structures are designed with two key parameters: economics and control. As Brad Feld of the Foundry Group points out, terms sheets are really simple if we focus on what matters:

1. *Ownership and economics.* Buying a meaningful slice of the company at the right price is the first step for any investor. But most savvy practitioners know that while valuation is important, the potential of the opportunity in the long run, as well as other investment terms, matters. In some investments, such as distressed real estate, the philosophy that "you make money when you buy" may be true; with VC investments, that may not necessarily be the case. A pre-money value of $8 million or $10 million is not that significant when the opportunity could potentially offer a billion-dollar exit. The price-based debate creates undue tension at the point when a relationship is being established.

2. *Governance and control.* Also described as protection or control aspects of an investment, these rights minimize risks, protect against any downside, and thereby potentially amplify the upside. Governance is established by the board of directors, which typically appoints the CEO and approves an annual plan, budget, and major business decisions. The board is controlled by investors and establishes certain protective provisions to ensure that the management does not jeopardize the security interests of the investors.

Exhibit 25.2 details the various investment terms.

Exhibit 25.2 **Summary of Key Investment Terms: Preferred Stock.**

Term	What It Means	Importance to Investors	Key Negotiation Variables
	Economic Terms: Those That Impact Financial Outcomes for Investors		
Valuation	Establishes value of a company	Project potential internal rate of return	Percentage of ownership, price per share
Liquidation preference	Creates a waterfall of distribution — who gets paid first and how much — when a liquidity event occurs	Improves returns at exit, protects investment at lower exit values	Multiple (1X, 2X), participating preferred, cap/no-cap
Antidilution	Prevents dilution of investors' ownership if a down-round occurs	Minimizes downside/protects ownership	Weighted average/ full ratchet
Dividends	Allows board/investors to declare dividends	Improves potential returns	Percentage, cumulative/noncumulative
Preemptive rights/right of first refusal (ROFR)	Allows investors to buy additional shares in future rounds	Ensures increasing ownership in winners	Time frame for decision, pro rata percentage
Redemption of shares	Allows investors to redeem their ownership/ shares after a certain time frame. Ensures that investors are able to trigger the timing and conditions of an exit; drag-along and tagalong rights allow one party to sell his or her shares if the other party is able to find a seller.	Allows for exits; redemption is especially important when the company has minimal upside potential. Registration rights depend on the strength of the company and state of the public markets.	Time period (number of years), fair market value
Registration rights, conversion to common at public offering, piggyback rights, drag-along rights/tag along rights, co-sale agreements	These are exit-related provisions that come into effect at the time of IPO. Savvy practitioners stick to standard language and do not waste much time negotiating these boilerplate terms at the early stages of the company's evolution, as the probability of a company going public is much lower.		

26

Structure of
the Term Sheet

OVERVIEW

A good investment structure allows an investor to double up and invest higher amounts as the opportunity progresses — or minimize the risks if it craters. The two major types of investment structures are (a) convertible loan, also called convertible note — which converts to preferred equity and (b) preferred equity. These are compared in Exhibit 26.1. Convertible notes are often termed as "company friendly" as investors have only economic upside with little recourse for recovering their investment, nor do they have any control provisions and hence are exposed to a high level of risk. At the seed and early stages, convertible notes are the de facto norm and considered as a standard structure.

CONVERTIBLE LOANS AND SAFE

The convertible loan (also called convertible note) is a simple and popular investment structure that is used more often by angel investors and early-stage investors.

A convertible loan starts with senior position on the balance sheet and drops down, or converts to equity, when the company meets certain milestones. Primarily used as a risk-mitigation tactic in the early stages of the company, a

Exhibit 26.1 **Convertible Loan and Preferred Equity.**

Terms	Convertible Loan	Preferred Equity	Remarks
Structure	Debt, if secured, is senior to all equity.	Preferred shares, junior to debt and senior to common equity	Convertible loans are used in earlier stages of the company. As the company progresses, later investments are structured as equity rounds. Bridge loans are structured in interim financing rounds. Most convertible loans are often unsecured, or companies have no substantial assets to offer as collateral, hence the notes and act like preferred equity.
Speed of closing	Fast — typically, in weeks	Slower — typically, months	Convertible loans require lighter legal inputs and regulatory filings.
Legal costs	Low	High	
Economics	Cap, interest rate, discount rate, and conversion triggers	Valuation, liquidation; preferences and anti-dilution	Typical terms for ensuring ownership is priced.
Control and governance	None until converted	Board seats, voting rights	Investors have full control provisions with preferred equity.

convertible note allows the investor to claim the assets of a startup if it fails. Alternatively, in certain conditions, the note holder can "call" the note, or ask for redemption under certain trigger conditions.

The key parameters that come into effect with convertible notes are principal, interest rate, and conversion trigger points. After the conversion, the interest payments are terminated, and appropriate changes on the balance sheet (the liabilities are shifted to the equity section) are duly recorded. Typical convertible note terms include the following:

- *Interest rate.* Depending on the risk investor's appetite, interest rates vary from 3 percent upward to as much as

10 percent; it is normal to accrue interest for most convertible notes.

- *Term.* Typical terms are one year, but notes can be as much as two years or longer.

- *Conversion triggers.* The note converts to preferred stock upon raising a predetermined amount in a Series A round.

- *Improving the returns.* Investors frequently add a few other terms in the mix to improve the returns.

  - *Discounts.* For example, a 20 percent discount is given to the share price of the next round.

  - *Warrants.* Warrants would act as sweeteners and help aggregate a higher ownership through additional shares at a lower price point.

- *Capped convertible notes.* A capped convertible note establishes a cap on valuation for the next round; for example, a cap at $20 million pre-money indirectly establishes the valuation of $20 million at the next round. VC Mark Suster warns, "A sword that can cut both ways, a convertible note with cap, could hurt the entrepreneur. It basically sets the maximum price rather than your actual price. Example: If you do a convertible note, raising $500,000 at a $5 million pre-money, your ceiling is 10 percent of the company ($500,000/$5 million post-money). But your actual next round might come in at $2 million pre-money. You might have been better just negotiating an agreed price in the first place. Not always, but sometimes."[1] Capped notes work in favor of investors in such situations.

Consider Exhibit 26.2, which assumes that each investor puts in $100,000. The cap on conversion moves steadily upward from $3 million to $20 million, as the company progresses with its milestones. The final investor comes in at 12 percent discount, but no cap. The effect of cap on conversion can be seen when a Series A round is closed at a $12 million pre-money valuation with an effective share price of $1.29. Only

Exhibit 26.2 **Impact of Capped Conversion.**

Investor	Cap	Discount (%)	Conversion Price ($)
Investor 1	$3,000,000	0	0.46
Investor 2	$5,000,000	0	0.77
Investor 3	$20,000,000	0	1.29
Investor 4	None	12	1.14

investor 1 and investor 2 benefit from the cap. Interestingly, investor 4, who negotiated a discount on the next-round price, benefits, too.

Similar to a convertible note, a bridge note is raised to meet certain short-term needs of a company. Typically used between financing rounds, a bridge loan bridges a company between its existing cash and a future financing round. Terms are similar to a convertible note. Investors are leery of a bridge to nowhere and may build in a stair-stepped interest rate, warrants, or incentives. Thus, if the bridging event does not occur as predicted, investors gain additional ownership.

Silicon Valley accelerator Y Combinator introduced the SAFE (simple agreement for future equity) — a simple and fast way to get that first money into the company. A convertible

Just Don't F— It Up

Peter Thiel was one of the first angel investors in Facebook. He invested $500,000 as a convertible loan that would convert to equity if Facebook achieved its milestone of 1.5 million users. "Just don't fuck it up," Thiel said to Mark Zuckerberg at the time of investing.

Since Thiel had a $5m cap on his note, when Accel invested at $100m valuation, Thiel's $500,000 got him 10.2 percent equity, implying an effective valuation of $4.9 million for his investment, while Accel paid $100 million premoney. Thiel's investment grew 20X in one year, and in six years, Facebook's value grew to an estimated $50 billion. Thiel's investment had grown by 10,000X.[2]

note is often unsecured but a form of debt, with an interest rate and maturity date, while a SAFE is a convertible security that is not debt. A SAFE is simpler and shorter than most convertible notes. Both SAFEs and convertible notes convert into equity in a future priced equity round and can have valuation caps, discounts, and most-favored-nation clauses. It is important to ensure that the SAFE applies post-money ownership so that founders and investors alike realize the impact of dilution of the SAFE round.

In summary, convertible notes are used when speed matters to both sides — the company as well as the investors, and valuation negotiations are postponed for another day. Or as some VCs say, you kick the can down the road. However, this creates a risk for VCs as the price for their ownership depends on (a) execution of milestones and (b) pricing of the next round. Most early-stage investors are often glad to get into a hot deal and bet that the execution and growth will counter the pricing risk, and that they will get a 10,000X outcome, just like Thiel did.

KEEPING TERM SHEETS SIMPLE

Seed investments often focus on a few key parameters such as amount of investment and valuation (and hence the percentage of investor ownership). Other terms such as liquidation preferences, antidilution, board seats, and information rights are mentioned for clarity but are not heavily negotiated.

A simple Series Seed term sheet[3] can be boiled down to one page as seen at the end of this chapter:

A simple summary term sheet is an elegant solution to the dense and onerous several-hundred-page term sheet. The model is better and minimizes legal expenses particularly for smaller seed investments. The law offices of Wilson Sonsini Goodrich and Rosati (WSGR) have developed an online tool that generates a venture financing term sheet based on inputs/responses to an online questionnaire.[4] Roald Dahl, popular writer of children's fiction (and Sequoia partner, Roelof Botha's favorite author), wrote a short story back in 1954 called "The Great Automatic Grammatizator," in which an inventor concludes that the rules of grammar follow mathematical principles. He creates a mammoth grammatizator — a machine that can write a prize-winning novel in 15 minutes. Wilson Sonsini has developed such an engine, a *termsheetizator* if you will, that takes a few inputs and magically outputs complete term sheets. The WSGR term sheet generator is free — and even has an informational component, with basic tutorials and annotations on financing terms. This term sheet generator is a modified version of a tool that the firm uses internally, which comprises document automation tools that the firm uses to generate startup and venture financing-related documents. Because it has been designed as a generic tool that takes into account a number of options, this version of the term sheet generator is fairly expansive and includes significantly more detail than would likely be found in a customized application.

SAMPLE SUMMARY TERM SHEET

Securities:	Shares of Series Seed Preferred Stock of the Company
Amount of This Round:	$1,000,000
Investors:	Name of funds and amounts committed by each
Price Per Share:	Price per share (the "***Original Issue Price***"), based on a pre-money valuation of _____, including an available option pool of __% of the fully diluted capitalization of the Company after giving effect to the proposed financing.
Liquidation Preference:	**One** times the Original Issue Price plus declared but unpaid dividends on each share of Series Seed, balance of proceeds paid to Common. A merger, reorganization, or similar transaction will be treated as liquidation.
Conversion:	Convertible into one share of Common (subject to proportional adjustments for stock splits, stock dividends, and the like) at any time at the option of the holder.

Voting Rights:	Votes together with the Common Stock on all matters on an as-converted basis. Approval of majority of Series Seed required to (a) adversely change rights of the Preferred Stock; (b) change the authorized number of shares; (c) authorize a new series of Preferred Stock having rights senior to or on parity with the Preferred Stock; (d) redeem or repurchase any shares (other than pursuant to the Company's right of repurchase at original cost); (e) declare or pay any dividend; (f) change the number of directors; or (g) liquidate or dissolve, including any change of control.
Financial Information:	Investors who have invested at least $____ will receive standard information and inspection rights and management rights letter.
Registration Rights:	Investors shall have standard registration rights.
Participation Right:	Major Investors will have the right to participate on a pro rata basis in subsequent issuances of equity securities.
Board of Directors:	Two directors elected by holders of a majority of common stock, the right to elect one by investors.
Expenses:	Company to reimburse investors for fees and expenses (not to exceed ____).
Future Rights:	The Series Seed will be given the same rights as the next series of Preferred Stock (with appropriate adjustments for economic terms).
Founder Matters	Each founder shall have four years vesting beginning from the date of his involvement with the company. Each founder shall have assigned all relevant IP to the company prior to closing.
Closing Date	No later than 30 days from the date of this terms sheet.

27

Buy Low, Sell High

Equity Preferred Stock

When any corporation is incorporated, the founders contribute capital and designate a certain number of shares. While at the time of formation only one class of shares may exist, typically common shares, this may change when investors come into the picture. Preferred stock is a separate class of shares for investors, which enjoys control and financial preferences over and above the common shareholders.

If the value of preferred stock grows, the ability to invest additional amounts of capital, such as with preemptive rights, helps investors maintain or build their position in a growing company. If it sours, the ability to gain control (via management changes), minimize the impact of downsides (via antidilution), and attempt to salvage the remains of the day is important. In reality, most practitioners agree that if any opportunity teeters, not much can be done to resurrect the remains. In any portfolio, at least a third of the investments will likely end up as write-offs.

Structuring an investment starts with valuation primarily, followed by liquidation and antidilution preferences (used to protect ownership), dividends, and rights of first refusal, or ROFR (pronounced as rofer, which sounds like an angry dog). These terms aligned effectively can help any investor (a) establish an ownership position and (b) build up ownership as the opportunity progresses. The lead investor, the one with the maximum investment amount in the round, typically sets the major terms.

The other syndicate investors have a choice — to accept those terms or not — but seldom have significant negotiating leverage.

It is important to establish "middle-of-the road" terms. Any exotic nonstandard terms will get cleaned up and renegotiated by future investors and will impact the reputation of the venture firm. In as much as 30 percent of subsequent financing, new investors renegotiated terms established at previous rounds. The most commonly renegotiated terms are (1) automatic conversion price, (2) liquidation preferences, (3) redemption maturity, and (4) funding milestones, vesting provisions, or performance benchmarks.[1]

VALUATION METHODS AND OTHER VOODOO ARTS

For those who have been in the business of venture capital long enough, many will ruefully reminisce about missed opportunities — some due to high valuations, and others due to timing.

Jim Bryer, when making the first investment in Facebook, remarked, "The price was way too high, but sometimes that's what it takes to do the deal." Accel's $12.7 million investment to acquire 15 percent of Facebook at approximately $100 million pre-money valuation grew by 50X in six years.[2] In hindsight, the price does not seem too high. Several investors had passed on Facebook — the opportunity of the decade. Josh Koppelman of First Round Capital missed investing in Twitter due to valuation concerns. "We offered Twitter a term sheet — $500,000 at a $5 million pre-money valuation." But Evan Williams, founder of Twitter, continued to fund it. Three months later, Union Square Ventures led the round at a $20 million valuation. Josh passed on Twitter, saying, "We thought the valuation was high."[3]

While valuation is one of the important terms for the entrepreneur as well as the investors, no simple method exists to calculate valuation at the seed- and early-stage of investments.

Valuation is primarily a function of market demand (*hot opportunity, must get in now*) and capital supply. For the more rational, valuation is a function of the sector, stage of the company, and the geography. Technology sectors often gain higher valuations as compared to medical devices or biotech sectors. In competitive geographies like Silicon Valley, valuations can soar quickly. In regions that suffer from paucity of capital, strong startups barely get what they deserve. Seasoned investors often think of valuation in simpler terms — instead of overthinking the numbers, a typical *"sounds about right"* reaction is often heard when numbers are tossed around.

Depending on the stage of the company, valuation can be a simple back-of-the-envelope calculation, based on comparable transactions, called "comps." Let us wear our academic hats and look at the approaches to valuation. However, bear in mind that valuation is a subjective art at an early stage of venture investing, rather than formulaic net present value (NPV)/ discounted cash flow (DCF) approach. Aswath Damodaran, author of *The Dark Side of Valuation*, writes, "There can be no denying the fact that young companies pose the most difficult estimation challenges in valuation. A combination of factors — short and not very informative histories, operating losses and the ... high probability of failure — all feed into valuation practices that try to avoid dealing with the uncertainty by using a combination of forward multiples and arbitrarily high discount rates."[4]

THE DRIVERS OF VALUATION

Valuation is often a function of several factors:

- The opportunity serves an *attractive market* with higher *growth potential*.
- The opportunity has *an established competitive position* via execution, market dominance, and low number of threats.

- A visionary CEO and a *strong team* — "an execution machine" — is in place.

- The opportunity demonstrates *strong financial metrics*, high growth rate of revenues, robust gross margins, and efficient uses of capital.

- A meaningful *exit potential within the target time frame* can be achieved: The universe of strategic buyers is large, accessible, and actively seeks growth opportunities via acquisition.

- Capital supply–demand drivers are in favor of the company and the sector/geography in which it operates. Valuation of startups is much higher in competitive markets like Silicon Valley.

- Finally, the state of the public markets, frothiness, or excessive capital supply, can often elevate valuations across the board and trounce all of the above criteria.

- When companies underperform, or markets slow down, down-round financings may occur. Try not to lose too much sleep over down rounds — because once you have invested, these are merely paper movements and the only valuation that matters is the one at the time of your exit.

For most investors, the exercise of establishing valuation begins with the end in mind. What is the target return that can be generated for such an investment? Valuation economics boil down to maximizing ownership while minimizing dilution as well as anticipated exit outcomes. Exhibits 27.1 and 27.2 show how valuation is often driven by anticipated exit values, often measured only by cash-on-cash multiples. Recall that in the LP fund-diligence section, several LPs described the importance of measuring both — cash-on-cash and IRR.

Exhibit 27.1 **Factors for setting valuation.**

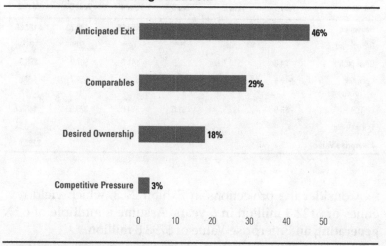

Anticipated Exit — 46%
Comparables — 29%
Desired Ownership — 18%
Competitive Pressure — 3%

Source: Based on Gompers, Paul A., William Gornall, Steven N. Kaplan, and Ilya A. Strebulaev. "How Do Venture Capitalists Make Decisions?" NBER Working Paper Series, No. 22587, September 2016.

Exhibit 27.2 **Financial metrics to analyze investments: Cash-on-cash matters more to GP.**

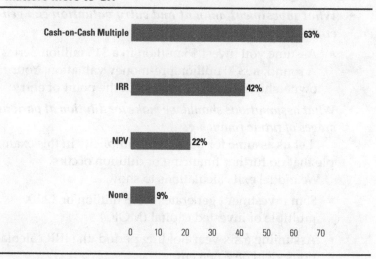

Cash-on-Cash Multiple — 63%
IRR — 42%
NPV — 22%
None — 9%

Exhibit 27.3 **Enterprise Value Based on Future Projections.**

$m	Year 1	Year 2	Year 3	Year 4	Year 5	Year 6
Revenues	$9.6	$21.1	$37.01	$59.99	$89.70	$122.98
Growth rate		120%	75%	62%	50%	37%
Gross profits	$4.8	$12.7	$25.9	$41.9	$67.2	$98.3
Operating expenses	$15.6	$23.5	$35.3	$45.9	$59.7	$77.6
EBITDA	–$5.9	–$2.3	$1.6	$14.05	$29.99	$45.27
Exit multiple						6.5x
Enterprise Value						**$798.8**

Consider the projections in Exhibit 27.3, which yield revenues of $122.8 million in 6 years. Assume a multiple of 6.5X generating an Enterprise Value of $798.8 million.

As you debate the valuation for this company, work your way backward from the exit value and ask these questions:

- *What should your ownership in this company be, at the time of its exit?* If we assume 10 percent ownership at exit, it generates $79.8 million in proceeds.
- *What investment amount and entry valuation can generate target returns?*
  - Assume you invest $5 million in a $15 million Series A round, at $30 million pre-money valuation. Your ownership is about 11 percent at the point of entry.
- *What assumptions should we make for dilution at various stages of future financing?*
    Let us assume for the sake of simplicity in this example that no further financing or dilution occurs.
    We model exit calculations to show:
  - $5m investment generates $79.8 million or 12.8X multiple of invested capital (MOIC).
  - Assuming a six-year holding period, the IRR calculations yield 56.7 percent.

- *Are these return-expectations (of both IRR and MOIC) sufficient?*
- *If variations in revenues and exit multiples were to occur, and they always do, how resilient is the potential for returns?*

If we assume the comparable exit multiples drop to 4.5X, how does that impact the returns?

Comparable Revenue Multiple	4.5x	6.5x	8.5x	10.5x
MOIC	8.8x	12.8x	16.7x	20.6x
Expected IRR (%)	46.9%	56.7%	64.3%	70.5%

Such a simple modeling exercise should allow any practitioner to assess whether the investment opportunity offers the expected target returns, and what expected ranges can be projected. This model does not factor in dilution of ownership across multiple rounds. The rule of thumb is to keep investing and building up ownership in winning companies at every round of investment.

As one venture capitalist pointed out, "I expect each of my portfolio companies to generate 10X or higher returns and make the fund whole — getting caught up in discount ratios and valuation techniques does not help. I seek the best in class and work hard to make them the *numero uno* of their category." Sir Michael Moritz of Sequoia Capital once remarked, "We are in the business of creating a large bonfire with a small matchstick."

Establishing a price for an illiquid security, with significant risk (management risk, market risk, technology risk, follow-on financing risk) is nebulous activity. At the early stages of investment, practitioners have honed the valuation process to an art form, a subjective technique at best. When valuation debates become prolonged, some practitioners consider using a blended approach that diffuses valuation issues. These include liquidation multiples and springing warrants, but these can create complexity in the legalese and deal structures.

For most practitioners, the ability to generate returns is what matters. For each investment, seasoned investors seek 10X or higher returns. As most agree, valuation is just a small, yet important, part of the overall structure.

While negotiating valuation, any practitioner keeps the following three variables in perspective: timing of exit, ownership at exit, and target IRR. The timing of an exit depends on several factors, both internal and external. Any rapid churn in the management team, unforeseen uses of cash, and changes in the burn rate will significantly affect the timing and value of the exit. At times, investor's tactfully force an exit, as they need to demonstrate liquidity and performance. External factors such as competitive threats, plateauing of growth, or competition can force an exit. The best scenario is, of course, an unsolicited offer to purchase the company.

COMPARABLE VALUATIONS OF SIMILAR INVESTMENTS (COMPS)

In the comparable valuation or comps method, valuation is determined by comparable transactions in the marketplace. Consider Exhibit 27.4, which shows a typical range of values. The revenues and the acquisition price are estimated, as these may not be declared or available publicly. A median and mean multiple is calculated that indicates a range of multiples that could be deployed in such a scenario.

In Exhibit 27.5, the universe of publicly traded companies is assessed. Critics argue that the method does not factor in

Exhibit 27.4 **Sample Comparable Method (Private Companies).**

Company	Acquisition Price	Estimated Revenue	Multiple
Tech Gizmo, USA	$550M	$50M	11X
Maps-R-Us, Germany	$225M	$28M	8X
Gemini Global, USA	$155M	$26.2M	5.9X
Pan Premier, Spain	$40M	$2M	20X

Valuation in 13 Short Tweets — Elizabeth Yin of Hustle Fund

@dunkhippo33 offers some advice to founders on early-stage valuation:

1. First and foremost, valuation is not actually about how much your company is worth.

2. Obviously if you have zero rev and you have raised money at a $4m post money, you are not currently worth $4m.

3. And using the public equities definition of market cap doesn't hold, either. A mkt cap of $50b in public equities is a reflection of how much investors believe your total revenues can amnt to.

4. So the best descriptor of what I think early stage valuation is — *it's just a supply and demand problem*. Supply of your round and investor demand of your round.

5. If you are raising say $200k and you have $500k of investor interest, your valuation can be bid up. If you are raising $2m and no one is interested, then your valuation is . . . well $0.

6. So it's less about your "actual" worth and more about what investors want to pay.

7. One could argue, "Well, what investors want to pay is based on what they think you are worth." And that's both true and false.

8. Where it's true: the more proof pts you have per your idea, the more investors will be interested, the more you can bid up the valuation. (Most early stage investors weight how big an idea is >> traction. But for two of the same idea, more traction is better.)

9. Where it's false: let's say that two funds are interested in the same company. One is a $100m fund. The other is a $1b fund. The latter is willing to pay a higher valuation, because this round is an option for the next. The former fund has to buy as much equity as possible now.

10. So you can see that willingness to pay higher valuations is not just about you as the company but also about the investor.

11. Another criteria is how valuable an investor is beyond money — a past portfolio co had two terms sheets: one from A16Z and another from someone else. In this case, A16Z was the lower valuation. The founder took it because he knew they would be really value add.

12. Lastly, sometimes investors are willing to pay a higher valuation to buy a logo or network w either the founders / investors in that round. This has nothing to do w the details of the business itself.

13. So as you think through valuation — it's less about how much am I "worth" and more about a) which investors do I want to work with? b) how quickly do I want to raise? c) how do I create a good supply vs demand dynamic in my round?

Exhibit 27.5 **Sample Comparable Method (Publicly Traded Companies).**

	TTM Revenues ($m)	TTM EBITDA ($m)	Enterprise Value ($m)	Enterprise Value (X Rev)	Enterprise Value (X EBIT)
ABC Technology	670	73	1,323	2.0	18.1
Street Group	433	99	1,220	2.8	12.3
Avalon Innovations	1229	114	3,600	2.9	31.6
Sapphire Technology	225	45	990	4.4	22.0

several risks, such as technology, market adoption, and liquidity risks. Furthermore, the growth rates and gross margins for each company are different.

While this method is used broadly in later-stage companies, it has its own set of fair challenges:

- *The universe of comparable transactions may be broad.* As they say, with a large data set, you can draw any conclusion you desire. When entrepreneurs present comparable transactions, and when investors dig into the data set, valuations can be surprisingly different.

- *Lack of transparency.* While the only data available are the pre-money valuation, the data do not depict the finer nuances of strengths and risks embedded within. For example, valuation skews toward the positive when an experienced entrepreneur may be leading an opportunity. Other factors that may affect value are the quality of technology and its attractiveness to customers or existing partnerships — these factors may be invisible from the comps data set.

- *The comparable data set in a frothy environment may not be relevant.*

Options Trading

Early-stage investors can seldom predict whether an opportunity will grow, gain momentum, and generate returns. A classic investment approach is to invest a small amount and gain a seat at the table. It is similar to buying an option to invest in future rounds. If the company grows fast, investors could maintain or build up their ownership position by investing additional amounts in future rounds.

DISCOUNTED CASH FLOW METHOD

If you have a master's in business administration, the DCF valuation technique would have been drilled into the depths of your cranium. Like most highly academic techniques, the DCF is irrelevant for early-stage venture capital on a number of counts. For one, at an early stage of any company, you really do not have comparable data, and the rest is projections. Thus, I have seen entrepreneurs conjure up projections and use extensive DCF models to develop precise valuation — a healthy exercise — but at the end of the day, value is what can be transacted up. A great model with multiple Excel spreadsheets is helpful, but if a transaction cannot be consummated, what good is all this idealism?

To calculate valuation of a firm using DCF, we estimate the percentage of growth and the number of years of such growth. The entrepreneur's estimates and practitioners' estimates on growth rates can vary significantly. But let us assume that the two parties agree upon a growth rate.

The second variable is free cash flows (FCF) available during such a period. FCF seems like a novel concept when we discuss startups and early-stage companies.

Finally, we assume a discount rate — you consider the terminal value and those FCFs and pull them all together to the present date. That rabbit you pull out of your hat is called net present value (NPV) — a formula that is an amalgamation of four different projected variables — the rate of growth, the time period of growth, the cash flows, and the cost of capital.

When all is said and done, you are trying to establish a value for the existing assets and future growth. The approach is well suited for more mature companies.

Startups have little or no revenues, no customers, and at times, operating losses. Even those young companies that are profitable have short histories, and most young firms depend on private capital, initially, owner savings, and venture capital investments later on. As a result, many of the standard techniques we use to estimate cash flows, growth rates, and discount rates either do not work or yield unrealistic numbers.

Researchers studied the survival rate of almost 9 million firms and concluded that only 38 percent of businesses survived over a five-year period. See Exhibit 27.6, which shows the survival rate of technology companies, which is substantially lower than health services.[6] In fact, at least two-thirds of technology companies die in five years, a higher mortality rate as compared to health services. Thus, astute practitioners factor this survival rate in the valuation negotiations.

Damodaran suggests that besides using "a combination of data on more mature companies in the business and the

---

How to Value Intel: Lessons from Arthur Rock

Bob Noyce called me one day and said, "We're thinking of leaving Fairchild Semiconductor to form a company," and I asked him how much money they thought they needed to get started, and they said, "$2.5 million." And I said, "Okay. You got it."

No — first, I think we first discussed the terms — how much of the company they would be willing to give to investors for putting up $2.5 million, and we agreed on 50 percent.

Then I said, "Okay, you're covered," and went about raising it.[5]

Exhibit 27.6 **Survival Rate of Firms.**

Sector	Year 1 (%)	Year 5 (%)	Year 7 (%)
Health services	86	50	44
Technology	81	31	25
Financial activities	84	44	37
Business services	82	38	31
All Firms	**81**	**38**	**31**

company's own characteristics to forecast revenues, earnings, and cash flows," we should "adjust the value for the possibility of failure."[7] He further points out that multiples of valuation should be considered at the point of exit, rather than present-day multiples. If the revenue of a start-up after year 5 were to drop to a compound annual growth rate (CAGR) of 10 percent, the multiple should reflect this growth as opposed to, say, 50 percent CAGR in earlier years. This would create an interesting conundrum where, besides revenues, practitioners would try to project the exit multiple five years down the road.

While this may not be adopted as easily, most practitioners use a rule of thumb to assert valuation while considering risks of technology failure, management churn, financing risk, and illiquidity premium.

LIQUIDATION PREFERENCE

Mark Suster of Upfront Ventures says that the second-most important term after valuation is liquidation preference.[8]

Liquidation preferences, often seen as an opportunity to juice up the returns, are rights to receive a return before the common shareholders do. These preferences come into play at the time of liquidating the assets of the company. Liquidation occurs under two scenarios: a sale via acquisition (presumably a good outcome if the sale price is right) or shutting down the company (and calling it a dog).

From a negotiation perspective, liquidation preferences have the following variables:

- *Liquidation multiple*. Defined as multiple of the amount invested, practitioners set a multiple of, say, one time the value of the original investment. This essentially translates to investors recovering the amount invested. The multiple is an indicator of market dynamics, and while one time (1X) is the standard norm in a healthy market, at times the multiple has scaled up to as much as 10 times.

- *Straight convertible preferred or nonparticipating*. In a non-participating liquidation preference, investors are entitled to the amount they invested and dividends, if any. That is it, they do not get anything more. Under certain circumstances, where an earn-out amount has been offered upon achieving certain milestones, investors can get a higher return when the preferred shares are converted to common. Thus, practitioners should ensure they have the option to choose the greater of the two scenarios.

- *Participating preferred (or, as entrepreneurs call it, a double dip)*. In this scenario, investors first recover the amount invested, dividends, and the multiple agreed on. The double dip occurs when the preferred shareholders get to take a share of the common shareholders on an as-converted basis. Market trends indicate that about 50 percent of the transactions fall in this category.

- *Capped participation*. A smart entrepreneur may have invented this term, which essentially caps the return any investor can get. A typical cap would be, say, 2.5X of the original amount invested. Typically, about 40 percent of participating transactions are capped.

As Exhibit 27.7 illustrates, liquidation preferences can have a significant impact on the rate of return, but it is primarily a downside protection mechanism for investors. At larger exit values, these preferences do not have any significant impact on the common shareholders or the IRR. These are just means of protecting an investors downside when the exit is not as high.

If you are a Series A investor, and a Series B investor stacks on their preferences on top of yours, the scenario could get complex due to the misalignment of interests between the various parties (two separate classes of preferred shareholders and common shareholders). Brad Feld of the Foundry Group writes:

As with many VC-related issues, the approach to liquidation preferences among multiple series of stock varies (and is often overly complex for no apparent reason). There are two primary approaches: (1) the follow-on investors will stack their preferences on top of each other: Series B gets its preference first, then series A, or (2) the series are equivalent in status (called *pari passu. . .*) so that Series A and B share proratably until the preferences are returned. *Determining which approach to use is a black art which is influenced by the relative negotiating power of the investors involved, ability of the company to go elsewhere for additional financing, economic dynamics of the existing capital structure, and the phase of the moon.*

Higher liquidation preferences = Demotivated founders and employees[9]

Exhibit 27.7 **Liquidation Preference Stack and Its Impact on IRR.**

Liquidation Preference	4X	2.5X Capped	1X
IRR to investors	87%	84%	81%
Multiple of invested capital (MOIC)	12.2X	11.4X	10.7X

Excessive liquidation preferences benefit only the investors and reduce the potential outcomes for common shareholders, including management and founders. When those who are working hard to create value see that all they would get is W2-like returns, the desire to perform and create significant value diminishes. Feld explains:

> The greater the liquidation preference ahead of management and employees, the lower the potential value of the management/employee equity. There's a fine balance here, and each case is situation specific, but *a rational investor will want a combination of "the best price" while insuring "maximum motivation" of management and employees*. Obviously what happens in the end is a negotiation and depends on the stage of the company, bargaining strength, and existing capital structure, but in general, most companies and their investors will reach a reasonable compromise regarding these provisions.

An elegant solution to protect the founders could be the founder's liquidity preference. Although rarely used, it is a creative approach to address the challenges wherein the founders can wash out completely. "Creating a special class of common stock for the founders with a special liquidation preference is not typical, but it is an option that offers investors a great deal of flexibility and creativity," writes attorney Jonathan Gworek. This can be a win–win approach where a founder's liquidity preference creates a financial threshold for the founders, especially if they have invested significant capital prior to any outside investments. Such a clause allows for the founders to retain a floor, a minimum position for value created by the entrepreneurs.[10]

Professors Colin Blaydon and Fred Wainwright, who head the Center for Private Equity and Entrepreneurship at the Tuck School of Business at Dartmouth, write that "risk-reducing mechanisms were seen to be counterproductive — an attempt to 'close the barn door after the horse was gone.'"

They conclude, "the continued prevalence of a participation feature in deal structures today indicates that the VC community either has less confidence in the potential growth of portfolio companies or a lower appetite for risk. This sets a precedent for terms in subsequent financing rounds" and that the "VCs who funded the earlier rounds . . . will now have to transfer some of that hard won value to the new investors."[11] It becomes a karmic cycle, as a Series A investor tries to squeeze the entrepreneur; when the Series B investors come in, they love to jump in and do the same. Jack Ahrens of TGap Ventures says, "It is best to avoid multiple liquidation preferences — it becomes a rat's nest and does not do anybody any good." At the early stage of investment, simpler is better. "You are betting on the market and the CEO — let's not get too tied up in preferences and such legalese when there are no revenues and no product," says Rick Heitzmann, FirstMark Capital.[12]

Typical trends of liquidation preferences vary with market conditions. Senior liquidation preferences are often seen in later stage investment rounds. Later stage investors are risk averse and often have lower ownership, and thus they demand better preferences. In certain market conditions, when capital supply shrinks, or if the company may have struggled, liquidation preferences as high as 5X preference have been observed.

ANTIDILUTION PROTECTIONS

Antidilution protection is a downside protection mechanism that protects existing investors when a company is forced to accept a down round, which is a lower share price compared to what the previous investors have paid. Existing investors receive additional shares, and their position is adjusted based on the price of the down round. The common shareholders, typically the management and founders, endure the maximum pain in such circumstances. An investor-friendly term, it forces the management team to retain value, execute on its milestones, and ensure value is created in an effective and timely manner. However, down rounds can occur with changes in burn rates (as unanticipated issues occur). Poor market conditions could significantly affect a company's ability to raise future rounds of capital.

Antidilution provisions fall into three categories:

1. *Full ratchet.* An investor-friendly provision, this has the largest impact on the common shareholders. The full ratchet converts the price of *all* the previously sold shares down to the price of the current round, irrespective of the amount raised or the number of shares issued.

2. *Broad-based weighted average.* A company-friendly provision (well, a true company-friendly provision equals no antidilution provisions), this clause has the least impact of all on common shareholders, as it is based on the weighted average of the outstanding shares, including options and warrants.

3. *Narrow-based weighted average.* The same as broad-based, this eliminates the options and warrants and thus has a lower impact on common shareholders.

The norm is weighted average (either broad-based or narrow-based), and thus practitioners are better off staying in the middle of the road.

As Exhibit 27.8 illustrates, the impact of antidilution on Series A would have been significant if there were no protective provisions. This is illustrated in the line "Additional ownership due to antidilution protection." The full ratchet offers maximum additional ownership, while the weighted average drops the ownership proportionally. Notice the significant drop in ownership for common shareholders.

Frank Demmler, who has participated in over 200 investments, points out that if Series A antidilution leaves little ownership for common/management, the Series B investors will have a due concern. Often, Series B investors will drive renegotiation between Series A and management to find a satisfactory middle ground. "The bottom line is that under

Exhibit 27.8 **Impact of Antidilution Provisions on Ownership.**

	Pre-round Ownership	Full Ratchet (%)	Weighted Average — Broad (%)
Series A preferred	47	17	17.8
Additional ownership due to antidilution protection		17	13.2
Common	43	18.9	19.8
Options	10	4.4	4.6

most circumstances, full ratchet antidilution protection will be completely waived, while weighted average is likely to be accepted."[13]

So why negotiate for something that will potentially be renegotiated anyway? *Over 90 percent of the financing rounds used weighted average antidilution.*[14] These percentages vary slightly as capital supply-and-demand conditions vary. It is best to stick with weighted average antidilution.

Dividends

While most early-stage practitioners know that dividends are neither expected nor declared by the board, the provision is included in the term sheet. The investor-friendly language is to seek cumulative dividends to juice up returns at the time of an exit. The data trends indicate that about 40 percent of Series A financings seek cumulative dividends. In some years, as much as 80 percent of Series A financings sought cumulative dividends.

As we can see in Exhibit 27.9, liquidation preferences, combined with the antidilution provisions, impact the overall economics significantly.

Pay-to-Play

Usually, this clause comes into effect when several investors have joined the club, say at Series B, Series C, or later. The

Exhibit 27.9 **Key Economic Terms and the Middle Path.**

Economics	Investor Friendly	Middle of the Road	Company Friendly
Liquidation preferences	2× or higher, no cap, participating preferred	1× participating preferred	1X nonparticipating
Antidilution preferences	Full ratchet	Weighted average — Broad	Weighted average — Narrow
Dividends (as and when declared by the board)	12% cumulative	8% noncumulative, as and when declared	None

Source: Adapted from Alex Wilmerding, *Term Sheets & Valuations: An Inside Look at the Intricacies of Term Sheets & Valuations* (Boston, MA: Aspatore Books, 2003).

provision tries to keep the syndicate together and ensure that all investors continue to participate in future rounds, especially when times are bad.

As venture funds of varying shapes, sizes, and motivations join the syndicate, it is likely that Fund A will not have as much ammunition as Fund B. Or, Fund A may no longer align with Fund B on the company's exit potential, execution plan, or business strategy. The pay-to-play provision would mean that if Fund A is unable to invest more capital in the following rounds for any reason, it will no longer be able to "play" and gets kicked out, wherein its ownership is converted to common stock, resulting in the loss of preferences and any substantial economic upside.

Preemptive Rights/Right of First Refusal

Seed- and early-stage investors seek a right of first refusal (ROFR) to ensure that they can maximize their upside. Thus, when a company is ready to offer additional securities, the first call would be placed to existing shareholders. In some situations, ROFR allows investors to purchase any founder's stock that may be up for sale. This tactic is used by early-stage investors who place a smaller amount of capital, and as the opportunity matures, they are able to increase their ownership and take advantage of the potential upside.

The Contentious Challenge — Right of First Refusal, Super Pro-Rata, and Future Financings

Jeremy Liew, partner at Lightspeed Venture Partners, reached out to Evan Spiegel, a Stanford University student who had recently started Snapchat with a fraternity brother. Evan's father was tired of paying Snapchat's bills, and Lightspeed promptly invested roughly $500,000 in Snapchat's seed round. In the terms, Lightspeed negotiated the right of first refusal to invest in a future round and the ability to take 50 percent of the future round.

A few months after Lightspeed completed its investment in Snapchat, another Silicon Valley venture firm, General Catalyst, offered Snapchat $2 million to $3 million, putting the company's valuation at $22 million, but did not close the investment, apparently due to the ROFR negotiated by Lightspeed. Evan Spiegel would say, "When we took financing, our lawyers would take us through the documents and they'd say: 'Oh, don't worry about it. It's all standard.' I've since learned that *standard* means either the person who's walking you through documents doesn't understand them or you could be getting taken advantage of. *When someone says something is standard, just ask why, and why and why and why, until you really understand how the deal is structured.*" Eventually, Evan struck a deal with Lightspeed, which would be able to buy a limited number of Snapchat shares at a discount. In exchange, the venture firm would remove its ROFR clause and other terms that the Snapchat founders considered onerous.[15]

Lightspeed's investment of a total of $8.1 million generated 250X from SNAP at IPO — its equity was valued at $2 billion.[16]

Options and Warrants

Stock options are incentive mechanisms granted to employees, advisors, and consultants, while a typical recipient of a warrant is an investor. From a VC perspective, both roughly translate to the same — they impact dilution of your ownership when these are exercised. Fully diluted ownership means when all preferred stock has been converted to common stock — stock options and warrants have been exercised and any reserved shares have been issued.

Employee stock options are offered as incentive tools to attract and retain talent. Incentive stock options are used for vendors, consultants, and the like. Typical option agreements include number of shares granted, strike price, term and vesting, and buyback provisions.

A warrant is a right to buy a security at a fixed price: the exercise or strike price. Typically, warrants are issued in conjunction with an existing investment — a security, such as a convertible note or venture debt. For investors, warrants provide the ability to increase the overall returns. Investors can improve their ownership positions at a suitable point in the future, as the opportunity matures.

A typical warrant would include terms such as the following:

- Percentage of investment or amount of investment:
  - *Percentage of investment*. If an investor issues a $500,000 convertible note with 10 percent warrants, the warrant allows the investor to invest $50,000 in the future.
  - *Amount of investment*. The warrant allows an investor to purchase shares worth $100,000.
- Strike price:
  - *Nominal value*. An example would be a value established at, say, $0.001 per share. An investor-friendly term, this would allow an investor to increase ownership at a certain point in the future.
  - *Share price of the next round*. A company-friendly term, this allows an investor to double up or increase the ownership position.
- Term:
  - *Time*. Term could be any time, say, up to 10 years; the longer the duration, the better for the investors.

- *Event-based triggers*. Events reduce the life of the warrant upon certain trigger conditions, such as future financing or value creation milestones. Such milestones reduce the overall liquidity that would affect the founders.

Springing Warrants

At the point of entry, valuation debates are the primary cause of tension. Founders believe that the value of the company should be as high as possible. It's a technological marvel — future revenue and growth projections are just a matter of time. For practitioners who have heard ample stories and burned their capital, the skepticism is obvious.

For John Neis of Venture Investors, the answer was simple — take the middle path. When the founders of Tomo Therapies came up to discuss an investment opportunity, Neis was intrigued, but like most practitioners, he looked at the financial projections with a degree of healthy skepticism. Typically, the struggle between the buyer and the seller is evident, as each side tries to extract the maximum value up front. Not in this case — Neis developed a structure of springing warrants.

In this structure, quite simply, the venture fund's ownership decreases as the founders and entrepreneurs meet their projections and milestones. A representative example is presented in Exhibit 27.10. It is an elegant model to balance the ownership struggles and provide adequate rewards if the founders meet their goals. The springing warrants are issued to founders, and these are exercisable (at a nominal exercise price) at certain milestones. The founders would thus acquire additional shares of common stock based on a predetermined formula. In the example in Exhibit 27.10, if the founders believe they can generate revenues of $30 million in Year 3, while the investors think it would be more like $23 million, the two parties can converge the valuation today with the assurance that as founders create value, investors relinquish a portion of their equity.

Exhibit 27.10 **Springing Warrants Can Be an Effective Way to Diffusive Valuation and Performance-Related Challenges.**

Revenues	Year 1	Year 2	Year 3
Baseline revenues	$5M	$12M	$23M
Upside case revenues	$7M	$15M	$30M
Additional equity granted to founder for meeting upside targets	3%	5%	3%

Tomo Therapies grew to $200 million in revenues in four years of commercial launch and was listed on Nasdaq. For Neis and Venture Investors, the largest shareholders, this investment yielded a solid outcome. In his modest style, John Neis says, "Tomo's technology saves lives — and bringing that to market — was the important goal for all. The financial returns are always a welcome byproduct of our efforts to change the world."

GOVERNANCE AND CONTROL: PROTECTING YOUR SECURITIES

All governance and control aspects in any term sheet are designed to protect the ownership interests of investors (Exhibit 27.11). Security ownership can be challenged because of internal performance issues (poor performance leads to cash challenges or lower valuation) or external financings (down rounds, debt obligations). An investor attempts to manage these conditions by controlling the board by governance and control mechanisms.

Consider the Series A investor in NewCo, who owns a 47 percent interest and thus is a minority ownership from a control perspective. But special voting rights and preferences allow such an investor to exercise control over key aspects of the company. As described in Exhibit 27.11, typical board approval items include the following:

- *Officers and management hiring, firing, and compensation.* These provisions allow the board to select the CEO, and if necessary, replace him or her if performance is lax.

Exhibit 27.11 **Key Governance Terms — Those That Impact Control of the Company.**

Term	What It Means	Importance to Investors	Key Negotiation Variables
Board composition	Number of seats for Series A, common, and independent shareholders	Allows for control and protection of security	Number of seats, how the board structure can be changed, rights of preferred shareholders vis-à-vis the rest
Board-approval items	Board approves hiring of executives, employment and compensation agreements, issuance of stock options, annual operating plan, and incurrence of debt obligations or contracts above a certain financial limit	To protect the ownership and equity, board would approve key business decisions that may impact the operations or the equity structure of the company.	David Cowan of Bessemer Venture Partners says, "As long as the ink is black — if the company is doing fine — I don't care much about control provisions."
Protective provisions	Provisions allow for protection of security interest.	Preferred shareholders will approve all changes to securities, board structure, mergers, redemption of stock, and amendments to articles of incorporation.	Most of these terms are standard, and very few practitioners open these up for negotiation.
Employment and vesting for management	Keeps management team focused on building the business	Aligns interests of founders and investor.	Includes employment agreements, stock vesting, restrictions on co-sale, creation of option pool, key man insurance, noncompete provisions

Source: Brad Feld, "Term Sheet: Liquidation Preference," *FeldThoughts* (blog).

- *Stock option programs.* These have a dilutive impact on the overall shareholders if an option pool is not established. Establishing an option pool may require shareholder approval. If an option pool is established, the board would approve grant of options to key executives.
- *Annual budgets.* As the annual budgets are directly related to the direction of the company and spend rates, the board typically approves all major budget items.

- *Debt obligations.* Any secured debt creates a lien on assets of a company and can be a drain on the cash. Under the right circumstances of growth, venture-backed companies raise debt. The board would approve any debt obligations to ensure they are aligned with the CEO/CFO's plans and performance.

Protective provisions included in the term sheet would minimize any impact to the value or preferences of the security:

- *Ownership/shares.* Any issuance of stock would impact the ownership and dilute current owners. Furthermore, the pricing of stock, the amount being raised, and the type of investors are all approved by existing investors/board members.
- *Mergers/acquisitions and co-sale.* Investors and all shareholders would approve such moves, as these impact ownership and economics.
- *Changes to the certificate of incorporation, voting, and bylaws.* Any changes in the corporate structure are typically approved by all shareholders and can impact the powers of the board.
- *Changes to board or election procedures.* Existing board members typically approve any changes to the board structure (additions of seats, observers) that occur as newer investors come to the table. Investors control the board dynamics closely, especially in the early stages of the development and growth.

EXIT-RELATED PROVISIONS

These provisions come into effect at the time of the sale of the company. As very few companies go public, savvy investors do not invest too much time and effort splitting hairs around these terms. For the most part, these are treated as boilerplate language. A brief description of the terms follows.

Redemption

Certain practitioners are tempted to sell the stock back to the company and redeem their investment at, say, the sixth anniversary. This provision is typically triggered when the company has made modest middle-of-the-road progress, but it is not going to be a significant exit for investors. Unkind expressions address these as the living dead. This provision implies that the investment is more a debt-like instrument and attempts to recover some or all of the investment.

Drag-Along Rights/Tagalong Rights and Co-Sale Agreements

These rights allow investors to "drag" the shareholders to an exit. The dragging comes in when a specified percentage of shareholders wants to sell the company when another group, typically, the founders or common shareholders, refuses to sell. The price may not be right, or they may see a bigger, better opportunity in the future. The investors may have given up on the opportunity and choose to get what they can. Drag-along provisions allow investors to sell the package as a whole — if any investor is unwilling to sell, it could block an exit, and this provision allows the sale to occur. In tagalong provisions, also called co-sale agreements, the founders or management either give up or find a third party to whom they can sell their shares. The tagalong rights allow investors to tag along with the founders and offer their shares for sale as well.

Conversion to Common at Public Offering, Registration Rights, and Piggyback Rights

In the rare event a portfolio company is ready to file for an IPO, all securities convert to one class: common stock. This allows for smoother marketing and share price establishment. Thus, the preferences established will vanish. In *Venture Capital Due Diligence*, Justin Camp writes, "Convertible instruments allow investors to take full advantage of the protections offered by preferred stock . . . until they are no longer necessary, and then allow them to forgo such protections. When investors invoke registration rights, they push the company to register the stock or piggyback on other registrations. Once registered, venture capitalists are able to sell their stock in the public markets."[17] Investors can demand registration, although several factors come into play, primarily the revenues, growth rate, and state of the public markets. Piggyback rights obligate companies to let investors piggyback on the registration.

OTHER IMPORTANT TERMS

These terms fall neither in the economic nor the governance category but are important to align the interest of investors and management.

Employment-Related Terms

All founders and key management team members should execute employment agreements. Other important terms such as stock vesting, restrictions on co-sale, key man insurance, and noncompete provisions are included to ensure management teams are aligned with the long-term goal of value creation.

Employment agreements clearly state a founder or manager's roles, responsibilities, and deliverables. These agreements incentivize the team to stay with the company, especially through tough times, and to create value. Stock vesting for founders is often negotiated aggressively to ensure that after the investment is made, the founders remain and continue to add value to the company. A separate stock option plan is typically created after investment and governed under the auspices of the board. This plan determines the dynamics of the employee stock options. Should an employee be terminated, his or her ability to exercise the balance of options will lapse.

Vesting for core team members can occur on a quarterly basis over a three-to four-year period. Acceleration of vesting upon acquisition is considered suitable to reward management for having created value. The contention is amplified when founders quit or are fired. The vesting debate can create a fair amount of distraction and hence needs to be addressed in employment agreements.

The restrictions on co-sale have been seen in a new light, especially when founders are allowed to take significant portions of their stock and liquidate it prior to a sale or IPO. Key man provisions are methods of ensuring that investors are protected if key management team members were to become unavailable due to death or disability.[18] Noncompete provisions can be enforced in certain states, but not all. The duration (number of years) and scope (geography, sector) of the noncompete agreement must be diligently negotiated.

The following miscellaneous conditions are prescribed in the term sheets:

- *Exclusivity and no-shop clause.* This clause is included to ensure entrepreneurs do not use the opportunity to get an auction going or to find better terms of investment by shopping the term sheet around.

- *Closing date and conditions.* This clause helps all parties, legal counsel for both sides especially, to complete the transaction on a certain date and meet any conditions prior to closing.

- *Nondisclosure, press/media.* Ensuring confidentiality, this is essentially an embargo on both parties to avoid making any premature public statements.

To summarize, in a survey of 889 venture firms,[19] as seen in Exhibit 27.12, terms that are most important include pro-rata rights, followed by participation rights and redemption rights. As seen in Exhibit 27.13, when it came time for negotiating these terms, VCs rarely gave up their pro-rata rights. This ensured they could increase their ownership of winners over time. Interestingly, valuation and ownership stake were not as important, likely due to pressures of getting in a hot deal.

Exhibit 27.12 **Terms that matter: Frequency with which terms are used.**

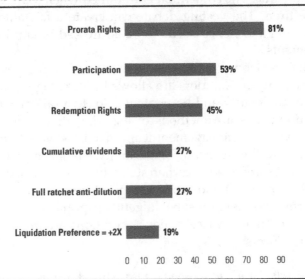

Source: Based on Gompers, Paul A., William Gornall, Steven N. Kaplan, and Ilya A. Strebulaev. "How Do Venture Capitalists Make Decisions?" NBER Working Paper Series, No. 22587, September 2016.

Exhibit 27.13 **Flexibility on terms: VCs rank these terms as least flexible.**

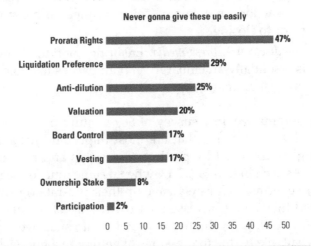

Source: Based on Gompers, Paul A., William Gornall, Steven N. Kaplan, and Ilya A. Strebulaev. "How Do Venture Capitalists Make Decisions?" NBER Working Paper Series, No. 22587, September 2016.

SYNDICATING INVESTMENTS

An analysis of over 2,000 venture transactions shows that syndication was found to be highest in biotechnology investments (in over 60 percent of investments) and lowest in the software sector (with only 37 percent of investments). Syndication was least at the seed stages and increased in later stages.[20] Capital constraints do bring investors together, as seen in Exhibit 27.14, especially in biotech sectors where capital intensity is significant. Past success makes good friends indeed as seen in Exhibit 27.15 from the results of a VC survey of over 800 investors.[21]

Whether seeking syndicate investors or being asked to be one, the simple rule applies: Does the combined intellectual and financial acumen allow for the better outcomes of the investment opportunity? When inviting syndicate investors into opportunities, look for complementary skill sets in syndicate investors so that the combined power of the board is higher in terms of value add. Mutual respect is important, as is the willingness to come up with a solution that is best for the company.

Exhibit 27.14 **Most important factors leading to syndication.**

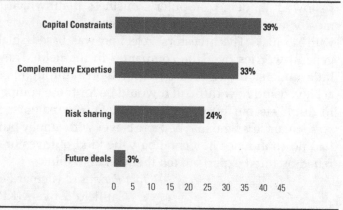

Source: Based on Gompers, Paul A., William Gornall, Steven N. Kaplan, and Ilya A. Strebulaev. "How Do Venture Capitalists Make Decisions?" NBER Working Paper Series, No. 22587, September 2016.

Exhibit 27.15 **Most important factors for choosing syndicate partners.**

Factor	Percentage
Past Shared Success	28%
Expertise	25%
Reputation	16%
Track Record	16%
Capital	9%
Social Connections	3%
Geography	2%

Source: Based on Gompers, Paul A., William Gornall, Steven N. Kaplan, and Ilya A. Strebulaev. "How Do Venture Capitalists Make Decisions?" NBER Working Paper Series, No. 22587, September 2016.

Those Clever Financiers . . .

I showed Tandem Computer's business plan, which I had mostly written myself, to all the local potential investors with no luck. The investors' rejection was based solely on general worries over the companies in the field. They had little understanding of the technical breakthrough we had achieved and how difficult it would be for those competitors to duplicate our effort and circumvent our patents. These were financiers who maybe were clever with money but who had no confidence in technology, the kind of investors who relied on hired experts to tell them what to think.

— *Tom Perkins* of Kleiner Perkins
Caufield & Byers (KPCB)[22]

Practitioners need to conduct due diligence on each other with the same rigor they would apply to looking at new opportunities, but add a few other parameters to the mix: What are the motives of the syndicate investor? Is it a true partnership? Are their interests aligned? Do they have the ability to play the long game and withstand the tremors?

Ideally, smaller funds would invite larger funds to participate with the optimistic outlook that as the capital needs for the company grow, the larger funds will be able to lead the future rounds. This can create a win–win situation for both funds. A smaller fund generates the opportunity and acts as a feeder to the larger fund. In turn, the larger fund can invest substantially higher amounts as needed by the company. The smaller fund needs to consider how antidilution and pay-to-play provisions could affect the smaller fund if the opportunity does not progress as desired. The appetite for loss also differs with the size and the stage of the fund.

Partnership of *unequals* can be challenging. As a practitioner remarked, "I would hope that we would get an equal ownership, but if Sequoia says they want 75 percent and we keep 25 percent, we'd be happy with that."[23] Syndication caveat: As in life, so in the syndicate round, choose your partners with care. The best syndicate opportunities are those where every investor has the same terms and economic interests. As they say, we are family and we eat from the same plate. Watch for investors who upsell their companies to you, or worse, try to pawn off their struggling companies. And finally, syndicate with the ones you trust will watch your back and play a fair game — you know how they will react in bad situations.

MILESTONE-BASED FINANCING: RISK MITIGATION OR DISTRACTION

Staged financing is used in seed- and early-stage investments, and the primary reason is to remove risk from the opportunity. Completion of a prototype and customer validations are a few examples of milestones that are typically used to structure investments. Recall Peter Thiel, who agreed to invest in Facebook with the precondition that his note would convert to equity after they reached a certain number of users. The company did not meet its milestone, and yet when the time came to convert, Thiel did not hold back. Staged financings can provide incentive for the teams to perform and move faster, and entrepreneurs can be assured that the tranches of capital will arrive as the milestones are completed. But is it that simple?

"Milestone-based financing forces the management to either declare victory too soon, or worse, it distracts them from a potentially bigger opportunity — in an evolutionary stage, milestones can push the founders in the wrong direction," says Jack Ahrens of TGap Ventures. If you choose to use milestone-based financing, consider the primary question: Can you disengage if the milestones are not met?

Furthermore, the caveats are as follows:

- *Definition of milestone.* Avoid ambiguity and insist on measurable and simple definitions. Instead of a broad, complete beta, it would be prudent to identify the top three key functions that the technology should meet.

- *Amount necessary to reach milestone.* If an entrepreneur prepares the budget, a practitioner needs to ensure that the resources, amounts, and line items are vetted. On the flip side, if you squeeze the amount down, be prepared to accept the blame: A common excuse from entrepreneurs can be "We couldn't meet the milestones because we did not have enough money to start with."

As with most terms, flexibility, speed, and simplicity are the keys to a successful start.

Key Takeaways

1. Focus on not just the price (valuation) but the upside potential (probability returns) of the investment. If the upside potential is significant, be willing to give up some levers of control. In some high-growth companies, investors have bought common shares, with no liquidation preferences nor any governance.

2. The single most important provision, after valuation, is pro-rata rights. Ensure you can build up your ownership position in rapidly growing companies. Liquidation preferences are standard 1X in most rounds, but can be higher in later-stage rounds.

3. Minimize your negotiations around other terms, such as antidilution, conversion, and drag-along rights, that rarely come into play. It's a binary game, where companies either die or have a huge outcome — everything else in between is a distraction.

28

The Closing Process

After the Term Sheet

To approve the investment, any company follows these steps:

- Board approval of the investment via formal resolution.
- Majority of shareholders consent via vote.
- Execution of detailed documents that include:
  - Share purchase agreement or subscription agreement including purchase details, company's representations and warranties, board composition, and voting matters.
  - Investor rights agreement (IRA) including information rights, preemptive rights, registration rights, and affirmative and negative covenants.
    - Affirmative covenants (or actions the company should take) include maintaining the existence of the corporation, paying taxes, maintaining insurance, complying with key agreements, maintaining accounts, and allowing access to premises.
    - Negative covenants (or actions the company should avoid) include changing the business, amending the charter, issuing stock, merging the company, conducting dealings with related parties, making investments, or incurring debt or financial liabilities.

- Modifications to the certificate of incorporation to allow for the new shareholders to be recognized as well as to ensure that the company does not take any actions that are not aligned with preferred shareholders' rights.
- Issuing of share certificates to shareholders/investors.

Part Four

The Art of
Value Creation

Do VCs create value for their portfolio companies at all? If you ask a star founder like Elon Musk, what answer might he have for such a question? Word on the street is that in its early years, Google board meetings were scheduled once every nine months. This was to avoid the VC noise that's often created in boardrooms — product-market fit, scaling, monetization, growth, and more. And the two VCs at the time were legends in their own right — Kleiner Perkins and Sequoia, but still. For one, founders with clear purpose, execution, and results are a rarity.

Most founders are good at a few things and investors can supplement their strengths in a number of ways. At earlier stages, companies may need a lot more engagement, guidance, and direction. This is where the upside is being designed, directions are being plotted, and early market experiments are being conducted. As the company grows and stabilizes, the board's involvement is mostly around staying the course, protecting the downside, governance, and reporting.

So how best can investors serve founders? The VC as a coach does not always play out well, because the VC may have never played the game. Or they played it in the days of past, with wooden sticks when the modern-day CEO has lasers. Their experience is not as relevant. The VC as a service provider is another option, but the role of money and its power dynamics can often create interesting challenges. Is it our duty to nurture the team? Challenge them? Or monitor and observe them without much interference, as they ride the roller coaster? If done right, with a healthy, balanced culture and thoughtful demands, the board can elevate the company and the CEO. Value creation need not be a formulaic approach to making a certain number of customer intros or helping hire engineers. In some cases, it's being present, when the CEO does not know how to tackle a rough patch. It can be helping the team overcome their fears and insecurities. But creating trust and engagement is not easy, especially when the two sides may have differing agendas.

Many board meetings have caused elevated levels of pain for all sides. This is often because the CEO is forced to prepare an elaborate, 70-slide deck every two months. And then get yelled at, or lorded over by five to seven people who may have very little understanding of the business. I have seen situations where some VCs take immense pride in catching the CEO off guard in the board meeting, with a clever-by-half question. Their goal is simple — to show how smart they are, so that the other VCs in the room could genuflect with admiration. It can devolve into an interesting theater, often at the expense of the founder. That is more like value destruction. Or subtraction. You get the point.

29

Serving on Boards

"The biggest consistent irritant in the boardroom were co-investors more intent on talking over management, rather than listening to them," Donald Valentine, founder, Sequoia Capital, would say. Echoing the sentiment was Vinod Khosla, who spent his early investment career at Kleiner Perkins. "Most VCs have not done shit . . . they have never been at a startup or through tough times. Most VCs add zero value, some add negative value while advising CEOs," complains Vinod Khosla, founder of Khosla Ventures.[1]

OVERVIEW

In a narrative account of a business, there is only one hero. When we look at the plucky startup or entrepreneurial business venture, the company founder or CEO is deified as a visionary who forges a groundbreaking idea into reality against all odds. In this account, the CEO is the captain of industry, creating a dent in the universe with mighty volition and against all odds, building a brilliant management team that works tirelessly to craft the idea into a viable business. Cast into a secondary supporting role is the venture capitalist. And most VCs do not know how best to play this supporting role. How should VCs understand their duties and, more importantly, draw the boundary lines of their role as a board member?

VCs have often acted as egotistical overlords, pushing the CEO and offering bad advice. Good role models are rare in the business of venture capital. Picking the right role models and understanding their *modus operandi* is an essential part of any self-development of an investor. No corporate governance textbook can prepare an investor for the challenges of the boardroom. Having seen several scenarios of toxic boardroom behavior, Brad Feld, partner at Foundry Group, and I co-authored a book, *Startup Boards*, which helps board members and founders manage the dynamics of a startup's board of directors.

This section is a summarized version of board roles, responsibilities, and, most importantly, guidelines on serving entrepreneurs. An investor, besides providing financial capital, is expected to offer strategic guidance, access to business relationships at every stage of development, while serving as a board member.

At the most basic level, board members are expected to adhere to *duty of care*, which calls for making prudent, informed decisions, and *duty of loyalty*, ensuring that directors act in the interest of all the shareholders. Above and beyond these duties, investors are expected to support the portfolio company CEO in a number of ways — providing strategic inputs where necessary, accessing networks of investors and customers, and identifying executives to build the management team. The challenge, though, is knowing one's limits and ensuring that you are not a distraction in the boardroom, causing confusion, derailing the management team while pontificating fantastical theories, and destroying value. Or as Khosla puts it, "creating negative value." And in such situations, CEOs will actively ignore your advice. One CEO put it succinctly: "My strategy is to minimize the value subtracted."[2]

Good governance is akin to parenting — lax behavior or micro-management leads to dysfunctional kids. A board member represents *all* shareholders — preferred and common, not just their own "Series B preferred" financial interests.

A good board member first orients, then engages. Experienced board members are adept at "pattern recognition," where lessons learned from various startups can be amalgamated to ensure mistakes are avoided. Rookie venture capitalists often stumble all over the boardroom, eager to display their acumen (or lack thereof). It gets worse if they have arrived only with an MBA, ready to divide the world into four magical quadrants. The only training ground for the novice practitioner is the battlefield. Having a view of apprenticeship, knowing your limits, and an attitude of servitude is better than an attitude of lordship. Entrepreneurs have often described rookie board members as "He learned how to be a director. We paid the tuition."[3]

LEGAL REQUIREMENTS OF BOARD SERVICE

Fiduciary Duties

Duty of care. Requires a director to act with the care that an ordinarily prudent person in a like position would exercise under similar circumstances.

Directors should:

- Obtain information they believe is reasonably necessary to make a decision.
- Make due inquiry.
- Make informed decisions in good faith.

Duty of loyalty. Requires a director to act in the best interests of the corporation and not in the interest of the director or a related party. Issues often arise where the director has a conflict of interest.

- Where the director or a related party has a personal financial interest in a transaction with the company (e.g., the inherent conflict between venture capitalists as directors and as representatives of their fund's interests).
- Where the director usurps a corporate opportunity that properly belongs to the company.
- Where the director serves as a representative of a third-party corporation and the third-party corporation's objectives conflict with the company's best interests.

- Where the director abdicates his or her oversight role or does not act in good faith.

Examples of not acting in good faith include the following:

- Consciously or recklessly not devoting sufficient time to required duties.
- Disregarding known risks.
- Failing to exercise oversight on a sustained basis.
- Failing to act in good faith, which can have serious adverse consequences to a director, such as being exposed to personal liability for breaches of the duty of care or losing coverage under indemnification provisions or insurance policies. Generally, state corporate laws have procedures for handling interested transactions and corporate opportunities, such as requiring full disclosure and disinterested director approval.

Confidentiality and Disclosure

Board members need to protect all information and at times push the management to share all material information with the shareholders. Often, first-time CEOs do not know the extent of information that needs to be shared. A prudent board lead member and lead counsel can mentor the CEO. But the judgment rule is one that needs to be exercised to ensure that board members are protected:

Duty of confidentiality. A subset of the duty of loyalty. Requires a director to maintain the confidentiality of nonpublic information about the company.

Duty of disclosure. Requires a director, pursuant to the duties of care and loyalty, to take reasonable steps to ensure that a company provides its stockholders with all material information relating to a matter for which stockholder action is sought.

Business judgment rule. Creates a presumption that in making a business decision, the directors of a company acted on an informed basis, in good faith, and in the honest belief that the action taken was in the company's best interests. The business judgment rule helps protect a director from personal liability for allegedly bad business decisions by essentially shifting the burden of proof to a plaintiff, alleging that the director did not satisfy his or her fiduciary duties. This presumption and the protections afforded by the business judgment rule are lost if the directors involved in the decision are not disinterested, do not make appropriate inquiry prior to making their decisions, or fail to establish adequate oversight mechanisms.

SELF-EDUCATION: PREPARING FOR YOUR BOARD ROLE

In early-stage companies, the business, its goals, and its challenges, complete with its cast of characters, are all visible. The purpose of the pointers listed here is to initiate steps into self-orientation and education. In addition to possessing a thorough understanding of the history and evolution of the company, any practitioner needs to consider the following:

- Develop a thorough 360-degree understanding of the business, including suppliers, customers, competitive threats, and replacements. The practitioner needs to understand the cycle of cash and friction therein. This is critical.

- Understand a company's strategy and key goals. Over the next 12 months and three years, how do you see your contribution vis-à-vis issues and challenges facing such a company? ("What would keep the CEO awake at night, and how can I help?")

- Ensure you have relevant expertise to affect the stated strategy. Prepare to impact the company's challenges and demands in a disciplined and consistent manner.

- Be aware of people and cash-related challenges. Does the team need to be augmented? What is the cash position, burn rate, and timing of next financing round?

- Understand the current board structure and how you fit in this context.

- What are the board's external and internal challenges? Examples may include the following:

  - *External*. Compliance with tax, civil, criminal, and employment laws, any legal matters or shareholder actions.

  - *Internal*. Emotional and power dynamics between board members, excessive churn of board members or CEO, strategy du jour, product development, and market adoption challenges, burn rate, and cash situation.

ROLES AND RESPONSIBILITIES OF A BOARD MEMBER

It is well known that venture capital is the financial fuel that kickstarted many great companies in the past decade, but there is less familiarity with what venture capitalists do once they sit on a company's board. Beyond financing, what kinds of support do they provide to startups? How do they use their investment muscle to attract and win more capital? To recruit a star management team? How do they winnow and champion the most promising drivers from the rest? "As a board, your role is to prove the business plan," says Lindsay Aspegren, founder of North Coast Technology Investors, "and your only two control levers are the CEO and the budget."

The primary role of any board member boils down to the following:

- *Shareholder value*. Create, sustain, and enhance shareholder value.

- *CEO selection and assessment.* Evaluate CEO performance, transition, assist in recruitment, succession planning.
- *Governance.* Manage risk via business strategy, finance, management, market insights, and legal compliance.

The boardroom is where the venture capitalist wields the greatest influence on a company's future growth. Typically, a company's board is a group of people who meet periodically and provide advice and guidance on the direction of the firm. For many startups and younger firms, venture capitalist board members are selected based on their influence and knowledge of the industry to help companies make a clear footprint on the market. Venture capitalist boards, therefore, do a lot: they attract, recruit, and retain an excellent management team and fellow board members; mentor and manage the executive team; provide advisory services and expertise outside the purview of the management team; and oversee adherence to fiscal, legal, and ethical governance standards. Brad Feld, managing director of the Foundry Group, points out the simple role of any board member: "With the exception of really two decisions, I'd like to think that we work for the CEO of the company. The two decisions we really make are, one, the capital allocation decision (do we want to keep funding the company?), and two, whether we keep and support the CEO."[4]

The board expertise, attributes, and roles of the board members shift as the company matures. Exhibit 29.1 demonstrates the minimum attributes required as the company evolves over time.

When there is ability and receptivity, any board member should, in conjunction with the CEO, identify the value creation milestones. If the CEO is on target and plan, the best way to serve is often to stay out of the way. Much damage has been done with the intention of doing good.

There are innumerable factors in determining whether a company succeeds — but none is as important as the role of the venture capitalist board member. Austen Arensberg, investor, says, "We need to be assertive and find a balanced, respectful

Exhibit 29.1 **Attributes of Board Members Across Stages of Company.**

	Seed and Early Stage	Growth Stage	Path to Liquidity
Management goals	Product development	Sales	Management of growth
Key metrics of the company	Burn rate, time to launch	Revenues, break-even	Growth, profitability, and gross margins
Evolution of management team attributes	Technical/product development, intellectual property	Operational, sales and marketing, finance, human resources	Management, investor relations, legal
Minimum board attributes	Relevant technical expertise	Business/financial expertise	Public company-like corporate governance
Number of board members	Three	Three to five	Seven or more
Culture of the board	Experimentation, nurturing, and openness	Expansion	Control and efficiencies
Governance via committees	Establish financial reporting and financial threshold levels; approval of key legal and shareholder agreements.	Establish compensation and audit committee, name formal board chairman, and perform additional financial and risk reporting.	Name lead director, establish public company-like internal controls and practices, and conduct Section 404 planning.
Examples of board's role in value creation	Provide access to scientific and technical luminaries, identify product development guidelines, attract first beta sites, and assess/identify development partners.	Advise on sales efficiencies, accelerate customer access, provide channel partnership insights, position competitively, provide access to future rounds of capital.	Maintain the course and develop regulatory and financial standards, practices, and policies.

Source: Adapted from Working Group on Director Accountability and Board Effectiveness, "A Simple Guide to the Basic Responsibilities of a VC-Backed Company Director," white paper.

way to support the CEO. How can we be objective in sharing options? In one scenario, we discussed what happens if we can raise the next round but we also had to be aware that we may have to shut down the company."

By their very nature, startups are not meant to be structured in a top-down, hierarchical way. More team-oriented than command-control, they must be managed from the ground up. A more engaged and flexible board member, ready to embrace and see opportunities in the challenges of growing a business, can be an asset to the firm. The key is to balance the interpersonal abilities with skills in order to stay focused on those three magic words: maximize shareholder value.

We start with the belief that we can help the company, but the most successful companies rarely need any help from the board. Opportunistic investors often take credit for value created by founders and prescribe blame to others for the failures. At times, we may find ourselves at the end of the rope and cannot do much, but we fail to admit it. Norman MacLean wrote in *A River Runs Through It*, "So it is, that we can seldom help anybody. Either we don't know what part to give or maybe we don't like to give any part of ourselves. Then, more often than not, the part that is needed is not wanted. And even more often, we do not have the part that is needed. It is like the auto-supply shop over the town where they always say, 'Sorry, we are just out of that part.'" Our goal is not to apologize — but to strive mightily. To help the founders with the best of our abilities. But knowing the finite edges of our universe is a sign of a responsible, even a wise board member.

30

Board Culture
and Orientation

Although in the early stages of a company's evolution, the largest shareholders might dominate the board composition, it is critical to structure the board with expertise necessary for the company's growth. If a board of a venture-backed company has five members — say, three investor representatives and two management team members — investors need to ask if they have the expertise to guide and help grow the company. "The board should have one expert each at the minimum from sales, strategy, industry expertise, and marketing areas. This allows for a balanced contribution, and the CEO can reach different experts as needed," says Rick Heitzmann of FirstMark Capital.

While board-member orientation is critical, it happens in a fairly ad hoc manner in most venture-backed companies. An orientation is essential to ensure that members understand their role and that they align their agenda with the overall mission. Members may have differing agendas: investors may seek exits at varying times, while the management team may have a desire to build the company.

On-Boarding a New Member

A typical orientation meeting could be one-on-one with the lead director and would include the following:

- Introduction of the current board members, if required
- Key goals and challenges of the company
- Board structure and goals
- Review of materials: handbook, policies, evaluation, and committees
- Attendance and performance expectations

TOWARD A BETTER BOARD CULTURE

An effective board is active, one in which members know their strengths as well as boundaries. Boards can be categorized as active, passive, or somewhere in between. While early-stage venture boards are predictably active, some board members can be more engaged than others. In a small family of five to seven board members, each member wields significant power, which if misused leads to distraction and the destruction of value. The cultural composition of any board includes the following five elements:

1. *Trust.* The ability to engage with the CEO and the board members in a manner that ensures common interests at heart, a level of transparency, and diligent actions that promote the greater good of the company.

2. *Communications.* Does the board discuss harder topics, challenge the management team's assumptions, and act in a nonthreatening and nonaccusatory manner?

3. *Active engagement.* Can the board members stay intellectually and emotionally engaged and vigorously support the company's growth?

4. *Alignment of interests.* Do all the board members oper- ate from a common thread of understanding — metrics, milestones, and expected outcomes?

5. *Independent observations.* Have the board members brought in an independent director early on, to ensure that there is a balance between the CEO's interests and the investors goals?

Healthy boards espouse these five key cultural aspects:

1. *Deep attention to details combined with macro views.* The ability to assess details and, at the same time, step back and look at the forest through these trees.

2. *Promote inquiry and dissent.* The ability to challenge man- agement assumptions and to act in a nonthreatening and nonaccusatory manner.

3. *Minimize the minutiae.* The ability to organize the qual- ity of information and discuss key issues, not irrelevant ones such as leases and janitorial services.

4. *Control the flow.* The ability to focus less on packaged information, leaving more room for open discussions.

5. *Establish a collegial atmosphere.* The personalities promote open and honest discussions in a respectful atmosphere; the CEO feels challenged but never threatened and is viewed as an extension of this team.[1]

Board member archetypes can fall into certain categories — these create the fabric of the boardroom dynamics. The ideal board member is one who combines the healthy aspects listed above. The negative archetypes often fall into these categories:

- *Authoritative pit bull.* A screamer who dominates all meetings, perpetually demanding higher sales revenues and lower burn rates, bent on creating a culture of fear.

- *An utterly disengaged, overstretched board member.* One practitioner describes this specimen as one who "starts every meeting by asking what the company does."[2] Not reading the board package or being prepared for the meeting is one thing; not knowing what the company does is unpardonable. Like the inability to recall the names of your own children.

- *Passive-aggressive board member.* Somewhere between the overstretched director and the micro-meddler sits the passive-aggressive member, who can do much harm by manipulative behavior.

Experience and luminary status of other board members, interpersonal relationships between board members, and board–CEO dynamics define the underlying ethos. Like all relationships, this fragile web has a finite life span. However, the interpersonal dynamics of mutual respect and trust, preparedness, the energy, and the work ethic of each board member determine the duration of the relationships beyond the life of the investment opportunity.

Honest self-assessment of individual members as well as the entire board is crucial — eager beavers and passive padres can never build a company, but in all likelihood, they will promptly take credit for all successes. Irrespective of the outcomes of the investment, the way board members engage and support the CEO in challenging times often defines their essence. As Andy Rappaport of August Capital noted, "A great board cannot make a great company, but a bad board can kill a good company."[3] A badly functioning board can be characterized in many ways, but the fundamental shortcoming is not performing the self-checks necessary to ensure that it stays cognizant of the real-time needs of company.

Very few CEOs survive the travails of a venture-backed company from seed stage to an exit. Like any relationship, the visions and plans for a company's future can become misaligned between investors and the CEO. Harvard Business School's Noam Wasserman has labeled this situation the "paradox of success," where during the course of trying to raise money, the founder-CEOs "put themselves at the mercy of capital providers, increasing the hazard of succession."[4]

As the company grows, any skill gaps between the abilities of the founder-CEOs and the organization's needs widen precariously. Venture capitalists should be quick to dispense with the unrealistic and romantic notion of the CEO who "goes all the way" in favor of a proactive approach that involves a candid evaluation of the CEO's strengths and weaknesses. Cracks in the relationship between the CEO and venture capitalist can easily lead to turmoil if not managed well.

A common mistake on boards in the venture capital business, according to Promod Haque at Norwest Venture Partners, is "not taking timely action to change a nonperforming CEO for fear that it will rock the boat."[5]

Board members can also become vulnerable to management spin on information, relying too heavily on their CEOs for the details of the business. Venture capitalists who appointed CEOs may be unable to offer dispassionate or unbiased criticism of management actions or decisions. This type of dependency quickly becomes dysfunctional and can lead to opacity and misunderstanding.

Being a good board member is simple as long as the focus is on shareholders' value maximization. However, bad board behavior abounds aplenty. Like dysfunctional families, each board has its own quirks and challenges. But where a culture of trust and open communication exists, the boardroom can be a productive arena.

Establish Trust with the CEO

Does the CEO know each board member's strengths and draw on these resources? Does the CEO feel secure and safe, discussing issues honestly and promptly? Does the CEO assign tasks to the board members effectively? "I really struggled to reconcile my role as a board member," says Brad Feld. Brad has formed companies, sat on boards and served as chair, and taken a few of the companies public. "It took me a while to firmly get my head set in one place where I focused on being the investor rather than the guy trying to run the company. It wasn't my responsibility to fix everything in the company, but to help the company win — I would provide feedback to the CEO and work for her. Trying to direct the CEO or entrepreneur does no good for any venture capitalist."

Build a Cadence of Healthy Communication

"The chairman's statements were guarded — guarded by enormous, labyrinthine fortifications that went on and on with such complexity and massiveness it was almost impossible to discover what in the world it was inside them he was guarding," writes Robert Pirsig in *Zen and the Art of Motorcycle Maintenance*. Communication between board members needs to be anything but guarded and labyrinthine. It needs to be open and frequent. The biggest mistake made by board members is to presume that there is consensus at the board and not bothering to ask others if they agree. If board members fail to communicate critical issues between board meetings, these can lead to surprises as well as inefficiencies. A common tactic employed is to discuss such surprises "offline" or delay the decision until a consensus is reached. Such behavior hurts the progress of the company, and very soon the CEO realizes that the board is playing the proverbial fiddle while Rome may be burning.

According to *A Simple Guide to the Basic Responsibilities of VC-Backed Company Directors*,[6] an open-door policy between management and the board is equally crucial. Venture capitalists can share their wide range of experiences in other portfolios to benefit a company, particularly during critical moments of transition (e.g., when a company is about to consider an initial public offering). Venture capitalists can also give advice on organizational planning and compensation structures. They should also serve as sounding boards for their CEOs and carve out opportunities to mentor them. This means making themselves available for broad-based consultations even outside normal board meeting schedules.

As Brad Feld puts it, "With some portfolio companies, the tempo of exchange is different, it could be daily — multiple times a day. Some want to meet. It is always useful to get face-to-face, but I let the entrepreneur decide the interaction."[7]

Exhibit 30.1 **Interaction with portfolio companies.**

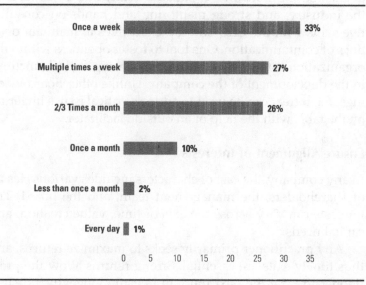

Once a week — 33%

Multiple times a week — 27%

2/3 Times a month — 26%

Once a month — 10%

Less than once a month — 2%

Every day — 1%

0 5 10 15 20 25 30 35

Source: Modified from Gompers, Paul A., William Gornall, Steven N. Kaplan, and Ilya A. Strebulaev. "How Do Venture Capitalists Make Decisions?" NBER Working Paper Series, No. 22587, September 2016.

A VC survey (see Exhibit 30.1) shows that most board members interact with companies multiple times a week.

A good board member invites and welcomes input from CEOs, non–venture capitalist directors, and other board members, including observers. Peer reviews and self-evaluations ensure greater accountability and better governance. Effective board members also avoid the distractions of boardroom intrigue and political maneuvering and focus on the operational goals of their roles: promoting the best interest of the company and maximizing value for shareholders.

Qualities to be nurtured among members for an effective, harmonious board include strong interpersonal skills to manage the team dynamics and the relationship with management; pattern recognition skills to anticipate events and make tough decisions, often with little information; partnering experience to work with other investors with different financial stakes and to manage board meetings without getting lost in the mundane details; strong networking skills to reach out to contacts in the industry; and strong mentoring and hands-on consultative skills with the CEO and top executives to maintain open lines of communication. One tool to foster openness within the organization is to hold board retreats during critical junctures in the development of the company. Unlike other board meetings, the retreat can be used to address critical issues lingering on the table with the help of an outside facilitator.

Ensure Alignment of Interests

In any company, the cast of characters includes various classes of shareholders, the management team, and the board. The interests can vary across the axis of time, value creation, and capital needs.

Any practitioner primarily seeks to maximize returns, and thus timely exits are essential. Strong returns allow the practitioner to raise the next fund and ensure longevity, possibly higher fees, and improved brand stature. Conflicts can arise when the following occur:

1. *Career interests.* A practitioner seeks attribution quickly in anticipation of moving on to another fund, collecting carried interest profits and seeking greener pastures.

2. *Fundraising drivers.* The next fund needs to be raised. We need an exit.

3. *Exit timing.* A practitioner cannot see the growth trajectory or strong exit value within a meaningful time frame. The founders are caught in self-preservation mode. Stalemate ensues.

4. *Financial.* This company is becoming a financial sinkhole and the practitioner has "checked out." Brad says, "Alignment does not matter when a company grows fast or craters quickly — you need alignment with the portfolio companies that are stuck in the middle."

The role of an independent director can alleviate any vested behavior. "Allocating a tie-breaking vote to an unbiased arbiter commits the entrepreneur and venture capitalists to more reasonable behavior and can reduce the opportunism that would result if either party were to control the board," writes Brian Broughman.[8]

Experts studied over 200 investments in over 100 companies and found that venture capitalists control board seats in 25 percent of the cases, the founders in 14 percent of the cases, and *neither controlled the board in 61 percent of the cases*.[9] In those 61 percent, the independent director acted as an adjudicator and likely brought the two sides to a common ground.

Various studies and anecdotal assessments show that independent directors were known by both parties in as many as 70 percent of the investments. Independent directors are brought in because they have the mutual respect of both the company and the investors, their behavior is objective and balanced, and they have strong reputations.

Avoid Complacency

In the beginning, a venture company gets by on the momentum of an exciting idea or concept. It is not unlike a heady romance, where the founder, who is consumed by passion for an idea, meets a venture capitalist interested in investing and taking the company forward. Their courtship is mostly driven by the CEO's charisma, technical expertise, and deep and narrow ambition. The board offers a steadying foundation. Andy Rappaport of August Capital observes that "a CEO has to be a person who . . . focuses on one issue, a single set of objectives," while a venture capitalist board member is someone "who likes to take a broad view," which "provides a check and balance" to the CEO's intensity.[10]

For any portfolio company, venture capitalists should have an understanding of the company's competitive position in the industry to help it stay nimble and to make inroads in the market. Venture capitalists are expected to keep abreast of specific industry developments, as well as the current regulatory environment, to maintain oversight of rules and regulations, and to understand the governance requirements throughout the development of the company.

ON-BOARDING CHECKLIST

The following orientation materials can be offered to a new board member, if and as needed:

- Company overview:
  - Business background, management team, and organization chart
  - Directors' biographies, listing, and contact information
  - Financial reports and projections
  - Capitalization table
- Board policies:
  - Conduct expectations, skills, knowledge, expertise of each board member
  - Frequency of meetings
  - Establishment process of committees: audit, compensation, governance
  - Decision-making procedures
  - Policy on observer roles
  - Legal responsibilities
  - Liabilities and insurance coverage, indemnification, confidentiality, conflict of interest matters, and resolution
  - Media and press policies
- Board committees:
  - Description (audit, governance, and compensation committees, are typically formed)
  - Composition, chaired by, purpose, and authority of each committee
- Board self-evaluation process

Let Me Know How I Can Be Helpful: Value Creation

VCs want to be helpful, but in that delusional arrogance (or neediness) they assume that everyone is groveling at their knees, seeking their help, while they sit on a high throne dispensing nuggets of wisdom. Now we have @vcstarterkit — a parody Twitter account ensuring that we don't do dumb stuff all day (like end every call with that annoying line, "Let me know how I can be helpful").

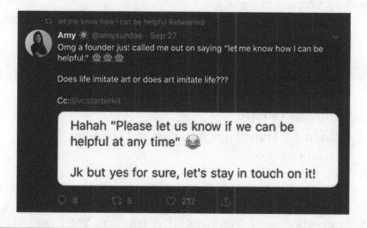

Source: vcstarterkit

As a board member, the best way to create value is to align closely the company's CEO, understand the key milestones, and support the short-term value drivers. For early-stage companies, these may be helping build the team or achieving product-market fit and early customer engagement. As the product gets ready for launch, access to beta sites or first customers takes priority. Risk mitigation is interwoven at all stages, with ongoing threats from competitors or substitutes. As the company grows, access to follow-on financial resources and scaling for growth becomes important. Finally, enabling exit negotiations requires the ability to align all stakeholders and ensure positive outcomes. Several variables affect this complex interplay, including the stage of the company, the CEO's ability and comfort in engaging the board, constitution of the board members and their skills, and investor alignment.

"The best VCs know how to market their companies really well to create a reality distortion field that can often become a self-fulfilling prophecy. Like the best managers, the best VCs help founders amplify strengths and defend against weaknesses, as opposed to trying to mold them into some idealized entrepreneur based on pattern matching," says Matthew Tamayo-Rios, a Silicon Valley founder backed by some of the leading venture investors.

Board members can support the CEO of a portfolio company in all major business matters, including:

- Talent attraction
- Revenue growth
- Business strategy
- Industry knowledge, insights, and strategic relationships

"The only reason top-tier venture capitalists invite you to coinvest is because of your ability to add value — be it your domain expertise or your network of contacts. You have to win their respect and gain confidence to be invited to participate in the future deals," says Lip-Bu Tan of Walden International. A board becomes a stage where relationships are forged.[1]

PricewaterhouseCoopers conducted a study of over 350 companies that had received seed or first-round financing[2] and identified three value-creation metrics:

1. *Strategy*. Market size, competitive position, and business model.
2. *Resources*. Cash flow, investor value contributed, and strength of management team.
3. *Performance*. Product development, channels/alliances, and customer acquisition.

Companies that grew rapidly and successfully attracted customers, built distribution channels, achieved healthy cash flow, and seized a strong competitive position very early became strong IPO outcomes while companies that were acquired had gradual ramp-up on product development, customer acquisition, and channel development.

On Value Creation

Andreessen Horowitz has an in-house market development team, which invites Fortune 1000 corporations, and the fund's portfolio companies to pitch products and develop business relationships. The firm does over a thousand such meetings a year.

GOOD GOVERNANCE AS THE FIRST STEP TOWARD VALUE CREATION

A McKinsey survey of over 2,500 directors and officers concluded that institutional investors are willing to pay a 14 percent premium for shares of a well-governed company.[3] On the flip side, poor governance translates to failed investments and, even worse, lawsuits.

Depending on the stage of venture investments, the role of directors is amplified in areas such as value identification, value enhancement, sustaining momentum, and risk mitigation. The concept of value is unique to each company's stage of evolution. Exploring the fit between the company's needs and the investor's expertise starts with the primary driver: capital. An investor "buys" their board seat and attempts to ensure value enhancement by offering intellectual and social capital.

Board Best Practices

Establish the following practices to ensure healthy board dynamics:

1. *Engagement.* Encourage the CEO to provide an annual board calendar that includes frequency of meetings, an annual strategy session where you can "go deep" and assess the company's progress and prepare a road map for the next 12 months.

2. *Preparation.* Read the board materials ahead of time. Besides agenda and minutes, emphasis is always placed on

    Business progress. Depending on the stage and evolution of the business, an overview could include the following:

    Progress against key milestones. Highlight delays and develop countermeasures.

    Product development road map. Present completed alpha, beta, pilot customer trials as well as future road maps.

    Sales and marketing. Pipeline, actual versus plan performance, gross margins, lead generation metrics.

    Financial status highlights. Provide the cash position and burn rate, cash-zero date, variations against budget.

3. *Follow-up/recordkeeping:* Begin board meetings by ensuring action items of the previous meetings were followed through. Ensure accountability, both with the CEO as well as other board members. The secretary of the company or legal counsel often records the minutes of all board meetings. Generally, these minutes are brief, factual statements that state the resolutions and outcomes. Records such as board books, minutes, and resolutions are important diligence materials, often needed in legal and acquisition-related discussions.

THE CEO'S PERSPECTIVE ON VENTURE CAPITALIST VALUE ADD

In an informal study, founders of venture capital–backed companies were asked to value the contributions of their venture capitalist counterparts.[4]

CEOs value contributions with respect to:

1. Financings, advice, and introductions.
2. Strategic focus.
3. Recruiting and hiring senior management — CEOs and VPs.

The areas where venture capitalists were least valued include the following:

- Selection of professionals, law, patent, accounting
- Strategic relations with other companies
- Functional advice in marketing, engineering

VCs believe and indeed invest a lot of time in "strategic guidance" with portfolio companies. Yet this can be an overarching term, often used to hide low-impact or even bad behavior. The best value a VC can bring to any CEO is connections to other investors.

Exhibit 31.1 **Value creation: VC activities in portfolio companies.**

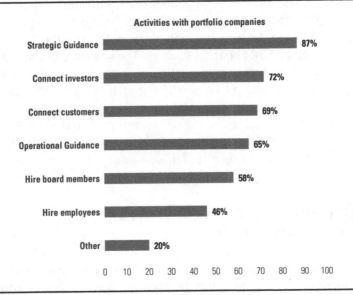

Activities with portfolio companies

Strategic Guidance	87%
Connect investors	72%
Connect customers	69%
Operational Guidance	65%
Hire board members	58%
Hire employees	46%
Other	20%

Source: Based on Gompers, Paul A., William Gornall, Steven N. Kaplan, and Ilya A. Strebulaev. "How Do Venture Capitalists Make Decisions?" NBER Working Paper Series, No. 22587, September 2016.

The challenge around rookie practitioners who do not have entrepreneurial background is widespread among boards. "I have seen situations where relatively junior board members get too caught up in what-if analysis and demand that the CEO prepare these unnecessary scenarios — what if a meteor hits the earth and such," says Rick Heitzmann of First-Mark Capital.

Hands Off

In a survey of over 150 CEOs, 58 percent said they want to work with venture capital firms that are entrepreneur friendly and collaborative . . . BUT *they are wary of firms that are too hands-on. Only 1 percent said "hands-on" was an important quality.*[5]

Another survey of over 300 companies shows that the best value a board member can offer is to assist with future financing. According to CEOs surveyed, lack of industry knowledge and inability to make meaningful time commitments were identified as the top two weaknesses of boards.

Free wristbands for VCs trying to be helpful. *Source:* Shrug Capital

Aydin Senkut of Felicis Ventures says, "I think portfolio value-add can be more strategic than just a function of time spent — for instance we have been able to help founders where it really matters — making a connection that resulted in an exit or to find that critical executive. Those valuable connections can sometimes be achieved with a mere 30-minute phone call, but it could be transformative in value."

Effective Board Meetings, the Sequoia Capital Way

The following is a summary of Sequoia Capital's thoughts and advice to founders on structuring the first few board meetings at early-stage startups. The underlying theme is clear: Board meetings are all about solving problems for the CEO.

While we focus on "decks," it's important to note: *Board decks don't actually have to be decks.* You could use Amazon-style "memos" that communicate the same information through text. It really comes down to the most efficient and effective mode of communication for the management team.

Prepare just enough. The goal of a board meeting should be to maximize the value the founder gets while minimizing the amount of time you spend preparing. Of course, if the founder doesn't prepare at all, they'll have a hard time keeping your board focused. That's why a good board deck is so important. It may sound odd that the presentation can contribute so much to the success of a board meeting. But consider this: *A board's job is to give advice, help solve problems, reinforce best practices,* and so on. When all of this is on topic, it can help guide you through the company-building process. When board members are left to explore whichever topics they choose . . . look out.

Focus on calibration. The primary difference between company meetings and board meetings is that your employees spend every day at your company, which even the most committed board members can't do. That means you'll need to effectively and efficiently calibrate your board every time you meet. Hopefully, you invited these people to your board because they have relevant experience in areas where you need help. The calibration will be worth the effort if it enables you to leverage the skills and experience in the room to help you think through problems in a different way.

Take a step back. Preparing a board deck is also an opportunity for the founders to take a big step back. This is incredibly important to do. And if you don't, no one else will. Treat board meeting prep as an opportunity to pull yourself out of the day to day and take a look at your company as if you were sitting on the moon viewing the earth: Are you executing? Are you innovating? Are you hiring? Are you building a management team? Are you growing the customer base? Are you doing so according to the last plan you laid out? And is that plan still good enough to win, or do you need a new plan and new targets?

Don't overthink it. This may sound like a significant undertaking for a three-hour meeting that happens four to six times per year — and it definitely is if you build a presentation from scratch every time. It's important, instead, to report to the board leveraging the materials you use to run the company. The Holy Grail is a board pack that is assembled by your assistant who simply prints the cover sheet(s) from weekly management-team reports and staples them together. Then you have no overhead and, even better, perfect alignment between the board and the management team.

Share materials early. Distribute the board materials one to two days in advance and ask your board members to study the material ahead of time so you can spend the meeting discussing rather than presenting.

Structure the meeting. Following is a general structure (see Exhibit 31.2) for an early board meeting/deck. We've seen our founders riff on this, and you can see some feedback from those CEOs below. In fact, Dropbox — where we partnered from the seed stage — has used this basic format from those early days onward, even as a public company today.

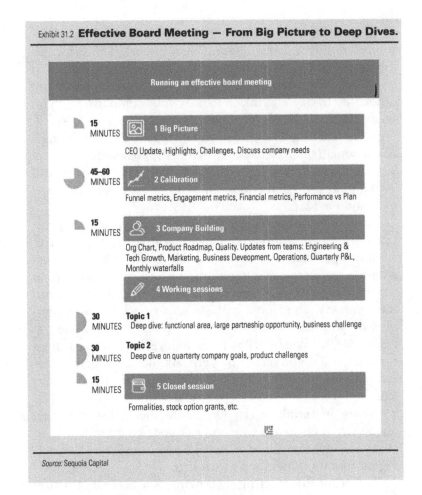

Exhibit 31.2 **Effective Board Meeting — From Big Picture to Deep Dives.**

Running an effective board meeting

15 MINUTES — **1 Big Picture**
CEO Update, Highlights, Challenges, Discuss company needs

45–60 MINUTES — **2 Calibration**
Funnel metrics, Engagement metrics, Financial metrics, Performance vs Plan

15 MINUTES — **3 Company Building**
Org Chart, Product Roadmap, Quality. Updates from teams: Engineering & Tech Growth, Marketing, Business Deveopment, Operations, Quarterly P&L, Monthly waterfalls

4 Working sessions

30 MINUTES **Topic 1** Deep dive: functional area, large partneship opportunity, business challenge

30 MINUTES **Topic 2** Deep dive on quarterty company goals, product challenges

15 MINUTES — **5 Closed session**
Formalities, stock option grants, etc.

Source: Sequoia Capital

Industry Expertise as a Value Driver

Industry knowledge, sector/domain expertise — the terms mean more or less the same in the venture business. Some practitioners have built their expertise by doing — starting companies — while others have gained awareness by observing — reading about trends and discussing opportunities with sector experts. The CEO of a portfolio company does not care as long as a practitioner is able to deliver tangible elements.

David Cowan of Bessemer Venture Partners was an expert on web security and has successfully morphed his expertise into other domains. "Over the years, Bessemer has made a number of investments in the Software as a Service (SaaS) arena. Our investments and knowledge within this arena has led to creation of unique metrics that are significant value drivers. We offer these to all our SaaS portfolio companies, and it helps them to assess their own performance vis-à-vis the rest of the SaaS universe," says David.

Customer Relationships as a Value Driver

Any venture-backed company needs rapid access to potential customers and vendors. A practitioner with a strong Rolodex can reduce some of this friction. "With one of our portfolio companies, I arranged and participated in at least 15 customer meetings in the first 12 months of our Series A investment. To get access to decision makers quickly is important for startups — essentially, you are accelerating the time to market." Lip-Bu emphasizes that a practitioner ought to be able to play a role in every stage of evolution — product planning, customer acquisition, manufacturing, and organizational development. However, a rookie practitioner can make a classic mistake of digging too deep. A mistake I have made too often is to assess the pipeline and challenge the CEO on the probabilities and timing of the sales. This becomes an exhausting affair for both parties and yields little positive outcome. Rather, a practitioner should understand the sales dynamics, as Ravi Mohan of Shasta Ventures suggests. "I recall my first board meeting where I wanted to conduct a review of the sales pipeline. It is a very common mistake and a low-level tactical move. I am now better in serving my CEOs by focusing on the high-level quarterly goals and by understanding the sell cycle, customers' buying motivations, and any friction therein. It is important to use the board meetings wisely so that the CEO can get the benefit of the board's time and intellect."

Work Product as a Value Driver

"During my early years, one of the CEOs of our portfolio company was in my face saying 'Hey, look, when have you done this before?' and my response was honest — I have not run a company before, but let me share a specific example. I described how I had developed a marketing campaign for a certain product line and its strong impact on sales." Providing a tangible example and supporting it with numbers helped Brent Ahrens of Canaan Partners to build a strong relationship with the CEO.

Business Strategy as a Value Driver

"One of the companies I invested in originally planned to develop a product — I convinced its leaders to build a services company. It was pretty clear that a services model would function efficiently and solve the problem the company was attempting to tackle," says Todd Dagres, founder of Spark Capital.[6] Todd got involved with the founders at a very early stage and helped shape the key elements of the company's business model. The company eventually went on to grow over $800 million in revenues.

As Brad Feld correctly points out, "Every CEO and company's needs are different, and there is no formulaic approach to value add. It is highly customized. A lot of VCs have a playbook of how they are going to add value. They are always asking for information — constantly probing and pushing, but never turning around and saying — let me help you solve that problem. It becomes a very time-consuming affair for the CEO, and it's a very selfish act on the part of the venture capitalists." If done right, it is the most rewarding part of a VC career. When I asked Pat Grady, partner at Sequoia for 12 years, on what keeps him going after all these years, he recalled an event that occurred several years ago. "It was a celebratory dinner with the founder of a company that had just gone public. He pulled me aside and said, *"This is all because of you. Thank you."*

But I was really supporting a senior partner who did most of the work. . . . Yet that CEO was so generous in his remark. That is a reward I carry with me — it keeps me going. Our purpose is noble — we can help founders to build great businesses, with enduring advantage."

32

Challenges
in the Boardroom

"The fundamental cause of the trouble is that in the modern world, the stupid are cocksure while the intelligent are full of doubt," philosopher and mathematician Bertrand Russell once wrote. And this battle of stupid and intelligent plays out in the boardroom at all levels. Between CEOs and VCs — between big-dog Type A VCs and other moderately chilled out VCs.

Arthur Rock resigned from the board of Apple when "Apple took a two-page ad in every newspaper you could think of, announcing that they were ready to ship the PowerPC, which I did not know they were going to manufacture — but that's not important — but that they were going to kill Intel. Literally — that's what it said. At that point, I resigned."[1] Yet it was the same Arthur Rock who once fired the CEO. He said, "Steve Jobs was a national treasure, he is a visionary — so bright — but I had to fire him from Apple."[2]

A board member needs to be prepared to face some rough times — either when companies enter the hyper-growth mode or when they fall apart. When Cisco's venture-backed board brought in a new CEO, his first job was to ensure there was no blood in the hallways. "The quarter that I arrived, we hired a shrink. He eliminated fighting in the open hallways. Physical fighting, I mean. I actually had the vice president of engineering deck the sales vice president in my office!"[3]

Venture-backed boards undergo considerable stresses when a portfolio company faces:

- CEO transitions
- Performance challenges
  - Slower sales growth/Loss of key accounts
  - Loss of key executives or churn of talent
  - CEO transitions
- Market-based/external challenges
  - Slower adoption and constrained market conditions affecting sales or future financing
  - Competitive forces disrupting the company's progress
  - IP-related matters causing unforeseen issues

In challenging times, patterns of emotional behavior manifest in ego games, actions taken to save face, self-interested moves, and personal vendettas. Left unchecked, the force of emotion may compromise directors' abilities to promote the shareholders' best interests.

CEO TRANSITIONS

Professor Noam Wasserman writes in his book, *The Founder's Dilemma*,[4] "Entrepreneurs face a choice, at every step, between making money and managing their ventures. Those who don't figure out which is more important to them often end up neither wealthy nor powerful." Several CEO behavioral characteristics act as warning signs leading to a potential transition. Pascal Levensohn points out that the CEO:

- Repudiates board input and stays the wrong course.
- Is often missing in action.
- Is defensive and combative with the board, stonewalling board inquiries.
- Is not proactive in keeping the board informed.
- Shirks responsibilities or passes the blame.

Exhibit 32.1 **Impact on Valuation When CEOs Gave Up Both Board Control and CEO Role.**

	Share of Company Valuation ($m)	Share of Company Valuation ($m)
Gave up both CEO role and board control	6.5	9.5
CEO role only	5	7.2
Board control only	4.1	6.1
Kept both CEO role and board control	3.3	4.8

Source: Based on Founder's Dilemma, 2012, Noam Wasserman, Sample size of ~200 companies © 2012 Princeton University Press

If ignored, these warning signs can deteriorate into more serious mismanagement problems such as revenue shortfalls, gaps, and delays in meeting purchase targets or in completing contracts, and an exodus of employees. Valuation is often impacted negatively when the CEOs do not relinquish control, as seen in Exhibit 32.1.

Almost two-thirds of all venture-backed startup companies replace their founding CEOs or top executives, as seen in Exhibit 32.2. Initiating and managing transitions during the changing of the guard is one of the most important decisions venture capitalists will make as board directors or members. Friction between the venture capitalist board members and CEO generally arises during these times. As CEOs build management teams by recruiting trusted team members, the risk of implosion during such times can be high. With their broader perspectives, venture capitalist board members can lobby to add talent outside the CEO's circle. This kind of strategic recruiting may call for the difficult task of moving founding

Exhibit 32.2 **CEO Changes over Series of Investments.**

	A Round	B Round	C Round	D Round
Founder still CEO	75%	62%	48%	39%
On 2nd CEO	19%	29%	35%	38%
On 3rd or more CEO	6%	9%	17%	23%

Source: Based on Founder's Dilemma, 2012, Noam Wasserman, Sample size of ~200 companies © 2012 Princeton University Press

members out of management seats and into more supportive, advisory roles.

Such transitions can be challenging for both sides — in the formative stages, the VCs mentor the CEO, act as sounding boards, and even joke that they act as corporate shrinks. This build-up leads to deepening personal ties, but a practitioner needs to realize the consequences of any friendship. "One of the mistakes I made early on was trying to become friends with the entrepreneurs. You eventually learn that you can like them and admire them, . . . and you get too close to them, and it sort of inhibits you in some ways," James Swartz of Accel Partners once stated.[5]

Exhibit 32.2 shows how founders change over rounds. The best way to manage these changes is to anticipate them, monitor for early signs of leadership problems, and act quickly and decisively before any shortfalls lead to irreparable damage. One way to do this is for both parties to establish specific performance expectations. Annual reviews of CEO performance, including management team feedback, board member feedback, and input from other key stakeholders, are critical.

Besides value creation, the role of the board member is critical in assessing the performance of the CEO and helping identify and recruit other suitable members of the management team. Studies have shown that in venture-backed companies, management turmoil and change are constant, and roughly half of the CEOs step away. it is rare that founders are able to retain their roles as CEOs during the rapid evolution stages of the company — managing people, budgets, and technology in a rapidly evolving marketplace is difficult. Thus, a practitioner needs to be prepared to identify and recruit key management talent. John Doerr of Kleiner Perkins identifies himself as the "glorious recruiter." Benchmark Capital went on to bring a top recruiter as a full partner in the firm. Leonard Bosack, along with his wife, Sandy Lerner, formed Cisco Systems. Their tenure with Cisco lasted for four years after they raised their first $2.5 million Series A round from Sequoia Capital.[6]

"It's a tough decision and very disruptive," says Deepak Kamra of Canaan Partners. He adds, "It's much easier to assume that the CEO will eventually work out, so let's keep him."

A Sand Hill Road investor pointed out that one of his port-folio companies had a very effective CEO who was able to build a world-class product. "The product risk was overcome and the team surpassed our expectations — the CEO was a great engineer who could get a product to market. After the IPO, we agreed that the founder would be better suited in the capacity of the chairman. Solidifying the company's position post-IPO required a different skill set." Organizational devel-opment and management, sustained growth, defending com-petitive jabs — all under the public glare of analysts — calls for a different timbre.

People seldom grow from managing product development, to managing people, to eventually managing expectations in post-IPO public glare. As human beings, we rarely recognize our own shortcomings and inabilities when it comes to manag-ing people, products, and capital.

As John Kenneth Galbraith once remarked, "The great entrepreneur must, in fact, be compared in life with the male *'epis mellifera.'* He accomplishes his act of conception at the price of his own extinction."[7]

BEST PRACTICES IN MANAGING CEO TRANSITIONS

While every investment starts with the assumption that the team will perform, a practitioner can manage transitions effec-tively by taking these action:

- Prioritize skills and experience essential to build the company.
- Enlist support from the board as well as the existing CEO.
- Establish a new role for the founder ahead of time. If the CEO initiates the change as seen in Exhibit 32.3, the CEO can stay in other executive roles and can continue to add value.
- Make the search priority one. One board member should lead the process.

Exhibit 32.3 **Triggers of Change and CEO Transition.**

	Moved to CTO or CSO	Other C-Level Role	Left the Company Immediately	Lower-Level Executive Role
Trigger of change Board	26%	25%	37%	13%
Trigger of change Founder CEO	24%	49%	24%	2%

Source: Based on Founder's Dilemma, 2012, Noam Wasserman, Sample size of ~200 companies © 2012 Princeton University Press

- Choose the closer: Prime candidates usually need persuasion. One board member — the best closer — works with the dream candidate to close.
- Ensure that the founder and the new CEO are aligned and an effective "hand-off" process is established.
- Stay close to the new CEO: To ensure a smooth transition, maintain a high-touch relationship in the first few months. Avoid complacency after the CEO arrives.

CEO ousters can occur by board, or by the CEO themselves — each of which can impact the value of the company, as seen in Exhibit 32.2. As one investor pointed out, "By far, this is the biggest service any venture practitioner can do for the CEO is to educate and alert the CEO, preferably prior to making the investment, that transition is normal."[8]

In a survey of over 300 participants, the National Association of Corporate Directors (NACD) Private Company Governance Survey concluded that *the three weakest areas of board effectiveness are director education, board evaluation, and CEO succession planning.* Often, venture-backed boards have little or no time to indulge in the luxury of education, development, and self-evaluation.

PERFORMANCE CHALLENGES

Multiple classes of shares with multiple preferences stacked on each other create a labyrinth wherein keeping track of each entity's agenda and economic interests can be challenging.

Furthermore, while the terms may be static, each practitioner and his or her fund's status is dynamic.

Any venture capital fund owns preferred stock, while the management may own common stock. Thus, any exit discussions where the management or common shareholders do not benefit would lead to frustration. In a few cases, the common shareholders have successfully negotiated additional cash prior to consenting to the sale of the company. According to one entrepreneur, the carveout was offered only because the venture capitalists (VCs) were concerned about a possible shareholder lawsuit challenging the terms of the sale. In another case where the VCs lacked board control, the VCs offered a carveout to obtain the support of the other directors for the sale.[9]

Cash Flow–Related Matters

If the burn rate is too high, management is seen as the primary culprit. The board and the CEO may disagree on the spend rate and priorities. Tension can arise over the priority of cash distribution at exit when the numbers are mediocre — for example, should accrued dividends, which primarily benefit investors, have a priority over management performance bonuses?

Follow-on Funding Challenges

Are you writing checks to defend sunk capital? Or to fuel growth? Consider the example of NEON, a health care IT company backed by ARCH Venture Partners. The company had developed tools for hospitals to organize data and increase transaction speed. The target market never developed because the hospitals' IT protocol had not reached the point at which they could maximize the potential of NEON's technology. And any IT company selling to hospitals is leery about the sales cycle, which can be as long as nine months or more. NEON was one of the larger investments for ARCH, and thus, the partners were investing a fair amount of time in trying to resurrect the opportunity. This conundrum has been faced by many practitioners when the initial thesis of an opportunity does not pan out. "The technology had to have a market somewhere . . . we just hadn't found it yet," Steven Lazarus, founder of ARCH, would recall. From hospitals, where the adoption for new technologies was sluggish, the company shifted its target market to Wall Street. Its technology was ideally suited for speedier transactions and messaging, and in five years the company grew to $180 million in revenues before it was acquired.[10] ARCH continued to support the company despite market-related challenges, and it paid off.

Compare NEON with the defunct online grocer Webvan — termed as one of the most epic failures in the dot-com bubble fiasco, this company sold groceries such as bread and vegetables. Within 18 months it had spent $1 billion on several futuristic warehouses, promising to offer groceries in 30 minutes or less. Webvan's investor list was the who's who of venture capital — Sequoia Capital, Benchmark Capital and several others. The company raised almost half a billion dollars from the public markets. However, the senior executives did not have any experience in the supermarket trade — Webvan went from being a $1.2 billion company with 4,500 employees to being liquidated in under two years. "The presumption that you needed to get big fast worked for Amazon.com and virtually no one else," commented Gartner analyst Whit Andrews at the time of Webvan's bankruptcy.[11]

In each of these examples, the underlying challenges of performance exist. Neither NEON nor Webvan was able to penetrate the market. However, the market conditions — the dot-com boom and bust — and capital needs of each business (Webvan needed a lot of money, NEON did not) impact investor outcomes. Whatever be the reasons, the Webvan boardroom may have been much more challenging as compared to NEON.

ALIGNMENT ON EXIT

Successful venture capitalist board members have alignment on timing, and value for a potential exit. If a company fails to accomplish milestones, encounters dwindling resources, or suffers from competitive pressures, the exit path and value may be severely compromised. On the other hand, with strong performance, selling to a corporate buyer or going public on the stock exchange at the right time is expected to yield a strong outcome.

But timing matters on exits, as does alignment of the stakeholders. If one venture investor is under more pressure to achieve an exit quickly than are other investors, the misalignment can impair the exit value. Further, if the CEO or the management team does not want to exit, the investors end up with another set of challenges. As the company evolves into maturation, it is rare and even unlikely that one individual will encompass all the skills necessary to guide the CEO and enhance value at every stage. Board members' ability to add value may diminish, and they need to cede their positions to more suitable peers within the firm. This rarely happens in practice — board members embed themselves within the company, especially as the company ascends to rapid growth. It's only during a crisis that disemboweling occurs.

At the heart of the challenge is the hero-worship *rock star* culture — CEOs who perform well when it comes to valuations and growth but are unable to maintain ethical and cultural boundaries. Boards have been challenged in a number of situations when fraud, misrepresentation, and harassment have occurred, often led by the CEOs themselves.

Venture capitalists, most of whom are trying to be supportive and nurturing without being overbearing, can be silent when a high-performing CEO delivers growth and stellar valuations.

Often, the executives can collude, cook books, and defraud investors. While rare, GCA Savvian's Steve Fletcher warns, "The CEO and CFO are the most important executives of a company. In reality, most of your information comes from them. If a company's executives really set out to defraud people, if they make up invoices or clients, it's difficult to detect as an auditor or a board member or an investment banker."[12]

Performance versus Governance: The Challenge of Rock Star CEOs

Company	Performance	Challenges
Uber	The world's fastest-growing rideshare company, raised ~$20 billion in 6 years and valued over $80bn at IPO	Misled regulators, evasion of law enforcement, shortchanged taxi drivers, overcharged customers, threatened journalists. Hostile work environment includes sexual harassment.
Zenefits	Fastest-growing SaaS company ever, providing online insurance to small businesses, raised ~$500 million and valued at ~$4.5 billion	Flouted insurance laws, skirted training requirements to sell insurance products. Reports of partying, alcohol consumption in the office.
Theranos	Charismatic 19-year-old Stanford dropout CEO, promises to offer superior blood tests. Raised $700 million and valued at ~$10 billion.	Lab-on-a-chip technology did not perform, endangered patient safety with misleading and fraudulent data. CEO indicted with multiple counts for defrauding investors, doctors, and patients.
Outcome Health	Installed flat-screen TVs in doctors' offices and patient waiting rooms, streaming pharma advertisements. Raised ~$500 million and valued at $5.5 billion.	Accusations of overcharging customers, falsifying documents showing inflated ad performance.
SoFi	Financial products such as student loans and mortgages. Raised $2.5 billion in debt and equity and valued ~$5 billion.	CEO resigns after allegations of sexual harassment, Federal Trade Commission charges company with false claims misrepresentation.
WeWork	Co-working space; expanded globally managing 40 million sq. ft. Raised $8 billion and was valued over ~$40 billion at its peak.	CEO controls the board, and received $300 million loan from company to exercise his stock options, complex corporate structure, self-dealings.

Fraud

From: Paul Johnston
To: Pete Solvik; Jonathan D. Roberts
Subject: Resignation
Jonathan and Pete:

This is a very difficult e-mail to write, but effective immediately both Parrish and I are tendering our resignation. We have both made a grave mistake by misrepresenting our revenue reporting to the board. Looking back at the time, we thought we would be able to right the wrong and correct our representation, but we have not been able to do this. Revenues have been overstated with a delta of approximately $400K a month. . . .

So begins the sordid nightmare for a group of venture capitalists that had invested $50 million in this company. Entellium, the Seattle-based company that was driving the next revolution of customer relationship management tools, came under intense fire. Entellium's four-year rise that garnered it numerous product design awards, accolades from *BusinessWeek* magazine and Forrester Research, and a CRM Market Leader designation, ended with the arrest of CEO Paul Johnston and CFO Parrish Jones.[13]

To any practitioner, such case studies offer expensive lessons:

- *Cover the blind spots.* Blind spots in business often occur both when things are going badly and when the business is going well. Assistant US Attorney Carl Blackstone, who prosecuted the case against Johnston and Jones, called Entellium a "legitimate company with a real product and real employees" with the only discordance being the inflated revenues, from which Johnston pocketed about $1.4 million.[14] In other words, there weren't explicit red flags to board members about something fishy in the books. The numbers — even the exaggerated versions hammed up by Johnston and Jones — made sense and fit the story of a robust company and its vibrant industry. As a venture capitalist, it may be hard to question your charismatic and driven founder and CEO, especially when the numbers look great! Venture capitalists can avoid being hoodwinked by learning to intelligently question all the facts. Safeguards like periodic in-depth reviews of sales to dig deeper into financial records can help.

- *Put healthy skepticism to work by putting periodic reviews in place.* A study found that among 1,770 VCs who have taken at least one of their portfolio firms public, 196 (11.07 percent) of them have funded a fraudulent IPO firm, and 154 (8.7 percent) of them have backed an IPO firm that committed fraud after their exit.[15] Obviously, the VCs who backed Entellium are not alone.

- *Enlist key players and enhance information flow.* A strong relationship with the business development team might have exposed deception sooner since collusion was largely confined to the CEO and CFO. Gathering inputs from people who aren't on the management team nor have any interest in sticking to the management team's story can be valuable.

- *Financial audits.* Despite the high costs of financial audits, this is an important step to ensure checks and balances.

BOARD EVALUATION

Self-evaluation of boards, while it seldom occurs, is a critical exercise. Venture-backed company boards tend to be smaller in size and are more interactive. Thus, the formal self-evaluation may never occur. Nevertheless, several CEOs of venture-backed companies express the challenges of time and attention. In a McKinsey study of 586 corporate directors, respondents pointed out that they would like to double their time on strategy and spend at least five times their time on talent management.[16]

Quotes such as, "He learned how to be a director. We paid the tuition," or "My strategy is to minimize the value subtracted"[17] are indicative of fundamental challenges that exist in the boardroom. In the white paper "A Simple Guide to Basic Responsibilities of a VC-Backed Director,"[18] guidelines for an annual self-review suggest the following criteria:

- Preparedness
  - Review all board materials prior to meetings.
  - Be aware of key challenges for the company, both short term and long term.
  - Communicate with other board members between meetings.
  - Complete any assignments in a timely and thorough fashion.
- Alignment
  - Align with other board members and CEO with respect to key performance indicators and challenges.
  - Ensure other board members are aligned with CEO and supportive, as well.
  - Raise any challenging issues related to performance and conflicts, which are not to be ignored or brushed under the carpet.
- Attention
  - Attend all board meetings, engaged in thoughtful manner without cell phone or email distractions.
- Contribution
  - Proactively seek ways of assisting the CEO to meet or exceed their goals. The CEO is at the center of the board's universe and a VC's role is to be supportive, staying behind the scenes as much as possible.

When time is the most critical resource, especially in early-stage companies, no director is going to raise his or her hand to take on any additional tasks. Board self-evaluation remains an academic exercise at best. After all, who will bell the proverbial cat? No CEO is going to push their board, even though they are the beneficiaries of a well-functioning board. Lead directors seem reluctant to create more work. In conversations with several board members, such a practice has yet to be suggested, leave alone being adopted with enthusiasm. Lindsay Aspegren of North Coast Technology Investors summarizes the challenges of a board member succinctly, "As board members, we are charged to make decisions amidst a dynamic and fast-changing microcosm. We have to manage change effectively. It is not only understanding this role but having the skills and the experience to do this job well. There is much emphasis on the front-end, the deal, in our business, but not enough on the post-investment plan."

Part Five

Exits: Liquidity Events and Champagne

"I remember one morning," writes Nikos Kazantzakis in *Zorba the Greek*, "when I discovered a cocoon in the back of a tree just as a butterfly was making a hole in its case and preparing to come out. I waited awhile, but it was too long appearing, and I was impatient. I bent over it and breathed on it to warm it. I warmed it as quickly as I could and the miracle began to happen before my eyes, faster than life. The case opened; the butterfly started slowly crawling out, and I shall never forget my horror when I saw how its wings were folded back and crumpled; the wretched butterfly tried with its whole trembling body to unfold them. Bending over it, I tried to help it with my breath, in vain. It needed to be hatched out patiently and the unfolding of the wings should be a gradual process in the sun. Now it was too late. My breath had forced the butterfly to appear all crumpled, before its time. It struggled desperately and, a few seconds later, died in the palm of my hand. That little body is, I do believe, the greatest weight I have on my conscience. For I realize today that it is a mortal sin to violate the great laws of nature. We should not hurry, we should not be impatient, but we should confidently obey the external rhythm."

Many startups have been killed while VCs, trying to do good, breathe their strategy, scaling, and other proxy-operational techniques to ensure a good and a speedy exit. This does not weigh on the capitalist conscience, though — we brush it away as risk, even the price of doing business.

The best VCs know that companies are always bought, never sold. In that vein, the singular goal is to not optimize for a premature exit — it is to ensure that the company has its fundamentals in place and is always playing from a position of strength. Good companies will always have plenty of options at every inflection point. But there may be only one such company — for the other nine companies in your portfolio, be prepared to earn your stripes. In this section, let us look at the various pathways to exits.

The business of VC is about liquidity events, which is more than drinking fine wine. You can declare success only when you have completed the full cycle of an investment and returned capital to your LPs, ideally more than what they gave you.

33

Exit Strategies

"For I must tell you friendly in your ear, Sell when you can, you are not for all markets," writes William Shakespeare, in *As You Like It* (Act 3 Scene V). The bard knew about the temptations of a VC. When a portfolio company is acquired, or its stock trades on the public exchanges, those rare (and hopefully happy) moments are what we live for, celebrate, and, at times, heave a sigh of relief. Capital invested comes back to LPs, completes a full circle, and an investor "exits the investment" by selling the stock of the portfolio company.

EXIT OPTIONS

The two primary exit options, acquisitions and initial public offerings (IPOs), are reviewed, along with private exchanges—an emerging option with implications for some highly sought-after technology companies. As seen in Exhibit 33.1, data from VentureSource samples show that 13 percent of exits end up in an IPO while 43 percent are acquisitions. A typical portfolio sees losses well above 40 percent of its companies.

Exhibit 33.1 **Frequency of portfolio outcomes.**

IPO	M&A	Failure
13%	43%	44%

Data: VentureSource

- *Mergers and acquisitions (M&A or trade-sale).* Mergers and acquisitions is the most popular path of exit for a venture-backed company. Also called *trade sale,* a portfolio company is sold to a larger company. The transaction nets a return for investors, who, in turn, share the spoils with their limited partners. Many M&A exits are disguised failures, where over 20 percent of investments have lost money on a cash-on-cash basis at another 19 percent have yielded outcomes between 1X and 2X.[1]

- *Initial public offering.* A highly desired badge of honor; investors list a company on a publicly traded stock exchange and sell privately owned shares for the first time to the public. Of course, fewer companies can demonstrate the growth and value to be considered IPO ready. And after they are ready, the Securities and Exchange Commission (SEC), the federal regulatory body, prescribes rules and regulations on public offerings to keep everyone honest and protect that little old lady. Some venture practitioners treat the public offering as a financing event and not an exit. Compared to acquisitions, IPOs typically deliver a higher return to investors, as seen in Exhibit 33.2.

- *Secondary markets and private exchanges.* Several options for secondary markets such as private exchanges have sprung up, offering shares of hot startups to eager buyers.

Exhibit 33.2 **Returns: Or why an IPO is better.**

Exit Path	Median IRR (%)	Mean IRR (%)	Standard Deviation
IPO	58.39 %	123.42 %	207.97
M&A	18.32 %	75.32 %	408.27

Source: CEPERS, Frankfurt. For exits between 1971 and 2003, with 100 to 400 observations. Data from Center for Private Equity Research, Frankfurt. Carsten Bienz and Tore E. Leite, "A Pecking Order of Venture Capital Exits "(April 2008). Available at SSRN: http://ssrn.com/abstract=916742.

- *Redemption of shares.* Remember that redemption clause you negotiated — the one where you can treat your equity much like a debt instrument and trigger the repayment after five years! That is technically an exit, but no venture practitioner worth his IRR speaks of redemption in public.

And yes, a write-off is technically an exit in disguise, but it doesn't need much deliberation. Be assured that in your portfolio, the lemons, as depicted in Exhibit 33.3, will always ripen much faster. Stated differently, the losses occur much faster.

Each exit path has its own advantages and challenges, as seen in Exhibit 33.4.

Exhibit 33.3 **Lemons ripen faster than pearls — or losses often come before profits.**

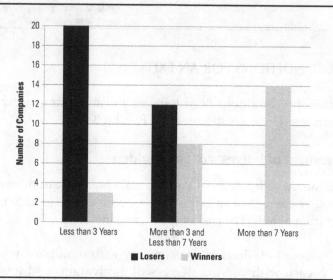

Source: Jeffry Timmons, *New Venture Creation: Entrepreneurship for the 21st Century,* 5th ed. (New York: McGraw Hill, 1999).

Exhibit 33.4 **Exit methods.**

Method of Exit	Pros	Cons
Acquisition (trade-sale)	Speed. Reduced regulatory challenges (assuming the FTC does not get involved!). Value can be lower in comparison to an IPO, but, as many practitioners point out, it is efficient.	Companies are always bought, never sold. Earnouts may be beyond the full control of current management or existing investors. Founders or any other shareholders cannot retain partial ownership.
Listing on public exchange or an IPO (initial public offering)	Larger valuation in stronger market conditions. Can use stock for acquisitions. Improves stature and morale. Founders can retain partial ownership	Company needs to achieve substantial growth rates. Expensive and complex process. Regulatory and market challenges.
Private exchanges	Rapid liquidity. Higher valuations.	Awareness and demand for the companies must be high. No one is looking to invest in no-name companies. Value is determined by sheer frothiness and public market-like speculation.
Redemption	Ability to recover capital, assuming company has cash at hand at the time of redemption.	Dependent on company's ability to redeem, as well as other balance sheet obligations and board composition. Payouts could be spread out over time to minimize cash impact, further reducing any IRR.

PRECONDITIONS FOR AN EXIT

Certain preconditions need to be established prior to any exit overtures. These are discussed in Exhibit 33.5.

Alignment of Interests of Stakeholders

Alignment of interests of various stakeholders can determine whether passage of an exit will be smooth or be a joyride to the suburbia of hell. The cast of characters includes:

- Board of directors, presumably with multiple investors, each with varying degrees of motivations and investor preferences
- Founders/chief executive officer motivations
- Common shareholders' interests

Exhibit 33.5 **Preconditions for an exit.**

Preconditions for an Exit	Favorable Conditions	Unfavorable Conditions
Value drivers	Rapid sales and expansion, market leadership and proprietary position.	Flat growth, limited potential. Sagging morale. A dog. A distraction.
Board-investor alignment	Board members/investors are aligned with respect to timing and value of exit.	The largest investor wants that quick hit — a fund-raise cycle is coming up and we need that IRR! You want to stay! Or the largest investor (and the chairman of the board) is fatigued and wants to get rid of this dog. You, on the other hand, are a seed investor and control a fraction of the shares. And the common shareholders want to block the sale because those 3X liquidation preferences do not leave any crumbs for them.
Board– management alignment	Board and CEO/founders are in agreement with respect to timing and value of exit.	The investors want to sell. The CEO wants to grow. Investors sell — unhappy CEO ends up writing a book. What a wicked world! The CEO wants to sell — the investors want to hold and build value. A premature liquidity event for VCs!
Market demand	Buyers are kicking the doors down. A nice auction process is driving price and IRR to all-time highs. Sell this — and get that PPM ready for the next fund raise?	No market demand, but we want to sell. Hire an I-banker, prepare a book, and start the selling process. With no bites and sinking cash position, attempt to raise a bridge note or swallow a down round. Eighteen months later, shut the company down.
Macro conditions	Strong public markets and economic conditions.	Competition, erosion of margins, regulatory changes.

Naturally, the board exerts the maximum influence, but the role of other stakeholders is important as exits are being planned. Consider a Cisco executive who, while conducting due diligence, assesses the quality and character of the target company's management team. Cisco interacts with the executives in an informal manner to explore short-term and long-term goals. "We look for culture, qualities, and leadership style. We don't care about the product that is on the manufacturing floor . . . the second- and third-generation product is locked up in their heads," a Cisco executive points out.[2] John Chambers, the CEO of Cisco, laid out five guidelines for acquiring companies, including the "chemistry between companies has to be right" and "long-term win for all four constituencies — shareholders, employees, customers, and business partners."[3] If the founders and CEO of the target company do not see the exit as a win, it may show during buyer diligence. When Ted Dacko, CEO of HealthMedia, was getting ready to complete the sale of his company to Johnson & Johnson, he was not worried about the exit value as much as the team culture. "I wanted to ensure everyone understood the exit strategy and was aligned — we did not have any passive aggressive behavior," he says.

Aligning the Board and the Management Team

We had a tough time convincing our board of directors who were also our investors to embrace many of our activities that would help build the Zappos brand and make the world a better place. The directors didn't fully understand or were convinced of things like brand or culture, dismissing many of these as "Tony's social experiments." Sequoia expected an exit in five years and hadn't signed up for these additional things. I was pretty close to being fired from the board. I was learning that alignment with shareholders and board of directors was just as important.[4]

Exit strategies, value, and timing evolve as the company matures. Practitioners have a strong sense of when a company has matured or is languishing toward failure. If a company fails to accomplish future-financing rounds, misses milestones and targets, exhausts ideas and resources, or sees its market shrink or shift, then it is critical to close down operations rather than to slowly wither into oblivion.[5] Conversely, selling to a corporate buyer or going public at the right time is certainly expected as a strong outcome. Timing matters. Premature efforts to drive exits can lead to depressed value or, worse, no buyer interest. Sell too late and the dynamics may shift — potential buyers,

Exhibit 33.6 **Diffusion of innovations — and the best exit window.**

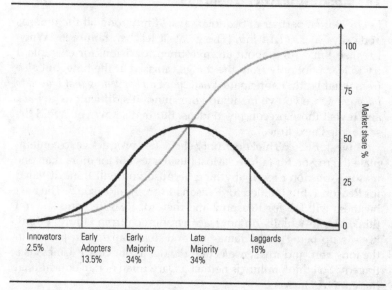

market conditions, and the arrival of competition could impair the value. Mitch Lasky of Benchmark Capital points out that the window of exit opportunity can be narrow. "Look for that S Curve when growth and exit multiples are on your side," he says. See Exhibit 33.6.

Alignment of Exit Value: What's a Few Hundred Million, Anyway?

At an appropriate time, specific exit values should also be discussed openly to ensure alignment with various stakeholders. For example, different investors may have conflicting valuations in mind. Examples abound where one venture capitalist was happy to part with the company for $100 million and another was expecting to turn at least $300 million.[6] If the liquidation preferences come into play and gravely impact the common shareholders, unpleasant situations, such as holdup of the voting process or, worse, lawsuits, can ensue.

The Greatest Teacher, Failure Is

Roelof Botha, partner at Sequoia, says, "I'm wrong all the time; as Yoda says in *The Last Jedi*, 'The greatest teacher, failure is.' When I realize I'm wrong about an investment decision, for example, I try to learn not only from the things I missed at the time, but also from what I didn't anticipate. *What ended up happening that I failed to imagine?* Once you've made up your mind, it's difficult to go back and revisit those preconceived ideas. But that's how you avoid the same traps next time."

Investor Peter Thiel does not believe it is productive to contemplate the reason for failure. "Most businesses fail for more than one reason. You don't learn anything because you will think it failed for Reason 1, but it failed for Reasons 1 through Reason 5. The next business will fail for Reason 2 and then for Reason 3 and so on. I think people actually do not learn very much from failure. I think it ends up being quite damaging and demoralizing to people in the long run, and my sense is that the death of every business is a tragedy. So I think failure is neither a Darwinian nor an educational imperative," he says.[7]

Marc Andreessen has a similar worldview. "Forward. We don't stop, slow down, or second guess. We don't revisit past decisions," he says.

In hospitals and doctors' residency training programs, a morbidity and mortality (M&M) conference is held. Surgeons and residents candidly discuss complications and deaths. Students are often present, as this is a great learning opportunity. The resident practitioner who performed the operation presents the summary of the case, pertinent history, physical examination findings, lab results, and images. Cases are presented and critiqued by the participants. Questions are asked on why the case was managed in a certain way. Other surgeons often chime in to share their views and learning from similar cases. Often, a consensus may be reached if the complication could have been prevented. Such honest and robust conversations often prevent the same mistakes from occurring and can save lives in the future. The atmosphere can be rich with debates, but the goal is not to blame any one person nor elicit retribution. Every attendee learns from the mistakes. The focus of such a conference is on education, improving quality of care, and saving lives.

When it comes to analyzing the cause of startup failures, can a venture capitalist learn from this model?

For any practitioner (and any LP), the exit of an investment is a much-anticipated event. But savvy practitioners do not necessarily aim for premature exits—rather, they work toward building stable and sound companies that generate value for customers. For such companies, exit options are always plentiful and never at the mercy of markets.

Acquisitions

THE PRIMARY PATH TO AN EXIT

Acquisitions are seen as the fastest way for larger companies to expand, whether vertically or horizontally. Such *growth by acquisition* strategies can bolster companies' revenues, profitability, and entry in new markets, or often fend off competition. VC-backed companies make strong acquisition candidates, as they often offer an established revenue/customer base and proprietary technology, are profitable and receptive to fair valuation metrics, have a unique and defensible market position, and employ strong management teams. For larger companies, especially the ones with significant cash, stagnant revenues, and limited growth potential, acquisitions is a core component of their growth strategy. Exhibit 34.1 lists motivations for buyers (acquirers), as well as sellers.

Exhibit 34.1 **Exit drivers.**

Acquirers' Motivations	Sellers' Motivations
Growth and increased revenues via access to new products, geographic markets	Positive market/macroeconomic conditions
Operational synergies and reduced risks via diversification	Financial trade-offs: time and capital required to create future value versus present value
Accelerating innovation, minimizing research, and development risks	Investor liquidity
Access to talent (or acqui-hires)	Inability to raise capital to fuel additional organic growth
Industry consolidation	Reduced pace of growth
Defensive / Competition	Ability to sustain competitive pressures
	Margin erosion
	Regulatory challenges
	Intellectual property landscape

When larger companies, often bereft of research budgets, seek rapid growth, new product lines, or technologies, the first choice may be to try and build innovative products in-house. Any chief technology officer (CTO) of a technology company will strongly assert that their team can develop new products internally, and do it faster and cheaper. However, except for a handful of nimble companies, there are not many examples of successful innovation in larger organizations. The innovator's dilemma plays out often, where the giants cannot dance. The potential for increased revenues, competitive dynamics, and financial growth and market timing comes into play. Often, this is where the CFO and the corporate development team display their acumen and go on a shopping spree.

Whatever the motivation — technological, market driven, or ego driven — target companies and venture practitioners benefit from such behavior. The search process starts where the acquirer establishes certain criteria to narrow down the universe of potential targets. At a very primal level, every CEO seeks to deploy excess cash to build a larger empire via acquisitions and demonstrate King Arthur–like prowess. Warren Buffett remarked, "Of one thing be certain: if a CEO is enthused about a particularly foolish acquisition, both his internal staff and his outside advisors will come up with whatever projections are needed to justify his stance. Only in fairy tales are emperors told that they are naked."

When any acquisition-related discussions occur, practitioners point to their duty to shareholders of maximizing the outcome for all. Thus, in certain situations, bringing in an investment banker would be appropriate. For the investment banker, the goal of such an exercise is to drive the price up, or run an auction. Daniel Axelsen, formerly with investment bank Qatalyst Partners, says, "The company and the board have a fiduciary obligation to all shareholders to maximize value. These processes are like a three-dimensional game of chess," Daniel says. In one transaction, Qatalyst drove the sale price from $1.15 billion to $2.4 billion, all in a matter of a few weeks.

If Google wants to buy a company, surely some competitors would love to jump into the fray. When Google did a

$900 million deal with MySpace, Microsoft followed soon thereafter and did a $300 million deal with Facebook. This move turned out to be a much better win for Microsoft. Investment bankers can often drive competing entities to bid, and can drum up additional interest from various acquirers and juggle with different interested buyers, all the time pushing the price as high as possible. The frenzy often culminates with a letter of intent (LOI) with one of the suitors. At times, the buyer promptly locks up the game by proposing a "no shop" clause, where the target cannot indulge in the shopping exercise. Axelsen says, "Exclusive processes are a lot harder and don't necessarily yield the best results."

A buyer's due diligence process will occur in phases. The primary goal of the buyer is to ensure that the technology and teams are a suitable fit within its existing fabric. Thus, while the product lines, revenues, and markets are tangible, the softer challenges of postmerger integration are important as well. For example, Cisco sets short-term and long-term joint initiatives with the target's management team as a way to assess culture, management qualities, and leadership styles. It looks for softer cues and watches if one person speaks over everyone else. Do some people roll their eyes when the other is talking? Cisco negotiates directly with key individuals to identify their post-acquisition intentions and also insists on employees waiving their accelerated vesting rights to ensure that they stay with the company post-integration.

Valuation is not the most important negotiating point.[1] One Cisco executive remarked, "*Acquisitions are not financial — we do not do them because we can swing a good deal — they are strategic and help grow our company in the right direction.*"[2] When a buyer seeks to make a strategic acquisition, the price is no longer a multiple, but could be significantly higher.

"As a practitioner, your goal is to understand that universe of strategic buyers," says Lindsay Aspegren of North Coast Technology Investors. For larger companies, effective integration is key, or else the entire exercise is deemed a failure. Cisco has a small army of employees to manage the post-integration process. An integration leader is appointed, and within

30 days of announcement, the human resources team lays out compensation plans for the team so that the talent pool can avoid uncertainty, stays, and focuses on creating value.

After the board approval and shareholder consents, the closing process begins.

A Big Fish Swallows a Small Fish

Acquisitions are seldom completed in five easy steps as described, followed by hugs and a friendly dinner. Often, people threaten, lose sleep and fret, wave their arms. It's a storm of greed, fear, and the desire to win. The stakes are high.

When Quidisi, a company that operated Diapers.com, reached $300 million in sales in a few years, Amazon took notice. Over an introductory lunch, an Amazon executive ominously informed the founders of Quidisi that the giant was getting ready to start selling diapers. They should consider selling to Amazon.

Quidisi had raised over $50 million from leading venture capitalists in Silicon Valley. The founders didn't jump in, and a few months later they noticed something strange — Amazon had dropped prices on diapers by as much as 30%. As an experiment, Quidisi changed prices, and voilà — Amazon's tracking bots monitored and changed its prices, too. For Quidisi, this price drop impacted growth and started to erode profit margins. Worse, its ability to raise additional equity capital or possibly consider an IPO was now slimmer than ever.

In the meantime, Walmart made an acquisition overture to Quidisi, and offered $450 million. Quidisi founders flew to Seattle to meet with Bezos to discuss Amazon's interest. To keep the heat, that morning, Amazon announced a service called Amazon Mom, where it offered a 30% discount and free shipping. When Quidisi factored these maneuvers in the costs of selling diapers, Amazon was on track to lose $100 million in three months on diapers alone. Amazon was doing about $34 billion in revenues, and Bezos wanted Diapers.com at a price. He was also not going to let this slip to Walmart, which did over $400 billion in revenues. Amazon's $540 million offer was open for 48 hours, and even as the offer was tentatively accepted, Walmart countered with $600 million. Executives at Amazon let Quidisi know that Bezos was such a furious competitor, that he would trigger a "thermo-nuclear" option and drive diaper prices to zero if they sold to Walmart. A lot of Amazon Moms would have been happier at free diapers. The move paid off and Quidisi was sold to Amazon, largely out of fear.[3]

As seen in Exhibit 34.2, acquisitions are significantly larger as compared to public offerings.

Acquisitions are the preferred path for most venture-backed companies due to speed and efficiency, as well as minimal regulatory challenges. Acquisitions offer larger companies much-needed growth and expansion opportunities. Consider Exhibits 34.3 and 34.4.

Most technology companies grow via acquisitions, and slower innovators like Amazon, Google, Facebook, and Apple have acquired 445 companies in 2007–2019. IBM acquired over 70 companies in seven years, spending about $14 billion.[4] By pushing these newly acquired products through an existing global sales force, IBM estimates it increased its revenue by almost 50 percent in the first two years after each acquisition and an average of more than 10 percent over the next three years.[5]

Exhibit 34.2 **Liquidity events of VC-backed companies.**

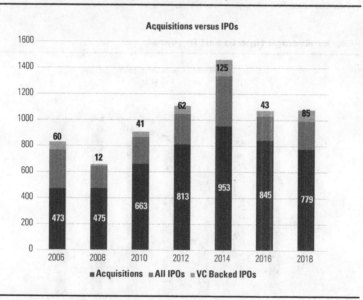

Acquisitions versus IPOs

Source: Modified from NVCA 2019 Yearbook, Data provided by Pitchbook.

Exhibit 34.3 **Acquisitions — Mean deal values.**

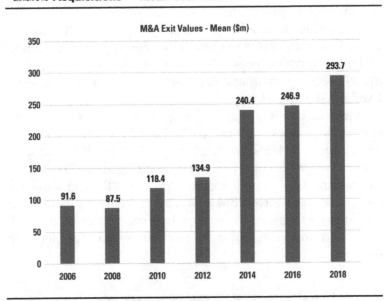

Exhibit 34.4 **Average time to exit in years.**

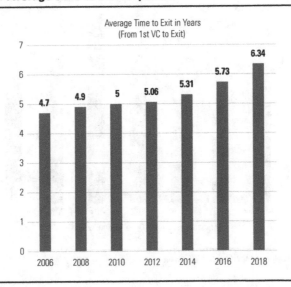

By rough estimates, Cisco acquired over 120 companies over a 15-year span — roughly an average of 8–12 companies each year. The first 71 companies acquired within an eight-year period[6] were at an average price of approximately $350 million. In that same period, Cisco's sales increased from $650 million to $22 billion, with nearly 40 percent revenue coming directly from these acquisitions.[7]

Google acquired 131 companies over a 12-year period,[8] an average of 10 companies a year. For Google, the technology drivers have opened up new revenue sources. Its acquisition of Applied Semantics helped Google develop a text-advertising network called AdSense, now a multibillion-dollar revenue generator. Andy Rubin's startup, Android Inc., was snapped up by Google and led to the development of Android, a leading operating system for smartphones.[9]

Key drivers for acquisitions are:

- *Improved revenues and profitability.*
- *Operational synergies.* Larger companies seek to reduce costs and expand revenues and profitability by seeking synergistic companies that feed their value chain.
  - *Vertical.* Vertical synergies occur when an acquirer moves vertically — up or down the value chain or supply chain. Also called forward integration or backward integration.
  - *Horizontal.* Horizontal synergies occur when an acquirer moves to buy another company within an adjacent domain.
  - *Diversification of product lines to increase revenues.*
  - *Geographic penetration.* Access to a new geographic territory, when conducted internationally, is also referred to as cross-border transactions.
  - *Quash any rising threats:* Apple bought Lala, a cloud-based web streaming music service, and within a few months shut it down. Lala users are angry; yet Apple bought Lala simply to take it offline because it

Three Hidden Motivators of Acquisitions

The real reasons companies are acquired

Warren Buffett describes the three primary drivers of acquisitions — animal spirits (Don't just stand there, do something. Buy a company), bigger is better (Ego. Larger acquisitions are better), and undue optimism on post-merger integration (It will all work out — if not, all we lose is shareholder capital). He writes, "We suspect three motivations — usually unspoken — to be, singly or in combination, at work in high-premium takeovers."

This is Buffett's take:

Leaders, business or otherwise, seldom are deficient in animal spirits and often relish increased activity and challenge.

All the other kids have one, what about me?

When a CEO is encouraged by his advisors to make deals, he responds much as would a teenage boy who is encouraged by his father to have a normal sex life. It's not a push he needs. Some years back, a CEO friend of mine — in jest, it must be said — unintentionally described the pathology of many big deals. This friend, who ran a property-casualty insurer, was explaining to his directors why he wanted to acquire a certain life insurance company. After droning rather unpersuasively through the economics and strategic rationale for the acquisition, he abruptly abandoned the script. With an impish look, he simply said: "Aw, fellas, all the other kids have one."

I am bigger. . . .

Most organizations, business or otherwise, measure themselves, are measured by others, and compensate their managers far more by the yardstick of size than by any other yardstick. (Ask a *Fortune 500* manager where his corporation stands on that famous list and, invariably, the number will be ranked by size of sales; he may well not even know where his corporation places on the list by profitability.)

Kissing toads, optimistically. . . .

Many managers apparently were overexposed in impressionable childhood years to the story in which the imprisoned handsome prince is released from a toad's body by a kiss from a beautiful princess. Consequently, they are certain their managerial kiss will do wonders for the profitability of Company T(arget). Such optimism is essential. Absent that rosy view, why else should the shareholders of Company A(cquisitor) want to own an interest in T at the 2X takeover cost rather than at the x market price they would pay if they made direct purchases on their own? In other words, investors can always buy toads at the going price for toads. If investors instead bankroll princesses who wish to pay double for the right to kiss the toad, those kisses had better pack some real dynamite. We've observed many kisses but very few miracles. Nevertheless, many managerial princesses remain serenely confident about the future potency of their kisses — even after their corporate backyards are knee-deep in unresponsive toads.[10]

didn't like the price erosion — Lala was charging 10 cents per track as compared to 99 cents on the iTunes music store.[11] Google snapped up reMail, a popular iPhone application that provides "lightning fast" full-text search. reMail was yanked from the iTunes App Store soon thereafter and no predictions were made on the future of reMail. As TechCrunch's MG Siegler predicted, "Google is just as happy to kill one of the best email applications on the iPhone — much better than the iPhone's native email app."

If acquisitions offer an efficient mechanism for generating returns, who are GPs to judge these human fallacies of ego, mindless activity, and undue optimism? As cash piles are hoarded by public companies, the animal spirits for acquisitions will continue. Rich Levandov, an investor in several technology start-ups says, "Venture capital is about asymmetrical information and value — you know something that the buyer does not and you have something that a buyer wants — and wants it now," he says. One of his portfolio companies was a startup with no revenues. Yet five buyers jostled over each other to snag the company. For one of his companies that got an unsolicited soft overture, First Mark Capital's Rick Heitzmann politely demurred, "We do not wish to sell, but if you are aggressive about buying, let's see your offer."

PUTTING THE COMPANY UP FOR SALE

Should the board decide to put the company for sale, the process, as seen in Exhibit 34.5, starts with testing the market conditions — or dipping your toe in the water.

Exhibit 34.5 **Typical trade sale process.**

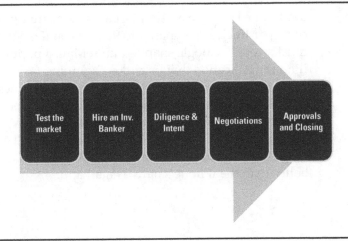

Step 1: Test the Market Conditions

Companies considering a sale generally hire a "sell-side" investment bank to oversee the process of the company in a timely and efficient manner. Investment bankers charge a fee, typically, around 4–7 percent of the transaction amount, along with a retainership. At this stage, a company would invite investment bankers to propose terms and timelines and to demonstrate their industry awareness and connections. While these discussions ensue, the ineffective bankers will be eager to take the assignment and, after collecting substantial retainer fees, fail to deliver value. The low-level tactics include proposing significantly higher valuations to snag the assignment, and later, point to the buyer universe for poor outcomes. On the other hand, the best of the breed may not be willing to engage or sell something unless they believe the opportunity is meaningfully attractive to the universe of acquirers — and if they do, may propose a lower number to get the transaction completed fast. The company should seek the right balance between investment banker industry expertise, fee structures, target valuation range, and target timelines of transaction.

Company boards identify the investment bankers who have relevant knowledge of the challenges and opportunities of a particular sector and market conditions. Investment bankers are able to gauge the field, identify potential buyers, and know the potential hurdles and buyer objections. In determining the company's selling price, investment banks can provide fair assessments of value by analyzing the company's long-term prospects and current financials. Beyond providing these financial advisory services, investment banks identify potential buyers, solicit bids and review proposals, help companies select the most attractive candidates, and participate in the negotiations with interested parties.

At times, the value and visibility of the company may be such that an investment banker may be unnecessary. Or consider the approach of Heitzmann: "We deliberately built a board with tentacles in the potential buyer's market. You generally know someone — first-time entrepreneurs do not have much of a network — and that's where we come in. One of our board members knew people at the acquiring company, and that's how it started," he says.

Step 2: Formalize the Process — Hire an Investment Banker

At this stage, the board would hire an investment banker who will proceed within the following framework:

- *Process metrics and timelines.* Establish valuation guidelines, universe of potential acquirers, and steps/timelines for the process.
- *Presentation materials.* A teaser sheet, a set of slides, and relevant information memorandum.
- *First contact.* At this point, the I-banker blasts emails to the universe of acquirers, using teasers, which provide high-level information to acquirers. Teasers are typically a page or two long, with key highlights of the technology, revenues, and growth potential. Teasers do not disclose the name of the company and offer only some key points that get the buyers to the door to sign a nondisclosure agreement.
- *Screening the parties interested in the company.* Once the interested parties have been identified and have signed nondisclosure agreements, these would be prescreened. This can be a nebulous step, as the goal of prescreening is to eliminate those who are merely seeking information without providing any insights into their process, motivations, or criteria. And beware of tire kickers. Brad Feld cautions that expressions of interest occur many times along the way. "It could well be corporate development guys from large companies just sucking info from entrepreneurs, or staying busy, doing their job. They may have no money but are wasting an entrepreneur's time. We see many tire kickers and can help our entrepreneurs to cut through the noise — we know a lot of natural acquirers and we don't hesitate to call them when the time comes." Also, after the prescreening stage, companies choose to negotiate the terms themselves, without any substantial involvement

from the I-bankers. Many intermediaries prefer to offer advice on the various potential outcomes based on negotiation parameters — mature I-bankers will seldom prescribe one path over another. The ultimate decision lies with the company. Gaurav Bhasin, managing director of Allied Advisers, a Silicon Valley–based advisory firm, has closed the sales of multiple VC-backed companies in the United States, Europe, and Asia. He works with founders and investors as a close confidant. "My role is to establish trust with the founders and help them understand the buyer's viewpoint" he says. "We run a tight process with our established and deep contacts in the buyer universe. Bringing relationships to bear is an advantage, but we also make sure founders can make data driven decisions. For example, we analyzed over 13044 exit transactions over a five year period and found that 89 percent of exits are below $100m price points. If founders get emotionally attached to irrationally large exit amounts, such details can help them see the bigger picture."

After a suitable buyer has been zeroed in on, the parties proceed to stage two of the process:

- *Execute a letter of intent.* A letter of intent (LOI) establishes a level of commitment on both sides to proceed in a diligent and a timely fashion to finish what has been initiated. The LOI would include:
  - *Exclusivity.* The seller is engaging with only one party. This clause tilts the axis in favor of the buyer.
  - *Confidentiality.* This clause protects the seller's information. A must-have clause that does not impact the economic terms.
  - Broad parameters of transaction terms.
    - Due diligence
    - Conditions to closing
    - Employee matters
  - Suggested timelines

- Buyers may choose to offer a *nonbinding* LOI, which is a two-edged sword. Further, a weak yet binding LOI does not accomplish much for the seller.

- Once the LOI has been executed, the buyer is aware of the negotiating advantage that starts therein. Other suitors usually step back at this point and the dance frenzy intensifies. A seller needs to ensure that the LOI has enough teeth in it to protect valuation and ensure that the diligence is completed with a sense of urgency.

In describing the role of investment bankers, author Karen Ho takes a scalpel to cut some carcasses open. Here is an honest take on the "Process for a High Yield Deal" (from the desk of an investment banking associate), which was symptomatic malaise in the industry leading up to the 2008 financial crisis.[12]

Investment Banking Process	The Real Deal
Pitch prospective client. Tell them how great we are at raising junk.	Lie, cheat, steal, and bad-mouth your competitors to win the business.
Build financial model: historical performance and projected earnings and leverage ratios.	Manipulate projection so credit ratings are reasonable.
Analyze comparable high-yield issues to understand market rates and returns.	Select the most aggressive companies to show the client.
Due diligence: Analyze the company and understand why it exists and will it exist tomorrow.	Boondoggle: Build up your frequent-flyer miles.
Drafting sessions: Craft the perfect marketing document to bring to market.	Eat M&M's, ice cream bars, and cookies. Get fat!!!
Prepare rating agency presentation.	Mask the company's weaknesses by concentrating on one or two strengths.
Prepare road show presentation.	Same as above — Goal: To fool the investor.
Road show: Grueling 8 days on the road.	Expense account: Go crazy with the client's money!!!

Most processes follow a similar undertone but occasionally you may find a good banker, who is less about lying, cheating, and bad mouthing and more about ensuring all parties walk away with a fair advantage.

Step 3: Do Your Due Diligence

Larger companies, and the buyer's counsel, will engage in deep due diligence. Sellers establish a data room with relevant documents, which include:

- *Corporate records*. Certificate of incorporation, bylaws, board minutes, and shareholders' list.
- *Business records*. All material contracts of purchase, sale, and supply agreements, research agreements, licensing and distribution agreements and government contracts, list of all assets and intellectual property.
- *Financial records*. All financial statements, receivables, loan and equity agreements, tax records. Copies of all placement memorandums, capitalization schedules, and equity amounts.
- *Employee records*. All employee agreements, consultant agreements, details of option plans and benefits (pension, health care) offered.
- *Legal*. Details of any litigation, pending or foreseen.

Step 4: Negotiate/Structure the Transaction

Typical elements of negotiation during the sell process include, besides valuation, the following:

- Asset purchase versus stock purchase:
  - *Most acquisitions occur as asset purchases*. This eliminates any unknown or contingent liabilities that a seller may assume as a result of stock purchase. Assets can be chosen ("You keep those

desks and phone systems, we keep the IP and the customers") and allow for depreciation — a tax advantage.

- *In a stock purchase, the buyer can assume net operating losses (NOL) that the seller may have accrued.* These may reduce the buyer's tax liabilities and augment the value. On the flip side, the buyer also assumes all liabilities, known or unknown. And yes, those old desks and archaic phone systems are a part of the deal.

- Cash offering, part cash and part stock, or all-stock transaction:

  - All-cash transaction is preferred by sellers and venture investors. Buyers can finance such transactions via external financings.

  - Stock transactions allow the seller to gain long-term economic advantages and to be a shareholder to enjoy any advantages.

- *Earnouts and escrows.* A buyer may believe that the value of the company lies in executing certain orders that generate revenues and cash flows or profits. Further, a buyer may establish certain targets and milestones for such an earnout. Jack Ahrens of TGap Ventures tries to minimize any earnouts: "The company is going to be controlled largely by the acquirer, and so are the resources — people as well as cash. Things can get sticky pretty quickly when motivations change," he says. Depending on the sector, practitioners advise that approximately 15 percent of the value in earnouts is acceptable. In the pharmaceutical sector, these percentages vary significantly and depend on the stage of drug development. Escrow percentages are 5–15 percent and periods (12–24 months) are negotiated as buyer attempts to protect from any surprises and contingencies.

- Other terms:
  - Representations and warranties made by the target company
  - Employees: Who stays, who goes
  - Employee options: Vesting schedule and acceleration
  - Indemnities offered by the target company

Step 5: Approvals and Closing

The board and shareholders approve the transaction. The closing, a process during which the attorneys and key stakeholders execute final agreements, occurs on a set date. While these would historically happen in person, typically at an attorney's office, many of these are done virtually nowadays. After all, if signatures can be scanned and money can be wired, we do not need the general assembly.

DEAL KILLERS

Acquirers walk away from opportunities for several reasons, but the most critical deal-breakers are often alignment of interests and financial terms. For investors, the primary deal killer is the value of an exit. Yet a young CEO may find an *acqui-hire* offer appealing.

Understanding the buyer's motivations is critical. The value of the acquisition, pace of transaction, terms, and conditions are often driven by the buyer's ambitions.

Good recordkeeping is often underestimated by startup CEOs, and it is often the onus of the board and investors to ensure that all records are up to date. Material contracts, cap tables, intellectual property assignments, and even timely payment of taxes can cause irritants in this process.

35

Initial Public Offering

The initial public offering (IPO), or "going public," holds a special cachet in the world of VC-backed companies. Often marking the coming of age of companies, entrepreneurs see it as the epitome of success. But the regulatory and market complexities are significant and have impacted the IPO dynamics significantly.

In the 1990s, an IPO was within reach for companies with annual revenues of $30–50 million that showed a profitable quarter and had a good board and management team. After the dot-com crash of the 1990s, it was the larger, more mature companies with revenues of $150+ million that were seen as suitable candidates for public offering. This, combined with regulatory challenges, had the effect of stretching out IPO timelines for companies.

Ninety percent of firms surveyed separately indicate pursuing dual strategies in which they consider both an IPO filing and a trade sale for their portfolios.[1] Dual tracks offer a better negotiation leverage. "Dual track for an exit? Now that is a problem we'd love to have," says Bryce Roberts of O'Relly AlphaTech Ventures (OATV), an early-stage venture fund.

If the company is ready and the markets are favorable, the public offering is certainly a better option because most acquisitions don't generate the killer returns that public offerings do. Because IPO-ready companies can be affected by market downturns and regulations, the volume of investment returns for investors may be driven more by acquisitions than public offerings. Consequently, acquisitions are efficient and faster exit options.

When a company decides to file for a public offering in the United States, it registers its securities with the Securities and Exchange Commission (SEC) for sale to the general public. From a business perspective, it is a culmination of a longer strategic plan for the company. For entrepreneurs, the priority is to expand capital resources by tapping into the public equity markets for additional investors.

The benefits and costs are manifold. The advantages are evident, including enabling access to capital, exposure, and prestige; facilitating future acquisitions of other companies (via partial payments in shares); enjoying access to multiple financing opportunities such as equity, convertible debt, and cheaper bank loans; and developing increased liquidity.[2] The costs are also not to be ignored: loss of privacy as to matters regarding business operations; competition; disclosure of executive officers' compensation, material contracts, and customers; pressure from shareholders to perform and meet market expectations; time-consuming diplomacy in undergoing periodic reporting to investors; and shareholder and regulatory compliance.

THE IPO PROCESS: THE LONG AND WINDING ROAD

The IPO journey can be divided into many different phases in which the actual IPO is seen as a significant milestone in an otherwise-complex structural transformation. According to *Ernst & Young's Guide to Going Public*, there are essentially three main stages:[3]

1. *Planning stage.* The company commits to diligent preparation that includes conducting feasibility studies and readiness checks on the business and financials itself, as well as the market.

2. *Execution or implementation stage.* The right management and advisory teams are established; financial infrastructure and accounting, tax, operational, and IT processes and systems are assessed; corporate structure

and governance are established; and investor relations and corporate communication strategies and plans are managed.

3. *Realization stage.* Finally, the company reaches the realization phase, where shares are priced and the IPO transaction closes.

In the preparatory, planning stage, which takes place about one to two years before the IPO is set to take place, a company does its homework to assess the readiness to go IPO:

- *Prepare a compelling business plan.* The business plan should be long-term, covering 24 to 36 months before and after the IPO to provide a clear road map that can be embedded early in the organization.

- *Benchmark the portfolio company's performance.* Before deciding to go public, companies monitor their performance, tracking growth rates, sales performance, profitability, and market share. Companies should also measure themselves on other benchmarks, such as ensuring that their products and services are well defined and assessing their reputation among various market stakeholders (e.g., customers, analysts, and investment banks). Aside from financials, reputation and brand name are important intangibles for leveraging a company's strength in the public markets.

- *Is this a public-ready company?* A compelling business track record and a plan to demonstrate how IPO funds will fuel growth is key. Is there growth? Rising profits? In the management team, what expertise gaps need to be filled for operating a public company? Also, does the company have adequate budgetary systems in place with financial information readily available on a monthly and quarterly basis? What are the state of investor relationships and the corporate structure for transparent reporting to shareholders? In a survey of global institutional investors, respondents ranked the top nonfinancial factors leading to IPO success.[4] In order of priority, these are:

- *Management credibility and experience*
- *Quality of corporate strategy and its execution*
- *Brand strength and market position*
- *Operational effectiveness*
- *Corporate governance practices*

In reviewing IPO trends of over 7,500 companies from 1980 to 2010, the median age of a company is eight years. The lowest median age during these three decades was five years and the highest median age was 15 years.[5]

After this soul-searching stage, the second stage is where the company begins the practical preparation toward going IPO.

STEPS TO AN IPO

After an IPO readiness assessment is completed, the steps to an IPO, as presented in Exhibit 35.1, include selection of underwriters, conducting the road show, and demand assessment.

Exhibit 35.1 **Steps to an IPO.**

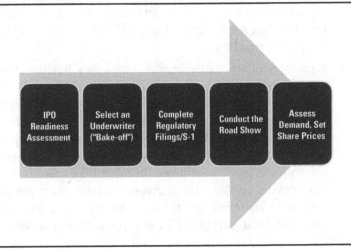

Consider the road map to IPO for a company like Google. To comply with SEC rules, Google had to consider disclosing its financial information. It found itself in a position where it had more than 500 shareholders and had 120 days from the end of the year to file the financial statements. Google faced three choices: buy back shares from some shareholders, report financials publicly without selling any shares, or go public. Google had to present its financials by 2:00 P.M. and three hours ahead of this deadline, at 11:00 A.M., the company announced that it would be going public.[6] Prior to filing, Google realized neither of the exchanges NASDAQ or NYSE would list the offering, as they were short of three board members. Google was able to add three heavy hitters quickly — the president of Stanford University, the president of Intel, and the CEO of Genentech. Companies preparing for IPO take special care in building an independent and a strong board that offers a broad mix of skills — from industry networks, technical knowledge, and expertise in business development to acquisition integration and financial analysis.

Hire an Underwriter: The "Bake-Off"

Investment banks compete for the issuing company's business during a process known as the "beauty contest" or "bake-off." The investment banks present their credentials to the company's board of directors, as well as their view of market conditions and challenges.

The word *underwriter* is said to have come from the practice of having each risk-taker write his or her name under the total amount of risk that they were willing to accept at a specified premium. In a way, this is still true today. An underwriting syndicate brings new issues to market. Each firm takes the responsibility (and risk) of selling its specific allotment.

Underwriters or investment banks are hired to raise investment capital from investors on behalf of the company. This is a way of selling a newly issued security, such as common stock, to investors. Syndicates of banks (the lead managers) typically underwrite the transaction, which means they have taken on the risk of distributing the securities. Underwriters make their income from the price difference (the underwriting spread) between the price they pay the issuer and what they collect from investors or from broker-dealers who buy portions of the offering.

Google ended up with 31 underwriters — a long list, indicative of the eagerness of the middlemen. Several would drop off eventually. Credit Suisse and Morgan Stanley ended up with their names on the S1 filings.

File the S-1/Prospectus and Avoid the Media

Any company intending to go public is required to file a legal document known as the prospectus with the SEC. Registration is a two-part documentation process that involves Form S-1. Part 1 covers the prospectus, which serves as the primary documentation of disclosure to investors, detailing the operations and financial conditions of the company. Part 2 covers the supplemental information furnished to the SEC (copies of contracts, etc.). Once the SEC approves the company's registration statement, a final prospectus is released to investors.

The prospectus, which reads much like a business plan, includes the company's financial history and growth strategy, the details of its offering, and information on company management. It also outlines industry competition and other risk factors that investors would want to know in advance. In essence, the prospectus provides all the information investors need to know in order to decide whether to participate in the IPO. The preliminary prospectus is also known as a *red herring* because of the red ink used on the front page, which indicates that some information — including the price and size of the offering — is subject to change.

As soon as a company files a preliminary prospectus with the SEC, the quiet period begins. The company is prohibited from distributing any information not included in the prospectus. This period lasts for 25 days post-IPO, after the shares start trading.

Sergey Brin and Larry Page did several things noteworthy at the time of the Google IPO, but the *Playboy* interview was the one that almost got them crossways with the SEC during the quiet period. A week before its celebrated IPO, the SEC caught wind of this interview, which had been conducted about five months prior. Eventually, this interview was included in its entirety in the S-1 Prospectus as Appendix B. *Playboy* lost the exclusive interview to an inane SEC rule, and the media made some hay about it, as did the late-night comedians. As CEO Eric Schmidt quipped, it was a generic article, "without any pictures, I might add."[7] Phew!

The Road Show: Which City Are We In, Again?

Google did not have to struggle much with a road show, as it decided to go down the Dutch auction path for selling its shares to the public. But the underwriter typically schedules dozens of meetings across the country. The CEO, and typically also the CFO and other key executives, will join the tour, during which the company pitches its business plan to institutional investors: mutual funds, endowments, or pension funds. At these meetings, the underwriter attempts to gauge the level of interest in the IPO, which helps lead to a decision on how to price the stock offering.

Book building is the process by which an underwriter attempts to determine at what price to offer an IPO based on demand from institutional investors. An underwriter builds a book by accepting orders from fund managers indicating the number of shares they desire and the price they are willing to pay. The book runner is the managing or lead underwriter who maintains, or runs, the books of securities sold for a new issue. Often, the book runner is given credit for the total size of the deal.[8] Following the road show, the company prints its final prospectus, distributes it to potential investors, and files it with the SEC.

Great Demand, or Put It on Ice?

After all the road show presentations are complete, if the demand from the institutions is feeble, the underwriters will recommend that you put the offering on ice. Let it chill. And someday, hopefully, it will be springtime. On some occasions, you might find a competing company go public at the same time, causing some unintended effects. "We went public the same day that Playboy Enterprises went public. At the same price. And one of the analysts says, 'The market has spoken. It's memories over mammaries, 10-to-1,'" Gordon Moore, co-founder of Intel recalled their IPO with a chuckle.[9]

Not an Endgame but a Financing Event   According to Ernst & Young, around 70 percent of startup companies fail before they reach their IPO potential, with the majority of successful IPOs mostly around for at least five years before the transition.[10] Once on the public market, these companies must compete with other IPOs. Only 8 percent of offerings are competitive in terms of value and fair market value offered by peers in the industry.[11]

The metamorphosis from a private company to a publicly listed company is a daunting process, requiring massive strategic planning and cost-benefit analysis of markets and products, value chain activities, infrastructure (e.g., business information systems, compensation, plans, and redundant assets), governance and management structures, and other business components — from both financial and legal perspectives.[12] The process itself, timed from the decision to go public to the day the IPO transactions are closed, varies significantly. Several factors will affect the timeline, such as how well the process is planned, how well the company is positioned in the market, the abilities of the management team and advisors, as well as factors outside the control of companies, such as market conditions and the current regulatory environment.[13]

Timing the Market   Researchers point out that when public markets are favorable, the experienced venture capitalists are quick to take advantage. After assessing over 40,000 transactions spanning over two decades, the authors concluded that not only are the investments of the specialized VC organizations more successful, but there is no appreciable degradation with changing conditions.[14]

IPO UNDERPRICING AND DUTCH AUCTIONS

The goal when pricing an IPO should be to establish an offering price that is low enough to stimulate interest in the stock but high enough to raise an adequate amount of capital for the company. The process of determining an optimal price usually involves the underwriters (syndicate) arranging share purchase commitments from leading institutional investors.

In order to balance the needs of the investor and the issuing company, the investment bank traditionally tries to price a deal so that the first-day pop is about 15 percent.[15] This is a nice gift that benefits underwriters (the company pays the price) and their institutional investor friends — this incestuous cycle may seal the next investment opportunity that may be led by the underwriter.

Underwriters may claim that the effect of initial underpricing of an IPO generates additional interest in the stock when it first becomes publicly traded. But in reality, those institutional friends make an instant 15 percent. This results in money left on the table — lost capital that could have gone to the company had the stock been offered at a higher price. The company all along believes that the underwriters are representing its interests, but in reality, the underwriters want to just get the deal done quickly — the costs can be borne by the company, after all.

According to Professor Jay Ritter, over 50 years, IPOs in the United States have been underpriced by 16.8 percent on average. This translates to more than $125 billion that companies have left on the table. IPO pricing is also a worldwide phenomenon. In China, the underpricing has been severe, averaging 137.4 percent from 1990 to 2010. This compares with 16.3 percent in Britain from 1959 to 2009. In most other countries, IPO underpricing averages above 20 percent.[16]

The danger of overpricing is an important consideration for venture investors. If a stock is offered to the public at a higher price than the market will pay, the underwriters may have trouble meeting their commitments to sell shares. Even if they sell all the issued shares, if the stock falls in value on the first day of trading, it may lose its marketability and hence even more of its value. This can have emotional consequences, and hence most companies would rather succumb to the 15 percent loss.

Information Asymmetry: The Bigger Fool Theory of IPO Underpricing

Kevin Rock of Harvard Business School pointed out that the IPO price is observable and does not correspond to a unique level of demand, which is unobservable. Like a one-sided marketplace, buyers still don't know who is willing to buy at the set share price and if the offering will be accepted en masse or selectively.

Until this asymmetry resolves, there is an inequilibrium. During this time, the informed investor has an opportunity to profit from his knowledge by bidding for "mispriced" securities. In this way, the informed investor is compensated for his due diligence into the asset's value and obtains some upside for showing where capital should best be allocated. The uninformed investors compete with the informed, and the issuer must ultimately compensate them for their disadvantage. In other words, the bigger fools pay the price. But we need the fools so that the smarter investors can make money.

"The underwriters, however, need the uninformed investors to bid, since informed investors do not exist in sufficient number. To solve this problem, the underwriter reprices the IPO to bring in these investors and ensure that uninformed investors bid. The consequence is underpricing," writes Professor Steven Davidoff.[17] If the investment bankers tilt the scale to only the smarter buyers, the advantages evaporate. For the pop to occur, you need the foolish and the greedy in large quantities. Davidoff writes, "When investment banks can allocate shares in greater measure to informed investors, the underpricing is reduced since the compensation needed to draw uninformed investors is lower. Underpricing has also been found to be lower when information about the issuer is more freely available so that uninformed investors are at less of a disadvantage."[18]

The Dutch Auction: Eliminate the Pop and Those Middlemen

Google is an unconventional company in every way — even its IPO was a case study of sorts. Eric Schmidt, CEO of Google, did not like this pop — this 15 percent that should be in the hands of the company — and pushed for a Dutch auction. "I know this may sound like baloney, but we settled decisively on the Dutch auction after we got a letter from a little old lady who asked why she couldn't make money from the IPO the way the stockbrokers would. We thought she had a point about the basic fairness of the system," he wrote.[19]

A Dutch auction is an attempt to minimize the extreme underpricing that underwriters establish. In a Dutch auction, individuals could log on to their brokerage accounts and bid for a certain number of shares, say 500 shares. Or bid for shares for a certain amount, say $1,000. After the auction was completed, the company would establish a price and the individual bidders would receive a certain allocation of shares. "We liked this approach because it was consistent with the auction-based business model we used to sell our ads — it had a strong intuitive appeal for us," Schmidt would say.[20]

Such auctions threaten large fees otherwise payable to underwriter syndicates. Google had as many as 31 underwriters at the table when contemplating the IPO path, but it ignored the conventional. Although not the first company to use Dutch auction, no company the size of Google had ever done such a thing. Google's share price rose 17 percent in its first day of trading despite the auction method. Wall Street was angry — it felt left out of one of the biggest IPOs of the time. "Don't bother to bid on this shot-in-the-dark IPO," said *BusinessWeek*. *The Wall Street Journal* ran a front-page article, "How Miscalculation and Hubris Hobbled Celebrated Google IPO." Miffed underwriters actively discouraged institutional investors from buying, to punish Google, reduce demand, and send the initial price down. But for Google, a successful IPO was one where average investors, not necessarily big institutions, eventually gained from the underpricing.

POST IPO: SHOULD VCs STAY ENGAGED?

After the rapture and thrill of the IPO settles and the tombstones have been proudly distributed, a question comes up: Should a VC stay involved with a public company? A successful IPO outcome is a financing event and not a guarantee of long-term success of the company. With analysts and shareholders eagerly watching the ticker price run across the board at the stock exchange, the CEO is under pressure to deliver consistent earnings and growth. And this leads to an interesting conundrum for any practitioner: Should I stay and help the CEO become successful? Or should I keep my fiduciary responsibility to my LPs and move on to the next portfolio company? No easy answers here. Lip-Bu Tan of Walden International says, "I think it is a big mistake when a VC resigns from the board when a company is going public. That's when the CEO needs the most help. Being a public company is very unforgiving — the CEO is in the public eye and trying to live life by the quarterly earnings, and with a VC's skills and expertise, you can help the CEO and the company to become a stable and a strong company."[21]

Seth Rudnick of Canaan Partners, who has led at least half a dozen companies to the IPO stage, differs in his views. "As a venture investor, you're looking at a number of metrics: What's best for the company, what's the IRR that you're getting for your investors? How do all the other investors in the company benefit? And those are all very complicated decisions." Rudnick says, "Frankly, at Canaan Partners we strongly urge all of our partners who are in companies that go public to get off the boards so that the decisions then become simply those that you would make as an investor rather than as a board member." He observed, "I think you get too confounded, you know; you love the company, you want to stay on it, you want to stay involved but the dynamics are much different now."[22]

For Brad Feld of the Foundry Group, the choice is easy. "Forget your ego, do what your LPs want you to do," he says.[23] For a VC who is engaged with a public company, the responsibilities and liabilities become significant. Reporting, disclosures, insurance, insider trading issues — the game changes substantially. Factors such as the performance of the company, publicity, and liability risk are key parameters of consideration for any VC who wishes to stay on the board of a publicly traded company. In the proverbial limelight, public companies have a strong incentive to avoid any negative publicity that will adversely affect the stock price. Delivering financial statements in a transparent and timely way, whether annually or quarterly, gives investors and analysts continued assurance and confidence in the company.

As companies are traded publicly, limited partners often pressure VCs to sell these stocks and return capital to investors. While these dynamics are dependent on LP–GP terms, investors are eager to gain liquidity, especially after a long investment horizon. On the flip side, the VCs may believe these stocks have latent value and the price can only go up. For some VCs, their IRR, and their careers are also at stake. The timing and decision of sale is a perennial debate. Diana Frazier of FLAG Capital, a fund of funds managing over $6 billion, points out, "There were two venture funds that had significant investments in Google. One fund sold their stock at the time of the IPO, the other one held on for much longer. No marks for guessing who made more money."

While IPOs are the pinnacle of all exits, secondary sales and private exchanges have evolved. Early investors and founders can enjoy partial liquidity, thanks to these exit options.

36

Secondary Sales

Until recently, the prospect of selling shares of private companies could have been a challenge. A few big-name companies in the past decade have allowed for the creation of secondary markets, prior to which it was inefficient for the investors on Sand Hill Road to enjoy a partial liquidity event. Wide-open exchanges for private company shares were pretty much nonexistent.

Now the trading of shares for private technology firms is becoming more the norm, with Nasdaq SecondMarkets, EquitZen, Forge (formerly Equidate), and SharesPost. Venture capitalists have relied on two primary exit options: a trade sale via an acquisition or the IPO. Most firms that remain private offer some kind of ownership or stake to employees, venture capitalists, and other institutional investors. Some of these want to cash out, while others want to buy more. In the past, employees in private companies couldn't sell their shares. Also, VC funds are 10-year closed-end funds. Finally, in an economic environment hostile to IPOs, a venue for entrepreneurs, venture capitalists, and employees to cash out makes sense. All these challenges presented a ripe opportunity for innovative trading solutions — an if-you-build-it-they-will-come proposition.

Private exchanges generally function by having an intermediary take shares from sellers or companies and actively find buyers, a process that can drag into weeks — completely out of sync with the fast-paced world of trading. Such exchanges simplify the process by offering an auction-style system, formalizing the market-clearing process with more ease and transparency. Greg Brogger of SharesPost has cited angel investors and senior management of private companies as big users: "Those people are not necessarily looking to sell all of their position in a company, but want some amount of liquidity for their shares."[1]

Early investors are especially keen on the legitimate transition/exit as a way to cash in some of their earnings. Accel Partners sold about 15 percent of its stake in Facebook, then valued over $500 million, via secondary markets.[2] While still a fraction of what is traded in public exchanges like the New York Stock Exchange and Nasdaq, private exchanges have brought a much-needed third exit option to venture practitioners.

Strong investor attention to companies on private exchanges acts as a barometer of success and could prompt bullish interest in firms before they debut on the public market. Yet, according to reports in the *Wall Street Journal*,[3] companies have attempted to control pre-IPO trading, as online trading could lead to speculative swings in share price affecting companies' stock-based incentives for employees, and spread information about privately held companies too widely. Individual investors are often excluded from purchasing shares of some of the most popular private technology companies before they have held an IPO, with institutions preferred as buyers. Widespread online sales of private shares placed the burden on companies to approve scores of transactions and brought in an unwieldy mass of shareholders with varying agendas. Such trading avenues also impacted employee morale and caused distraction where employees would sell their shares and quit. Companies now allow employees and other stakeholders to sell shares in narrow windows of time.

Any investor would welcome these models where friction in venture capital transactions is minimized and holdings need not be locked up for as much as 10 years.

Notes

Preface

1. C. P. Cavafy, "Ithaka," Collected Poems Revised Edition, translated by Edmund Keeley and Philip Sherrard, edited by George Savidis. Translation copyright © 1975, 1992 by Edmund Keeley and Philip Sherrard. Princeton University Press. https://www.onassis.org/initiatives/cavafy-archive/the-canon/ithaka.

2. "James 4:13–14," *Holy Bible, English Standard Version UK* (London: Harper Collins, 2012).

3. José Luis A. Fermosel, "Jorge Lui Borges: 'No estoy seguro de que yo exista en realidad,'" El País, September 25, 1981.

4. Rudyard Kipling, "If," Rewards and Fairies. (Garden City, NY: Doubleday, Page & Company, 1910).

5. Ashwin Rodrigues, "Group of White Men in Patagonia Vests Confused for VC Fund, Raise $500 Million," Fortune, September 29, 2017.

Chapter 1: The Business of Cash and Carry

1. "SoftBank: Inside the 'Wild West' $100bn Fund Shaking up the Tech World," *Financial Times*, June 19, 2018: https://www.ft.com/content/71ad7cda-6ef4-11e8-92d3-6c13e5c92914.

Chapter 2: Why Choose a Career in VC

1. Donald T. Valentine, "Early Bay Area Venture Capitalists: Shaping the Economic and Business Landscape," an oral

history conducted by Sally Smith Hughes in 2009, Regional Oral History Office, The Bancroft Library, University of California, Berkeley, 2010.

2. Author interview, October 2010.

3. CNNMoney, "The Keys to Andreessen Horowitz's Success," YouTube video, February 6, 2012, http://www .youtube.com/watch?v=PbW-1k3ZOA4.

Chapter 4: Welcome to the Land of Ad-Venture

1. Hank Paulson, 2004 — this was well before the 2008 financial crisis, during which Goldman Sachs was described as a giant vampire squid.

2. Sarah Tavel, Adenturista blog, accessed on July 3, 2010, www.adventurista.com/2008/04/vc-pre-mba-hiring.html.

3. This bizarre position description was posted on LinkedIn for a family office based in California. I could NOT make this up.

4. Gary Rivlin, "So You Want to Be a Venture Capitalist," *New York Times*, May 22, 2005, accessed January 13, 2011, www.nytimes.com/2005/05/22/business/ yourmoney/22venture.html.

5. Michael Carney, "At Benchmark, "Good Judgment Comes from Experience, Which Comes from Bad Judgment," July 26, 2013, Pandodaily website, http://pandodaily. com/2013/07/26/at-benchmark-good-judgment-comes-from-experience-which-comes-from-bad-judgement/.

6 John Doerr, "Kleiner Perkins Caufield & Byers," in *Done Deals — Venture Capitalists Tell Their Stories*, ed. Udayan Gupta (Boston: Harvard Business School Press, 2000), 374.

7. Robert Nelsen (ARCH Venture Partners) in discussions with the author, December 2010.

8. David Cowan (Bessemer Venture Partners) in discussions with the author, December 2010.

9. Union Square Ventures, "We're Hiring," accessed November 23, 2010, unionsquareventures.com/2008/02/were-hiring.php.

10. A remora, also called a suckerfish, grows to about three feet in length. Using its suction cups, it attaches itself to a larger fish, typically a shark. The relationship, termed as *commensalism*, is a one-way benefit to the remora with no distinct advantage to the shark. The remora hitches a ride and feeds off the shark's leftovers. In fact, there is a controversy as to whether a remora's diet is primarily leftover fragments or its host's feces.

11. Rahim 2003, *The Daily Princetonian*.

12. Rajeev Batra (Mayfield Fund) in discussions with the author, December 2010.

13. Steve Arnold, Jonathan Flint, and Terrance McGuire, "Polaris Venture Partners," in *Done Deals—Venture Capitalists Tell Their Stories*, ed. Udayan Gupta (Boston: Harvard Business School Press, 2000), 281

14. Source: http://paulgraham.com/startupfunding.html.

15. Blake Masters, "Class 8 Notes Essay—The Pitch," May 2, 2012, http://blakemasters.com/post/22271192791/peter-thiels-cs183-startup-class-8-notes-essay.

16. Punit Chiniwalla in discussions with the author, September 2010.

17. Society of Kauffman Fellows, "Frequently Asked Questions," accessed January 13, 2011, www.kauffmanfellows.org/faq.aspx.

18. David Cassak, "John Simpson: Reluctant Entrepreneur," *In Vivo: The Business & Medicine Report* 21, no. 3 (April 2003), accessed January 13, 2011, www.denovovc.com/press/denovo-simpson.pdf.

19. Peter J. Tanous, *Investment Visionaries: Lessons in Creating Wealth from the World's Greatest Risk Takers* (Upper Saddle River, NJ: Prentice Hall, 2003), 69.

20. C. Richard Kramlich, "Venture Capital Greats: A Conversation with C. Richard Kramlich," interview by Mauree Jane Perry, 2006, accessed January 13, 2011, http://digitalassets.lib.berkeley.edu/roho/ucb/text/kramlich_dick_donated.pdf.

21. NEA was then a mere $125 million fund. Today, NEA's committed capital exceeds $11 billion.

22. "Boston Scientific Announces Offer to Acquire Guidant at $80 per Share," news release, http://bostonscientific.mediaroom.com/index.php?s=43&item=376.

23. Gary Rivlin, "So You Want to Be a Venture Capitalist."

24. Ibid.

25. Jan expressed this at the board meeting of Michigan Venture Capital Association. Trust me, I was in the room when she said that.

26. Seth Levine's VC Adventure blog, "How to Become a Venture Capitalist," accessed on November 23, 2010, http://www.sethlevine.com/wp/2005/05/how-to-become-a-venture-capitalist.

27. Source: From the documentary *Something Ventured*, 2011, Produced by Paul Holland, Foundation Capital.

Chapter 5: Developing Your Investment Career

1. William H. Draper, III, "Early Bay Area Venture Capitalists: Shaping the Economic and Business Landscape," interview by Sally Smith Hughes, 2008, accessed January 13, 2011, http://digitalassets.lib.berkeley.edu/roho/ucb/text/draper_william.pdf.

2. Andrew Adams Schoen, "Quantum Computing: Time for Venture Capitalists to Put Chips on the Table," LinkedIn, March 19, 2016, www.linkedin.com/pulse/quantum-computing-time-venture-capitalists-put-chips-table-schoen/ accessed on August 25, 2019.

3. C. Richard Kramlich, "Venture Capital Greats: A Conversation with C. Richard Kramlich," interview by Mauree Jane Perry.

4. Donald T. Valentine, "Early Bay Area Venture Capitalists: Shaping the Economic and Business Landscape," interview by Sally Smith Hughes, 2009, accessed January 13, 2011, http://digitalassets.lib.berkeley.edu/roho/ucb/text/valentine_donald.pdf.

5. Rob Hayes, in discussion with the author, October 2010.

6. Paul Bancroft III, "Early Bay Area Venture Capitalists: Shaping the Economic and Business Landscape," interview by Sally Smith Hughes, 2010, accessed January 13, 2011, http://digitalassets.lib.berkeley.edu/roho/ucb/text/bancroft_pete.pdf.

7. Tim Ferris, *Tribe of Mentors* (New York: Houghton Mifflin Harcourt, 2017).

8. McRaney describes the case of a brain-tumor patient who lost his emotional responses and became a complete wreck, as he could not make any decisions.

9. Source: http://www.paulgraham.com/guidetoinvestors.html

10. Rivlin, "So You Want to Be a Venture Capitalist," *New York Times*, May 22, 2005.

11. James R. Swartz, "Venture Capital Greats: A Conversation with James R. Swartz," interview by Mauree Jane Perry, 2006, accessed January 13, 2011, http://digitalassets.lib.berkeley.edu/roho/ucb/text/swartz_james_donated.pdf.

12. Reid Dennis, "Early Bay Area Venture Capitalists: Shaping the Economic and Business Landscape," interview by Sally Smith Hughes, 2009, accessed January 13, 2011, http://digitalassets.lib.berkeley.edu/roho/ucb/text/dennis_reid.pdf.

13. William K. Bowes, Jr., "Early Bay Area Venture Capitalists: Shaping the Economic and Business Landscape," interview by Sally Smith Hughes, 2008, accessed January 13, 2011, http://digitalassets.lib.berkeley.edu/roho/ucb/text/bowes_william.pdf.

14. Source: Malcolm Gladwell, *The Tipping Point: How Little Things Can Make a Difference* (New York: Little Brown, 2000).

15. Terry McGuire (Co-Founder, Polaris Ventures, and Chairman Emeritus of the National Venture Capital Association), in discussion with the author, November 2010.

16. Blake Masters, "Peter Thiel's CS183: Startup Class 8 Notes Essay," May 2, 2012, blog, http://blakemasters.com/post/22271192791/peter-thiels-cs183-startup-class-8-notes-essay.

Chapter 6: A Career Where Enemies Accumulate

1. Michael Moritz, *Return to the Little Kingdom: How Apple and Steve Jobs Changed the World* (New York: Overlook Press, 2009), 89.

2. *Inside the Minds: Venture Capitalists* (ebrandedbooks.com, 2000).

3. Blake Masters, "Peter Thiel's CS183: Startup — Class 7 Notes Essay," April 26, 2012, blog, http://blakemasters. com/post/21869934240/peter-thiels-cs183-startup-class-7-notes-essay.

4. Marc Andreessen, "A Panorama of Venture Capital and Beyond." Stanford University's Entrepreneurship Corner, May 13, 2010, http://ecorner.stanford.edu/authorMaterial-Info.html?mid=2457.

5. Tarang Shah and Sheetal Shah, *Venture Capitalists at Work* (New York: APress, 2011).

6. A fictional town in the US state of Minnesota. Garrison Keillor made this term popular as he reports the news from Lake Wobegon on the radio show *A Prairie Home Companion*.

7. Chris Dixon, "Being Friendly Has Become a Competitive Advantage in VC," January 29, 2010, blog, http://cdixon. org/2010/01/29/being-friendly-has-become-a-competitive-advantage-in-vc/.

Chapter 7: Generational Transfer and Succession

1. The Tim Ferris Show #373: Interview with Jerry Colonna.

Chapter 8: LP Universe

1. YaleNEWS, "Yale Endowment Grows by 8.9%, a Gain of $1.4 Billion," September 24, 2010, Asset Allocation Data as of June 30, 2010, http://opac.yale.edu/news/article. aspx?id=7789.

2. How Do Sovereign Wealth Funds Invest? by Elliot Hentov, PhD, head of Policy and Research, Official Institutions Group, and Alexander Petrov, Associate (who probably did all the hard work), Policy Research, Official Institutions Group — State Street Global Advisors, 2019.

Chapter 10: How LPs Conduct Fund Due Diligence

1. Paul A. Gompers and Josh Lerner, "What Drives Venture Capital Fundraising?" January 1999, available at http://ssrn.com/abstract=57935.

2. Sources of Capital for Michigan Venture Capital Firms and Entrepreneurial Companies. Research report, Professor Zsuzsanna Fluck, director — Center for Venture Capital, Private Equity and Entrepreneurial Finance, Michigan State University, 2007.

3. Lisa Edgar (Top Tier Capital Partners) in discussion with the author, March 2011.

4. Georganne Perkins (Fisher Lynch Capital) in discussion with the author, January 2011.

5. Kenneth Van Heel (Dow Chemical Company) in discussions with the author, June 2010.

6. Private Equity International, *The Guide to Private Equity Fund Investment Due Diligence* (London: PEI Media, 2003), 91. The survey included responses from 313 institutions, of which 70 percent were North America–based, with primary investing in PE and venture capital.

Chapter 11: Defining Your Fund's Investment Strategy

1. Peter F. Drucker, *Innovation and Entrepreneurship* (Oxford: Butterworth-Heinemann, 1985), xiv.

2. Ibid.

3. David Cowan, "Road Map Investing," *Who Has Time for This?*, August 12, 2005, blog, http://whohastimeforthis.blogspot.com/2005/08/road-map-investing.html.

4. Ibid.

Chapter 12: Investment Team Diligence

1. Kelly DePonte (Probitas Partners) in discussions with the author, September 2010.

2. AltAssets, "Institutional Investor Profile: Clint Harris, Managing Partner, Grove Street Advisors," September 4, 2002.

3. Paul Bancroft III, "Early Bay Area Venture Capitalists: Shaping the Economic and Business Landscape," interview by Sally Smith Hughes, 2010, accessed January 13, 2011, http://digitalassets.lib.berkeley.edu/roho/ucb/text/bancroft_pete.pdf.

4. Geoffrey H. Smart, Steven N. Payne, and Hidehiko Yuzaki, "What Makes a Successful Venture Capitalist?" *The Journal of Private Equity* 3, no. 4 (2000): 7–29.

5. Paul Gompers, Anna Kovner, and Josh Lerner, "Specialization and Success: Evidence from Venture Capital," *Journal of Economics & Management Strategy* 18, no. 3 (2009): 817–844.

6. *Young Venture Capital Society Newsletter* 1, no. 2.

7. Zarutskie Rebecca, "The Role of Top Management Team Human Capital in Venture Capital Markets: Evidence from First-Time Funds," *Journal of Business Venturing* 25 (2010): 155–172.

8. Yael V. Hochberg, Alexander Ljungqvist, and Yang Lu, "Networking as a Barrier to Entry and the Competitive Supply of Venture Capital," *Journal of Finance* 65, no. 3 (2010): 829–859. The authors conclude that there is less entry in venture capital markets in which incumbents are more tightly networked with each other. And the relationship factor seems to work both ways: a venture capital firm is significantly more likely to enter a market if it has previously established ties to incumbents by inviting them into syndicates in its own home market. In other words, VCs will not cooperate with an outsider until they have quid pro quo access to the outsider's markets.

9. Ibid.

10. Alan Frazier, "Venture Capital Greats: A Conversation with Alan Frazier," interview by Carole Kolker, 2009, accessed January 13, 2011, http://digitalassets.lib.berkeley.edu/roho/ucb/text/frazier_alan_donated.pdf.

11. Steve Bird, "Private Equity . . . or Personal Equity? Why Who You Know Still Drives Venture Capital Returns," July 7, 2005, accessed February 20, 2011, www.go4venture.com/content/Case%20for%20Late%20Stage%20VC%20(July%202005).pdf.

Chapter 13: Fund Size and Portfolio Construction

1. Source: NVCA Yearbook, 2018 and Pitchbook

2. Lisa Edgar, "Are We Going to Make Money in This Fund?" *PEHub* (blog), www.pehub.com/81521/are-we-going-to-make-money-in-this-fund.

Chapter 14: Performance Analysis

1. John C. Kelleher and Justin J. MacCormack, "Internal Rate of Return: A Cautionary Tale," *McKinsey Quarterly*, August 2004, accessed February 20, 2011, http://www.mckinseyquarterly.com Internal rate_of_return_A_cautionary_tale_1481.

2. FLAG Capital Management, "Behind the Benchmarks: The Art of Private Capital Performance Assessment," November 2009, accessed February 20, 2011, www.flagcapital.com/pdf/Insights%202009%20November%20-%20Behind%20the%20Benchmarks.pdf.

3. AltAssets, "Institutional Investor Profile: Clint Harris, Managing Partner, Grove Street Advisors," September 4, 2002, accessed February 20, 2011, www.altassets.com/private-equity-features/by-author-name/article/nz1183.html.

4. Robert S. Harris, Tim Jenkinson, and Steven N. Kaplan, "Private Equity Performance: What Do We Know?" (July 2013). *Journal of Finance*, forthcoming. Fama-Miller Working Paper; Chicago Booth Research Paper No. 11-44; Darden Business School Working Paper No. 1932316.

Available at SSRN: http://ssrn.com/abstract=1932316 or http://dx.doi.org/10.2139/ssrn.1932316.

5. These can be accessed at http://ilpa.org/ilpa-standard ized-reporting-templates.

6. FLAG Capital Management, "Behind the Benchmarks: The Art of Private Capital Performance Assessment," November 2009, accessed February 20, 2011, www.flagcapi tal.com/pdf/Insights%202009%20November%20-%20 Behind%20the%20Benchmarks.pdf.

7. David F. Swensen, *Pioneering Portfolio Management: An Unconventional Approach to Institutional Investment* (New York: Free Press, 2009), 75.

8. Ibid.

9. Ibid.

10. Anonymous institutional investor in discussions with the author, September 2010.

Chapter 15: Terms of Fund Investment

1. Seth Levine (Foundry Group) in discussions with the author, December 2010.

2. Kelly DePonte (Probitas Partners), in discussion with the author, August 2010.

3. ILPA, "Private Equity Principles 2.0," accessed January 17, 2011, http://ilpa.org/wp-content/uploads/2011/01/ ILPA-Private-Equity-Principles-2.0.pdf.

4. Timothy Recker, in discussion with the author, December 2010.

5. Liam Donohue (.406 Ventures) in discussions with the author, December 2010.

6. Colin Blaydon and Fred Wainwright, Tuck School of Business at Dartmouth, "Limited Partnership Agreement Project: Results of GP and LP Survey," accessed January 17, 2011, http://mba.tuck.dartmouth.edu/pecenter/research/ pdfs/LPA_survey_summary.pdf.

7. Kelly Williams (Credit Suisse), in discussions with the author, February 2011.

8. Anonymous institutional LP, managing $30 billion in assets, in discussions with the author, October 2010.

9. Preqin Investor Outlook: Private Equity, "The Opinions of 100 Leading Private Equity LPs on the Market and Their Plans in 2011." https://docs.preqin.com/reports/Preqin_ Private_Equity_Investor_Survey_Q1_2011x.pdf.

Chapter 16: The Venture Firm's Ethos, Culture, and Values

1. Draw the Owländ Other Company Values You Didn't Know You Should Have, Jeff Lawson, as presented in *First Round Essentials, Management*.

2. And the Children Shall Lead: Gender Diversity and Performance in Venture Capital, Working Paper 17-103, May 2017, Paul A. Gompers, Harvard Business School and Sophie Q. Wang, Harvard University.

3. Us Too: A Due Diligence Survey and Analysis on the Current State of Sexual Harassment In the Investment Management Industry, February 2018, Conducted by The Investment Management Due Diligence Association.

4. https://www.bloomberg.com/news/articles/2019-07-29/ sequoia-s-first-woman-partner-is-raising-capital-and- standards. Accessed on September 14, 2019. Investor respondents included endowments, pensions, insurance companies, private banks, and funds of funds. The geographic breakdown of the respondents is as follows: 68 percent US/Canada, 25 percent Europe, and 7 percent Asia/ Australia. This report is based on the results of the survey.

5. Gupta Udayan, *Done Deals — Venture Capitalists Tell Their Stories* (HBS Press, 2000).

6. NVCA, Branding and Venture Capital: Research Preview, July 2013, Survey conducted by DeSantis Breindel.

7. Source: CNN Money, February 6, 2013, accessed January 3, 2014, http://www.youtube.com/watch?v=PbW-1k3ZOA4.

8. Ibid.

9. *Forbes*, "Forbes Q and A with Andreessen Horowitz's Secret Agent," February 2011, accessed on January 3, 2014, http://www.forbes.com/sites/nicoleperlroth/2011/02/04/forbes-q-and-a-with-andreessen-horowitzs-secret-agent.

10. Mark Boslet, *The New Full Service VC*, VCJ, June 2013, https://www.fenwick.com/FenwickDocuments/VCJ%20June%202013_cover%20story.pdf.

11. Harry Cendrowski, *Private Equity: History, Governance, and Operations* (Hoboken, NJ: John Wiley & Sons, 2008).

Chapter 17: Raising Your First Fund

1. AltAssets, "Investor Profile: Christophe Nicolas, executive director, Morgan Stanley Alternative Investment Partners," December 8, 2009, accessed February 20, 2011, www.altassets.com/private-equity-investor-profiles/article/nz17499.html.

2. Thomas Meyer and Pierre-Yves Mathonet, *Beyond the J Curve: Managing a Portfolio of Venture Capital and Private Equity Funds* (West Sussex: John Wiley & Sons, 2005).

3. AltAssets, "Institutional Investor Profile: Peter Keehn, Head of Alternative Investments, Allstate Investments, LLC," June 29, 2006, accessed February 20, 2011, www.altassets.com/private-equity-features/by-author-name/article/nz8835.html.

Chapter 18: The Fundraising Roadshow

1. Thomas Doyal in discussions with the author, January 2011.

2. Source: Luisa Beltran, peHub reporting from Venture Alpha East PartnerConnect panel, "Roadshow Workshop: Dos and Don'ts Advice from Top LPs," April 2013.

3. Ibid.

4. Source: Preqin 2018 survey of all PE funds, https://www.preqin.com/insights/blogs/placement-agent-success-in-2018/22795 accessed on September 29, 2019.

5. "What to Expect from a Placement Agent: Things You Should Know," Probitas Partners, accessed January 19, 2011, http://probitaspartners.com/pdfs/whattoexpect_deponte.pdf.

6. Source: "What to Expect from a Placement Agent: Things You Should Know," Probitas Partners, as quoted in The Definitive Guide to PE Fundraising, PE Media.

7. Robert Finkel and David Greising, *The Masters of Private Equity and Venture Capital* (New York: McGraw-Hill, 2009), 216.

8. Source: C. Richard Kramlich, "Venture Capital Greats: A Conversation with C. Richard Kramlich," interviewed by Mauree Jane Perry on August 31, 2006, in San Francisco, National Venture Capital Association, Arlington, Virginia.

9. Source: William H. Draper, III, "Early Bay Area Venture Capitalists: Shaping the Economic and Business Landscape," oral history conducted by Sally Smith Hughes in 2009, Regional Oral History Office, The Bancroft Library, University of California, Berkeley, 2008, p. 31.

Chapter 19: Why LPs Seek First-Time Funds

1. Robert Finkel and David Greising, *The Masters of Private Equity and Venture Capital* (New York: McGraw-Hill, 2009), 210.

2. Steven Lazarus, From IP to IPO, Key Issues in Commercializing University Technology, in "The VC View," supplement, *Intellectual Asset Management Magazine*, March 2005, accessed March 12, 2011, www.archventure.com/archview.html.

3. Grove Street Advisors, "Case Study 1," May 10, 2001, accessed February 20, 2011, www.grovestreetadvisors.com/news/gsa_case_study_01.pdf.

4. Kelvin Liu, "The Growing Importance of New and Emerging Managers in Private Equity," accessed February 20, 2011, www.institutional.invesco.com/portal/.../II-IPCEM-IVP-1-E%5B1%5D.pdf.

5. Ann Grimes, "New Kids Arrive On the Venture-Capital Block," *Wall Street Journal*, February 25, 2005, accessed February 20, 2011, http://online.wsj.com/article/0, SB110928737299763683,00.html.

6. John Coelho, speaking at Venture Alpha West, October 2013 conference.

7. John Coelho, speaking at Venture Alpha West, October 2013 conference.

8. Amit Tiwari, speaking at Venture Alpha West, October 2013 conference.

9. Jean-Pierre Pipaud, "Emerging Managers: Elizabeth Flisser, Capital Z Asset Management," *Emerging Managers Incubation* (blog), September 22, 2008, http://emerging-managers.blogspot.com/2008/09/emerging-managers-elizabeth-flisser.html.

10. "CalSTRS AND CalPERS Unveil Emerging Managers and Financial Services Database," January 17, 2007, accessed February 20, 2011, www.calstrs.com/newsroom/2007/news011707.aspx.

11. Ibid.

12. Women in Investments, Alternative Investment Management Program (CalPERS) presentation, February 10, 2009, www.calpers.ca.gov/eip-docs/.../womens.../wiic-private-equity.pdf.

13. Kenneth Smith, speaking at Venture Alpha West, October 2013 conference.

14. Sara Behunek and Mary Kathleen Flynn, "Closing the VC Gender Gap," *The Deal*, July 2, 2010, accessed February 20, 2011, www.thedeal.com/newsweekly/dealmakers/weekly-movers-and-shakers/closing-the-vc-gender-gap.php.

Chapter 20: Sourcing Investment Opportunities

1. Erik Lundberg, CIO (University of Michigan Endowment), in discussions with the author, December 2010.

2. https://www.wsj.com/articles/signalfire-raises-330-million-for-data-centric-venture-capital-1494415804 accessed on September 2, 2019.

3. The Information https://www.theinformation.com/articles/ in-ambitious-gamble-hedge-fund-coatue-launches-700-million-early-stage-venture-fund accessed on September 2, 2019.

4. Claire Cain Miller, "Google Ventures Stresses Science of Deal, Not Art of the Deal," *The New York Times*, June 23, 2013.

5. Paul A. Gompers, William Gornall, Steven N. Kaplan, and Ilya A. Strebulaev. "How Do Venture Capitalists Make Decisions?" NBER Working Paper Series, No. 22587, September 2016.

6. From the documentary, *Something Ventured*, 2011, produced by Paul Holland.

7. David Kirkpatrick, *The Facebook Effect: The Inside Story of the Company That Is Connecting the World* (New York: Simon & Schuster, 2010), 116–121. In recreating this section, I have relied extensively on this book.

8. James R. Swartz, interview by Mauree Jane Perry, "National Venture Capital Association Venture Capital Oral History Project," 2006, accessed January 30, 2011, http://digitalassets.lib.berkeley.edu/roho/ucb/text/swartz_james_donated.pdf.

9. *The Startup of You: Adapt to the Future, Invest in Yourself, and Transform Your Career*, Reid Hoffman and Ben Casnocha (New York: Crown Business, 2012), 122. (See Kevin's video of the product at http://www.youtube.com/watch?v=3BP5ax1qs5o.)

10. Randall E. Stross, *eBoys: The First Inside Account of Venture Capitalists at Work* (New York: Crown Business, 2000), 216, 291.

11. Michael Moritz, *Return to the Little Kingdom: Steve Jobs, The Creation of Apple and How It Changed the World* (New York: Overlook Press, 2009), 237.

12. William Elkus (Clearstone Partners) in discussions with the author, September 2008.

13. Chris Douvos in discussion with the author, December 2010.

14. Christopher Rizik (Renaissance Venture Capital Fund) in discussions with the author, February 2011.

15. Data from http://www.angelsoft.net, a leading software-as-a-service tool for managing angel networks.

16. Statistics from www.angelcapitalassociation.org.

17. A well-managed network has a streamlined decision-making and negotiation process, typically managed by one angel representative. If each angel is to decide on his or her own the terms, amounts, and so forth, the process can be fraught with challenges for both investors and entrepreneurs.

18. Tony Stanco and Uto Akah, *Survey: The Relationship Between Angels and Venture Capitalists in the Venture Industry* (2005). The survey was sent to 2,156 venture capitalists and angels; 14 percent responded.

19. William R. Kerr, Josh Lerner, and Antoinette Schoar, "The Consequences of Entrepreneurial Finance: A Regression Discontinuity Analysis" (working paper No. 10–086, Harvard Business School Entrepreneurial Management), March 16, 2010. Available at SSRN: http://ssrn.com/abstract=1574358.

20. Tony Stanco and Uto Akah, *Survey*.

21. AUTM 2011 data.

22. Robert Finkel and David Greising, *The Masters of Private Equity and Venture Capital* (New York: McGraw-Hill, 2009).

23. Damon Darlin, "It Came from Their Lab. But How to Take It to the Bank?" *The New York Times*, March 12, 2011.

24. Barry Jaruzelski and Kevin Dehoff, 2010. "THE GLOBAL INNOVATION 1000: How the Top Innovators Keep Winning, Booz & Company's Annual Study of the World's Biggest R&D Spenders Shows How the Most Innovative Companies Consistently Outperform Competitors, Even When Total R&D Investments Fall. Their Secret? They're Good at the Right Things, Not at Everything," *Strategy and Business*, (61), p.48.

25. Quoted in *Mac Week*, March 14, 1989.

26. David Scheer (Scheer and Company) in discussions with the author, August 2008. "Cholesterol Champions," accessed

December 26, 2010, http://pharmexec.findpharma.com/pharmexec/article/articleDetail.jsp?id=109681.

27. Arthur Rock, interview by Sally Smith Hughes, 2008–2009, "Early Bay Area Venture Capitalists: Shaping the Economic and Business Landscape," accessed January 30, 2011, http://digitalassets.lib.berkeley.edu/roho/ucb/text/rock_arthur.pdf.

28. William H. Draper, III, "Early Bay Area Venture Capitalists: Shaping the Economic and Business Landscape," oral history conducted by Sally Smith Hughes in 2009, Regional Oral History Office, The Bancroft Library, University of California, Berkeley, 2008. Accessed on July 3, 2010.

29. John Jarve (Menlo Ventures) in discussion with the author, September 2008.

30. Doc Searls, "A Talk with Tim O'Reilly," *Linux Journal*, February 1, 2001, accessed February 1, 2011, www.linuxjournal.com/article/4467.

31. "About O'Reilly," O'Reilly Media, accessed January 28, 2011, http://oreilly.com/about/.

32. Chris Douvos (TIFF) in discussion with the author, December 2010.

33. Robin Wauters, "Venture Capitalists Get Grilled (and Pitched at Urinals) at *#TCDisrupt*," *TechCrunch* (blog), May 26, 2010, accessed on December 12, 2010, http://techcrunch.com/2010/05/26/venture-capitalists-get-grilled-and-pitched-at-urinals-at-tcdisrupt.

34. Cromwell Schubarth, "New Menlo VC Venky Ganesan on Idolizing Warren Buffett and Avoiding 'The Social Network,'" *Business Review*, March 5, 2013, accessed on October 6, 2013, http://businessreview.org/new-menlo-vc-venky-ganesan-on-idolizing-warren-buffett-and-avoiding-the-social-network.

35. Source: Josh Koppelman at Upround Conference, San Francisco http://www.youtube.com/watch?v=CaX_2n9iAxI.

36. Bessemer Venture Partners, "Anti-Portfolio," web page, accessed February 1, 2011, www.bvp.com/Portfolio/Anti-Portfolio.aspx.

37. OVP Venure Partners, "Deals Missed," web page, accessed January 6, 2014, http://www.ovp.com/deals-missed.

38. Scott Duke Harris, "The Venture Deals That Got Away," *Mercury News*, August 10, 2008, accessed February 1, 2011, www.mercurynews.com/ci_10156479?nclick_check=1.

39. Alice Schroeder, *The Snowball: Warren Buffett and the Business of Life* (New York: Bantam Dell, 2008), 320.

40. Peter O. Crisp, interview by Carole Kolker, October 21, 2008, "Venture Capital Greats: A Conversation with Peter O. Crisp," accessed February 1, 2011, http://digitalassets.lib.berkeley.edu/roho/ucb/text/vcg-crisp.pdf.

41. Robert Finkel and David Greising, *The Masters of Private Equity and Venture Capital*, 215.

42. A virtualization software company formed in 1998, now a publicly traded company in 2019, had over $8 billion in revenues and $60 billion market capitalization.

43. David Kirkpatrick, *The Facebook Effect: The Inside Story of the Company That Is Connecting the World* (New York: Simon & Schuster, 2010), 120–122.

44. Scott Austin, "Kleiner Perkins Invested in Facebook at $52 Billion Valuation," *Wall Street Journal*, February 14, 2011, accessed April 2, 2011, http://blogs.wsj.com/venturecapital/2011/02/14/kleiner-perkins-invests-in-facebook-at-52-billion-valuation.

45. Keynote Speech, Michigan Growth Capital Symposium, University of Michigan, Ann Arbor, 2007. The full video can be found at iTunes: "Michigan Growth Capital Symposium 2007 Keynote Speaker — Ram Shriram, Founder Sherpalo Ventures."

46. TechCrunch TV, Nolan Bushnell's New Book, Finding the Next Steve Jobs," http://www.youtube.com/watch?v=dWpu62yEpTI, accessed on January 2, 2014.

47. From the documentary, *Something Ventured*, 2011, produced by Paul Holland, Foundation Capital, and Molly Davis, Rainmaker Communications.

48. Charles D. Ellis, *The Partnership: The Making of Goldman Sachs* (New York: Penguin, 2008), 188.

Chapter 21: Due Diligence Cheat Sheet

1. Tarang and Sheetal Shah, *Venture Capitalists at Work: How VCs Identify and Build Billion-Dollar Successes* (New York: APress, 2011).

Chapter 22: Diligence

1. Peter Bevelin, *Seeking Wisdom: From Darwin to Munger* (San Marino, CA: PCA Publications, 2007), 220. Buffett mentioned these criteria at a press conference in 2001.

2. Warren Buffett, *The Essays of Warren Buffett: Lessons for Corporate America*, ed. Lawrence A. Cunningham, 2nd ed. (New York: L. Cunningham, 2008). Buffett defines "understanding a business" as "we have a reasonable probability of being able to assess where it will be in 10 years."

3. Blake Masters, notes from Stanford class, Startup:CS183, as recorded by Blake Masters in Spring 2012, http://blakemasters.com/post/20955341708/peter-thiels-cs183-startup-class-3-notes-essay.

4. Nassim Nicholas Taleb, *The Bed of Procrustes: Philosophical and Practical Aphorisms* (New York: Random House, 2010), 78.

5. *Linda Werfelmen — Bad Habits,* November 17, 2016. https://flightsafety.org/asw-article/bad-habits/ accessed on August 2019. Study conducted by National Business Aviation Association (NBAA) analysis of 143,756 business aviation flights conducted in 379 business aircraft during the three-year period 2013–2015.

Chapter 23: Management Team Diligence: Assessing the Intangible

1. Jim Rasmussen, "Billionaire Talks Strategy with Students," *Omaha World-Herald,* January 2, 1994, 178.

2. PBS, "William Shockley," accessed April 12, 2011, www.pbs.org/transistor/album1/shockley/shockley3.html.

3. Joel N. Shurkin, *Broken Genius: The Rise and Fall of William Shockley, Creator of the Electronic Age* (New York: Macmillan, 2008), 181.

4. Ibid., 251.

5. Joel Shurkin, www.pbs.org/transistor/album1/addlbios/shurkin.html, accessed February 6, 2011.

6. Arthur Rock, interview by Sally Smith Hughes, 2008–2009, "Early Bay Area Venture Capitalists: Shaping the Economic and Business Landscape," accessed February 6, 2011, http://digitalassets.lib.berkeley.edu/roho/ucb/text/rock_arthur.pdf.

7. Source: Ben Horowitz, "How Andreessen Horowitz Evaluates CEOs," Ben's Blog (blog), May 10, 2010, accessed February 6, 2011, http://bhorowitz.com/2010/05/30/how-andreessen-horowitz-evaluates-ceos/.

8. Geoff Smart and Randy Street, *Who: The A Method for Hiring* (New York: Ballantine Books, 2008), 160.

9. Geoff Smart (ghSMART), in discussion with the author, December 2010.

10. Smart and Street, *Who: The A Method for Hiring*, 161–162.

11. Ibid., 162.

12. Steven N. Kaplan, Mark M. Kiebanov, and Morten Sorensen, "Which CEO Characteristics and Abilities Matter?" (working paper no. 14195, National Bureau of Economic Research) 2008, accessed February 7, 2011, www.nber.org/papers/w14195.pdf.

13. Peter F. Drucker, *The Effective Executive* (New York: HarperCollins, 2002), 1.

14. Paul A. Gompers, Anna Kovner, Josh Lerner, and David Scharfstein, "Skill vs. Luck in Entrepreneurship and Venture Capital: Evidence from Serial Entrepreneurs," July 2006. Available at SSRN: http://ssrn.com/abstract=933932.

15. Alison Wood Brooks, Laura Huang, Sarah Wood Kearney, and Fiona Murray. "Investors Prefer Entrepreneurial Ventures Pitched by Attractive Men." *Proceedings of the National*

Academy of Sciences of the United States of America 111 (10) (March 11, 2014).

16. Alex Pentland, "Defend Your Research: We Can Measure the Power of Charisma," *Harvard Business Review*, January–February 2010, accessed February 7, 2011, http://hbr.org/2010/01/defend-your-research-we-can-measure-the-power-of-charisma/ar/1.

17. Ibid.

18. Patricia Sabatini, "Fibs on Resumes Commonplace," *Pittsburgh Post-Gazette*, February 24, 2006.

19. Tom Perkins, Valley Boy: The Education of Tom Perkins (New York: Gotham Books, 2007), 137–138.

20. Interview with Theresa Mack, CPA, CFF, CAMS, CFCI, PI of Cendrowski Corporate Advisors in Chicago, Illinois, and Bloomfield Hills, Michigan.

21. Smith & Wesson Chief Quits Over Crime." CNN Money.com. February 27, 2004, http://money.cnn.com/2004/02/27/news/smith_wesson/.

22. Geoffrey H. Smart, "The Art and Science of Human Capital Valuation," 1998, accessed February 6, 2011, www.ghsmart.com/media/press/human_capital.pdf.

23. Ibid.

24. Ibid.

25. Source: Geoff Smart, "The Art and Science of Human Capital Valuation," 1998, accessed February 6, 2011, www.ghsmart.com/media/press/human_capital.pdf.

26. As one VC told me, "It's mostly a feel-good thing. I have yet to find a coach who will honestly state the shortcomings of their own process. They all seem very happy to take my $15,000 and offer a half a day of subjective analysis. I only get to see if this really works after several years."

27. The Myers & Briggs Foundation, "The 16 MBTI® Types: ESTJ," accessed April 12, 2011, www.myersbriggs.org/my-mbti-personality-type/mbti-basics/the-16-mbti-types.asp.

28. Kaplan, Kiebanov, and Sorensen, "Which CEO Characteristics and Abilities Matter?"

29. Steven N. Kaplan, "Bet on the Horse: Determining Success Factors of New Businesses," *Capital Ideas*, accessed February 6, 2011, www.chicagobooth.edu/capideas/dec05/1.aspx.

30. Speaking at Stanford Business School, October 2011, accessed on January 2, 2014, http://www.youtube.com/watch?v=nKN-abRJMEw#t=368.

31. Tarang and Sheetal Shah, *Venture Capitalists at Work* (New York: APress, 2011).

32. Scott Shane, *Born Entrepreneurs, Born Leaders – How Genes Affect your Work Life* (New York: Oxford University Press, 2010).

Chapter 24: Market, Product, and Business Model Analysis

1. Tarang and Sheetal Shah, *Venture Capitalists at Work: How VCs Identify and Build Billion-Dollar Successes* (New York: Apress, 2011).

2. Speaking at VentureAlpha East, April 2013, Boston, MA. Trust me, I was in the audience.

3. Tarang and Sheetal Shah.

4. Todd Dagres (Spark Capital) in discussions and e-mail communications with the author, 2008 and 2011.

5. Tim Ferris, *Tribe of Mentors: Short Life Advice from the Best in the World* (New York: Houghton Mifflin Harcourt, 2017).

6. Terry McGuire (Polaris Ventures) in discussions with the author, January 2011.

7. Saras D. Sarasvathy, "What Makes Entrepreneurs Entrepreneurial?" Accessed February 6, 2011, available at www.effectuation.org/sites/default/files/research_papers/what-makes-entrepreneurs-entrepreneurial-sarasvathy_0.pdf.

8. Antoine de Saint Exupéry, *Flight to Arras*, trans. Lewis Galantiére (New York: Harcourt Brace, 1942), 129.

9. http://davidgcohen.com/2013/03/07/vc-asshat-move-1/ Accessed on September 2, 2019.

10. "Inside the Mind of Google," 2010, CNBC Interview with Maria Bartiromo.

11. Modified from Douglas Macmillan, "Andreessen: Bubble Believers 'Don't Know What They're Talking About'— Venture Capitalist Discusses the Current State of Tech Investing," Wall Street Journal, January 3, 2014.

12. Arthur Rock, interview by Sally Smith Hughes, http://digitalassets.lib.berkeley.edu/roho/ucb/text/rock_arthur.pdf.

13. Nichomachean Ethics, Book I, passage 3, accessed February 9, 2011, http://classics.mit.edu/Aristotle/nicomachaen.mb.txt.

Chapter 26: Structure of the Term Sheet

1. Mark Suster, "Is Convertible Debt Preferable to Equity?" *Both Sides of the Table* (blog), August 30, 2010, http://www.bothsidesofthetable.com/2010/08/30/is-convertible-debt-preferable-to-equity.

2. Source: David Kirkpatrick, *The Facebook Effect* (New York: Simon & Schuster, 2010), p. 89.

3. Source: Based on Series Seed, developed by Fenwick & West, LLP, www.seriesseed.com.

4. See "Emerging Companies," Wilson Sonsini, www.wsgr.com/wsgr/display.aspx?sectionname=practice/termsheet.htm.

Chapter 27: Buy Low, Sell High

1. Steven N. Kaplan and Per Stromberg, "Financial Contracting Theory Meets the Real World: An Empirical Analysis of Venture Capital Contracts" (CRSP working paper 513), April 26, 2000, accessed February 11, 2011, http://ssrn.com/abstract=218175.

2. David Kirkpatrick, *The Facebook Effect: The Inside Story of the Company That Is Connecting the World* (New York: Simon & Schuster, 2010).

3. Josh Koppelman, speaking at Upround Conference, San Francisco, 2013.

4. Aswath Damodaran, "Valuing Young, Start-Up and Growth Companies: Estimation Issues and Valuation Challenges," June 12, 2009, available at SSRN: http://ssrn.com/abstract=1418687.

5. Source: Arthur Rock, interview by Sally Smith Hughes, 2008–2009, "Early Bay Area Venture Capitalists: Shaping the Economic and Business Landscape," accessed February 10, 2011, http://digitalassets.lib.berkeley.edu/roho/ucb/text/rock_arthur.pdf.

6. Amy E. Knaup, "Survival and Longevity in the Business Employment Dynamics Data," *Monthly Labor Review* (May 2005), 50–56; Amy E. Knaup and M. C. Piazza, "Business Employment Dynamics Data: Survival and Longevity," *Monthly Labor Review* (September 2007), 3–10.

7. Aswath Damodaran, "Valuing Young, Start-Up and Growth Companies."

8. Mark Suster, "Want to Know How VC's Calculate Valuation?"

9. Brad Feld's blog, Feld Thoughts blogs.

10. Jonathan D. Gworek, "The Making of a Winning Term Sheet: Understanding What Founders Want," Morse Barnes-Brown Pendleton PC, June 2007, accessed February 9, 2011, www.mbbp.com/resources/business/founder_termsheet.html.

11. Colin Blaydon and Fred Wainwright, "It's Time to Do Away with Participating Preferred," *Venture Capital Journal*, July 2006, accessed February 11, 2011, http://mba.tuck.dartmouth.edu/pecenter/research/VCJ_July_2006.pdf.

12. Rick Heitzmann, First Mark Capital, in discussions with the author.

13. Frank Demmler, "Practical Implications of Anti-Dilution Protection," accessed February 10, 2011, www.andrew.cmu.edu/user/fd0n/54%20Practical%20Implications%20Anti-dilution%20excel.htm.

14. Based on a survey conducted by law firm, Wilmer Hale and Fenwick & West.

15. Snapchat Founders' Grip Tightened After a Spat with an Early Investor by Katie Benner, *The New York Times*, dated February 23, 2017, https://nyti.ms/2lB5TnG Accessed on March 2, 2017

16. https://www.cnbc.com/2017/03/02/snap-ipo-huge-exits-for-lightspeed-benchmark.html Accessed on September 14, 2019.

17. Justin J. Camp, *Venture Capital Due Diligence: A Guide to Making Smart Investment Choices and Increasing Your Portfolio Returns* (Hoboken, NJ: John Wiley and Sons, 2002), 140.

18. While this may seem unimportant, I am aware of at least one situation where the founder of a venture-backed company died in a car accident. In another situation, the founder had an ugly divorce case that caused undue distraction to the board, shareholders, and the company while his ownership in the company was being divvied up.

19. Paul A. Gompers, William Gornall, Steven N. Kaplan, and Ilya A. Strebulaev. "How Do Venture Capitalists Make Decisions?" NBER Working Paper Series, No. 22587, September 2016.

20. Ibid.

21. Ibid

22. Tom Perkins, *Valley Boy: The Education of Tom Perkins* (New York: Gotham Books, 2007), 112.

23. Ibid.

Chapter 29: Serving on Boards

1. https://venturebeat.com/2013/09/11/vinod-khosla-vcs-should-hush-up-because-they-havent-done-sht/ Accessed on Aug 23, 2019.

2. William D. Bygrave and Jeffry A. Timmons, *Venture Capital at the Crossroads* (Watertown, MA: Harvard Business Press, 1992), 220.

3. Ibid.

4. Brad Feld (Foundry Group) in discussions with the author, December 2010.

Chapter 30: Board Culture and Orientation

1. Allison Leopold Tilley, "Best Practices for the High Performance Board," podcast, accessed January 30, 2011.

2. Ibid.

3. Dennis T. Jaffe and Paul N. Levensohn, "After the Term Sheet: How Venture Boards Influence the Success or Failure of Technology Companies," November 2003, accessed January 30, 2011, www.equitynet.com/media/pdf/How%20 Venture%20Boards%20Influence%20The%20Success%20 or%20Failure%20of%20Technology%20Companies%20 (Dennis%20Jaffe,%20et%20al,%202003).pdf.

4. Pascal N. Levensohn, "Rites of Passage: Managing CEO Transition in Venture-Backed Technology Companies," January 2006, accessed January 30, 2011, www.levp.com/ news/whitepapers.shtml.

5. Ibid.

6. Working Group on Director Accountability and Board Effectiveness, "A Simple Guide to the Basic Responsibilities of VC-Backed Company Directors," accessed January 31, 2011, www.nvca.org/index.php?option=com_ docman&task=doc_download&gid=78&Itemid=93.

7. Brad Feld (Foundry Group) in discussions with the author, December 2010.

8. Brian J. Broughman, "The Role of Independent Directors in VC-Backed Firms," October 13, 2008, available at SSRN: http://ssrn.com/abstract=1162372.

9. Steven N. Kaplan and Per Johan Strömberg, "Financial Contracting Theory Meets the Real World: An Empirical Analysis of Venture Capital Contracts," March 2000 (CRSP working paper No. 513), available at SSRN: http://ssrn. com/abstract=218175 or doi:10.2139/ssrn.218175.

10. Ibid.

Chapter 31: Let Me Know How I Can Be Helpful: Value Creation

1. Lip-Bu Tan (Walden International) in discussions with the author, December 2008.

2. PricewaterhouseCoopers, "Paths to Value," 2002. The Paths to Value study analyzed more than 350 R&D and services-intensive companies in the United States, Europe, and Israel that received seed or first-round private financing between 1999 and 2001.

3. McKinsey & Company, The State of the Corporate Board, 2007: A McKinsey Global Survey, accessed January 30, 2011, www.mckinseyquarterly.com/The_state_of_the_corporate_board_2007_A_McKinsey_Global_Survey_2011. A total of 2,268 respondents, including 825 directors and officers, contributed to this survey.

4. Fred Dotzler, "What Do Venture Capitalists Really Do, and Where Do They Learn to Do It?" De Novo Ventures, accessed January 30, 2011, www.denovovc.com/articles/2001_Dotzler.pdf.

5. NVCA, Branding and Venture Capital: Research Preview, July 2013, survey conducted by DeSantis Breindel.http://nvcatoday.nvca.org/index.php/nvca-study-explores-the-importance-of-brand-management-in-the-venture-capital-industry.html Accessed on April 8, 2014.

6. Akamai went on to become a global Internet/web company and celebrated its IPO in two years from launch.

Chapter 32: Challenges in the Boardroom

1. Arthur Rock, interview by Sally Smith Hughes, 2008–2009, "Early Bay Area Venture Capitalists: Shaping the Economic and Business Landscape," accessed January 30, 2011, http://digitalassets.lib.berkeley.edu/roho/ucb/text/rock_arthur.pdf.

2. From the documentary, Something Ventured, 2011, produced by Paul Holland.

3. Ibid.

4. Harvard Business Review, February 2008.

5. James R. Swartz, interview by Mauree Jane Perry, 2006, "National Venture Capital Association Venture Capital Oral History Project," accessed January 30, 2011, http://digitalassets.lib.berkeley.edu/roho/ucb/text/rock_arthur.pdf.

6. Carey, Pete, "A start-up's true tale: Often-told story of Cisco's launch leaves out the drama, intrigue," *Mercury News*, December 1, 2001.

7. John Kenneth Galbraith, *The New Industrial State* (Boston: Houghton Mifflin, 1971).

8. Thomas Bredt (Menlo Ventures) in discussions with the author, July 2008.

9. Brian J. Broughman and Jesse M. Fried, "Renegotiation of Cash Flow Rights in the Sale of VC-Backed Firms," *Journal of Financial Economics*, Vol. 95, pp. 384–399, 2010; UC Berkeley Public Law Research Paper No. 956243. Available at SSRN: http://ssrn.com/abstract=956243.

10. Robert Finkel and David Greising, *The Masters of Private Equity and Venture Capital* (McGraw-Hill; 1st ed., November 2009), 216.

11. "The Greatest Defunct Web Sites and -Dotcom Disasters," CNET. June 5, 2008. Archived from the original on 2008-06-07. Accessed March 21, 2011, http://web.archive.org/web/20080607211840/http://crave.cnet.co.uk/0,39029477,49296926-6,00.htm.

12. Constance Loizos, "Could It Happen to You?" *Venture Capital Journal*, November 1, 2008, accessed January 30, 2011, www.jphibbard.com/uploads/VCJ%2011-01-08.pdf.

13. Kristi Heim, "Entellium CEO Pleads Guilty to Wire Fraud," *Seattle Times*, December 12, 2008, accessed January 30, 2011, http://seattletimes.nwsource.com/html/businesstechnology/2008499215_entellium120.html.

14. Ibid.

15. Xuan Tian, Gregory F. Udell, and Xiaoyun Yu, "Disciplining Delegated Monitors: Evidence from Venture Capital," January 23, 2011. Available at SSRN: http://ssrn.com/abstract=1746461.

16.. *McKinsey Quarterly*, February 2008 Survey on Governance. Of the 586 respondents, 378 were privately held companies, making it a relevant sample for the purposes of our discussion.

17. William D. Bygrave and Jeffry A. Timmons, *Venture Capital at the Crossroads* (Harvard Business Press, 1992), 220.

18. Working Group on Director Accountability and Board Effectiveness, "A Simple Guide to the Basic Responsibilities of VC-Backed Company Directors," October 2007, www.nvca.org/index.php?option=com_docman&task=doc_download&gid=78&Itemid=93.

Chapter 33: Exit Strategies

1. How Do Venture Capitalists Make Decisions? by Paul Gompers, William Gornall, Steven N. Kaplan, Ilya A. Strebulaev, NATIONAL BUREAU OF ECONOMIC RESEARCH (NBER) Working Paper No. 22587, Issued in September 2016, Survey 885 institutional venture capitalists (VCs) at 681 firms.

2. David Mayer and Martin F. Kenney, professor, Department of Human and Community Development, University of California, Davis, "Economic Action does not take place in a Vacuum: Understanding Cisco's Acquisition and Development Strategy," BRIE working paper 148, September 2002.

3. Glenn Rifkin, "Growth by Acquisition," The Case of Cisco Systems," *Strategy and Business* (Booz Allen Hamilton, 1997) http://www.strategy-business.com/article/15617?gko=3ec0c accessed on December 13, 2010.

4. Tony Hsieh (CEO, Zappos), *Delivering Happiness: A Path to Profits, Passion, and Purpose* (New York: Hachette Book

Group, 2010), 209–211. Tony tried to buy Sequoia's stock for $200 million, but eventually Zappos was sold to Amazon for $1.2 billion.

5. Paul Stavrand, "Best Practice Guide for Angel Groups—Post Investment Monitoring," accessed January 30, 2011, www.angelcapitalassociation.org/data/Documents/Resources/AngelCapitalEducation/ACEF_BEST_PRACTICES_Post_Investment.pdf.

6. Working Group on Director Accountability and Board Effectiveness, "A Simple Guide to the Basic Responsibilities of VC-Backed Company Directors," www.nvca.org/index.php?option=com_docman&task=doc_download&gid=78&Itemid=93.

7. Tim Ferris, *Tribe of Mentors: Short Life Advice from the Best in the World* (New York: Houghton Mifflin Harcourt, 2017).

Chapter 34: Acquisitions

1. David Mayer and Martin F. Kenney, "Economic Action Does Not Take Place in a Vacuum," BRIE Working paper 148, September 2002.

2. Ibid., attributed to Michael Volpi, chief strategic officer.

3. Source: Brad Stone, "The Secrets of Bezos," Bloomberg Businessweek, October 2013.

4. Between 2002 and 2009.

5. Marc Goedhart, Tim Koller, and David Wessels, "The Five Types of Successful Acquisitions," *McKinsey Quarterly*, July 2010, accessed February 10, 2011, www.mckinseyquarterly.com/The_five_types_of_successful_acquisitions_2635.

6. Between 1993 and 2001.

7. David Mayer and Martin F. Kenney, "Economic Action Does Not Take Place in a Vacuum."

8. Between 2001 and 2013.

9. Amir Efrati, "Google Cranks Up M&A Machine," *Wall Street Journal*, March 5, 2011.

10. Source: www.berkshirehathaway.com/letters/1994.html, accessed March 5, 2011.

11. www.wired.com/epicenter/2010/04/apple-kills-lala-music-service/ Accessed February 21, 2011.

12. Karen Ho, *Liquidated — An Ethnography of Wall Street* (Durham, NC: Duke University Press, 2009), 106.

13. Source: Adapted from Tony Hsieh, *Delivering Happiness: A Path to Profits, Passion, and Purpose* (New York: Hachette Book Group, 2010), 45–46.

Chapter 35: Initial Public Offering

1. Center for Private Equity and Entrepreneurship, Tuck School of Business at Dartmouth, "Results of Survey of Private Equity Funds," April 2005, accessed February 11, 2011, http://mba.tuck.dartmouth.edu/pecenter/research/pdfs/exits_survey.pdf.

2. KPMG, LLP, "Going Public," accessed February 11, 2011, www.kpmg.com/Ca/en/IssuesAndInsights/ArticlesPublications/Documents/Going%20Public.pdf; Ernst & Young, *Ernst & Young's Guide to Going Public: Lessons from the Leaders*, accessed February 11, 2011, www.ey.com/Publication/vwLUAssets/Lessons_from_the_leaders/$FILE/BE0067.pdf.

3. Ernst & Young, *Ernst & Young's Guide to Going Public.*

4. Ibid.

5. Initial Public Offerings: 1980–2010 Tables Updated Through 2010, as of January 2011. Jay R. Ritter, Cordell Professor of Finance, University of Florida.

6. This was announced on April 29, 2004.

7. Eric Schmidt, "Google's CEO on the Enduring Lessons of a Quirky IPO," *Harvard Business Review,* May 2010.

8. www.investopedia.com/terms/b/bookrunner.asp, accessed February 21, 2011.

9. From the documentary, *Something Ventured,* 2011. Produced by Paul Holland.

10. Ernst & Young, *Ernst & Young's Guide to Going Public*, www.ey.com/Publication/vwLUAssets/Lessons_from_the_leaders/$FILE/BE0067.pdf.

11. Roman Binder, Patrick Steiner, and Jonathan Woetzel, "A New Way to Measure IPO Success," *McKinsey Quarterly*, January 2002, accessed February 11, 2011, http://mkqpreview1.qdweb.net/A_new_way_to_measure_IPO_success_1538.

12. KPMG, LLP, *Going Public*.

13. Ibid., Ernst & Young, *Ernst & Young's Guide to Going Public*.

14. Paul A. Gompers, Anna Kovner, Josh Lerner, and David Scharfstein, "Venture Capital Investment Cycles: The Impact of Public Markets" (May 2005). NBER Working Paper Series, Vol. w11385, 2005. Available at SSRN: http://ssrn.com/abstract=731040.

15. www.pbs.org/wgbh/pages/frontline/shows/dotcon/thinking/primer.html, accessed February 22, 2011.

16. Steven Davidoff, "Why I.P.O.s Get Underpriced," *New York Times*, May 2011.

17. Ibid.

18. Ibid.

19. Eric Schmidt, "Google's CEO on the Enduring Lessons of a Quirky IPO."

20. Ibid.

21. Lip-Bu Tan (Walden International) in discussion with the author, August 2008.

22. Seth Rudnick (Canaan Partners) in discussion with the author, August 2008.

23. Brad Feld (The Foundry Group) in discussion with the author, December 2010.

Chapter 36: Secondary Sales

1. Benjamin F. Kuo, "Interview with Greg Brogger, SharesPost," Socaltech, June 17, 2009, accessed February 11, 2011,

http://www.socaltech.com/interview_with_greg_brog-ger_sharespost/s-0022276.html.

2. Pui-Wing Tam and Geoffrey Fowler, "Hot Trade in Private Shares of Facebook," *Wall Street Journal,* December 28, 2010, https://www.wsj.com/articles/SB100014240529702 04685004576045943100180026.

3. Yuliya Chernova, "Trading Pre-IPO Shares Gets Trickier — Investors Wanting to Get in Early on the next Twitter Find a Tougher Path," *Wall Street Journal.* October 29, 2013.

Index

485